Essays On the Intellectual Powers of Man

ESSAYS

ON THE

INTELLECTUAL POWERS OF MAN.

BY

THOMAS REID, D. D., F. R. S. E.

ABRIDGED.

WITH NOTES AND ILLUSTRATIONS FROM SIR WILLIAM HAMILTON
AND OTHERS.

EDITED

By JAMES WALKER, D. D.,

PROFESSOR OF INTELLECTUAL AND MORAL PHILOSOPHY IN HARVARD COLLEGE.

Third Edition.

CAMBRIDGE:
PUBLISHED BY JOHN BARTLETT.
Bookseller to the University.
1852.

Entered according to Act of Congress, in the year 1850, by

JOHN BARTLETT,

In the Clerk's Office of the District Court of the District of Massachusetts.

CAMBRIDGE:
STEREOTYPED AND PRINTED BY
METCALF AND COMPANY,
PRINTERS TO THE UNIVERSITY.

EDITOR'S NOTICE.

THE psychology generally taught in England and this country for the last fifty years has been that of the Scotch school, of which Dr. Reid is the acknowledged head. The influence of the same doctrines is also apparent in the improved state of philosophy in several of the Continental nations, and particularly in France. Sir W. Hamilton dedicates his annotated edition of Reid's works to M. Cousin, the distinguished philosopher and statesman " through whom Scotland has been again united intellectually to her old political ally, and the author's writings (the best result of Scottish speculation) made the basis of academical instruction in philosophy throughout the central nation of Europe."

The name of Reid, therefore, historically considered, is second to none among British psychologists and metaphysicians, with perhaps the single exception of Locke. His *Essays on the Intellectual Powers of Man* have likewise intrinsic and peculiar merits, especially as a manual to be used by those who are just entering on the study. The spirit and tone are unexceptionable; the style has a freshness and an interest which betoken the original thinker; technicalities are also avoided to a great degree, by which means, and by the frequent use of familiar and sometimes homely comparisons and illustrations, much of the obscurity, and perplexity, commonly objected to in metaphysical discussion, is removed.

The notes are intended either to correct mistakes and supply defects in the text, or to bring down the history of the speculation to the present day. Most of them are from Sir W. Hamilton's edition of Reid, mentioned above, and are marked by his initial. These, together with the extracts occasionally made from the supplementary dissertations, can hardly fail to convince the reader, that, when the whole of that work, as yet incomplete, is given to the public, it will constitute one of the most important contributions ever made to intellectual science.

In order to make room for these additions, and, at the same time, keep the volume within the limits proper for a text-book, it has been found necessary materially to abridge some portions of the original; but the omitted passages consist almost exclusively of repetitions, or of historical or merely critical digressions, in which the author did not excel. On account of these changes, the division and numbering of the chapters have been altered in several instances, and some passages have been transposed. To give greater distinctness to the argument or exposition, sections have also been introduced.

The references in the notes are generally for beginners, and not for proficients. They will be found convenient where students are required, under the form of dissertations or forensics, to collect and weigh the various opinions which have been entertained respecting the disputed question.

CAMBRIDGE, February 15, 1850.

CONTENTS.

a*

CHAPTER III.

CHAPTER IV.

CHAPTER V.

CHAPTER VI.

CHAPTER VII.

CHAPTER VIII.

CHAPTER IX.

CHAPTER X.

CHAPTER XI.

CHAPTER XII.

ESSAY III.

OF MEMORY.

CHAPTER I.

CHAPTER II.

CHAPTER III.

ESSAY IV.

OF CONCEPTION.

CHAPTER I.

CHAPTER II.

ESSAY V.

OF ABSTRACTION.

CHAPTER I.

CHAPTER II.

CHAPTER III.

ESSAY VI.

OF JUDGMENT.

CHAPTER I.

viii

CHAPTER II.

skip 351-362

CHAPTER III.

skip 392-422

ESSAY VII.
OF REASONING.

CHAPTER I.

CHAPTER II.

CHAPTER III.

ESSAY VIII.
OF TASTE.

CHAPTER I.

CHAPTER II.

APPENDIX.

PREFACE.

I. *Distribution of the Sciences.*] Human knowledge
may be reduced to two general heads, according as it
relates to *body* or to *mind;* to things material, or to
things intellectual.

The whole system of bodies in the universe, of which
we know but a very small part, may be called the material world ; the whole system of minds, from the infinite Creator to the meanest creature endowed with
thought, may be called the intellectual world. These
are the two great kingdoms of nature* that fall within
our notice ; and about the one or the other, or things
pertaining to them, every art, every science, and every
human thought are employed ; nor can the boldest
flight of imagination carry us beyond their limits.

Many things there are, indeed, regarding the nature
and the structure both of body and of mind, which our
faculties cannot reach ; many difficulties which the

---

* The term *nature* is used sometimes in a wider, sometimes in a nar-
rower extension. When employed in its most extensive meaning, it em-
braces the two worlds of mind and matter. When employed in its more
restricted signification, it is a synonyme for the latter only, and is then
used in contradistinction to the former. In the Greek philosophy, the
word φύσις was general in its meaning ; and the great branch of philosophy styled *physical* or *physiological* included under it, not only the sciences
of matter, but also those of mind. With us the term *nature* is more vaguely extensive than the terms *physics, physical, physiology, physiological,* or even
than the adjective *natural ;* whereas, in the philosophy of Germany, *Natur,*
and its correlatives, whether of Greek or Latin derivation, are, in general,
expressive of the world of matter, in contrast to the world of intelligence.
—H.

ablest philosopher cannot resolve; but of other natures, if any other there be, we have no knowledge, no conception at all.

That every thing that exists must be either corporeal or incorporeal, is evident. But it is not so evident, that every thing that exists must either be corporeal or endowed with thought. Whether there be in the universe beings which are neither extended, solid, and inert, like body, nor active and intelligent, like mind, seems to be beyond the reach of our knowledge. There appears to be a vast interval between body and mind; and whether there be any intermediate nature that connects them together, we know not.

We have no reason to ascribe intelligence, or even sensation, to *plants;* yet there appears in them an active force and energy, which cannot be the result of any arrangement or combination of inert matter. The same thing may be said of those powers by which animals are *nourished and grow,* by which matter *gravitates,* by which magnetical and electrical bodies *attract* and *repel* each other, and by which the parts of solid bodies *cohere.*

Some have conjectured, that the phenomena of the material world which require active force are produced by *the continual operation of intelligent beings.* Others have conjectured, that there may be in the universe beings that are *active without intelligence,* which, as a kind of incorporeal machinery, contrived by the Supreme Wisdom, perform their destined task without any knowledge or intention. But, laying aside conjecture, and all pretences to determine in things beyond our reach, we must rest in this, — that body and mind are the only kinds of being of which we can have any knowledge, or can form any conception. If there be other kinds, they are not discoverable by the faculties which God has given us; and, with regard to us, are as if they were not.

As, therefore, all our knowledge is confined to body and mind, or things belonging to them, there are two great branches of philosophy, one relating to body, the other to mind. The properties of body, and the laws that obtain in the material system, are the objects of *natural philosophy*, as that term is now used. The branch which treats of the nature and operations of minds has by some been called *pneumatology.** And to the one or the other of these branches, the principles of all the sciences belong.

What variety there may be of minds or thinking beings throughout this vast universe, we cannot pretend to say. We dwell in a little corner of God's dominion, disjoined from the rest of it. The globe which we inhabit is but one of seven planets that encircle our sun. What various orders of beings may inhabit the other six, their secondaries, and the comets belonging to our system, and how many other suns may be encircled with like systems, are things altogether hid from us. Although human reason and industry have discovered, with great accuracy, the order and distances of the planets, and the laws of their motion, we have no means of corresponding with them. That they may be the habitation of animated beings is very probable ; but of the nature or powers of their inhabitants, we are perfectly ignorant. Every man is conscious of a thinking principle or mind in himself, and we have sufficient evidence of a like principle in other men. The actions of brute animals show that they have some thinking principle, though of a nature far inferior to the human mind. And every thing about us may convince us of the existence of a Supreme Mind, the Maker and Governor of the universe. These are all the minds of which reason can give us any certain knowledge.

II. *General Prejudice against the Study of Psychology.*] The mind of man is the noblest work of God which reason discovers to us, and therefore, on account

---

* Now properly superseded by the term *psychology ;* to which no competent objection can be made, and which affords — what the various clumsy periphrases in use do not — a convenient adjective, *psychological.* — H.

of its dignity, deserves our study. It must, indeed, be
acknowledged, that although it is of all objects the
nearest to us, and seems the most within our reach,
it is very difficult to attend to its operations, so as to
form a distinct notion of them; and on that account
there is no branch of knowledge in which the ingenious and speculative have fallen into so great errors,
and even absurdities.   These errors and absurdities
have given rise to *a general prejudice against all inquiries of this nature;* and because ingenious men
have, for many ages, given different and contradictory
accounts of the powers of the mind, it is concluded that
all speculations concerning them are chimerical and
visionary.

But whatever effect this prejudice may have with
superficial thinkers, the judicious will not be apt to be
carried away with it. About two hundred years ago
the opinions of men in natural philosophy were as
various and as contradictory as they are now concerning the powers of the mind. Galileo, Torricelli, Kep-
ler, Bacon, and Newton had the same discouragement
in their attempts to throw light upon the material system, as we have with regard to the intellectual. If
they had been deterred by such prejudices, we should
never have reaped the benefit of their discoveries, which
do honor to human nature, and will make their names
immortal. The motto which Lord Bacon prefixed to
some of his writings was worthy of his genius, *Inve-
niam viam aut faciam.*

There is a natural order in the progress of the sciences, and good reasons may be assigned why the
philosophy of body should be *elder sister* to that of
mind, and of a quicker growth; but the last has the
principle of life no less than the first, and will grow
up, though slowly, to maturity. The remains of ancient philosophy upon this subject are venerable ruins,
carrying the marks of genius and industry, sufficient
to inflame, but not to satisfy, our curiosity. In later
ages, Descartes was the first that pointed out the
road we ought to take in these dark regions. Male-

branche, Arnauld, Locke, Berkeley, Buffier, Hutcheson, Butler, Hume, Price, Lord Kames, have labored
to make discoveries; nor have they labored in vain.
For, however different and contrary their conclusions
are, however skeptical some of them, they have all
given new light, and helped to clear the way for their
successors.

We ought never to despair of human genius, but
rather to hope, that, in time, it may produce a system
of the powers and operations of the human mind, no
less certain than those of optics or astronomy.

III. *Grounds on which the Study is recommended.*]
This is the more devoutly to be wished, as a distinct
knowledge of the powers of the mind would undoubtedly *give great light to many other branches of science.*
Mr. Hume has justly observed, that " all the sciences
have a relation to *human nature;* and, however wide
any of them may seem to run from it, they still return back by one passage or another. This is the centre and capitol of the sciences, which being once masters
of, we may easily extend our conquests everywhere."

The faculties of our minds are the tools and engines
we must use in every disquisition; and the better we
understand their nature and force, the more successfully we shall be able to apply them. Mr. Locke gives
this account of the occasion of his entering upon his
Essay concerning Human Understanding: — " Five or
six friends," says he, " meeting at my chamber, and
discoursing on a subject very remote from this, found
themselves quickly at a stand, by the difficulties that
rose on every side. After we had for a while puzzled
ourselves, without coming any nearer to a resolution
of those doubts that perplexed us, it came into my
thoughts that we took a wrong course; and that,
before we set ourselves upon inquiries of that nature,
it was necessary to examine our own abilities, and
see what objects our understandings were fitted or not
fitted to deal with. This I proposed to the company,
who all readily assented; and thereupon it was agreed

h

that this should be our *first* inquiry." If this be commonly the cause of perplexity in those disquisitions which have least relation to the mind, it must be so much more in those that have an immediate connection with it.

The sciences may be distinguished into two classes, according as they pertain to the material or to the intellectual world. The various parts of natural philosophy, the mechanical arts, chemistry, medicine, and agriculture, belong to the first; but to the last belong grammar, logic, rhetoric, natural theology, morals, jurisprudence, law, politics, and the fine arts. The knowledge of the human mind is the root from which these grow and draw their nourishment.* Whether, therefore, we consider the dignity of this subject, or its subserviency to science in general, and to the noblest branches of science in particular, it highly deserves to be cultivated.

---

* It is justly observed by M. Jouffroy, that the division here enounced is not in principle identical with that previously propounded. — H.

Jouffroy objects to the distinction made by the Scotch philosophers between the physical sciences, and the moral or philosophical sciences, as not being sufficiently exact and precise. He says : — " In this world there are two orders of phenomena perfectly distinct, — physical phenomena, and intellectual and moral phenomena, which I shall call, for brevity's sake, *material phenomena* and *mental phenomena.* It is by the senses and in the external world that we apprehend and know the first; it is by consciousness and within our own minds that we attain to the second, for in the theatre of consciousness alone are we able to observe them immediately and in themselves. Elsewhere we see the effects or the material symbols of mental phenomena, but we could not comprehend the cause of these effects, or the meaning of these symbols, except by the knowledge which we first acquire in ourselves of this order of phenomena. Now every possible scientific question is resolved by a knowledge of the laws of one or the other of these two orders of phenomena. Every question which finds its solution in the laws of material phenomena belongs to *physics;* every question which finds its solution in the laws of mental phenomena belongs to *philosophy;* every question, in fine, the solution of which presupposes at the same time a knowledge of the laws of some material phenomena and of some mental phenomena, is *mixed,* and partakes of the double nature of philosophical questions and physical questions. On what, then, depends the nature of any given question, and consequently that of the science which is to resolve it? On the nature of the phenomena; and as these phenomena are perfectly distinct, and apprehended by faculties which are equally so, the separation established by common sense between the philosophical sciences and the physical sciences is at once completely justified, and clearly explained and defined." — Preface to his *Œuvres Complètes de Thomas Reid,* p. xlii. — ED.

A very elegant writer on the sublime and beautiful concludes his account of the passions thus : — " The variety of the passions is great, and worthy, in every branch of that variety, of the most diligent investigation. The more accurately we search into the human mind, the stronger traces we *everywhere find of His wisdom who made it.* If a discourse on the use of the parts of the body may be considered as a hymn to the Creator, the use of the passions, which are the organs of the mind, cannot be barren of praise to Him, nor unproductive to ourselves of that noble and uncommon union of science and admiration, which a contemplation of the works of Infinite Wisdom alone can afford to a rational mind ; whilst referring to Him whatever we find of right, or good, or fair, in ourselves, discovering his strength and wisdom even in our own weakness and imperfection, honoring them where we discover them clearly, and adoring their profundity where we are lost in our search, we may be inquisitive without impertinence, and elevated without pride ; we may be admitted, if I may dare to say so, into the counsels of the Almighty, by a consideration of his works. This elevation of the mind ought to be the principal end of all our studies, which, if they do not in some measure effect, they are of very little service to us."*

---

* Burke's *Origin of our Ideas of the Sublime and Beautiful*, Part I. Sect. XIX.

For ampler discussion of the topics in this Preface, see Descartes, *Discours de la Méthode.* Stewart, *Elements of the Philosophy of the Human Mind*, Introduction ; and *Philosophical Essays*, Preliminary Dissertation. Brown, *Lectures on the Philosophy of the Human Mind*, Lect. I.-IV. Cousin, *Cours de* 1828, Leçons I. et II. This volume has been translated into English by Mr. Linberg, under the title of *Introduction to the History of Philosophy.* Jouffroy, Prefaces to his *Esquisses de Philosophie Morale de Dugald Stewart*, and *Œuvres de Reid.* Mr. Ripley has given an English version of the former in his *Philosophical Miscellanies*, Vol. II. Sir W. Hamilton says also of the latter, that it " will soon be made generally accessible to the British public by a highly competent translator."

On the division and organization of the sciences, and the relation of psychology to the rest, compare Jouffroy, *Nouveaux Mélanges Philosophiques.* Comte, *Philosophie Positive*, Leçon II. Coleridge, General Introduction to *The Encyclopædia Metropolitana.* — ED.

ESSAYS

INTELLECTUAL POWERS OF MAN.

PRELIMINARY ESSAY.

CHAPTER I.

EXPLICATION OF WORDS.

I. *On the Definition of Terms.*]   There is no greater impediment to the advancement of knowledge than the *ambiguity of words.*   To this chiefly it is owing that we find sects and parties in most branches of science, and disputes, which are carried on from age to age, without being brought to an issue.

Sophistry has been more effectually excluded from mathematics and natural philosophy than from other sciences.   In mathematics it had no place from the beginning; mathematicians having had the wisdom *to define accurately the terms they use,* and to lay down, as axioms, the first principles on which their reasoning is grounded.   Accordingly, we find no parties among mathematicians, and hardly any disputes.*

In natural philosophy there was no less sophistry, no less dispute and uncertainty, than in other sciences, until, about a century and a half ago, this science began to be built upon the foundation of clear defini-

---

* It was not the superior wisdom of mathematicians, but the simple and palpable character of their object-matter, which determined the difference. — H.

1

tions and self-evident axioms. Since that time, the
science, as if watered with the dew of heaven, has
grown apace; disputes have ceased, truth has prevailed,
and the science has received greater increase in two
centuries than in two thousand years before.

It were to be wished that this method, which has
been so successful in those branches of science, were
attempted in others; for definitions and axioms are the
foundations of all science. But that definitions may
not be sought where no definition can be given, nor
logical definitions be attempted where the subject does
not admit of them, it may be proper to lay down some
general principles concerning definition, for the sake of
those who are less conversant in this branch of logic.

When one undertakes to explain any art or science,
he will have occasion to use many words that are common to all who use the same language, and some that
are peculiar to that art or science. Words of the last
kind are called *terms of the art*, and ought to be distinctly explained, that their meaning may be understood.

A definition is nothing else but an explication of the
meaning of a word, by words whose meaning is already
known. Hence it is evident, that *every word cannot be
defined;* for the definition must consist of words; and
there could be no definition, if there were not words
previously understood without definition. Common
words, therefore, ought to be used in their common acceptation; and when they have different acceptations
in common language, these, when it is necessary, ought
to be distinguished. But they require no definition.
It is sufficient to define words that are uncommon, or
that are used in an uncommon meaning.

It may further be observed, that there are many
words which, though they may need explication, cannot
be logically defined. A logical definition, that is, a
strict and proper definition, must express the *kind*
(*genus*) of the thing defined, and the *specific difference*
by which the species defined is distinguished from every
other species belonging to that kind. It is natural to

the mind of man to class things under various kinds, and again to subdivide every kind into its various species. A species may often be subdivided into subordinate species, and then it is considered as a kind.

From what has been said of logical definition, it is evident that no word can be logically defined which does not denote a species; because such things only can have a specific difference; and a specific difference is essential to a logical definition. On this account there can be no logical definition of *individual things,* such as London or Paris. *Individuals* are distinguished either by proper names, or by accidental circumstances of time or place; but they have no specific difference; and therefore, though they may be known by proper names, or *may be described* by circumstances or relations, they cannot be defined. It is no less evident, that *the most general words* cannot be logically defined, because there is not a more general term of which they are a species.

Nay, we cannot define every *species of things,* because it happens sometimes that *we have not words to express the specific difference.* Thus a scarlet color is, no doubt, a species of color; but how shall we express the specific difference by which scarlet is distinguished from green or blue? The difference between them is immediately perceived by the eye; but we have not words to express it. These things we are taught by logic.

Without having recourse to the principles of logic, we may easily be satisfied that words cannot be defined which signify things perfectly simple, and void of all composition. This observation, I think, was first made by Descartes, and afterwards more fully illustrated by Locke.* But however obvious it appears to be, many

---

* This is incorrect. Descartes has little and Locke no title to praise for this observation. It had been made by Aristotle, and after him by many others; while, subsequent to Descartes, and *previous to Locke,* Pascal and the Port-Royal logicians, to say nothing of a paper of Leibnitz, in 1681, had reduced it to a matter of commonplace. In this instance Locke can, indeed, be *proved* a borrower. Mr. Stewart, *Philosophical Essays,* Note

instances may be given of great philosophers who
have perplexed and darkened the subjects they have
treated, by not knowing or not attending to it.

When men attempt to define things which cannot
be defined, their definitions will always be either obscure or false. It was one of the capital defects of
Aristotle's philosophy, that he pretended to define the
simplest things, which neither can be nor need to be
defined; such as *time* and *motion.* Among modern
philosophers, I know none that has abused definition
so much as Wolf, the famous German philosopher,
who, in a work on the human mind, called *Psychologia
Empirica*, consisting of many hundred propositions,
fortified by demonstrations, with a proportional accom-
paniment of definitions, corollaries, and scholia, has
given so many definitions of things which cannot be
defined, and so many demonstrations of things self-
evident, that the greatest part of the work consists of
tautology, and ringing changes upon words.

II. *Explication of some of the most frequently recur-
ring Terms in Psychology.*] There is no subject in
which there is more frequent occasion to use words
that cannot be logically defined, than in treating of the
powers and operations of the mind. The simplest
operations of our minds must all be expressed by words
of this kind. No man can explain by a logical definition what it is to *think*, to *apprehend*, to *believe*, to *will*,
to *desire.* Every man who understands the language
has some notion of the meaning of these words; and
every man who is capable of reflection may, by attending to the operations of his own mind which are signified by them, form a clear and distinct notion of them;
but they cannot be logically defined.

Since, therefore, it is often impossible to define words
which we must use on this subject, we must as much

A, is wrong in thinking that, after Descartes, Lord Stair is the earliest
philosopher by whom this logical principle was enounced; for Stair, as
a writer, is subsequent to the authors adduced. — H.

as possible use *common words in their common acceptation*, pointing out their various senses where they are ambiguous; and when we are obliged to use words less common, we must endeavour to explain them as well as we can, without affecting to give logical definitions, when the nature of the thing does not admit of them.

The following observations on the meaning of certain words are intended to supply, as far as we can, the want of definitions, by preventing ambiguity or obscurity in the use of them.

1. *The Mind.* — By the *mind* of a man we understand that in him which thinks, remembers, reasons, wills. The essence both of body and of mind is unknown to us. We know certain properties of the first, and certain operations of the last, and by these only we can define or describe them. We define *body* to be *that which is extended, solid, movable, divisible.* In like manner we define *mind* to be *that which thinks.* We are conscious that we think, and that we have a variety of thoughts of different kinds; such as seeing, hearing, remembering, deliberating, resolving, loving, hating, and many other kinds of thought, all which we are taught by nature to attribute to one internal principle; and this principle of thought we call the *mind* or *soul* of a man.

2. *Operations of the Mind.* — By the *operations** of the mind, we understand every mode of thinking of which we are conscious.

It deserves our notice, that the various modes of thinking have always, and in all languages, as far as we know, been called by the name of *operations of the mind*, or by names of the same import. To body we ascribe various *properties*, but not operations, properly so called; it is extended, divisible, movable, inert; it continues in any state in which it is put; every change of its state is the effect of some force impressed upon it, and is exactly proportional to the force impressed,

* *Operation, act, energy,* are nearly convertible terms; and are opposed to *faculty* (of which anon), as the *actual* to the *potential.* — H.

1*

and in the precise direction of that force. These are the general properties of matter, and these are not operations; on the contrary, they all imply its being a dead, inactive thing, which moves only as it is moved, and acts only by being acted upon.

But the mind is, from its very nature, a living and active being. Every thing we know of it implies life and active energy; and the reason why all its modes of thinking are called its operations is, that in all, or in most of them, it is not merely passive, as body is, but is really and properly active.

In all ages, and in all languages, ancient and modern, the various modes of thinking have been expressed by words of active signification, such as seeing, hearing, reasoning, willing, and the like. It seems, therefore, to be the natural judgment of mankind, that the mind is active in its various ways of thinking; and for this reason they are called its *operations*, and are expressed by *active* verbs.

It may be made a question, What regard is to be paid to this natural judgment? May it not be a vulgar error? Philosophers who think so have, no doubt, a right to be heard. But until it is *proved* that the mind is not active in thinking, but merely passive, the common language with regard to its operations ought to be used, and ought not to give place to a phraseology invented by philosophers, which implies its being merely passive.

3. *Powers and Faculties of the Mind.* — The words *power* and *faculty*, which are often used in speaking of the mind, need little explication. Every operation supposes a power in the being that operates; for to suppose any thing to operate which has no power to operate is manifestly absurd. But, on the other hand, there is no absurdity in supposing a being to have power to operate when it does not operate. Thus, I may have power to walk when I sit, or to speak when I am silent. Every operation, therefore, implies power; but the power does not imply the operation.

The *faculties* of the mind, and its *powers*, are often

used as synonymous expressions. But as most synonymes have some minute distinction that deserves notice, I apprehend that the word *faculty* is most properly applied to those powers of the mind which are *original* and *natural*, and which make a part of the constitution of the mind. There are other powers which are *acquired* by use, exercise, or study, which are not called faculties, but *habits*. There must be something in the constitution of the mind necessary to our being able to acquire habits, and this is commonly called *capacity*.*

4. *Subject and Object.* — We frequently meet with a distinction, in writers upon this subject, between things *in the mind* and things *external* to the mind. The powers, faculties, and operations of the mind are things in the mind. Every thing is said to be *in the mind* of which the mind is the *subject*. It is self-evident, that there are some things which cannot exist without a subject to which they belong, and of which they are attributes. Thus, color must be in something colored; figure in something figured; thought can only be in something that thinks; wisdom and virtue cannot exist but in some being that is wise and virtuous. When, therefore, we speak of things in the mind, we understand by this, things of which the mind is the subject. Excepting the mind itself and things in the mind, all other things are said to be external. It ought, therefore, to be remembered, that this distinction between things in the mind and things external is not meant to signify the *place* of the things we speak of, but their *subject*.

There is a figurative sense in which things are said to be in the mind, which it is sufficient barely to mention. We say, Such a thing was not in my mind,

---

* These terms properly stand in the following relations : — *powers* are *active* and *passive, natural* and *acquired*. Powers natural and active are called *faculties ;* powers natural and passive, *capacities* or *receptivities ;* powers acquired are *habits,* and habit is used both in an active and in a passive sense. The power, again, of acquiring a habit, is called a *disposition.* — H.

meaning no more than that we had not the least thought
of it. By a figure, we put the thing for the thought of
it. In this sense, external things are in the mind as
often as they are the objects of our thought.

Most of the operations of the mind, from their very
nature, must have *objects* to which they are directed,
and about which they are employed. He that perceives
must perceive something; and that which he perceives
is called the object of his perception. To perceive,
without having any object of perception, is impossible.
The mind that perceives, the object perceived, and the
operation of perceiving that object, are distinct things,
and are distinguished in the structure of all languages.
In this sentence, " I see or perceive the moon," *I* is the
person or *mind;* the active verb *see* denotes the operation
of that mind, and the *moon* denotes the object. What
we have said of perceiving is equally applicable to
most operations of the mind. Such operations are, in
all languages, expressed by active transitive verbs; and
we know that, in all languages, such verbs require a
thing or person, which is the agent, and a noun following in an oblique case, which is the object. Whence
it is evident that all mankind, both those who have
contrived language, and those who use it with understanding, have distinguished these three things as different, — to wit, the *operations* of the mind, which are
expressed by active verbs, the *mind* itself, which is the
nominative to those verbs, and the *object*, which is, in
the oblique case, governed by them.*

---

* *Subject* and *object* are correlative terms. The former is properly *id in
quo;* the latter, *id circa quod.* Hence, in psychological language, the subject, absolutely, is the mind that knows or thinks, — i. e. the mind considered as the subject of knowledge or thought; the *object*, that which is
known, or thought about. The adjectives *subjective* and *objective* are convenient, if not indispensable expressions.

The antithesis between *myself* and *what is not myself* is sometimes expressed by an awkward use of the pronoun *I.* In English we cannot say *the I*
and *the not-I* so happily as the French *le moi* and *le non-moi*, or even the
German *das Ich* and *das nicht-Ich.* The ambiguity arising from the identity of sound between *the I* and *the eye* would of itself preclude the ordinary employment of the former. *The ego* and *the non-ego* are the best
terms *we* can use; and as the expressions are scientific, it is perhaps no loss
that their technical precision is guarded by their non-vernacularity. — H.

5. *Idea.* — When, in common language, we speak of *having an idea* of any thing, we mean no more by that expression than *thinking* of it. The vulgar allow, that this expression implies a mind that thinks, an act of that mind which we call thinking, and an object about which it thinks. But, besides these three, the philosopher conceives that there is a fourth, — to wit, the *idea*, which is the *immediate* object. The idea is in the mind itself, and can have no existence but in the mind that thinks; but the *remote* or *mediate* object may be something external, as the sun or moon; it may be something past or future; it may be something which never existed. This is the philosophical meaning of the word *idea;* and we may observe, that this meaning of that word is built upon a philosophical opinion; for, if philosophers had not believed that there are such immediate objects of all our thoughts in the mind, they would never have used the word *idea* to express them.*

I shall only add on this article, that, although I may have occasion to use the word *idea* in this philosophical sense in explaining the opinions of others, I shall have no occasion to use it in expressing my own, because I believe *ideas*, taken in this sense, to be a mere fiction of philosophers. And in the popular meaning of the word there is the less occasion to use it, because the English words *thought, notion, apprehension,* answer the purpose as well as the Greek word *idea*, with this advantage, that they are less ambiguous. There is, indeed, a meaning of the word *idea*, which I think most agreeable to its use in ancient philosophy, and which I would willingly adopt, if use, the arbiter of language, did permit. But this will come to be explained afterwards.

I have premised these observations on the meaning of certain words that frequently occur in treating of this subject, for two reasons: *first*, that I may be the

---

* As we proceed, we shall have frequent occasion to notice the limited meaning attached by Reid to the term *idea*, viz. something in or present to the mind, but not a mere modification of the mind; and also his error in supposing that all the philosophers who accepted the theory of ideas accepted it under this crude form. — ED.

better understood when I use them; and *secondly*, that those who would make any progress in this branch of science may accustom themselves to attend very carefully to the meaning of words that are used in it. They may be assured of this, that the *ambiguity of words*, and the vague and improper application of them, have thrown more darkness upon this subject than the subtilty and intricacy of things.

When we use common words, we ought to use them in the sense in which they are most commonly used by the best and purest writers in the language; and when we have occasion to enlarge or restrict the meaning of a common word, or to give it more precision than it has in common language, the reader ought to have warning of this, otherwise we shall impose upon ourselves and upon him.

Other words that need explication shall be explained as they occur.*

CHAPTER II.

OF HYPOTHESES.

I. *Proneness of Philosophers to build on Hypotheses.*] Every branch of human knowledge has its proper principles, its proper foundation and method of reasoning; and if we endeavour to build it upon any other foundation, it will never stand firm and stable. Thus the historian builds upon testimony, and rarely indulges conjecture. The antiquarian mixes conjecture with testimony; and the former often makes the larger ingredient. The mathematician pays not the least regard

---

* As a convenient manual for the explication of technical terms in psychology we can recommend Isaac Taylor's *Elements of Thought; or, Concise Explanations (alphabetically arranged) of the Principal Terms employed in the Several Branches of Intellectual Philosophy.* Still better for this purpose is the *Dictionnaire des Sciences Philosophiques*, now in course of publication. — ED.

either to testimony or conjecture, but deduces every thing, by demonstrative reasoning, from his definitions and axioms. Indeed, whatever is built upon conjecture is improperly called science; for conjecture may beget opinion, but cannot produce knowledge. Natural philosophy must be built upon the phenomena of the material system, discovered by observation and experiment.

When men first began to philosophize, that is, to carry their thoughts beyond the objects of sense, and to inquire into the causes of things, and the secret operations of nature, it was very natural for them to indulge conjecture; nor was it to be expected that, in many ages, they should discover the proper and scientific way of proceeding in philosophical disquisitions. Accordingly, we find that the most ancient systems in every branch of philosophy were nothing but the conjectures of men famous for their wisdom, whose fame gave authority to their opinions. Thus, in early ages, wise men conjectured that this earth is a vast plain, surrounded on all hands by a boundless ocean; that from this ocean the sun, moon, and stars emerge at their rising, and plunge into it again at their setting.

With regard to the mind, men in their rudest state are apt to conjecture, that the principle of life in a man is his breath; because the most obvious distinction between a living and a dead man is, that the one breathes and the other does not. To this it is owing, that, in ancient languages, the word which denotes the soul is that which properly signifies breath or air.

As men advance in knowledge, their first conjectures appear silly and childish, and give place to others which tally better with later observations and discoveries. Thus, one system of philosophy succeeds another, without any claim to superior merit but this, that it is a more ingenious system of conjectures, and accounts better for common appearances.

To omit many ancient systems of this kind, Descartes, about the middle of the last century, dissatisfied with the *materia prima*, the *substantial forms*, and the *occult qualities* of the Peripatetics, conjectured boldly, that the heavenly bodies of our system are carried round by a vortex or whirlpool of subtile matter, just as straws and chaff are carried round in a tub of water. He conjectured that the soul is seated in a small gland in the brain, called the *pineal gland;* that there, as in her chamber of presence, she receives intelligence of every thing that affects the senses, by means of a subtile fluid contained in the nerves, called *the animal spirits;* and that she despatches these animal spirits, as her messengers, to put in motion the several muscles of the body, as there is occasion.* By such conjectures as these, Descartes could account for every phenomenon in nature in such a plausible manner as gave satisfaction to a great part of the learned world for more than half a century.

Such conjectures in philosophical matters have commonly got the name of *hypotheses* or *theories.*† And the invention of an hypothesis, founded on some slight probabilities, which accounts for many appearances of nature, has been considered as the highest attainment of a philosopher. If the hypothesis hangs well together, is embellished by a lively imagination, and serves to account for common appearances, it is considered by many as having all the qualities that should recommend it to our belief, and all that ought to be required in a philosophical system.

There is *such proneness in men of genius to invent*

---

* It is not, however, to be supposed that Descartes allowed the soul to be seated by local presence in any part of the body; for the smallest point of body is still extended, and mind is absolutely simple and incapable of occupying place. The pineal gland, in the Cartesian doctrine, is only analogically called the seat of the soul, inasmuch as this is viewed as the central point of the corporeal organism; but while through this point the mind and body are mutually connected, that connection is not one of a mere physical dependence, as they do not operate on each other by direct and natural causation. — H.

† Reid uses the terms *theory, hypothesis,* and *conjecture* as convertible, and always in an unfavorable acceptation. Herein there is a double inaccuracy. But of this again. — H.

Almost every *theory,* e. g. that of gravitation, or the Copernican system, was an hypothesis in the beginning, but after being verified by facts it ceased to be an *hypothesis.* — Ed.

hypotheses, and *in others to acquiesce in them* as the utmost which the human faculties can attain in philosophy, that it is of the last consequence to the progress of real knowledge, that men should have a clear and distinct understanding of the nature of hypotheses in philosophy, and of the regard that is due to them.

II. *A priori Improbability of such Hypotheses.*] Although some conjectures may have a considerable degree of probability, yet it is evidently in the nature of conjecture to be uncertain. In every case, the assent ought to be proportioned to the evidence; for to believe firmly what has but a small degree of probability is a manifest abuse of our understanding. Now, though we may, in many cases, form very probable conjectures concerning the works of men, every conjecture we can form with regard to the works of God has as little probability as the conjectures of a child with regard to the works of a man. The wisdom of God exceeds that of the wisest man, more than that of the wisest man exceeds the wisdom of a child. If a child were to conjecture how an army is to be formed in the day of battle, how a city is to be fortified, or a state governed, what chance has he to guess right? As little chance has the wisest man, when he pretends to conjecture how the planets move in their courses, how the sea ebbs and flows, and how our minds act upon our bodies.

If a thousand of the greatest wits that ever the world produced were, without any previous knowledge in anatomy, to sit down and contrive how, and by what internal organs, the various functions of the human body are carried on, — how the blood is made to circulate, and the limbs to move, — they would not in a thousand years hit upon any thing like the truth.* Of

---

* " Nothing can be juster than this remark; but does it authorize the conclusion, that, *to an experienced and skilful anatomist,* conjectures founded on analogy and the consideration of uses are of no avail as media of discovery ? The logical inference, indeed, from Dr. Reid's own statement is, not against anatomical conjectures in general, but against the anatomical

2

all the discoveries that have been made concerning the inward structure of the human body, never one was made by conjecture. Accurate observations of anatomists have brought to light innumerable artifices of nature in the contrivance of this machine of the human body, which we cannot but admire as excellently adapted to their several purposes. But the most sagacious physiologist never dreamed of them till they were discovered. On the other hand, innumerable conjectures, formed in different ages, with regard to the structure of the body, have been confuted by observation, and none ever confirmed. What we have said of the internal structure of the human body may be said, with justice, of every other part of the works of God, wherein any real discovery has been made. Such discoveries have always been made by patient observation, by accurate experiments, or by conclusions drawn by strict reasoning from observations and experiments; and such discoveries have always tended to refute, and not to confirm, the theories and hypotheses which ingenious men had invented.

As this is a fact confirmed by the history of philosophy in all past ages, it ought to have taught men, long ago, to treat with just contempt hypotheses in every branch of philosophy, and to despair of ever advancing real knowledge in that way. The Indian philosopher, being at a loss to know how the earth was supported, invented the hypothesis of a huge elephant; and this elephant he supposed to stand upon the back of a huge tortoise. This hypothesis, however ridiculous it appears to us, might seem very reasonable to other Indians, who knew no more than the inventor of it; and the same will be the fate of all hypotheses invented by men to account for the works of God: they may have a decent and plausible appearance to those who are not more knowing than the inventor; but when

---

conjectures of those who are ignorant of anatomy." — Stewart's *Elements*, Part II. Chap. IX. § 2. Harvey's theory of the circulation of the blood began in a conjecture founded on the doctrine of final causes. — ED.

men come to be more enlightened, they will always appear ridiculous and childish.

This has been the case with regard to hypotheses that have been revered by the most enlightened part of mankind for hundreds of years; and it will always be the case to the end of the world. For until the wisdom of men bear some proportion to the wisdom of God, their attempts to find out the structure of his works by the force of their wit and genius will be vain.

The world has been so long befooled by hypotheses in all parts of philosophy, that it is of the utmost consequence to every man, who would make any progress in real knowledge, to treat them with just contempt, as the reveries of vain and fanciful men, whose pride makes them conceive themselves able to unfold the mysteries of nature by the force of their genius. A learned man, in an epistle to Descartes, has the following observation, which very much deserved the attention of that philosopher, and of all that come after him: — "When men, sitting in their closet, and consulting only their books, attempt disquisitions into nature, they may, indeed, tell how they would have made the world, if God had given them that in commission; that is, they may describe chimeras which correspond with the imbecility of their own minds, no less than the admirable beauty of the universe corresponds with the infinite perfection of its Creator; but without an understanding truly divine, they can never form such an idea to themselves as the Deity had in creating things."

III. *The only Legitimate Rules of Philosophizing.*] Let us, therefore, lay down this as a fundamental principle in our inquiries into the structure of the mind and its operations, that no regard is due to the conjectures or hypotheses of philosophers, however ancient, however generally received. Let us accustom ourselves to try every opinion by the touchstone of fact and experience. What can fairly be deduced from facts duly observed, or sufficiently attested, is genuine and pure; it is the voice of God, and no fiction of human imagination.

The first rule of philosophizing laid down by the great Newton is this:— *Causas rerum naturalium, non plures admitti debere, quam quæ et vera sint, et earum phænomenis explicandis sufficiant,* — "No more causes, nor any other causes of natural effects, ought to be admitted, but such as are both true, and are sufficient for explaining their appearances." This is a golden rule; it is the true and proper test, by which what is sound and solid in philosophy may be distinguished from what is hollow and vain.*

If a philosopher, therefore, pretend to show us the cause of any natural effect, whether relating to matter or to mind, let us *first consider whether there be sufficient evidence that the cause he assigns does really exist.* If there be not, reject it with disdain, as a fiction which ought to have no place in genuine philosophy. If the cause assigned really exist, *consider in the next place whether the effect it is brought to explain necessarily follows from it.* Unless it have these two conditions, it is good for nothing.

When Newton had shown the admirable effects of gravitation in our planetary system, he must have felt a strong desire to know its cause. He could have invented a hypothesis for this purpose, as many had done before him. But his philosophy was of another complexion. Let us hear what he says:— *Rationem harum gravitatis proprietatum ex phænomenis non potui deducere, et hypotheses non fingo. Quicquid enim ex phænomenis non deducitur, hypothesis vocanda est. Et hypotheses, seu metaphysicæ, seu physicæ, seu qualitatum occultarium, seu mechanicæ, in philosophia experimentali locum non habent.†*

---

* For this rule we are not indebted to Newton. It is only the old *law of parsimony,* and that ambiguously expressed. For in their plain meaning, the words *et vera sint* are redundant; or what follows is redundant, and the whole rule a barren truism.— H. [Compare Whewell, *Philosophy of the Inductive Sciences,* Book XII. Chap. XIII.— Ed.]

† "I have not been able to deduce from phenomena the cause of these properties of gravity, and *I do not frame hypotheses.* For whatever is not

CHAPTER III.

OF ANALOGY.

I. *Nature and Uses of Analogical Reasoning*.] It is natural to men to judge of things less known by some similitude they observe, or think they observe, between

---

deduced from phenomena must be termed *hypothesis*. And hypotheses, whether regarding physics, metaphysics, occult qualities, or mechanics, have no place in experimental philosophy."

On the use of hypotheses, with its just limitations, compare Stewart, *Elements*, Part II. Chap. IX. § 2; Herschel, *Preliminary Discourse*, Part II. Chap. VII.; Mill, *System of Logic*, Book III. Chap. XIII. §§ 4–7. The latter observes:—"When Newton said, *Hypotheses non fingo*, he did not mean, that he deprived himself of the facilities of investigation afforded by assuming, in the first instance, what he hoped ultimately to be able to prove. Without such assumptions, science could never have attained its present state: they are necessary steps in the progress to something more certain; and nearly every thing which is now theory was once hypothesis. Even in purely experimental science, some inducement is necessary for trying one experiment rather than another; and although it is abstractedly possible that all the experiments which have been tried *might* have been produced by the mere desire to ascertain what would happen in certain circumstances, without any previous conjecture as to the result, yet, in point of fact, those unobvious, delicate, and often cumbrous and tedious processes of experiment, which have thrown most light upon the general constitution of nature, would hardly ever have been undertaken by the persons or at the time they were, unless it had seemed to depend on them whether some general doctrine or theory which had been suggested, but not yet proved, should be admitted or not. If this be true even of merely experimental inquiry, the conversion of experimental into inductive truths could still less have been effected without large temporary assistance from hypotheses. The process of tracing regularity in any complicated, and at first sight confused, set of appearances, is necessarily *tentative*; we begin by making any supposition, even a false one, to see what consequences will follow from it; and by observing how these differ from the real phenomena, we learn what corrections to make in our supposition. Let any one watch the manner in which he himself unravels any complicated mass of evidence; let him observe how, for instance, he elicits the true history of any occurrence from the involved statements of one or of many witnesses. He will find, that he does not take all the items of evidence into his mind at once, and attempt to weave them together: the human faculties are not equal to such an undertaking: he extemporizes, from a few of the particulars, a first rude theory of the mode in which the facts took place, and then looks at the other statements, one by one, to try whether they can be reconciled with that provisional theory, or what corrections or additions it requires to make it square with them. In this way, which, as M. Comte remarks, has some resemblance to the methods of approxima-

2 *

them and things more familiar or better known. In
many cases, we have no better way of judging. And
where the things compared have really a great similitude in their nature, when there is reason to think that
they are subject to the same laws, there may be a considerable degree of probability in conclusions drawn
from analogy.

Thus, we may observe a very great similitude between this earth which we inhabit, and the other planets, Saturn, Jupiter, Mars, Venus, and Mercury. They
all revolve round the sun, as the earth does, although at
different distances, and in different periods. They borrow all their light from the sun, as the earth does.
Several of them are known to revolve round their axes
like the earth, and, by that means, must have a like
succession of day and night. Some of them have
moons, that serve to give them light in the absence of
the sun, as our moon does to us. They are all, in
their motions, subject to the same law of gravitation
as the earth is. From all this similitude, it is not unreasonable to think, that those planets may, like our

tion of mathematicians, we arrive, by means of hypotheses, at conclusions
not hypothetical."

In a note he adds : — " The attempt to localize, in different regions of the
brain, the physical organs of our different mental faculties and propensities, was, on the part of its original author, a strictly legitimate example of
a scientific hypothesis; and we ought not, therefore, to blame him for the
extremely slight grounds on which he often proceeded, in an operation
which could only be tentative, though we may regret that materials barely
sufficient for a first rude hypothesis should have been hastily worked up
by his successors *into the vain semblance of a science.* Whatever there may
be of reality in the connection between the scale of mental endowments
and the various degrees of complication in the cerebral system (and that
there is some such connection, comparative anatomy seems strongly to indicate), it was in no other way so likely to be brought to light as by framing, in the first instance, an hypothesis similar to that of Gall. But the
verification of any such hypothesis is attended, from the peculiar nature of
the phenomena, with difficulties which phrenologists have not hitherto
shown themselves even competent to appreciate, much less to overcome."

That Dr. Reid has pushed his objections too far must be admitted.
Still, the very example which Mr. Mill has given of a legitimate hypothesis admonishes us with how much danger to science the resort is attended,
and strengthens our conviction that the *spirit* which dictated these objections, and which they, in turn, are adapted to inspire, cannot be too highly
commended. — ED.

earth, be the habitation of various orders of living creatures. There is some probability in this conclusion from analogy.

In medicine, physicians must, for the most part, be directed in their prescriptions by analogy. The constitution of one human body is so like to that of another, that it is reasonable to think, that what is the cause of health or sickness to one may have the same effect upon another. And this generally is found true, though not without some exceptions.

In politics we reason, for the most part, from analogy. The constitution of human nature is so similar in different societies or commonwealths, that the causes of peace and war, of tranquillity and sedition, of riches and poverty, of improvement and degeneracy, are much the same in all.

Analogical reasoning, therefore, is not in all cases to be rejected. It may afford a greater or a less degree of probability, according as the things compared are more or less similar in their nature. But it ought to be observed, that, as this kind of reasoning can afford only probable evidence at best, so, unless great caution be used, we are apt to be led into error by it. *For men are naturally disposed to conceive a greater similitude in things than there really is.*

To give an instance of this. Anatomists, in ancient ages, seldom dissected human bodies; but very often the bodies of those quadrupeds whose internal structure was thought to approach nearest to that of the human body. Modern anatomists have discovered many mistakes the ancients were led into, by their conceiving a greater similitude between the structure of men and of some beasts than there is in reality. By this, and many other instances that might be given, it appears that conclusions built on analogy stand on a

---

* Berkeley says: — "We should proceed warily in such things, for we are apt to lay too great a stress on *analogies*, and, to the prejudice of truth, humor that eagerness of mind whereby it is carried to extend its knowledge into general theorems." — *Principles of Human Knowledge*, Part I. § 106. — ED.

slippery foundation; and that we ought never to rest
upon evidence of this kind, when we can have more
direct evidence.

I know no author who has made a more just and a
more happy use of this mode of reasoning than Bishop
Butler, in his *Analogy of Religion, Natural and Re-
vealed, to the Constitution and Course of Nature.* In
that excellent work, the author does not ground any of
the truths of religion upon analogy, as their proper
evidence. He only makes use of analogy to answer
objections against them. When objections are made
against the truths of religion, which may be made with
equal strength against what we know to be true in the
course of nature, such objections can have no weight.

Analogical reasoning, therefore, may be of excellent
use, (1.) in answering objections against truths which
have *other* evidence. It may likewise (2.) give a greater
or a less degree of probability in cases where we can
find no other evidence. But all arguments drawn from
analogy are still the weaker, the greater disparity there
is between the things compared; and therefore must
be weakest of all when we compare body with mind,
because there are no two things in nature more unlike.

II. *Why a frequent Source of Error in Mental Science.*] There is no subject in which men have always
been so prone to form their notions by analogies of this
kind as in what relates to the mind. We form an early
acquaintance with material things by means of our
senses, and are bred up in a constant familiarity with
them. Hence we are apt to measure all things by
them, and to ascribe to things most remote from matter
the qualities that belong to material things. It is for
this reason, that mankind have, in all ages, been so
prone to conceive the *mind itself to be some subtile kind
of matter;* that they have been disposed to ascribe *human figure,* and *human organs,* not only to *angels,* but
even to the *Deity.* Though we are conscious of the
operations of our own minds when they are exerted,

and are capable of attending to them so as to form a
distinct notion of them, this is so difficult a work to
men whose attention is constantly solicited by external
objects, that *we give them names from things that are
familiar*, and which are *conceived to have some similitude to them;* and the notions we form of them are no
less analogical than the names we give them. Almost
all the words by which we express the operations of
the mind are borrowed from material objects. To *understand*, to *conceive*, to *imagine*, to *comprehend*, to *deliberate*, to *infer*, and many others, are words of this
kind; so that the very language of mankind, with
regard to the operations of our minds, is analogical.
Because bodies are affected only by contact and pressure, *we are apt to conceive that what* is an immediate
object of thought, and *affects the mind, must be in contact with it*, and make some impression upon it. When
we imagine any thing, the very word leads us to think
that there must be some image in the mind of the thing
conceived. It is evident that these notions are drawn
from some similitude conceived between body and
mind, and between the properties of body and the operations of mind.

To illustrate more fully that analogical reasoning
from a supposed similitude of mind to body, which I
conceive to be the most fruitful source of errors with
regard to the operations of our minds, I shall give an
instance of it.

When a man is urged by contrary motives, those on
one hand inciting him to do some action, those on the
other to forbear it, he deliberates about it, and at last
resolves to do it, or not to do it. The contrary motives
are here compared to the weights in the opposite scales
of a balance; and there is not, perhaps, any instance
that can be named of a more striking analogy between
body and mind. Hence the phrases of *weighing motives*,
of deliberating upon actions, are common to all languages.

From this analogy some philosophers draw very important conclusions. They say, that, as the balance

cannot incline to one side more than the other, when
the opposite weights are equal, so a man cannot possibly determine himself, if the motives on both hands
are equal; and, as the balance must necessarily turn to
that side which has most weight, so the man must
necessarily be determined to that hand where the motive is strongest.   And on this foundation, some of the
schoolmen* maintained, that, if a hungry ass were
placed between two bundles of hay equally inviting,
the beast must stand still and starve to death, being
unable to turn to either, because there are equal motives to both.   This is an instance of that analogical
reasoning which I conceive ought never to be trusted;
for the analogy between a balance and a man deliberating, though one of the strongest that can be found
between matter and mind, is too weak to support any
argument.   A piece of dead, inactive matter, and an
active, intelligent being, are things very unlike; and
because the one would remain at rest in a certain case,
it does not follow that the other would be inactive in a
case somewhat similar.   The argument is no better
than this: that, because a dead animal moves only as
it is pushed, and, if pushed with equal force in contrary directions, must remain at rest, therefore the same
thing must happen to a living animal; for surely the
similitude between a dead animal and a living is as
great as that between a balance and a man.

The conclusion I would draw from all that has been
said on analogy is, that, in our inquiries concerning the

---

* This illustration is specially associated with Joannes Buridanus, a
celebrated nominalist of the fourteenth century, and one of the acutest
reasoners on the great question of moral liberty.   The supposition of the
ass, &c., is not, however, as I have ascertained, to be found in his writings.
Perhaps it was orally advanced in disputation or in lecturing as an example in illustration of his *determinism;* perhaps it was employed by his
opponents as an instance to reduce that doctrine to absurdity.   With this
latter view, a similar refutation of the principles of our modern fatalists
was ingeniously essayed by Reid's friend and kinsman, Dr. James Gregory.—H.

For further illustrations of the grounds and scope of analogical reasoning, see Archbishop Whately's *Rhetoric*, Part I. Chap. II. § 6, and Mill's
System of Logic, Book III. Chap. XX.—Ed.

mind and its operations, (1.) we ought never to trust to reasonings drawn from some *supposed similitude of body to mind;* and (2.) that we ought to be very much upon our guard, that we be not imposed upon by those *analogical terms and phrases* by which the operations of the mind are expressed in all languages.

CHAPTER IV.

ON THE PROPER MEANS OF KNOWING THE OPERATIONS OF THE MIND.

I. *Subsidiary Sources of Knowledge respecting the Mind.*] Since we ought to pay no regard to hypotheses, and to be very suspicious of analogical reasoning, it may be asked, From what source must the knowledge of the mind and its faculties be drawn?

I answer, the chief and proper source of this branch of knowledge is accurate reflection upon the operations of our own minds. Of this source we shall speak more fully, after making some remarks upon two others that may be subservient to it.

1. The first of them is *attention to the structure of language.* The language of mankind is expressive of their thoughts, and of the various operations of their minds. The various operations of the understanding, will, and passions, which are common to mankind, have various forms of speech corresponding to them in all languages, which are the signs of them, and by which they are expressed; and a due attention to the *signs* may, in many cases, give considerable light to the things signified by them.

There are in all languages modes of speech by which men signify their judgment or give their testimony; by which they accept or refuse; by which they ask information or advice; by which they command, or threaten, or supplicate; by which they plight their faith in promises and contracts. If such operations were not common to mankind, we should not find in all languages forms of speech by which they are expressed. All languages, indeed, have their imperfections; they can never be adequate to all the varieties of human thought; and therefore things may be really distinct in their nature, and capable of being distinguished by the human mind, which are not distinguished in common language. We can only expect, in the structure of languages, those distinctions which all mankind in the common business of life have occasion to make. There may be peculiarities in a particular language, of the causes of which we are ignorant, and from which, therefore, we can draw no conclusion. But whatever we find common to all languages must have a common cause; must be owing to *some common notion or sentiment of the human mind.*

2. Another source of information on this subject is *a due attention to the course of human actions and opinions.* The actions of men are effects; their sentiments, their passions, and their affections are the causes of those effects; and we may, in many cases, form a judgment of the cause from the effect. The behaviour of parents towards their children gives sufficient evidence, even to those who never had children, that the parental affection is common to mankind. It is easy to see, from the general conduct of men, what are the natural objects of their esteem, their admiration, their love, their approbation, their resentment, and of all their other original dispositions. It is obvious, from the conduct of men in all ages, that man is, by his nature, a social animal; that he delights to associate with his species, — to converse and to exchange good offices with them.

Not only the *actions*, but even the *opinions*, of men may sometimes give light into the frame of the human mind. The opinions of men may be considered as the effects of their *intellectual* powers, as their actions are the effects of their *active* principles. Even the prejudices and errors of mankind, when they are general, must have some cause no less general, the discovery of which will throw some light upon the frame of the human understanding.

I conceive this to be the principal use of the *history of philosophy.* When we trace the history of the various philosophical opinions that have sprung up among thinking men, we are led into a labyrinth of fanciful opinions, contradictions, and absurdities, intermixed with some truths; yet we may sometimes find a clew to lead us through the several windings of this labyrinth; we may find that point of view which presented things to the author of the system in the light in which they appeared to him. This will often give a consistency to things seemingly contradictory, and some degree of probability to those that appeared most fanciful.* The history of philosophy, considered as a map of the intellectual operations of men of genius, must always be entertaining, and may sometimes give us views of the human understanding which could not easily be had any other way.

II. *Consciousness and Reflection.*] I return to what I mentioned as the main source of information on this subject, — *attentive reflection upon the operations of our own minds.*

All the notions we have of mind and of its operations are, by Mr. Locke, called *ideas of reflection.*† A man may have as distinct notions of remembrance, of judgment, of will, of desire, as he has of any object whatever. Such notions, as Mr. Locke justly observes, are got by the power of reflection. But what is this power of reflection? It is, says the same author, " that power by which the mind turns its view inward, and observes its own actions and operations." He observes elsewhere, that the understanding, like the eye, whilst it makes us see and perceive all other things, takes no

---

* "Every error," says Bossuet, " is a truth abused." — H.
† Locke is not (as Reid seems to think, and as Mr. Stewart expressly says) the first who introduced *reflection*, either as a psychological term or as a psychological principle. See Note I. — H.

3

notice of itself;* and that it requires art and pains to
set it at a distance, and make it its own object.

This *reflection* ought to be distinguished from *consciousness*, with which it is too often confounded, even
by Mr. Locke. From infancy, till we come to the
years of understanding, we are employed solely about
external objects; and, although the mind is conscious
of its operations, it does not *attend* to them; its attention is turned solely to the external objects about which
those operations are employed. Thus, when a man is
angry, he is conscious of his passion; but his attention is turned to the person who offended him, and the
circumstances of the offence, while the passion of anger
is not in the least the object of his attention.

I conceive this is sufficient to show the difference
between consciousness of the operations of our minds,
and reflection upon them; and to show that we may
have the former without any degree of the latter. The
difference between *consciousness* and *reflection* is like to
the difference between a superficial view of an object
which presents itself to the eye while we are engaged
about something else, and that attentive examination
which we give to an object when we are wholly employed in surveying it. Attention is a *voluntary* act;
it requires an active exertion to begin and to continue
it, and it may be *continued* as long as we will; but
consciousness is *involuntary* and of no continuance,
changing with every thought.

The power of reflection upon the operations of their
own minds does not appear at all in children. Men
must be come to some ripeness of understanding before they are capable of it. Of all the powers of the
human mind, it seems to be the *last that unfolds itself.* Most men seem incapable of acquiring it in any
considerable degree. Like all our other powers, it
is greatly improved by exercise; and, until a man
has got the habit of attending to the operations of his

---

* After Cicero : — "At ut oculus, sic animus se non videns alia cernit."
Tusc., I. 28. — Ed.

own mind, he can never have clear and distinct notions
of them, nor form any steady judgment concerning
them. His opinions must be borrowed from others,
his notions confused and indistinct, and he may easily
be led to swallow very gross absurdities. To acquire
this habit is a work of time and labor, even in those
who begin it early, and whose natural talents are tol-
erably fitted for it; but the difficulty will be daily diminishing, and the advantage of it is great. They will
thereby be enabled to think with precision and accuracy on every subject, especially on those subjects that
are more abstract. They will be able to judge for
themselves in many important points, wherein others
must blindly follow a leader.*

---

* Consciousness is not a special faculty coördinate with perception and
memory, but a general condition of mind considered as self-knowing, by
which all the mental faculties are made available. Through consciousness
the mind not only knows itself and the changes it undergoes, but also
whatever it knows by means of any of its special faculties. We are conscious of remembering as we do; we are conscious of perceiving as we do;
we are conscious of feeling as we do. Accordingly, as Sir W. Hamilton
intimates elsewhere, the various faculties may be regarded as special modifications of consciousness. If consciousness fails, all the special faculties fail.
Very frequently, however, the term is used in a restricted sense, signifying
the notice which the mind takes of itself and its operations and affections;
or *internal observation* in contradistinction to *external observation*, its acts
being called by some, not perceptions, but *apperceptions*. So understood,
consciousness is the witness and authority of all proper psychological facts.

Thus Jouffroy: — "What is consciousness? It is the feeling which the
intelligent principle has of itself. This principle has the feeling of itself,
and hence the consciousness of all the changes, all the modifications,
which it undergoes. The only phenomena, then, of which it can have the
consciousness, are those which are produced *within itself*. Those which
are produced *beyond itself*, it can *see;* but it cannot *feel* them. It can, then,
have the consciousness of its sensations, because it is itself which enjoys or
suffers; or of its thoughts, its determinations, because it is itself which
thinks and determines: but it can have no consciousness of muscular con-
traction, of digestion, of the circulation of the blood, because it is the mus-
cle which contracts, the stomach which digests, the blood which circulates,
and not itself. These phenomena, then, are precisely in the same relation
to it as the phenomena of external nature; they are produced *beyond it*,
and it can have no consciousness of them. Such is the true reason of the
incapability of the consciousness to seize a multitude of phenomena which
take place *in the body*, but which, on that account, are none the less exterior to the intelligent principle, to the real *me* [*ego*]. On the other hand,
the phenomena of consciousness being only the inward modifications of
the intelligent principle, that alone can perceive them, because it is that
alone which experiences them, and because, in order to perceive them, it

CHAPTER V.

DIVISION OF THE POWERS OF THE MIND.

I. *Division of the Mental Powers into Understanding and Will.*] The powers of the mind are so many, so various, and so connected and complicated in most of its operations, that there never has been any division of them proposed which is not liable to considerable objection. We shall therefore take that general division which is the most common, into the powers of *understanding* and those of *will.* Under the will we comprehend our *active* powers, and all that lead to action, or influence the mind to act, such as appetites, passions, affections. The understanding comprehends our *contemplative* powers; by which we perceive objects; by which we conceive or remember them; by which we analyze or compound them; and by which we judge and reason concerning them.

---

is necessary to feel them. For this reason, the phenomena of consciousness necessarily escape all external observation." — Ripley's *Philosophical Miscellanies*, Vol. II. p. 15.

To the same effect Cousin: — "But is a knowledge of human nature, is psychology, possible? Without doubt it is; for it is an undeniable fact, that nothing passes within us which we do not know, of which we have not a consciousness. Consciousness is a witness which gives us information of every thing which takes place in the interior of our minds. It is not the principle of any of our faculties, but is a light to them all. It is not because we have the consciousness of it, that any thing goes on within us; but that which goes on within us would be to us as though it did not take place, if it were not attested by consciousness. It is not by consciousness that we feel, or will, or think; but it is by it that we know that we do all this. . . . . . Consciousness is indeed more or less distinct, more or less vivid, but it is in all men. No one is unknown to himself, although very few know themselves perfectly, because all, or nearly all, make use of consciousness without applying themselves to perfect, unfold, and understand it, *by voluntary effort and attention.* In all men consciousness is a natural process; some elevate this natural process to the degree of an art, a method, by reflection, which is a sort of second consciousness, a free reproduction of the first; and as *consciousness* gives to all men a knowledge of what passes within them, so *reflection* gives the philosopher a *certain* knowledge of every thing which falls under the eye of consciousness. It is to be observed, that the question here is not concerning hypotheses or conjectures; for it is not even a question concerning a process of reasoning. It is solely

Although this general division may be of use in order to our proceeding more methodically in our subject, we are not to understand it as if, in those operations which are ascribed to the understanding, there were no exertion of will or activity, or as if the understanding were not employed in the operations ascribed to the will; for I conceive there is no operation of the understanding wherein the mind is not active in some degree. We have some command over our thoughts, and can attend to this or that, of many objects which present themselves to our senses, to our memory, or to our imagination. We can survey an object on this side or that, superficially or accurately, for a longer or a shorter time; so that our *contemplative* powers are under the guidance and direction of the *active;* and the former never pursue their object, without being led and directed, urged or restrained, by the latter: and because the understanding is always more or less directed by the will, mankind have ascribed some degree of activity to the mind in its intellectual operations, as well as in those which belong to the will, and have ex-

---

a question of facts, and of facts that are equally capable of being observed as those which come to pass on the scene of the outward world. The only difference is, the one is exterior, the other interior; and as the natural action of our faculties carries us outward, it is more easy to observe the one than the other. But with a little attention, voluntary exertion, and practice, one may succeed in internal observation as well as in external. The talent for the latter is not more common than for the former. The number of Bacons is not greater than the number of Descarteses."

In a note the translator, Professor Henry, adds: — " In regard to the distinction between the natural or spontaneous, and the philosophical or reflected consciousness, it may be remarked, that, while Locke uses the word *reflection* to signify the *natural* consciousness common to all reflecting beings, Cousin uses it above to imply *a particular determination of consciousness by the will.* Coleridge makes the same distinction with Cousin; but he does not consider the power of philosophical insight to be as common as Cousin would make it. 'It is neither possible,' says he, 'nor necessary for all men, or for many, to be philosophers. There is a *philosophic* (and, inasmuch as it is actualized by an effort of freedom, an *artificial*) consciousness which lies beneath, or, as it were, *behind*, the spontaneous consciousness natural to all reflecting beings.' " — *Elements of Psychology,* Chap. I. Compare Brown, *Lectures*, Lect. XI.; Fearn, *Essay on Consciousness,* p. 15 *et seq.; Dictionnaire des Sciences Philosophiques,* Art. *Conscience;* also, in *Blackwood's Edinburgh Magazine,* Vol. XLIII. - XLV., a series of ingenious papers, entitled *An Introduction to the Philosophy of Consciousness.* — ED.

3 *

pressed them by active verbs, such as *seeing, hearing, judging, reasoning*, and the like.

And as the mind exerts some degree of activity even in the operations of understanding, so it is certain that there can be no act of will which is not accompanied with some act of understanding. The will must have ∨ an object, and that object must be apprehended or conceived in the understanding. It is therefore to be remembered, that in most, if not all, operations of the mind, *both faculties concur;* and we range the operation under that faculty which has the largest share in it.*

II. *Subdivision of the Powers of the Understanding.*] There is not a more fruitful source of error in this branch of philosophy, than divisions of things which

---

* It would be out of place to enter on the extensive field of history and discussion relative to the distribution of our mental powers. It is sufficient to say, that the vulgar division of the faculties, adopted by Reid, into those of the *understanding* and those of the *will*, is to be traced to the classification, taken in the Aristotelic school, of the powers into *gnostic*, or cognitive, and *orectic*, or appetent. On this the reader may consult the admirable introduction of Philoponus — or rather of Ammonius Hermiæ — to the books of Aristotle *Upon the Soul.* — H.

The threefold division of the mind into *intellect, sensibility*, and *will* — to think, to feel, and to act — is now generally adopted by psychologists. See it stated and defended in *Dictionnaire des Sciences Philosophiques*, Art. *Facultés de l'Ame.* Also in Upham's *Mental Philosophy*, Introduction, Chap. IV.

Another classification is given by Jouffroy: — "In the actual state of human knowledge, the irreducible capacities of the human mind appear to me to be the following. First, *the personal faculty*, or the supreme power of taking possession of ourselves and of our capacities, and of controlling them: this faculty is known by the name of *liberty* or *will*, which designates it but imperfectly. Secondly, *the primitive inclinations* of our nature, or that aggregate of *instincts* or tendencies which impel us towards certain ends and in certain directions, prior to all experience, and which at once suggest to reason the destiny of our being, and animate our activity to pursue it. Thirdly, *the locomotive faculty*, or that energy by means of which we move the locomotive nerves, and produce all the voluntary bodily movements. Fourthly, *the expressive faculty*, or the power of representing by external signs that which takes place within us, and of thus holding communication with our fellow-men. Fifthly, *sensibility*, or the capacity of being agreeably or disagreeably affected by all external or internal causes, and of reacting in relation to them by movements of love or hatred, of desire or aversion, which are the principle of all passion. Sixthly, *the intellectual faculties:* this term comprises many distinct faculties, which can only be enumerated and described in a treatise on *Intelligence*." — Ripley's *Philosophical Miscellanies*, Vol. I. p. 382. — ED.

are taken to be complete when they are not really so. To make a perfect division of any class of things, a man ought to have the whole under his view at once. But the greatest capacity very often is not sufficient for this. Something is left out which did not come under the philosopher's view when he made his division; and to suit this to the division, it must be made what nature never made it. This has been so common a fault of philosophers, that one who would avoid error ought to be suspicious of divisions; though long received and of great authority, especially when they are grounded on a theory that may be called in question. In a subject imperfectly known, we ought not to pretend to perfect divisions, but to leave room for such additions or alterations as a more perfect view of the subject may afterwards suggest.

I shall not, therefore, attempt a complete enumeration of the *powers of the human understanding*. I shall only mention those which I propose to explain, and they are the following: —

First, The powers we have by means of our external senses. *Secondly*, Memory. *Thirdly*, Conception. *Fourthly*, The powers of resolving and analyzing complex objects, and compounding those that are more simple. *Fifthly*, Judging. *Sixthly*, Reasoning. *Seventhly*, Taste.*

---

* To these Dr. Reid added, — "*Eighthly*, Moral Perception; and, *last of all*, Consciousness." I omit the clause, because Moral Perception is not treated by him in this work, but in another, *On the Active Powers*, Essay V.; and Consciousness obtains only an incidental consideration, under Judgment, in the sixth Essay. On the impropriety of regarding *consciousness* as one of the coördinate special faculties of the understanding, see p. 27, note.

Dr. Brown reduces all the proper intellectual powers (or "states," as he prefers to call them) to *simple* and *relative suggestion*. To the former he refers *perception* (as distinguished from *sensation*), *conception*, *memory*, *imagination*, and *habit*; to the latter, *judgment*, *reason*, and *abstraction*. *Lectures*, Lect. XVI. *et passim*. For a defence of the same, see Payne's *Elements of Mental and Moral Science*, Chap. VI. — ED.

ESSAY II.

OF THE POWERS WE HAVE BY MEANS OF OUR EXTERNAL SENSES.

CHAPTER I.

OF THE ORGANS OF SENSE.

I. *General Remarks.*] Of all the operations of our minds, the *perception of external objects* is the most familiar. The senses come to maturity even in infancy, when other powers have not yet sprung up. They are common to us with brute animals, and furnish us with the objects about which our other powers are the most frequently employed. We find it easy to attend to their operations; and because they are familiar, the names which properly belong to them are applied to other powers which are thought to resemble them. For these reasons they claim to be first considered.

The perception of external objects is one main link of that mysterious chain which connects the material world with the intellectual. We shall find many things in this operation unaccountable; sufficient to convince us, that we know but little of our own frame, and that a perfect comprehension of our mental powers, and of the manner of their operation, is beyond the reach of our understanding.

In perception there are impressions upon the organs of sense, the nerves, and brain, which, by the laws of our nature, are followed by certain operations of mind. These two things are apt to be confounded, but ought most carefully to be distinguished. Some philosophers, without good reason, have concluded that the impressions made on the body are the proper efficient cause of perception. Others, with as little reason, have concluded that impressions are made on the mind similar to those made on the body. From these mistakes, many others have arisen. The wrong notions men have rashly taken up with regard to the senses have led to wrong notions with regard to other powers which are conceived to resemble them. Many important powers of mind have, especially of late, been called *internal senses*, from a supposed resemblance to the external; such as the *sense of beauty*, the *sense of harmony*, the *moral sense*. And it is to be apprehended, that errors with regard to the external have, from analogy, led to similar errors with regard to the internal; it is therefore of some consequence, even with regard to other branches of our subject, to have just notions concerning the external senses.

II. *The Laws of Perception considered in Relation to the Organs of Sense.*] In order to this, we shall begin with some observations on the organs of sense, and on the impressions which in perception are made upon them, and upon the nerves and brain.

1. *We perceive no external object but by means of certain bodily organs which God has given us for that purpose.* The Supreme Being who made us, and placed us in this world, has given us such powers of mind as he saw to be suited to our state and rank in his creation. He has given us the power of perceiving many objects around us, — the sun, moon, and stars, the earth and sea, and a variety of animals, vegetables, and inanimate bodies. But our power of perceiving these objects is limited in various ways, and particularly in this, that without the organs of the several senses we perceive no external object. We cannot see without eyes, nor hear without ears: it is not only necessary that we should have these organs, but that they should be in a sound and natural state. There are many disorders of the eye that cause total blindness; others

that impair the powers of vision, without destroying it altogether; and the same may be said of the organs of all the other senses.

All this is so well known from experience, that it needs no proof; but it ought to be observed, that we know it from *experience only*. We can give no reason for it, but that such is the will of our Maker. No man can show it to be impossible to the Supreme Being to have given us the power of perceiving external objects without such organs. We have reason to believe, that, when we put off these bodies, and all the organs belonging to them, our perceptive powers shall rather be improved than destroyed or impaired. We have reason to believe that the Supreme Being perceives every thing in a much more perfect manner than we do, without bodily organs. We have reason to believe that there are other created beings endowed with powers of perception more perfect and more extensive than ours, without any such organs as we find necessary.

We ought not, therefore, to conclude, that such bodily organs are, in their own nature, necessary to perception; but rather, that, by the will of God, our power of perceiving external objects is limited to and circumscribed by our organs of sense; so that we perceive objects in a certain manner, and in certain circumstances, and in no other.*

---

* "Among the well-attested facts of physiology," says Müller, perhaps the highest authority on the subject, "there is not one to support the belief that one nerve of sense can assume the functions of another. The exaggeration of the sense of touch in the blind will not, in these days, be called *seeing with the fingers;* the accounts of the power of vision by the fingers and epigastrium, said to be possessed in the so-called magnetic state, appear to be mere fables, and the instances in which it has been pretended to practise it, cases of deception." And again: — "It is quite in accordance with the laws of science, that a person sleeping shall have ocular spectra, — we experience them sometimes when the eyes are closed, even before falling asleep, — for the nerves of vision may be excited to sensation by internal as well as by external causes; and so long as a magnetic patient manifests merely the ordinary phenomena of nervous action that are seen in other disorders of the nervous system, it is all creditable enough. But when such a person pretends to see through a bandage placed before the eyes, or by means of the fingers or the epigastrium, or to see round a corner and into a neighbouring house, or to become pro-

If a man were shut up in a dark room, so that he could see nothing but through one small hole in the shutter of a window, would he conclude that the hole was the cause of his seeing, and that it is impossible to see any other way? Perhaps, if he had never in his life seen but in this way, he might be apt to think so; but the conclusion is rash and groundless. He sees because God has given him the power of seeing; and he sees only through this small hole, because his power of seeing is circumscribed by impediments on all other hands.

Another necessary caution in this matter is, that we ought *not to confound the organs of perception with the being that perceives.* Perception must be the act of some being that perceives. The eye is not that which sees; it is only the organ by which we see. The ear is not that which hears, but the organ by which we hear. And so of the rest.*

A man cannot see the satellites of Jupiter but by a telescope. Does he conclude from this, that it is the telescope that sees those stars? By no means; such a conclusion would be absurd. It is no less absurd to conclude that it is the eye that sees or the ear that hears. The telescope is an artificial organ of sight, but it sees not. The eye is a natural organ of sight, by which we see; but the natural organ sees as little as the artificial.

The eye is a machine most admirably contrived for refracting the rays of light, and forming a distinct picture of objects upon the retina; but it sees neither the object nor the picture. It can form the picture after it

---

phetic, such arrant imposture no longer deserves forbearance, and an open and sound exposure of the deception is called for." — *Elements of Physiology,* Vol. II. pp. 1071, 1125. See also Carpenter's *Principles of Human Physiology,* § 311.

* This doctrine may be traced back to Aristotle and his school, and even higher. "There is extant," says Plutarch, "a discourse of Strato Physicus, demonstrating *that a sensitive apprehension is wholly impossible without an act of intellect.*" (*Op. Mor.,* p. 961.) And as to Aristotle himself: — " To divorce," he says, " sensation from understanding, is to reduce sensation to an insensible process; wherefore it has been said, *intellect sees, and intellect hears.*" (*Probl.,* XI. 33.) — H.

is taken out of the head; but no vision ensues. Even when it is in its proper place, and perfectly sound, it is well known that an obstruction in the optic nerve takes away vision, though the eye has performed all that belongs to it.

If any thing more were necessary to be said on a point so evident, we might observe, that, if the faculty of seeing were in the eye, that of hearing in the ear, and so of the other senses, the necessary consequence of this would be, that the thinking principle, which I call *myself*, is not one, but many. But this is contrary to the irresistible conviction of every man. When I say, *I* see, *I* hear, *I* feel, *I* remember, this implies that it is one and the same self that performs all these operations; and as it would be absurd to say, that my memory, another man's imagination, and a third man's reason, may make one individual intelligent being, it would be equally absurd to say, that one piece of matter seeing, another hearing, and a third feeling, may make one and the same percipient being.

2. A second law of our nature regarding perception is, *that we perceive no object, unless some impression is made upon the organ of sense, either by the immediate application of the object, or by some medium which passes between the object and the organ.*

In two of our senses, to wit, touch and taste, there must be an *immediate application of the object to the organ.* In the other three, the object is perceived at a distance, but still by means of a medium by which some impression is made upon the organ.*

The effluvia of bodies drawn into the nostrils with

---

* This distinction of a *mediate* and *immediate* object, or of an object and a medium, in perception, is inaccurate, and a source of sad confusion. We perceive, and can perceive, nothing but what is in relation to the organ, and nothing is in relation to the organ that is not present to it. All the senses are, in fact, *modifications of touch*, as Democritus of old taught. We reach the distant reality, not by sense, not by perception, but by *inference*. Thus it is inaccurate to say, as Reid does in the next sentence, that "the effluvia of bodies" are "the medium of smell." Nothing is smelt but the effluvia themselves. They constitute the total object of *perception* in smell. Reid, however, in this only follows his predecessors. — H.

the breath are the medium of smell; the undulations of the air are the medium of hearing; and the rays of light passing from visible objects to the eye are the medium of sight. We see no object unless rays of light come from it to the eye. We hear not the sound of any body, unless the vibrations of some elastic medium, occasioned by the tremulous motion of the sounding body, reach our ear. We perceive no smell, unless the effluvia of the smelling body enter into the nostrils. We perceive no taste, unless the sapid body be applied to the tongue, or some part of the organ of taste. Nor do we perceive any tangible quality of a body, unless it touch the hands, or some part of our body.

These are facts known from experience to hold universally and invariably, both in men and brutes. By this law of our nature, our powers of perceiving external objects are further limited and circumscribed. Nor can we give any other reason for this, than that it is the will of our Maker, who knows best what powers, and what degrees of them, are suited to our state. We were once in a state, (I mean in the womb,) wherein our powers of perception were more limited than in the present, and in a future state they may be more enlarged.

3. It is likewise a law of our nature, that, in order to our perceiving objects, *the impressions made upon the organs of sense must be communicated to the nerves, and by them to the brain.* This is perfectly known to those who know any thing of anatomy.

The nerves are fine cords, which pass from the brain, or from the spinal marrow, which is a prolongation of the brain, to all parts of the body, dividing into smaller branches as they proceed, until at last they escape our eyesight; and it is found by experience, that all the voluntary and involuntary motions of the body are performed by their means. When the nerves that serve any limb are cut, or tied hard, we have then no more power to move that limb than if it was no part of the body.

4

As there are nerves that serve the muscular motions, so there are others that serve the several senses; and as without the former we cannot move a limb, so without the latter we can have no perception.

This train of machinery the wisdom of God has made necessary to our perceiving objects. Various parts of the body concur to it, and each has its own function. First the object, either immediately or by some medium, must make an impression on the organ. The organ serves only as a medium, by which an impression is made on the nerve; and the nerve serves as a medium to make an impression upon the brain. Here the material part ends; at least, we can trace it no farther; the rest is all intellectual.

The proof of these impressions upon the nerves and brain in perception is this, — that, from many observations and experiments, it is found, that, when the organ of any sense is perfectly sound, and has the impression made upon it by the object ever so strongly, yet, if the nerve which serves that organ be cut or tied hard, there is no perception; and it is well known, that disorders in the brain deprive us of the power of perception, when both the organ and its nerve are sound.

There is, therefore, sufficient reason to conclude, that, in perception, the object produces some change in the organ; that the organ produces some change upon the nerve; and that the nerve produces some change in the brain. And we give the name of an *impression* to those changes, because we have not a name more proper to express, in a general manner, any change produced in a body by an external cause, without specifying the nature of that change. Whether it be pressure, or attraction, or repulsion, or vibration, or something unknown, for which we have no name, still it may be called an impression. But with regard to the particular kind of this change or impression, philosophers have never been able to discover any thing at all.

But, whatever be the nature of those impressions upon the organs, nerves, and brain, we perceive nothing without them. Experience informs us that it is so;

but we cannot give a reason why it is so. In the constitution of man, perception, by fixed laws of nature, is connected with those impressions; but we can discover no necessary connection. The Supreme Being has seen fit to limit our power of perception, so that we perceive not without such impressions; and this is all we know of the matter.

This, however, we have reason to conclude in general, — that, as the *impressions* on the organs, nerves, and brain, correspond exactly to the nature and conditions of the objects by which they are made, so our *perceptions* and *sensations* correspond to those impressions, and vary in *kind*, and in *degree*, as they vary. Without this exact correspondence, the information we receive by our senses would not only be imperfect, as it undoubtedly is, but would be fallacious, which we have no reason to think it is.*

---

* Physiologists will not allow us to hold the doctrine taught in this chapter in such a sense as to exclude what are called *subjective sensations*. "Every one," says Müller, " is aware how common it is to see bright colors while the eyes are closed, particularly in the morning, when the irritability of the nerves is still considerable. These phenomena are very frequent in children after waking from sleep. Through the sense of vision, we receive from external nature no impressions which we may not also experience from internal excitement of our nerves; and it is evident that a person blind from infancy, in consequence of opacity of the transparent media of the eye, must have a perfect internal conception of light and colors, provided the retina and optic nerve be free from lesion. The prevalent notions with regard to the wonderful sensations supposed to be experienced by persons blind from birth, when their sight is restored by operation, are exaggerated and incorrect. The elements of the sensation of vision, namely, the sensations of light, color, and darkness, must have been previously as well known to such persons as to those of whom the sight has always been perfect. The sensations of hearing, also, are excited as well by internal as by external causes; for whenever the auditory nerve is in a state of excitement, the sensations peculiar to it, as the sounds of ringing, humming, &c., are produced. No further proof is wanting, to show that external influences give rise in our senses to no other sensations than those which may be excited in the corresponding nerves by internal causes." — *Elements*, Vol. II. p. 1060.

Carpenter explains the possibility of these phenomena by observing, — " With regard to all kinds of sensation, it is to be remembered that the change of which the mind is informed is *not* the change at the peripheral extremities of the nerves, but the change communicated to the sensorium; hence it results, that external agencies can give rise to no kind of sensation which cannot also be produced by internal causes, exciting changes in the condition of the nerves in their course." — *Principles*, § 310. — ED.

CHAPTER II.

HARTLEY'S THEORY OF VIBRATIONS.

I. *Historical Notices.*] We are informed by anatomists, that although the two coats which inclose a nerve, and which it derives from the coats of the brain, are tough and elastic, yet the nerve itself has a very small degree of consistence, being almost like marrow. It has, however, a fibrous texture, and may be divided and subdivided, till its fibres escape our senses. And as we know so very little about the texture of the nerves, there is great room left for those who choose to indulge themselves in conjecture.

The ancients conjectured that the nervous fibres are fine tubes, filled with a very subtile spirit or vapor, which they called *animal spirits;* that the brain is a gland, by which the animal spirits are secreted from the finer part of the blood, and their continual waste repaired; and that it is by these animal spirits that the nerves perform their functions. Descartes has shown how, by these animal spirits going and returning in the nerves, muscular motion, perception, memory, and imagination are effected. All this he has described as distinctly as if he had been an eyewitness of all those operations. But it happens that the tubular structure of the nerves was never perceived by the human eye, nor shown by the nicest injections; and all that has been said about animal spirits, through more than fifteen centuries, is mere conjecture.

Dr. Briggs, who was Sir Isaac Newton's master in anatomy, was the first, as far as I know, who advanced a new system concerning the nerves.* He conceived

---

* Briggs was not the first. The Jesuit, Honoratus Fabry, had before him denied the old hypothesis of *spirits;* and the new hypothesis of cerebral fibres or fibrils, by which he explains the phenomena of sense, imagination, and memory, is not only the first, but perhaps the most ingenious of the class that has been proposed. Yet the very name of Fabry is

them to be solid filaments of prodigious tenuity; and this opinion, as it accords better with observation, seems to have been more generally received since his time. As to the manner of performing their office, Dr. Briggs thought, that, like musical cords, they have vibrations differing according to their length and tension. They seem, however, very unfit for this purpose, on account of their want of tenacity, their moisture, and being through their whole length in contact with moist substances: so that, although Dr. Briggs wrote a book upon this system, called *Nova Visionis Theoria*, it seems not to have been much followed.

Sir Isaac Newton, in all his philosophical writings, took great care to distinguish his doctrines, which he intended to prove by just induction, from his conjectures, which were to stand or fall, according as future experiments and observations should establish or refute them. His conjectures he has put in the form of queries, that they might not be received as truths, but be inquired into, and determined according to the evidence to be found for or against them. Those who mistake his queries for a part of his doctrine do him great injustice, and degrade him to the rank of the common herd of philosophers, who have, in all ages, adulterated philosophy by mixing conjecture with truth, and their own fancies with the oracles of nature. Among other queries, this truly great philosopher proposed this, — Whether there may not be an elastic medium, or ether, immensely more rare than air, which pervades all bodies, and which is the cause of gravitation; of the refraction and reflection of the rays of light; of the transmission of heat, through spaces void of air; and of many other phenomena? In the 23d query subjoined to his *Optics*, he puts this question, with regard to the impressions made on the nerves and brain in perception, — Whether vision is effected chiefly by the

---

wholly unnoticed by those historians of philosophy who do not deem it superfluous to dwell on the tiresome reveries of Briggs, Hartley, and Bonnet. — H.

4 *

vibrations of this medium, excited in the bottom of the eye by the rays of light, and propagated along the solid, pellucid, and uniform capillaments of the optic nerve?   And whether hearing is effected by the vibrations of this or some other medium, excited by the tremor of the air in the auditory nerves, and propagated along the solid, pellucid, and uniform capillaments of those nerves?   And so with regard to the other senses.

What Newton only proposed as a matter to be inquired into, Dr. Hartley conceived to have such evidence, that, in his *Observations on Man*, he has deduced, in a mathematical form, a very ample system concerning the faculties of the mind, from the doctrine of vibrations, joined with that of association.*

His notion of the vibrations excited in the nerves is expressed in the fourth and fifth Propositions in Part I. Chap. I. Sect. I. " Proposition 4. External objects impressed on the senses occasion, first in the nerves on which they are impressed, and then in the brain, vibrations of the small, and, as one may say, infinitesimal medullary particles.   Proposition 5. The vibrations mentioned in the last proposition are excited, propagated, and kept up, partly by the ether, that is, by a very subtile elastic fluid; partly by the uniformity, continuity, softness, and active powers of the medullary substance of the brain, spinal marrow, and nerves."

The modesty and diffidence with which Dr. Hartley offers his system to the world, by desiring his reader " to expect nothing but hints and conjectures in difficult and obscure matters, and a short detail of the principal reasons and evidences in those that are clear; by acknowledging that he shall not be able to execute, with any accuracy, the proper method of philosophiz-

---

* David Hartley was born at Armley, in the county of York, August 30, 1705, and died at Bath, August 28, 1757. His *Observations* were first published in 1749. Pistorius translated the work into German, with valuable " Notes and Additions," which are now commonly appended, in English, to the best editions of the original. In the *Metaphysical Tracts by English Philosophers of the Eighteenth Century*, there is one, *Conjecturæ quædam de Sensu, Motu, et Idearum Generatione*, which is ascribed to Hartley. — ED.

ing, recommended and followed by Sir Isaac Newton; and that he will attempt a sketch only for the benefit of future inquirers," — seem to forbid any criticism upon it. One cannot, without reluctance, criticize what is proposed in such a manner, and with so good intention; yet, as the tendency of this system of vibrations is to make all the operations of the mind mere mechanism, dependent on the laws of matter and motion, and as it has been held forth by its votaries *as in a manner demonstrated*, I shall make some remarks on that part of the system which relates to the impressions made on the nerves and brain in perception.

II. *Refutation of the Theory.*] It may be observed, in general, that Dr. Hartley's work consists of a chain of propositions, with their proofs and corollaries, digested in good order, and in a scientific form. A great part of them, however, are, as he candidly acknowledges, conjectures and hints only; yet these are mixed with the propositions legitimately proved, without any distinction. Corollaries are drawn from them, and other propositions grounded upon them, which, all taken together, *make up a system.* A system of this kind resembles a chain, of which some links are abundantly strong, others very weak. The strength of the chain is determined by that of the weakest links; for if they give way, the whole falls to pieces, and the weight supported by it falls to the ground.

As to the vibrations and vibratiuncles, whether of an elastic ether, or of the infinitesimal particles of the brain and nerves, there may be such things for what we know, and men may rationally inquire whether they can find any evidence of their existence; but while we have no proof of their existence, to apply them to the solution of phenomena, and to build a system upon them, is what I conceive we call building a castle in the air.

When men pretend to account for any of the operations of nature, the causes assigned by them ought, as Sir Isaac Newton has taught us, to have two conditions, otherwise they are good for nothing. *First*, They ought to be true, to have a real existence, and not to be barely conjectured to exist, without proof. *Secondly*, They ought to be sufficient to produce the effect.

As to the existence of vibratory motions in the medullary substance of the nerves and brain, the evidence produced is this:— *First*, It is observed, that the sensations of seeing and hearing, and some sensations of touch, have some short duration and continuance. *Secondly*, Though there be no direct evidence that the sensations of taste and smell, and the greater part of those of touch, have the like continuance; yet, says the author, analogy would incline one to believe, that they must resemble the sensations of sight and hearing in this particular. *Thirdly*, The continuance of all our sensations being thus established, it follows that external objects impress vibratory motions on the medullary substance of the nerves and brain; because no motion besides a vibratory one can reside in any part for a moment of time.

This is the chain of proof; in which the first link is strong, being confirmed by experience; the second is very weak; and the third still weaker. For other kinds of motion, besides that of vibration, may have some continuance, such as rotation, bending or unbending of a spring, and perhaps others which we are unacquainted with: nor do we know whether it is motion that is produced in the nerves; it may be pressure, attraction, repulsion, or something we do not know. This, indeed, is the common refuge of all hypotheses, that we know no other way in which the phenomena may be produced, and therefore they must be produced in this way. There is, therefore, no proof of vibrations in the infinitesimal particles of the brain and nerves.

It may be thought that the existence of an elastic vibrating ether stands on a firmer foundation, having the authority of Sir Isaac Newton. But it ought to be observed, that although this great man had formed conjectures about this ether near fifty years before he died, and had it in his eye during that long space as a sub-

ject of inquiry, yet it does not appear that he ever
found any convincing proof of its existence, but considered it to the last as a question whether there be such
an ether or not. In the premonition to the reader, prefixed to the second edition of his *Optics*, *anno* 1717, he
expresses himself thus with regard to it : — " Lest any
one should think that I place gravity among the essential properties of bodies, I have subjoined one question
concerning its cause ; a question, I say, for I do not
hold it as a thing established." If, therefore, we regard
the authority of Sir Isaac Newton, we ought to hold
the existence of such an ether as a matter not established by proof, but to be examined into by experiments ; and I have never heard that, since his time, any
new evidence has been found of its existence.

Vibrations and vibratiuncles of the medullary substance of the nerves and brain are assigned by Dr.
Hartley to account for all our sensations and ideas,
and, in a word, for all the operations of our minds.
Let us consider very briefly how far they are sufficient
for that purpose.

He proposes his sentiments with great candor, and
they ought not to be carried beyond what his words
express. He thinks it a consequence of his theory, that
matter, if it can be endued with the most simple kinds
of sensation, might arrive at all that intelligence of
which the human mind is possessed. He thinks that
his theory overturns all the arguments that are usually
brought for the immateriality of the soul, from the subtilty of the internal senses, and of the rational faculty ;
but he does not take upon him to determine whether
matter can be endued with sensation or no. He even
acknowledges, that matter and motion, however subtilely divided and reasoned upon, yield nothing more
than matter and motion still ; and therefore he would
not be any way interpreted so as to oppose the immateriality of the soul.

It would, therefore, be unreasonable to require that
his theory of vibrations should, in the proper sense, account for our sensations. It would, indeed, be ridicu-

lous in any man to pretend, that thought of any kind must necessarily result from motion, or that vibrations in the nerves must necessarily produce thought, any more than the vibrations of a pendulum. Dr. Hartley disclaims this way of thinking, and therefore it ought not to be imputed to him. All that he pretends is, that, in the human constitution, there is a certain connection between vibrations in the medullary substance of the nerves and brain, and the thoughts of the mind; so that the last depend entirely upon the first, and every kind of thought in the mind arises in consequence of a corresponding vibration, or vibratiuncle, in the nerves and brain. Our sensations arise from *vibrations*, and our ideas from *vibratiuncles*, or miniature vibrations; and he comprehends, under these two words of *sensations* and *ideas*, all the operations of the mind.

But how can we expect any proof of the connection between vibrations and thought, when the existence of such vibrations was never proved. The proof of their connection cannot be stronger than the proof of their existence: for, as the author acknowledges that we cannot infer the existence of the thoughts from the existence of the vibrations, it is no less evident that we cannot infer the existence of vibrations from the existence of our thoughts. The existence of both must be known before we can know their connection. As to the existence of our thoughts, we have the evidence of consciousness; a kind of evidence that never was called in question. But as to the existence of vibrations in the medullary substance of the nerves and brain, no proof has yet been brought.

All, therefore, we have to expect from this hypothesis is, that, in vibrations considered abstractly, there should be a variety in kind and degree, which tallies so exactly with the varieties of the thoughts they are to account for, as may lead us to suspect some connection between the one and the other. If the divisions and subdivisions of thought be found to run parallel with the divisions and subdivisions of vibrations, this would give that kind of plausibility to the hypothesis of their connection which we commonly expect in *a mere hypothesis;* but we do not find even this.

Philosophers have accounted in some degree for our various sensations of *sound,* by the vibrations of elastic *air.* But it is to be observed, *first,* that we know that such vibrations do really exist; and, *secondly,* that they tally exactly with the most remarkable phenomena of sound. We cannot, indeed, show how any vibration should produce the sensation of sound. This must be resolved into the will of God, or into some cause altogether unknown. But we know, that as the vibration is strong or weak, the sound is loud or soft. We know, that as the vibration is quick or slow, the sound is acute or grave. We can point out that relation of synchronous vibrations which produces harmony or discord, and that relation of successive vibrations which produces melody: and all this is not conjectured, but proved by a sufficient induction. This account of sounds, therefore, is philosophical; although, perhaps, there may be many things relating to sound that we cannot account for, and of which the causes remain latent. The connections described in this branch of philosophy are the work of God, and not the fancy of men.

If any thing similar to this could be shown in accounting for all our sensations by vibrations in *the medullary substance of the nerve and brain,* it would deserve a place in sound philosophy. But when we are told of vibrations in a substance, *which no man could ever prove to have vibrations, or to be capable of them;* when such imaginary vibrations are brought to account for all our sensations, *though we can perceive no correspondence, in their variety of kind and degree, to the variety of sensations;* the connections described in such a system are the creatures of human imagination, not the work of God.

The rays of light make an impression upon the optic nerves; but they make none upon the auditory or olfactory. The vibrations of the air make an impression upon the auditory nerves; but none upon the op-

tic or the olfactory. The effluvia of bodies make an
impression upon the olfactory nerves; but make none
upon the optic or auditory. No man has been able to
give a shadow of reason for this. While this is the
case, is it not better to confess our ignorance of the
nature of those impressions made upon the nerves and
brain in perception, than to flatter our pride with the
conceit of knowledge which we have not, and to adul-
terate philosophy with the spurious brood of hypotheses? *

CHAPTER III.

FALSE CONCLUSIONS DRAWN FROM THE CONNECTION
BETWEEN PERCEPTION AND IMPRESSIONS MADE ON
THE ORGANS OF SENSE.

I. (1.) *That the Mind is Material, and Perception the
Result of Mechanism.*] Some philosophers among the
ancients, as well as among the moderns, imagined that
man is nothing but *a piece of matter so curiously organized, that the impressions of external objects produce
in it sensation, perception, remembrance, and all the other
operations we are conscious of.* This foolish opinion
could only take its rise from observing the constant
connection which the Author of nature has established
between certain impressions made upon our senses,
and our perception of the objects by which the impression is made; from which they weakly inferred, that

---

* Reid appears to have been unacquainted with the works and theory of
Bonnet. With our author's strictures on the physiological hypotheses, the
reader may compare those of Tetens, in his *Versuche*, and of Stewart, in
his *Philosophical Essays.* — H.
   Haller took pains to refute the theory of vibrations in his *Elementa Phy-
siologiæ*, Vol. IV. Sect. VIII., Art. *Conjecturæ*. For some account of the
writers who have advocated it, see Blakey's *History of the Philosophy of
Mind*, Vol. III. Chap. XVII. Dr. Priestley published an octavo volume,
in 1775, containing a portion of Dr. Hartley's great work, with this title:
*Hartley's Theory of the Human Mind, on the Principle of the Association of
Ideas, with Essays on the Subject of it.* — ED.

those impressions were the proper efficient causes of the corresponding perception.

But no reasoning is more fallacious than this, that, because two things are always conjoined, therefore one must be the cause of the other. Day and night have been joined in a constant succession since the beginning of the world; but who is so foolish as to conclude from this that day is the cause of night, or night the cause of the following day? There is indeed nothing more ridiculous than to imagine that any motion or modification of matter should produce thought.

If one should tell of a telescope so exactly made as to have the power of seeing; of a whispering gallery that had the power of hearing; of a cabinet so nicely framed as to have the power of memory; or of a machine so delicate as to feel pain when it was touched, —such absurdities are so shocking to common sense, that they would not find belief even among savages: yet it is the same absurdity to think that the impressions of external objects upon the machine of our bodies can be the real efficient cause of thought and perception.

II. (2.) *That an Impression is made on the Mind, as well as on the Organs of Sense.*] Another conclusion sometimes drawn by philosophers is, *that in perception an impression is made upon the mind, as well as upon the organ, nerves, and brain.* Mr. Locke affirms very positively, that the ideas of external objects are produced in our minds by impulse, " that being the only way we can conceive bodies to operate in." It ought, however, to be observed, in justice to Mr. Locke, that he retracted this notion in his first letter to the Bishop of Worcester, and promised in the next edition of his *Essay* to have that passage rectified; but either from forgetfulness in the author, or negligence in the printer, the passage remains in all the subsequent editions I have seen.

There is no prejudice more natural to man, than to conceive of the mind as having some similitude to

5

body in its operations. Hence men have been prone
to imagine, that, as bodies are put in motion by some
impulse or impression made upon them by contiguous
bodies, so the mind is made to think and to perceive
by some impression made upon it, or some impulse
given to it, by contiguous objects. If we have such a
notion of the mind as Homer had of his gods, who
might be bruised or wounded with swords and spears,
we may then understand what is meant by impressions
made upon it by a body. But if we conceive the mind
to be *immaterial*, of which I think we have very strong
proofs, we shall find it difficult to affix a meaning to
impressions made upon it.

There is a *figurative* meaning of impressions on the
mind which is well authorized, but this meaning applies only to objects that are *interesting*. To say that
an object which I see with perfect indifference makes
an impression upon my mind, is not, as I apprehend,
good English. If philosophers mean no more than
that I see the object, why should they invent an improper phrase to express what every man knows how
to express in plain English?

But it is evident, from the manner in which this
phrase is used by modern philosophers, that they mean
not merely to express by it my perceiving an object,
but to explain the manner of perception. They think
that the object perceived acts upon the mind, in some
way similar to that in which one body acts upon
another, by making an impression upon it. The impression upon the mind is conceived to be something
wherein the mind is altogether passive, and has some
effect produced on it by the object. But this is a hy-.
pothesis which contradicts the common sense of mankind, and which ought not to be admitted without
proof. When I look upon the wall of my room, the
wall does not act at all, nor is it capable of acting; the
perceiving it is an act or operation in me. That this
is the common apprehension of mankind with regard
to perception, is evident from the manner of expressing
it in all languages.

The vulgar give themselves no trouble how they perceive objects. They express what they are conscious of, and they express it with propriety; but philosophers have an avidity to know *how* we perceive objects; and, conceiving some similitude between a body that is put in motion and a mind that is made to perceive, they are led to think, that, as the body must receive some impulse to make it move, so the mind must receive some impulse or impression to make it perceive. This analogy seems to be confirmed, by observing that we perceive objects only when they make some impression upon the organs of sense, and upon the nerves and brain; but it ought to be observed, that such is the nature of *body*, that it cannot change its state, *but by some force impressed upon it.* This is not the nature of *mind.* All that we know about it shows it to be in its nature *living and active,* and to have the power of perception in its constitution, but still within those limits to which it is confined by the laws of nature.

It appears, therefore, that this phrase of the mind's having impressions made upon it by corporeal objects in perception, is either a phrase without any distinct meaning, and contrary to the propriety of the English language, or it is grounded upon an hypothesis which is destitute of proof. On that account, though we grant that in perception there is an impression made upon *the organ of sense,* and upon *the nerves and brain,* we do not admit that the object makes any impression upon the *mind.*

III. (3.) *That these Impressions leave Images in the Brain which are the only Immediate Objects of Perception.*] There is another conclusion drawn from the impressions made upon the brain in perception, which I conceive to have no solid foundation, though it has been adopted very generally by philosophers. It is, *that by the impressions made on the brain, images are formed of the object perceived; and that the mind, being seated in the brain as its chamber of presence, immediately perceives those images only, and has no perception of the external object but by them.*

Now, with regard to this hypothesis, there are three things that deserve to be considered, because the hypothesis leans upon them; and if any one of them fail, it must fall to the ground. The *first* is, that the soul has its seat, or, as Mr. Locke calls it, "its presence-room," in the brain. The *second,* that there are images formed in the brain of all the objects of sense. The *third,* that the mind or soul perceives these images in the brain; and that it perceives not external objects immediately, but only by means of their images.

As to the *first* point, that the soul has its seat in the brain, this, surely, is not so well established as that we can safely build other principles upon it. There have been various opinions and much disputation about the place of spirits; whether they have a place, and if they have, how they occupy that place. After men had fought in the dark about these points for ages, the wiser part seem to have left off disputing about them, as matters beyond the reach of the human faculties.

As to the *second* point, that images of all the objects of sense are formed in the brain, we may venture to affirm that there is no proof nor probability of this, with regard to *any* of the objects of sense; and that with regard to the *greater part* of them, it is words without any meaning.

That external objects make some impression on the organs of sense, and by them on the nerves and brain, is granted; but that those impressions resemble the objects they are made by, so as that they may be called *images of the objects,* is most improbable. Every hypothesis that has been contrived shows that there can be no such resemblance; for neither the motions of animal spirits, nor the vibrations of elastic chords, or of elastic ether, or of the infinitesimal particles of the nerves, can be supposed to resemble the objects by which they are excited.

We know that, in vision, an image of the visible object is formed in the bottom of the eye by the rays of light. But we know also, that this image cannot be conveyed to the brain, because the optic nerve, and all the parts that surround it, are opaque and impervious to the rays of light; and there is no other organ of sense in which any image of the object is formed.

It is further to be observed, that, with regard to some objects of sense, we may understand what is meant by an image of them imprinted on the brain; but with regard to most objects of sense, the phrase is absolutely unintelligible, and conveys no meaning at all. As to objects of sight, I understand what is meant by an image of their *figure* in the brain. But how shall we conceive an image of their *color*, where there is absolute darkness? And as to all other objects of sense, except figure and color, I am unable to conceive what is meant by an image of them. Let any man say what he means by an image of heat or cold, an image of hardness or softness, an image of sound, of smell, or taste. The word *image*, when applied to these objects of sense, has absolutely no meaning. Upon what a weak foundation, then, does this hypothesis stand, when it supposes that images of all the objects of sense are imprinted on the brain, being conveyed thither by the conduits of the organs and nerves.

The *third* point in this hypothesis is, that the mind perceives the images in the brain, and external objects only by means of them. This is as improbable, as that there are such images to be perceived. If our powers of perception be not altogether fallacious, the objects we perceive are not in our brain, but without us. We are so far from perceiving images in the brain, that we do not perceive our brain at all; nor would any man ever have known that he had a brain, if anatomy had not discovered, by dissection, that the brain is a constituent part of the human body.

To sum up what has been said with regard to the organs of perception, and the impressions made upon our nerves and brain. It is a law of our nature, established by the will of the Supreme Being, that we perceive no external object but by means of the organs given us for that purpose. But these organs do not perceive. The eye is the organ of sight, but it sees not.

5 *

A telescope is an artificial organ of sight. The eye is a natural organ of sight, but it sees as little as the telescope. We know how the eye forms a picture of the visible object upon the retina; but how this picture makes us see the object we know not; and if experience had not informed us that such a picture is necessary to vision, we should never have known it. We can give no reason why the picture on the retina should be followed by vision, while a like picture on any other part of the body produces nothing like vision.

It is likewise a law of our nature, that we perceive not external objects, unless certain impressions be made by the object upon the organ, and by means of the organ upon the nerves and brain. But of the nature of those impressions we are perfectly ignorant; and though they are *conjoined with perception* by the will of our Maker, yet it does not appear that they have any *necessary* connection with it in their own nature, *far less that they can be the proper efficient cause of it.* We perceive, because God has given us the power of perceiving, and not because we have impressions from objects. We perceive nothing without those impressions, because our Maker has limited and circumscribed our powers of perception by such laws of nature as to his wisdom seemed meet, and such as suited our rank in his creation.*

---

* In noticing the benefit accruing to psychology from recent physiological investigations, Mr. Morell observes: — "The phantasms of Aristotle, the animal spirits of Descartes, the vibrations of Hartley, and all such speculations, are virtually moved out of the road by a closer examination of the *facts* of the case, and thus prevented from encumbering the movements of scientific research. In opposition to such notions, it has been discovered that the different kinds of nerves have specific qualities of their own, and that, instead of *conveying* impressions, they give rise to certain phenomena simply *by the excitement of their own properties.*"

He adds: — "At the same time, it is of great importance that the two sciences should each hold their proper limits, and that the one should not be allowed to assume the ground which peculiarly belongs to the other. To mark the boundaries of physiology and psychology we must simply inquire, what are the phenomena which we learn by *consciousness*, and what those which we learn by *outward observation.* These two regions lie entirely without each other; so much so, that there is not a single fact known by consciousness, which we should ever have learned by external obser-

CHAPTER IV.

OF PERCEPTION, PROPERLY SO CALLED.

I. *Known by Consciousness and Reflection alone.*] In speaking of the impressions made on our organs in per-

---

vation, and not a single fact known by external observation of which we are ever conscious. A sensation, for example, is known simply by consciousness; the material conditions of it, as seen in the organ and the nervous system, simply by external observation. No one could ever *see* a sensation, or be *conscious* of the organic action; accordingly, the one fact belongs to psychology, the other to physiology."

On this distinction he refers to a passage in Jouffroy, given by us in a note to Chap. IV. of the Preliminary Essay, but remarks, that "Jouffroy carries his views on this point too far. In the phenomena of muscular action, we have the uniting point of the two sciences, the link which indissolubly connects the science of mind with that of organic matter."

In this connection he also speaks of phrenology, the real merit of which is, as he contends, "that it has directed inquiry to the structure of the brain and the nervous system, and succeeded in drawing forth many interesting facts, which otherwise would have been to this time enveloped in darkness. Had it been content with taking its place as one peculiar branch of human physiology, it would have appeared in a light perfectly unobjectionable to the most rigidly philosophical minds; but its ambition has, to a great extent, been its bane."

He then shows, at some length, that it can never serve as the basis of a new system of intellectual philosophy. A brief extract must suffice:— "I will suppose, for a moment, that we knew nothing whatever *reflectively* of our own mental operations; that the study of the human mind had not yet been commenced; that none of its phenomena had been classified; and that we were to *begin* our investigation of them upon the phrenological system, some notion of which had been previously communicated to us: we might in this case proceed with our operations with the greatest ardor, and examine skull after skull for a century; but *this would not give us the least notion of any peculiar mental faculty, or aid us in the smallest degree in classifying mental phenomena.* We could never know that the organs of the reasoning powers were in front, and those of the moral feelings upon the top of the head, unless we had first made those powers and feelings *independently* the objects of our examination. The whole march of phrenology goes upon the supposition, that there is a system of intellectual philosophy already in the mind, and its whole aim is to show where the seat, materially speaking, of the faculties we have *already* observed really is to be found."

"The *Phrenological Journal* admits," he adds in a note to his second edition, "that we must know our mental phenomena *reflectively*, before we can allocate them,—but still persists in calling cerebral observation a *method* of studying psychology. I confess myself unable to see what *psychological* truth it unfolds, that is not clear without it. Does it reveal a

ception, we build upon facts borrowed from anatomy
and physiology, for which we have the testimony of
our senses. But being now to speak of perception
itself, which is solely an act of the mind, we must
appeal to another authority. The operations of our
minds are known, not by sense, but by consciousness,
the authority of which is as certain and as irresistible
as that of sense.*

---

mental fact? Not one, These are all facts of *consciousness.* Does it give
us a classification? No. 'We must know,' (I quote the critic,) 'from
our consciousness, the distinction between thoughts and feelings, before we
can trace their connection with particular parts of the brain.' Does it
define a single faculty or feeling, or give us any clew to the class of phenomena to which it should belong? No. The decision as to the class of
phenomena to which any mental fact belongs is left to the mind's reflective
judgment, which would be quite unaltered wherever the organ of it might
be found." — *Historical and Critical View of the Speculative Philosophy of
Europe in the Nineteenth Century,* Chap. IV. Sect. I.

For further information respecting the physiological conditions of perception and the other mental phenomena, see a small tract by Dr. Barlow,
On the Connection between Physiology and Intellectual Science. Muller's *Elements,* already referred to. The American edition of the English translation omits many passages interesting to the psychologist. Tissot, *Anthropologie.* Virey, *Physiologie dans ses Rapports avec la Philosophie.* Pritch-
ard's *Review of the Doctrine of a Vital Principle.* Green's *Vital Dynamics.*
Lawrence's *Introduction to Comparative Anatomy and Physiology.* Maine de
Biran, *Nouvelles Considérations sur les Rapports du Physique et du Moral de
l'Homme.* Jouffroy, *Nouveaux Mélanges Philosophiques,* Art. *De la Légiti-
meté de la Distinction de la Psychologie et de la Physiologie.* Comte, *Philosophie Positive,* Vol. III. Leçon XLV. — ED.

* It is more so. There is no skepticism *possible* touching the facts of
consciousness in themselves. We cannot doubt that the phenomena of
consciousness are real, in so far as we are conscious of them. I cannot
doubt, for example, that I am actually conscious of a certain feeling of
fragrance, and of certain perceptions of color, figure, &c., when I see and
smell a rose. Of the reality of these, as experienced, I cannot doubt, because they are facts of consciousness; and of consciousness I cannot
doubt, because such doubt, being itself an act of consciousness, would contradict, and consequently annihilate, itself. But of all beyond the mere
phenomena of which we are conscious, we may — without fear of self-
contradiction at least — doubt. I may, for instance, doubt whether the
rose I see and smell has any existence, beyond a phenomenal existence in
my consciousness. I cannot doubt that I am conscious of it *as* something
different from self, but whether it have, indeed, any reality beyond my
mind, — whether the *not-self* be not in truth only *self,* — that I may philosophically question. In like manner, I am conscious of the memory of a
certain past event. Of the contents of this memory, as a phenomenon
given by consciousness, skepticism is impossible. But I may by possibility demur to the reality of all beyond these contents, and the sphere of
present consciousness. — H.

In order, however, to our having a distinct notion of any of the operations of our own minds, it is not enough that we be conscious of them, for all men have this consciousness: it is further necessary that we attend to them while they are exerted, and reflect upon them with care, while they are recent and fresh in our memory. It is necessary that, by employing ourselves frequently in this way, we get the habit of this attention and reflection; and therefore, for the proof of facts which I shall have occasion to mention upon this subject, I can only appeal to the reader's own thoughts, whether such facts are not agreeable to what he is conscious of in his own mind.

II. *Three Things implied in every Act of Perception.*] If, therefore, we attend to that act of our mind which we call the perception of an external object of sense, we shall find in it these three things. *First*, some conception or notion of the object perceived. *Secondly*, a strong and irresistible conviction and belief of its present existence. And, *thirdly*, that this conviction and belief are *immediate*, and not the effect of reasoning.

First, It is impossible to perceive an object without having some *notion* or *conception* of that which we perceive. We may indeed conceive an object which we do not perceive; but when we perceive the object, we must have some conception of it at the same time; and we have commonly a more clear and steady notion of the object while we perceive it, than we have from memory or imagination when it is not perceived. Yet, even in perception, the notion which our senses give of the object may be more or less clear, more or less distinct, in all possible degrees.

Thus we see more distinctly an object at a small than at a great distance. An object at a great distance is seen more distinctly in a clear than in a foggy day. An object seen indistinctly with the naked eye, on account of its smallness, may be seen distinctly with a microscope. The objects in this room will be seen by a person in the room less and less distinctly as the light of the day fails; they pass through all the various degrees of distinctness according to the degrees of the light, and at last, in total darkness, they are not seen at all. What has been said of the objects of sight is so easily applied to the objects of the other senses, that the application may be left to the reader.

In a matter so obvious to every person capable of reflection, it is only necessary further to observe, that the notion which we get of an object merely by our external sense ought not to be confounded with that more scientific notion which a man, come to the years of understanding, may have of the same object, by attending to its various attributes, or to its various parts, and their relation to each other and to the whole. Thus the notion which a child has of a jack for roasting meat will be acknowledged to be very different from that of a man who understands its construction, and perceives the relation of the parts to one another and to the whole. The child sees the jack, and every part of it, as well as the man: the child, therefore, has all the notion of it which sight gives; whatever there is more in the notion which the man forms of it must be derived from other powers of the mind, which may afterwards be explained. This observation is made here only that we may not confound the operations of different powers of the mind, which, by being always conjoined after we grow up to understanding, are apt to pass for one and the same.

Secondly, In perception we not only have a notion more or less distinct of the object perceived, but *also an irresistible conviction and belief of its existence.* This is always the case when we are certain that we perceive it. There may be a perception so faint and indistinct, as to leave us in doubt whether we perceive the object or not. Thus, when a star begins to twinkle as the light of the sun withdraws, one may, for a short time, think he sees it, without being certain, until the perception acquires some strength and steadiness. When a ship just begins to appear on the utmost verge of the horizon, we may at first be dubious whether we perceive it or not; but when the perception is in any degree clear and steady, there remains no doubt of its reality; and when the reality of the perception is ascertained, the existence of the object perceived can no longer be doubted.

By the laws of all nations, in the most solemn judicial trials, wherein men's fortunes and lives are at stake, the sentence passes according to the testimony of eye or ear witnesses of good credit. An upright judge will give a fair hearing to every objection that can be made to the integrity of a witness, and allow it to be possible that he may be corrupted; but no judge will ever suppose that witnesses may be imposed upon by trusting to their eyes and ears: and if a skeptical counsel should plead against the testimony of the witnesses, that they had no other evidence for what they declared than the testimony of their eyes and ears, and that we ought not to put so much faith in our senses as to deprive men of life or fortune upon their testimony, surely no upright judge would admit a plea of this kind. I believe no counsel, however skeptical, ever dared to offer such an argument; and, if it was offered, it would be rejected with disdain.

Can any stronger proof be given, that it is the universal judgment of mankind, that the evidence of sense is a kind of evidence which we may securely rest upon, in the most momentous concerns of mankind, — that it is a kind of evidence against which we ought not to admit any reasoning, and therefore, that to reason either for or against it is an insult to common sense?

The whole conduct of mankind, in the daily occurrences of life, as well as the solemn procedure of judicatories in the trial of causes civil and criminal, demonstrates this. I know of only two exceptions that may be offered against this being the universal belief of mankind.

The first exception is that of some lunatics, who have been persuaded of things that seem to contradict the clear testimony of their senses. It is said there have been lunatics and hypochondriacal persons, who seriously believed themselves to be made of glass; and, in consequence of this, lived in continual terror of having their brittle frame shivered to pieces.

All I have to say to this is, that our minds, in our present state, are, as well as our bodies, liable to strange disorders; and as we do not judge of the natural constitution of the body from the disorders or diseases to which it is subject from accidents, so neither ought we to judge of the natural powers of the mind from its disorders, but from its sound state. It is natural to man, and common to the species, to have two hands and two feet; yet I have seen a man, and a very ingenious one, who was born without either hands or feet. It is natural to man to have faculties superior to those of brutes; yet we see some individuals, whose faculties are not equal to those of many brutes; and the wisest man may, by various accidents, be reduced to this state. General rules that regard those whose intellects are sound are not overthrown by instances of men whose intellects are hurt by any constitutional or accidental disorder.

The other exception that may be made to the principle we have laid down is that of some philosophers, who have maintained that the testimony of sense is fallacious, and therefore ought never to be trusted. Perhaps it might be a sufficient answer to this to say, that there is no absurdity, however great, which some philosophers have not maintained. It is one thing to *profess* a doctrine of this kind, another seriously to *believe* it, and to be governed by it in the conduct of life. It is evident, that a man who did not believe his senses could not keep out of harm's way an hour of his life; yet, in all the history of philosophy, we never read of any skeptic that ever stepped into fire or water because he did not believe his senses, or that showed, in the conduct of life, less trust in his senses than other men have.* This gives us just ground to apprehend that

* All this we read, however, in Laërtius, of Pyrrho; and on the authority of Antigonus Carystius, the great skeptic's contemporary. Whether we are to believe the narrative is another question. — H.

philosophy was never able to conquer that natural belief which men have in their senses; and that all their subtile reasonings against this belief were never able to persuade themselves.

It appears, therefore, that the clear and distinct testimony of our senses carries irresistible conviction along with it, to every man in his right judgment.

I observed, *thirdly*, that this conviction is not only irresistible, but it is *immediate ;* that is, *it is not by a train of reasoning and argumentation* that we come to be convinced of the existence of what we perceive. We ask no argument for the existence of the object, but that we perceive it; perception commands our belief upon its own authority, and disdains to rest its authority upon any reasoning whatsoever.

The conviction of a truth may be irresistible, and yet not immediate. Thus, my conviction that the three angles of every plane triangle are equal to two right angles, is irresistible, but it is not immediate: I am convinced of it by demonstrative reasoning. There are other truths in mathematics of which we have not only an irresistible, but an immediate conviction. Such are the axioms. Our belief of the axioms in mathematics is not grounded upon argument, — arguments are grounded upon them; but their evidence is discerned immediately by the human understanding.

It is, no doubt, one thing to have an immediate conviction of a self-evident axiom ; it is another thing to have an immediate conviction of the existence of what we see : but the conviction is *equally immediate* and *equally irresistible* in both cases. No man thinks of seeking a reason for believing what he sees; and before we are capable of reasoning, we put no less confidence in our senses than after. The rudest savage is as fully convinced of what he sees, and hears, and feels, as the most expert logician. The constitution of our understanding determines us to hold the truth of a mathematical axiom as a first principle, from which other truths may be deduced, but it is deduced from none; and the constitution of our power of perception deter-

6

mines us to hold the existence of what we distinctly perceive as a first principle, from which other truths may be deduced, but it is deduced from none.

What has been said of the irresistible and immediate belief of the existence of objects distinctly perceived, I mean only to affirm with regard to persons so far advanced in understanding as *to distinguish objects of mere imagination from things which have a real existence.* Every man knows that he may have a notion of Don Quixote or of Gargantua, without any belief that such persons ever existed; and that of Julius Cæsar and of Oliver Cromwell he has not only a notion, but a belief that they did really exist. But whether children, from the time that they begin to use their senses, make a distinction between things which are only conceived or imagined, and things which really exist, may be doubted. Until we are able to make this distinction, we cannot properly be said to believe or to disbelieve the existence of any thing. The belief of the existence of any thing seems to suppose a notion of *existence;* a notion too abstract, perhaps, to enter into the mind of an infant. I speak of the power of perception in those that are adult, and of a sound mind, who believe that there are some things which do really exist; and that there are many things conceived by themselves, and by others, which have no existence. That such persons do invariably ascribe existence to every thing which they distinctly perceive, without seeking reasons or arguments for doing so, is perfectly evident from the whole tenor of human life.

III. *How we are able to perceive by Means of the Senses is beyond our Comprehension.*] The account I have given of our perception of external objects is intended as a faithful delineation of what every man, come to years of understanding, and capable of giving attention to what passes in his own mind, may feel in himself. In *what manner* the notion of external objects, and the immediate belief of their existence, is produced by means of our senses, I am not able to show, and I do not pretend to show. If the power of perceiving external objects in certain circumstances be a part of the original constitution of the human mind, all attempts to account for it will be vain : no other account can be given of the constitution of things, but the will of Him that made them. As we can give no reason why matter is extended and inert, why the mind thinks, and is conscious of its thoughts, but the will of Him who made both, so, I suspect, we can give no other reason why, in certain circumstances, we perceive external objects, and in others do not.

The Supreme Being intended that we should have such knowledge of the material objects that surround us as is necessary in order to our supplying the wants of nature, and avoiding the dangers to which we are constantly exposed; and he has admirably fitted our powers of perception to this purpose. If the intelligence we have of external objects were to be got by reasoning only, the greatest part of men would be destitute of it; for the greatest part of men hardly ever learn to reason; and in infancy and childhood no man can reason : therefore, as this intelligence of the objects that surround us, and from which we may receive so much benefit or harm, is equally necessary to children and to men, to the ignorant and to the learned, God in his wisdom conveys it to us in a way that puts all upon a level. The information of the senses is as perfect, and gives as full conviction, to the most ignorant as to the most learned.

CHAPTER V.

THEORIES OF PERCEPTION.

I. *Plato's Theory.*] An object placed at a proper distance, and in a good light, while the eyes are shut, is not perceived at all; but no sooner do we open our eyes upon it, than we have, as it were by inspiration, a certain knowledge of its existence, of its color, figure, and distance. This is a fact which every one knows. The vulgar are satisfied with knowing the fact, and give themselves no trouble about the cause of it; but a philosopher is impatient to know how this event is produced, to account for it, or assign its cause.

This avidity to know the causes of things is the parent of all philosophy, true and false. Men of speculation place a great part of their happiness in such knowledge. *Felix qui potuit rerum cognoscere causas,* has always been a sentiment of human nature.

Many philosophers, ancient and modern, have employed their invention to discover how we are made to perceive external objects by our senses: and there appears to be a very great uniformity in their sentiments in the main, notwithstanding their variations in particular points.*

Plato illustrates our manner of perceiving the objects of sense in this manner. He supposes a dark subterraneous cave, in which men lie bound in such a manner that they can direct their eyes only to one part of the cave: far behind, there is a light, some rays of which come over a wall to that part of the cave which is before the eyes of our prisoners. A number of persons, variously employed, pass between them and the light, whose shadows are seen by the prisoners, but not the persons themselves.

In this manner that philosopher conceived that, by our senses, we perceive the shadows of things only, and not things themselves. He seems to have borrowed his notions on this subject from the Pythagore-

---

* It is not easy to conceive by what principle the order of the history of opinions touching perception, as given by Reid, is determined. It is not chronological, and it is not systematic. Of these theories, there is a very able survey, by M. Royer-Collard, among the fragments of his lectures in the third volume of Jouffroy's *Œuvres de Reid.* That distinguished philosopher has, however, placed too great a reliance upon the accuracy of Reid. — H.

Reid's historico-critical account of the theories of perception is materially abridged in this edition, and the order in one or two cases is changed, for the reason intimated above. — ED.

ans, and they very probably from Pythagoras himself. If we make allowance for Plato's allegorical genius, his sentiments on this subject correspond very well with those of his scholar Aristotle, and of the Peripatetics. The shadows of Plato may very well represent the species and phantasms of the Peripatetic school, and the ideas and impressions of modern philosophers.*

---

* This interpretation of the meaning of Plato's comparison of the cave exhibits a curious mistake, in which Reid is followed by Mr. Stewart and many others, and which, it is remarkable, has never yet been detected. In the similitude in question (which will be found in the seventh book of the Republic), Plato is supposed to intend an illustration of the mode in which the shadows or vicarious images of external things are admitted into the mind, — to typify, in short, an hypothesis of sensitive perception. On this supposition, the identity of the Platonic, Pythagorean, and Peripatetic theories of this process is inferred. Nothing can, however, be more groundless than the supposition; nothing more erroneous than the inference. By his *cave, images*, and *shadows*, Plato meant simply to illustrate the grand principle of his philosophy, that the *sensible* or *ectypal* world (phenomenal, transitory, γιγνόμενον, ὃν καὶ μὴ ὄν) stands to the *noetic* or *archetypal* (substantial, permanent, ὄντως ὄν) in the same relation of comparative unreality in which the *shadows of the images* of sensible existences themselves stand to the things of which they are the dim and distinct adumbrations. And as the comparison is misunderstood, so nothing can be conceived more adverse to the doctrine of Plato than the theory it is supposed to elucidate. It is here sufficient to state, that the εἴδωλα, the λόγοι γνωστικοί, the forms representative of external things, and corresponding to the *species sensiles expressæ* of the schoolmen, were *not held by the Platonists to be derived from without*. Prior to the act of perception, they have a latent but real existence in the soul; and, by the impassive energy of the mind itself, are elicited into consciousness, on occasion of the *impression* (κίνησις, πάθος, ἔμφασις) made on the external organ, and of the *vital form* (ζωτικὸν εἶδος), in consequence thereof, sublimated in the animal life.

I cannot now do more than *indicate* the contrast of this doctrine to the Peripatetic (I do not say, *Aristotelian*) theory, and its approximation to the Cartesian and Leibnitzian hypotheses; which, however, both attempt to explain what the Platonic did not, — how the mind (*ex hypothesi*, above all *physical influence*) is determined, on the presence of the unknown reality within the sphere of *sense*, to call into consciousness the representation through which that reality is made known to us. I may add, that not merely the Platonists, but some of the older Peripatetics, held that the soul virtually contained within itself representative forms, which were only excited by the external reality; as Theophrastus and Themistius, to say nothing of the Platonizing Porphyry, Simplicius, and Ammonius Hermiæ; and the same opinion, adopted probably from the latter by his pupil, the Arabian Adelandus, subsequently became even the common doctrine of the Moorish Aristotelians.

I shall afterwards have occasion to notice that Bacon has also wrested Plato's similitude of the cave from its genuine signification. — H.

On the subject of Plato's doctrines generally, and especially in respect to

Two thousand years after Plato, Mr. Locke, who studied the operations of the human mind so much, and with so great success, represents our manner of perceiving external objects by a similitude very much resembling that of the cave. " Methinks," says he, " the understanding is not much unlike a closet wholly shut from light, with only some little opening left to let in external visible resemblances or ideas of things without. Would the pictures coming into such a dark room but stay there, and lie so orderly as to be found upon occasion, it would very much resemble the understanding of a man, in reference to all objects of sight, and the ideas of them."

Plato's subterranean cave, and Mr. Locke's dark closet, may be applied with ease to all the systems of perception that have been invented: for they all suppose that we perceive not external objects immediately, and that the immediate objects of perception are only certain shadows of the external objects. Those shadows or images, which we immediately perceive, were by the ancients called *species, forms, phantasms.* Since the time of Descartes, they have commonly been called *ideas,* and by Mr. Hume *impressions.* But all philosophers, from Plato to Mr. Hume, agree in this, that we do not perceive external objects *immediately,* and that the immediate object of perception must be *some image present to the mind.* So far, there appears a unanimity rarely to be found among philosophers on such abstruse points.

II. *Theory of Aristotle and the Peripatetics.*] Aristotle taught, that all the objects of our thought enter at first by the senses; and, since the sense cannot receive external material objects themselves, it receives their species; that is, their images or *form,* without the matter, as wax receives the form of the seal, without any of the matter of it. These images or forms, impressed

sensible perception, and the similitude of the cave, compare Van Heusde, *Initia Philosophiæ Platonicæ.* — ED.

upon the senses, are called *sensible species*, and are the objects only of the sensitive part of the mind. But, by various internal powers, they are retained, refined, and spiritualized, so as to become objects of *memory* and *imagination*, and, at last, of pure *intellection*. When they are objects of memory and of imagination, they get the name of *phantasms*. When, by further refinement, and being stripped of their particularities, they become objects of *science*, they are called *intelligible species*. So that every immediate object, whether of sense, of memory, of imagination, or of reasoning, must be some phantasm or species in the mind itself.*

* This is a tolerable account of the doctrine *vulgarly* attributed to Aristotle. — H.

It is a common error to refer to Aristotle himself the refinements and subtilties introduced into his system by his followers. For a full and authentic view of the psychology of Aristotle, see the French translations of *De Anima* and of *Parva Naturalia*, with copious prefaces and notes, by J. Barthélemy Saint-Hilaire. The translator gives the following summary of Aristotle's doctrine respecting sensation and perception: —

"Aristotle considers each of the senses, in the following order, — sight, hearing, smell, taste, and touch. Omitting all details, we shall limit ourselves here to giving a general idea of his theory of sensibility.

"Sensibility, according to Aristotle, is a simple power, — a faculty which can always act, though it does not always act. Sensation is not, therefore, merely an alteration, as many have said: it is an act which completes the being who experiences it; in a particular act of sensation, he develops a faculty that is in him, he realizes what he can do. Thus, in sensation, a being does not suffer; he acts. Moreover, as in sensation there is always and necessarily an object felt, it must be admitted that the sensible being is in power very nearly as in reality the being felt. Before feeling, it is unlike the being which it feels; after having felt, it is, in some sense, like it. Sensibility is, therefore, that which receives *the form* of sensible objects, but not *the matter;* like wax which receives the impression of the ring, but not the iron or gold of which the ring is made. The sensibility does not become, strictly speaking, each of the objects which act upon it; but it becomes something analogous; and this something can be comprehended by the reason alone; that is to say, it is not a material phenomenon. The object is not truly sensible as long as it is not felt; sensibility, on its side, is a mere power as long as it feels not. The act of the object felt and the act of the sensibility are therefore blended together, and indissoluble. Hence a certain relation, a kind of harmony, is necessary between the sense and the object. A sensation, if too violent, is not perceived. Sensibility is, to speak properly, a mean; on this side or beyond a certain point, it no longer acts.

"But man has not only the faculty of feeling; he also has the faculty of feeling that he feels. He feels that he sees; he feels that he hears. Is it by the sight that he feels that he sees, or is it by some other sense? It is by the sight; or, to speak more correctly, the perceptions of sight, like

Aristotle seems .to have thought that the soul consists of two parts, or, rather, that 'we have two souls,
the animal and the rational; or, as he calls them, *the
soul* and *the intellect.** To the first belong the senses,

---

those of all the other senses, meet in a centre, in a single point, which
serves as a common limit to them all, and which compares and measures
them in an instant indivisible as is this point itself, indivisible as is the
principle which perceives and feels.

"Such is Aristotle's theory of sensibility. Not the least trace is found
there, as all will see, of those *sensible species*, of those *images*, of those *representative images*, as Reid calls them, without which, it has often been repeated, Aristotle could not explain perception. I do not deny that before
him some philosophers, Democritus and others, had supposed the intervention of images proceeding from objects to the mind, by means of which
the mind is enabled to comprehend the objects. Neither do I deny that,
after Aristotle, his commentators, and the schoolmen especially, have attributed to him, in trying to comprehend him, the views which Reid has
attacked and overthrown. But I think myself authorized to affirm that
these views were never held by Aristotle himself. He employed a metaphor to explain perception, and the use of metaphor (which he had formally proscribed and disowned in philosophy) has been unlucky in this
case, as it has caused his real thought to be misunderstood. But he went
no farther. As a perfectly faithful observer, he has stated the facts; he
has invented nothing. Before the great mystery of perception he paused,
with a prudence not exceeded by that of the Scotch school. Reid contents
himself, after having refuted all previous theories, with protesting against
them without pretending to substitute another more complete in their
place, declaring that perception, with all its ascertained characteristics, is a
fact irreducible to any other. With less profoundness and delicacy of
analysis, Aristotle has said precisely the same thing: — 'We experience in
sensation a modification which reason alone can apprehend.' Aristotle,
it is true, has gone farther than Reid, by adding, that, in perception, the
being which perceives becomes in some manner conformed to the being
perceived. This remark is perhaps more ingenious than solid; but it is
not the fault of Aristotle, if afterwards consequences were drawn from his
theories which he never attributed to them, and which even contradict
them. He no more held the doctrine of *idea-images, of representative ideas*,
than he admitted that confusion of sensation and thought which has so often
been ascribed to him, and which he refutes again and again in his treatise
On the Soul. Reid has certainly rendered a real service to science by dis-
embarrassing it of an hypothesis the source of so many errors, and entertained by some of the greatest thinkers, — by Descartes among the rest.
But this is an error into which Aristotle never fell; his theories do not
contain it: error may be there, but not that of which he is accused by
Reid." *Traité de l'Ame*, Preface, p. xxii. The same topics are treated
more fully in the editor's *Plan Général du Traité de l'Ame*, p. 35, *et seq.*;
and in the treatise itself, Liv. II. Chap. V.-XII., and Liv. III. Chap. I.,
II.—Ed.

* This is not correct. Instead of *two*, the *animal* and *rational*, Aristotle
gave to the soul *three* generic functions, the *vegetable*, the *animal* or *sensual*,
and the *rational;* but whether he supposes these to constitute three concen-

memory, and imagination; to the last, judgment, opinion, belief, and reasoning.   The first we have in common with brute animals; the last is peculiar to man. The animal soul he held to be a certain form of the body, which is inseparable from it, and perishes at death.   To this soul the senses belong: and he defines a sense to be that which is capable of receiving the sensible *forms*, or *species* of objects, without any of the *matter* of them, as wax receives the form of the seal without any of the matter of it.   The *forms* of sound, of color, of taste, and of other sensible qualities, are in like manner received by the senses.

It seems to be a necessary consequence of Aristotle's doctrine, that bodies are constantly sending forth, in all directions, as many different kinds of forms without matter as they have different sensible qualities; for the forms of color must enter by the eye, the forms of sound by the ear, and so of the other senses.   This accordingly was maintained by the followers of Aristotle, though not, as far as I know, expressly mentioned by himself.   They disputed concerning the nature of those forms, or species, whether they were real beings or nonentities; and some held them to be of an intermediate nature between the two.*   The whole doctrine of the Peripatetics and schoolmen concerning forms, substantial and accidental, and concerning the transmission of sensible species from objects of sense to the mind, if it be at all intelligible, is so far above my com-

---

tric potences, three separate parts, or three distinct souls, has divided his disciples.   He also defines the *soul in general*, and not, as Reid supposes, the mere "animal soul," to be the form or ἐντελέχεια of the body.   (*De Anima*, Lib. II. cap. 2.)   Intellect (νοῦς) he, however, thought was inorganic; but there is some ground for believing that he did not view this as personal, but harboured an opinion which, under various modifications, many of his followers also held, that the *active intellect* was common to all men, immortal and divine. — H.

* The question in the schools, among those who admitted species, was not whether species, *in general*, were *real* beings or *nonentities*, (which would have been, did they exist or not), but whether *sensible* species were *material*, *immaterial*, or of a nature *between* body and spirit, — a problem, it must be allowed, sufficiently futile, but not, like the other, self-contradictory. — H.

prehension, that I should perhaps do it injustice by entering into it more minutely. Malebranche, in his *Recherche de la Vérité*, has employed a chapter to show that material objects do not send forth sensible species of their several sensible qualities.

III. *Descartes's Theory.*] The great revolution which Descartes produced in philosophy was the effect of a superiority of genius, aided by the circumstances of the times.[*] Men had, for more than a thousand years, looked up to Aristotle as an oracle in philosophy. His authority was the test of truth. The small remains of the Platonic system were confined to a few mystics, whose principles and manner of life drew little attention. The feeble attempts of Ramus, and of some others, to make improvements in the system, had little effect. The Peripatetic doctrines were so interwoven with the whole system of scholastic theology, that to dissent from Aristotle was to alarm the Church. The most useful and intelligible parts, even of Aristotle's writings, were neglected, and philosophy was become an art of speaking learnedly, and disputing subtilely, without producing any invention of use in human life. It was fruitful of words, but barren of works, and admirably contrived for drawing a veil over human ignorance, and putting a stop to the progress of knowledge, by filling men with a conceit that they knew every thing. It was very fruitful, also, in controversies; but for the most part they were controversies about words, or about things of no moment, or things above the reach of the human faculties: and the issue of them was what might be expected, that the contending parties fought, without gaining or losing an inch of ground, till they were weary of the dispute, or their attention was called off to some other subject.[†]

---

[*] René Descartes was born at La Haye, in Touraine, March 31, 1596. Much of his life was passed in Holland. He died, February 14, 1650, at Stockholm, whither he had repaired at the invitation of Christina, queen of Sweden. — ED.

[†] This is the vulgar opinion in regard to the scholastic philosophy. The few are, however, now aware that the human mind, though partially, was never more powerfully developed than during the Middle Ages. — H.

Such was the philosophy of the schools of Europe, during many ages of darkness and barbarism that succeeded the decline of the Roman empire; so that there was great need of a reformation in philosophy as well as in religion. The light began to dawn at last; a spirit of inquiry sprang up, and men got the courage to doubt of the dogmas of Aristotle, as well as of the decrees of popes. The most important step in the reformation of religion was to destroy the claim of infallibility, which hindered men from using their judgment in matters of religion: and the most important step in the reformation of philosophy was to destroy the authority of which Aristotle had so long had peaceable possession. The last had been attempted by Lord Bacon and others, with no less zeal than the first by Luther and Calvin.

Descartes knew well the defects of the prevailing system, which had begun to lose its authority. His genius enabled him, and his spirit prompted him, to attempt a new one. He had applied himself much to the mathematical sciences, and had made considerable improvement in them. He wished to introduce that perspicuity and evidence into other branches of philosophy which he found in them. Being sensible how apt we are to be led astray by prejudices of education, he thought the only way to avoid error was, to resolve *to doubt of every thing*, — to hold every thing to be uncertain, even those things which he had been taught to hold as most certain, until he had such clear and cogent evidence as compelled his assent.

In this state of universal doubt, that which first appeared to him to be clear and certain was his own existence. Of this he was certain, because he was conscious that he thought, that he reasoned, and that he doubted. He used this argument, therefore, to prove his own existence, — *Cogito, ergo sum*. This he conceived to be the first of all truths, the foundation-stone upon which the whole fabric of human knowledge is built, and on which it must rest. And as Archimedes thought that, if he had one fixed point to rest his engines upon, he could move the earth; so Descartes, charmed with the discovery of one certain principle, by which he emerged from the state of universal doubt, believed that this principle alone would be a sufficient foundation on which he might build the whole system of science. He seems, therefore, to have taken no great trouble to examine whether there might not be other first principles, which, on account of their own light and evidence, ought to be admitted by every man of sound judgment. The love of simplicity, so natural to the mind of man, led him to apply the whole force of his mind to raise the fabric of knowledge upon this one principle, rather than seek a broader foundation.

Accordingly, he does not admit the evidence of sense to be a first principle, as he does that of consciousness. The arguments of the ancient skeptics here occurred to him;—that our senses often deceive us, and therefore ought never to be trusted on their own authority; that, in sleep, we often seem to see and hear things which we are convinced to have had no existence. But that which chiefly led Descartes to think that he ought not to trust to his senses, without proof of their veracity, was, that he took it for granted, as all philosophers had done before him, that he did not perceive external objects themselves, but certain images of them in his own mind, called *ideas*. He was certain, by consciousness, that he had the ideas of sun and moon, earth and sea; but how could he be assured that there really existed external objects like to these ideas?

Hitherto he was uncertain of every thing but of his own existence, and the existence of the operations and ideas of his own mind. Some of his disciples, it is said, remained at this stage of his system, and got the name of *Egoists.** They could not find evidence in the subsequent stages of his progress. But Descartes resolved not to stop here; he endeavoured to prove, by a

---

* Sir W. Hamilton can find no satisfactory evidence of the existence of this sect. — ED.

new argument, drawn from his idea of a Deity, the existence of an infinitely perfect Being, who made him and all his faculties. From the perfection of this Being, he inferred that he could be no deceiver; and therefore concluded, that his senses, and the other faculties he found in himself, are not fallacious, but may be trusted, when a proper use is made of them.

The merit of Descartes cannot be easily conceived by those who have not some notion of the Peripatetic system in which he was educated. To throw off the prejudices of education, and to create a system of nature totally different from that which had subdued the understanding of mankind, and kept it in subjection for so many centuries, required an uncommon force of mind.

In the world of Descartes we meet with two kinds of beings only, — to wit, *body* and *mind;* the first, the object of our senses, the other, of consciousness; both of them things of which we have a distinct apprehension, if the human mind be capable of distinct apprehension at all. To the first, no qualities are ascribed but extension, figure, and motion; to the last, nothing but thought, and its various modifications, of which we are conscious.* He could observe no common attribute, no resembling feature, in the attributes of body and mind, and therefore concluded them to be distinct substances, and totally of a different nature; and that body, from its very nature, is inanimate and inert, incapable of any kind of thought or sensation, or of producing any change or alteration in itself.

Descartes must be allowed the honor of being *the first who drew a distinct line between the material and intellectual world,* which, in all the old systems, were so blended together, that it was impossible to say where the one ends and the other begins.† How much this distinction has contributed to the improvements of

---

* In the Cartesian language, the term *thought* included all of which we are conscious. — H.

† This assertion is true in general; but some individual exceptions might be taken. — H.

7

modern times, in the philosophy both of body and of mind, it is not easy to say.

One obvious consequence of this distinction was, that *accurate reflection on the operations of our own mind is the only way to make any progress in the knowledge of it.* Malebranche, Locke, Berkeley, and Hume were taught this lesson by Descartes; and to it we owe their most valuable discoveries in this branch of philosophy. The analogical way of reasoning concerning the powers of the mind from the properties of body, which is the source of almost all the errors on this subject, and which is so natural to the bulk of mankind, was as contrary to the principles of Descartes as it was agreeable to the principles of the old philosophy. We may, therefore, truly say, that, in that part of philosophy which relates to the mind, Descartes laid the foundation, and put us into that track which all wise men now acknowledge to be the only one in which we can expect success.

To return to Descartes's notions of the manner of our perceiving external objects, from which a concern to do justice to the merits of that great reformer in philosophy has led me to digress, — he took it for granted, as the old philosophers had done, that what we immediately perceive must be either in the mind itself, or in the brain, to which the mind is immediately present. The impressions made upon our organs, nerves, and brain could be nothing, according to his philosophy, but various modifications of extension, figure, and motion. There could be nothing in the brain like sound or color, taste or smell, heat or cold; these are sensations in the mind, which, by the laws of the union of soul and body, are raised on occasion of certain traces in the brain; and although he gives the name of *ideas* to those traces in the brain, he does not think it necessary that they should be perfectly like to the things which they represent, any more than that words or signs should resemble the things they signify. But, says he, that we may follow the received opinion as far as is possible, we may allow a slight resemblance.

Thus we know that a print in a book may represent houses, temples, and groves; and so far is it from being necessary that the print should be perfectly like the thing it represents, that its perfection often requires the contrary. For a circle must often be represented by an ellipse, a square by a rhombus, and so of other things.*

It is to be observed, that Descartes rejected a part only of the ancient theory, concerning the perception of external objects by the senses, and that he adopted the other part. That theory may be divided into two parts: the first, that images, species, or forms of external objects come from the object, and enter by the avenues of the senses to the mind; the second part is, that the external object itself is not perceived, but only the species or image of it in the mind. The first part Descartes and his followers rejected, and refuted by solid arguments; but the second part, neither he nor his followers have thought of calling in question, being persuaded that it is only a representative image, in the mind, of the external object that we perceive, and not the object itself. And this image, which the Peripatetics called a *species*, he calls an *idea*, changing the name only, while he admits the thing.

It seems strange, that the great pains which the philosopher took to throw off the prejudices of education,

---

* But be it observed that Descartes did not allow, far less hold, that the mind had any cognizance of these organic motions, — of these material ideas. They were merely the antecedents, established by the law of union of soul and body, of the mental idea; which mental idea was nothing more than a modification of the mind itself. Reid, I may observe in general, does not distinguish, as it especially behooved him to do, between what were held by philosophers to be the proximate *causes* of our mental representations, and these representations themselves as the *objects* of cognition; i. e. between what are known in the schools as the *species impressæ*, and the *species expressæ*. The former, to which the name of *species, image, idea*, was often given, in common with the latter, was held on all hands to be unknown to consciousness, and generally supposed to be merely certain occult motions in the organism. The latter, the result determined by the former, is the mental representation, and the immediate or proper object in perception. Great confusion, to those who do not bear this distinction in mind, is, however, the consequence of the verbal ambiguity; and Reid's misrepresentations of the doctrine of the philosophers is, in a great measure, to be traced to this source. — H.

to dismiss all his former opinions, and to assent to
nothing till he found evidence that compelled his assent, should not have led him to doubt this opinion
of the ancient philosophy.   It is evidently a philosophical opinion; for the vulgar undoubtedly believe that it
is the external object which we immediately perceive,
and not a representative image of it only.   It is for
this reason that they look upon it as a perfect lunacy
to call in question the existence of external objects.

It seems to be admitted as a first principle by the
learned and the unlearned, that what is really perceived
must exist, and that to perceive what does not exist is
impossible.   So far the unlearned man and the philosopher agree.   The unlearned man says, I perceive the
external object, and I perceive it to exist.   Nothing
can be more absurd than to doubt it.   The Peripatetic
says, What I perceive is the very identical form of the
object, which came immediately from the object, and
makes an impression upon my mind, as a seal does
upon wax; and therefore I can have no doubt of the
existence of an object whose form I perceive.   But
what says the Cartesian?   I perceive not, says he, the
external object itself.   So far he agrees with the Peripatetic, and differs from the unlearned man.   But I
perceive an image, or form, or idea, in my own mind,
or in my brain.   I am certain of the existence of the
idea, because I immediately perceive it.   But how this
idea is formed, or what it represents, is not self-evident;
and therefore I must find arguments by which, from
the existence of the idea which I perceive, I can infer
the existence of an external object which it represents.

As I take this to be a just view of the principles
of the unlearned man, of the Peripatetic, and of the
Cartesian, so I think they all reason consequentially
from their several principles.   The Cartesian has strong
grounds to doubt of the existence of external objects,
the Peripatetic very little ground of doubt, and the
unlearned man none at all; and the difference of their
situation arises from this, — that the unlearned man
has no hypothesis, the Peripatetic leans upon an hy-

pothesis, and the Cartesian upon one half of that hypothesis.*

IV. *Malebranche's Theory.*] Malebranche, with a very penetrating genius, entered into a more minute examination of the powers of the human mind than any one before him.† He had the advantage of the discoveries made by Descartes, whom he followed without slavish attachment.

He lays it down as a principle admitted by all philosophers, and which could not be called in question, that we do not perceive external objects immediately, but by means of images or ideas of them present to the mind. "I suppose," says he, "that every one will grant that we perceive not the objects that are without us immediately, and of themselves.‡ We see the sun, the stars, and an infinity of objects without us; and it is not at all likely that the soul sallies out of the body, and, as it were, takes a walk through the heavens to contemplate all those objects. She sees them not, therefore, by themselves; and the immediate object of the mind, when it sees the sun, for example, is not the sun, but something which is intimately united to the soul; and it is that which I call an idea: so that by the word *idea* I understand nothing else here but that which is the immediate object, or nearest to the mind, when we perceive any object. It ought to be carefully observed, that, in order to the mind's perceiving any

---

* M. Garnier has published the best edition of Descartes's metaphysical writings, *Œuvres Philosophiques de Descartes* (4 vols., 8vo, Paris, 1835). For the best account of Cartesianism, and its influence on modern thought, see *Histoire et Critique de la Révolution Cartesienne*, par M. Francisque Bouillier. See, also, Stewart's *Dissertation*, Part I. Chap. II. Sect. II.; Hallam's *Literature of Europe*, from 1600 to 1650, Chap. III. Sect. III.; Damiron, *Essai sur l'Histoire de la Philosophie en France, au XVIIe Siècle*, Liv. II.

We have met with but two English translations from Descartes; his *Discourse of Method* (16mo, London, 1649), published anonymously, and his *Six Metaphysical Meditations*, by William Molyneux (16mo, London, 1680). — ED.

† Nicholas Malebranche, a priest of the Oratory, was born at Paris, August 6, 1638, and died in the same city, October 13, 1715. — ED.

‡ Rather *in* or *by themselves* (*par eux-mêmes*). — H.

7 *

object, it is absolutely necessary that the idea of that object be actually present to it. Of this it is not possible to doubt. The things which the soul perceives are of two kinds. They are either in the soul, or they are without the soul: those that are in the soul are its own thoughts, that is to say, all its different modifications. The soul has no need of ideas for perceiving these things. But with regard to things without the soul, we cannot perceive them but by means of ideas." *

Having laid this foundation, as a principle which was common to all philosophers, and which admitted of no doubt, he proceeds to enumerate all the possible ways by which the ideas of sensible objects may be presented to the mind: — Either, *first*, they come from the bodies which we perceive; or, *secondly*, the soul has the power of producing them in itself; or, *thirdly*, they are produced by the Deity, either in our creation, or occasionally, as there is use for them; or, *fourthly*, the soul has in itself virtually and eminently, as the schools speak, all the perfections which it perceives in bodies; or, *fifthly*, the soul is united with a being possessed of all perfection, who has in himself the ideas of all created things.

This he takes to be a complete enumeration of all the possible ways in which the ideas of external objects may be presented to our minds. He employs a whole chapter upon each; refuting the first four, and confirming the last by various arguments. The Deity, being always present to our minds in a more intimate manner than any other being, may, upon occasion of the impressions made on our bodies, discover to us, as far as he thinks proper, and according to fixed laws, his own ideas of the object; and thus " we see all things in God," or in the Divine ideas.†

---

* *De la Recherche de la Vérité*, Liv. III. Partie II. Chap. I.

† It should have been noticed that the Malebranchian philosophy is fundamentally Cartesian, and that, after De la Forge and Geulinx, the doctrine of *Divine Assistance*, implicitly maintained by Descartes, was most ably developed by Malebranche, to whom it owes, indeed, a principal share of its celebrity. — H.

However visionary this system may appear on a superficial view, yet when we consider that he agreed with the whole tribe of philosophers in conceiving ideas to be the immediate objects of perception, and that he found insuperable difficulties, and even absurdities, in every other hypothesis concerning them, it will not appear so wonderful that a man of very great genius should fall into this; and probably it pleased so devout a man the more, that it sets in the most striking light our dependence upon God, and his continual presence with us.

He distinguished, more accurately than any philosopher had done before, the *objects* which we perceive from the *sensations* in our own minds, which, by the laws of nature, always accompany the perception of the object. As in many things, so particularly in this, he has great merit: for this, I apprehend, is a key that opens the way to a right understanding both of our external senses and of other powers of the mind. The vulgar confound sensation with other powers of the mind, and with their objects, because the purposes of life do not make a distinction necessary. The confounding of these in common language has led philosophers, in one period, to make those things external which really are sensations in our own minds; and, in another period, running, as is usual, into the contrary extreme, to make almost every thing to be a sensation or feeling in our minds.

It is obvious, that the system of Malebranche leaves *no evidence of the existence of a material world* from what we perceive by our senses; for the Divine ideas, which are the objects immediately perceived, *were the same before the world was created.* Malebranche was too acute not to discern this consequence of his system, and too candid not to acknowledge it: he fairly owns it, and endeavours to make advantage of it, resting the complete evidence we have of the existence of matter upon *the authority of revelation.* He shows, that the arguments brought by Descartes to prove the existence of a material world, though as good as any that reason

could furnish, are not perfectly conclusive; and though
he acknowledges, with Descartes, that we feel a strong
propensity to believe the existence of a material world,
yet he thinks this is not sufficient, and that to yield to
such propensities without evidence is to expose ourselves to perpetual delusion.   He thinks, therefore, that
the only convincing evidence we have of the existence
of the material world is, that we are assured by revelation that "God created the heavens and the earth,"
and that "the Word was made flesh."   He is sensible
of the ridicule to which so strange an opinion may expose him among those who are guided by prejudice;
but, for the sake of truth, he is willing to bear it.   But
no author, not even Bishop Berkeley, has shown more
clearly, that, either upon his own system, or upon the
common principles of philosophers with regard to ideas,
we have no evidence left, either from reason or from
our senses, of the existence of a material world.   It is
no more than justice to Father Malebranche to acknowledge, that Bishop Berkeley's arguments are to
be found in him in their whole force.*

Malebranche's system was adopted by many devout
people in France, of both sexes; but it seems to have
had no great currency in other countries.   Mr. Locke
wrote a small tract against it, which is found among
his posthumous works; but whether it was written in
haste, or after the vigor of his understanding was impaired by age, there is less of strength and solidity in
it than in most of his writings.†   The most formidable
antagonist Malebranche met with was in his own
country, — Antony Arnauld, doctor of the Sorbonne,

---

* Once, and only once, these eminent philosophers had the pleasure of
an interview. " The conversation," we are told, " turned on the non-existence of matter. Malebranche, who had an inflammation in his lungs, and
whom Berkeley found preparing a medicine in his cell, and cooking it in a
small pipkin, exerted his voice so violently in the heat of their dispute,
that he increased his disorder, which carried him off in a few days after."
Biog. Brit., Art. *Berkeley*. — ED.

† In answer to Locke's *Examination of P. Malebranche's Opinions*, Leibnitz wrote *Remarques*, making No. LXVI. of Erdmann's edition of his
Opera Philosophica. — ED.

and one of the acutest writers the Jansenists have to boast of, though that sect has produced many. Those who choose to see this system attacked on the one hand, and defended on the other, with subtilty of argument and elegance of expression, and on the part of Arnauld with much wit and humor, may find satisfaction by reading Malebranche's *Inquiry after Truth*, Arnauld's book of *True and False Ideas*, Malebranche's *Defence*, and some subsequent replies and defences. In controversies of this kind, the assailant commonly has the advantage, if the parties are not unequally matched; for it is easier to overturn all the theories of philosophers upon this subject, than to defend any one of them. Mr. Bayle makes a very just remark upon this controversy, that the arguments of Mr. Arnauld against the system of Malebranche were often unanswerable, but they were capable of being retorted against his own system; and his ingenious antagonist knew well how to use this defence.*

V. *Arnauld's Theory.*] The controversy between Malebranche and Arnauld † necessarily led them to consider what kind of things ideas are, a point upon

---

* Independently of his principal hypothesis altogether, the works of Malebranche deserve the most attentive study, both on account of the many admirable thoughts and observations with which they abound, and because they are among the few consummate models of philosophical eloquence. — H.

Charpentier has published in his *Bibliothèque Philosophique* a good edition of Malebranche's metaphysical writings, — *Œuvres*, édition collationée sur les meilleurs textes, comprenant: les *Entretiens Métaphysiques*, les *Meditations*, le *Traité de l'Amour de Dieu*, *l'Entretien d'un Philosophe Chrétien et d'un Philosophe Chinois*, la *Recherche de la Vérité*, avec notes et introduction par J. Simon (2 vols., 12mo). For further information respecting Malebranche and his philosophy, see *Le Cartésianisme, ou la Véritable Renovation des Sciences*, par M. Bordas Demoulin; *Dictionnaire des Sciences Philosophiques*, Art. *Malebranche;* Damiron, *De la Philosophie en France, au XVIIe Siècle*, Liv. VI.; Stewart's *Dissertation*, Part I. Chap. II. Sect. II.

Malebranche's *Search after Truth* was translated into English by Richard Sault (2 vols., 12mo, London, 1694); and his *Treatise of Morality*, by James Shipton (12mo, London, 1699). Sault translated also his *Treatise of Nature and Grace.* — Ed.

† Antoine Arnauld, doctor of the Sorbonne, whom the Port-Royalists call "le grand," was born at Paris, February 8, 1612, and died at Brussels, August 8, 1694. — Ed.

which other philosophers had very generally been silent.
Both of them professed the doctrine universally received, that we perceive not material things immediately, that it is their ideas that are the immediate objects of our thought, and that it is in the idea of every
thing that we perceive its properties.

It is necessary to premise, that both these authors
use the word *perception*, as Descartes had done before
them, to signify every operation of the understanding.*
" To think, to know, to perceive, are the same thing,"
says Mr. Arnauld, Chap. V. Def. 2. It is likewise to
be observed, that the various operations of the mind
are by both called *modifications* of the mind. Perhaps
they were led into this phrase by the Cartesian doctrine, that the essence of the mind consists in thinking,
as that of body consists in extension. I apprehend,
therefore, that when they make sensation, perception,
memory, and imagination to be various modifications
of the mind, they mean no more than that these are
things which can only exist in the mind as their subject. We express the same thing by calling them
various modes of thinking, or various operations of the
mind.†

The things which the mind perceives, says Malebranche, are of two kinds. They are either in the
mind itself, or they are external to it. The things in
the mind are all its different modifications, its sensations, its imaginations, its pure intellections, its passions and affections. These are *immediately* perceived;
we are conscious of them, and have no need of ideas to
represent them to us.

Things external to the mind are either *corporeal* or
spiritual. With regard to the last, he thinks it possible, that, in another state, spirits may be an immediate

---

* Every *apprehensive*, or strictly *cognitive*, operation of the understanding. — H.

† *Modes* or *modifications of mind*, in the Cartesian school, mean merely
what some recent philosophers express by *states of mind*, and include both
the *active* and *passive* phenomena of the conscious subject. The terms
were used by Descartes as well as by his disciples. — H.

object of our understandings, and so be perceived without ideas; that there may be such a union of spirits as that they may immediately perceive each other, and communicate their thoughts mutually, without signs and without ideas. But leaving this as a problematical point, he holds it to be undeniable, that *material* things cannot be perceived immediately, but only by the *mediation of ideas*. He thought it likewise undeniable, that the idea must be immediately present to the mind, that it must touch the soul, as it were, and modify its perception of the object.

From these principles we must necessarily conclude, either that the idea is some modification of the human mind, or that it must be an idea in the Divine mind, which is always intimately present with our minds. The matter being brought to this alternative, Malebranche considers, first, all the possible ways such a modification may be produced in our mind as that we call an idea of a material object, taking it for granted always that it must be an object perceived, and *something different from the act of the mind in perceiving it*. He finds insuperable objections against every hypothesis of such ideas being produced in our minds, and therefore concludes, that the immediate objects of perception are the ideas of the Divine mind.

Against this system Arnauld wrote his book of *True and False Ideas*. He does not object to the alternative mentioned by Malebranche; but he maintains, that ideas are *modifications of our minds*. And finding no other modification of the human mind which can be called the *idea* of an external object, he says it is only another word for *perception*. (Chap. V. Def. 3.) " I take the idea of an object, and the perception of an object, to be the same thing. I do not say whether there may be other things to which the name of *idea* may be given. But it is certain that there are ideas taken in this sense, and that these ideas are either attributes or modifications of our minds." *

---

* Arnauld did not allow that perceptions and ideas are *really* or *numeri-*

This, I think, indeed, was to attack the system of Malebranche upon its weak side, and where, at the same time, an attack was least expected. Philosophers had been so unanimous in maintaining that we do not perceive external objects immediately, but by certain representative images of them called *ideas*, that Malebranche might well think his system secure upon that quarter, and that the only question to be determined was, in what *subject* those ideas are placed, whether in the human or in the Divine mind.

But, says Arnauld, these ideas are mere chimeras, fictions of philosophers; there are no such beings in nature; and therefore it is to no purpose to inquire whether they are in the Divine or in the human mind. The only true and real ideas are our perceptions, which are acknowledged by all philosophers, and Malebranche himself, to be acts or modifications of our own minds. He does not say that the fictitious ideas were a fiction of Malebranche. He acknowledges that they had been very generally maintained by the scholastic philosophers, and points out, very judiciously, the prejudices that had led them into the belief of such ideas.

Of all the powers of our mind, the external senses are thought to be the best understood, and their objects are the most familiar. Hence we measure other powers by them, and transfer to other powers the language which properly belongs to them. The objects of sense must be present to the sense, or within its sphere, in order to their being perceived. Hence, by analogy, we are led to say of every thing when we think of it, that it is *present* to the mind, or *in* the mind. But this presence is metaphorical or analogical only; and Arnauld calls it objective presence, to distinguish it from

---

cally distinguished,—i. e. as one thing from another thing; not even that they are *modally* distinguished,—i. e. as a thing from its mode. He maintained that they are *really* identical, and only *rationally* discriminated as viewed in different relations; the indivisible mental modification being called a *perception*, by reference to the mind or thinking subject,—an *idea*, by reference to the mediate object or thing thought. Arnauld everywhere avows that he denies ideas, only as existences distinct from the act itself of perception.—H.

that local presence which is required in objects that are perceived by sense. But both being called by the same name, they are confounded together, and those things that belong only to real or local presence are attributed to the metaphorical. We are likewise accustomed to see objects by their images in a mirror, or in water; and hence are led, by analogy, to think that objects may be presented to the memory or imagination, in some similar manner, by *images*, which philosophers have called *ideas*.

By such prejudices and analogies, Arnauld conceives, men have been led to believe that the objects of memory and imagination must be presented to the mind by images or ideas; and the philosophers have been more carried away by these prejudices than even the vulgar, because the use made of this theory was to explain and account for the various operations of the mind, a matter in which the vulgar take no concern. He thinks, however, that Descartes had got the better of these prejudices, and that he uses the word *idea* as signifying the same thing with *perception*, and is therefore surprised that a disciple of Descartes, and one who was so great an admirer of him as Malebranche, should be carried away by them. It is strange, indeed, that the two most eminent disciples of Descartes, and his contemporaries, should differ so essentially with regard to his doctrine concerning ideas.

I shall not attempt to give the reader an account of the continuation of this controversy between those two acute philosophers, in the subsequent defences and replies, because I have not access to them. After much reasoning, and some animosity, each continued in his own opinion, and left his antagonist where he found him. Malebranche's opinion of our seeing all things in God soon died away of itself, and Arnauld's notion of ideas seems to have been less regarded than it deserved by the philosophers that came after him; perhaps for this reason, among others, that it seemed to be in some sort given up by himself, in his attempting

8

to reconcile it to the common doctrine concerning ideas.*

Arnauld has employed the whole of his sixth chapter to show that these ways of speaking, common among philosophers, — to wit, *that we perceive not things immediately; that it is their ideas that are the immediate objects of our thoughts; that it is in the idea of every thing that we perceive its properties,* — are not to be rejected, but are true when rightly understood. He labors to reconcile these expressions to his own definition of ideas, by observing, that every perception and every thought is necessarily conscious of itself, and reflects upon itself; and that, by this consciousness and reflection, it is its own immediate object. Whence he in-

---

* The opinion of Arnauld in regard to the nature of ideas was by no means overlooked by subsequent philosophers. It is found fully detailed in almost every systematic course or compend of philosophy which appeared for a long time after its first promulgation, and in many of these it is the doctrine recommended as the true. Arnauld's was indeed the opinion which latterly prevailed in the Cartesian school. From this it passed into other schools. Leibnitz, like Arnauld, regarded *ideas, notions, representations,* as mere modifications of the mind, (what by his disciples were called *material* ideas, like the cerebral ideas of Descartes, are out of the question,) and no cruder opinion than this has ever subsequently found a footing in any of the German systems.

"I don't know," says Mr. Stewart, "of any author who, prior to Dr. Reid, has expressed himself on this subject with so much justness and precision as Father Buffier, in the following passage of his *Treatise on First Truths* (p. 311): — 'If we confine ourselves to what is intelligible in our observations on *ideas,* we will say, they are nothing but mere modifications of the mind as a thinking being.' They are called *ideas* with regard to the object represented, and *perceptions* with regard to the faculty representing. It is manifest that our ideas, considered in this sense, are not more distinguished than motion is from the body moved.' " — *Elements,* Add. to note to Part I. Chap. IV. Sect. II.

In this passage, Buffier only repeats the doctrine of Arnauld, in Arnauld's own words.

Dr. Thomas Brown, on the other hand, has endeavoured to show that this doctrine (which he identifies with Reid's) had been long the catholic opinion, and that Reid, in his attack on the ideal system, only refuted what had been already almost universally exploded. In this attempt he is, however, singularly unfortunate; for, with the exception of Crousaz, all the examples he adduces to evince the prevalence of Arnauld's doctrine are only so many mistakes, so many instances, in fact, which might be alleged in confirmation of the very opposite conclusion. See *Edinburgh Review,* Vol. LII. pp. 181 - 196. — H.

fers, that the idea — that is, the perception — is the immediate object of perception.*

VI. *Leibnitz's Theory.*] The next system concerning perception, of which I shall give some account, is the invention of the famous German philosopher, Leibnitz,† who, while he lived, held the first rank among the Germans in all parts of philosophy, as well as in mathematics, in jurisprudence, in the knowledge of antiquities, and in every branch both of science and of literature. He was highly respected by emperors, and by many kings and princes, who bestowed upon him singular marks of their esteem. ·He was a particular favorite of our Queen Caroline, consort of George II., with whom he continued his correspondence by letters after she came to the crown of Britain, till his death.

The famous controversy between him and the British mathematicians, whether he or Sir Isaac Newton was the inventor of that noble improvement in mathemat-

---

* Reid's discontent with Arnauld's opinion — an opinion which is stated with great perspicuity by its author — may be used as an argument to show that his own doctrine is, however ambiguous, that of intuitive or immediate perception. (See Note C.) Arnauld's theory is identical with the finer form of representative or mediate perception, and the difficulties of that doctrine were not overlooked by his great antagonist. Arnauld well objected, that, when we see a horse, according to Malebranche, what we see is in reality God himself; but Malebranche well rejoined, that, when we see a horse, according to Arnauld, what we see is in reality only a modification of ourselves. — H.

Charpentier has published in his *Bibliothèque Philosophique* the metaphysical writings of Arnauld, *Œuvres Philosophiques, collationnées sur les meilleurs Textes, avec une Introduction par J. Simon* (12mo). Arnauld, with the assistance of Nicole, was the author of *La Logique, ou l'Art de Penser*, of which, under the name of the *Port-Royal Logic*, there have been several editions in English. Arnauld assisted Pascal in the composition of several of the *Lettres Provinciales*. His entire works fill forty-five closely printed quarto volumes. His whole life was consumed in controversies, and distracted by the persecutions to which these controversies led. "Nicole, who bore a share in most of his literary labors, but was of a milder character than Arnauld, told him one day, that he was weary of this incessant warfare, and wished to rest. 'Rest!' said Arnauld; 'will you not have the whole of eternity to rest in?'" See Bayle, *Dict.*, Art. *Arnauld, Ant.*; and *The Biographical Dictionary* of the Society for the Diffusion of Useful Knowledge, under his name. — ED.

† Gottfried Wilhelm Leibnitz was born at Leipzig, July 3, 1646, and died at Hanover, November 14, 1714. — ED.

ics, called by Newton *the Method of Fluxions*, and by Leibnitz *the Differential Method*, engaged the attention of the mathematicians in Europe for several years. He had likewise a controversy with the learned and judicious Dr. Samuel Clarke, about several points of the Newtonian philosophy which he disapproved. The papers which gave occasion to this controversy, with all the replies and rejoinders, had the honor to be transmitted from the one party to the other through the hands of Queen Caroline, and were afterwards published.

His authority, in all matters of philosophy, is still so great in most parts of Germany, that they are considered as bold spirits, and a kind of heretics, who dissent from him in any thing. Christian Wolf, the most voluminous writer in philosophy of this age, is considered as the great interpreter and advocate of the Leibnitzian system, and reveres as an oracle whatever has dropped from the pen of Leibnitz. This author proposed two great works upon the mind. The first, which I have seen, he published with the title of *Psychologia Empirica*. The other was to have the title of *Psychologia Rationalis;* and to it he refers for his explication of the theory of Leibnitz with regard to the mind. But whether it was published I have not learned.*

I must, therefore, take the short account I am to give of this system from the writings of Leibnitz himself, without the light which his interpreter, Wolff, may have thrown upon it.

Leibnitz conceived the whole universe, bodies as well as minds, to be made up of *monads,* that is, simple substances, each of which is by the Creator, in the be-

---

* It was published in 1734. Such careless ignorance of the most distinguished works on the subject of an author's speculations is peculiarly British. -- H.

Wolf, who died in 1754, was succeeded by Kant, whose *Kritik der reinen Vernunft* appeared in 1781, and commenced a new philosophical era in Germany, corresponding to that which the writings of Reid commenced in Great Britain. The French eclectics of the present day claim to be heirs of what is good and enduring in both of these movements. — ED.

ginning of its existence, endowed with certain active and perceptive powers. A *monad*, therefore, is an active substance, simple, without parts or figure, *which has within itself the power to produce all the changes it undergoes from the beginning of its existence to eternity.* The changes which the monad undergoes, of what kind soever, though they may seem to us the effect of causes operating from without, yet they are only the gradual and successive *evolutions of its own internal powers,* which would have produced all the same changes and motions, although there had been no other being in the universe.

Every human soul is a monad joined to an organized body, which organized body consists of an infinite number of monads, each having some degree of active and of perceptive power in itself. But the whole machine of the body has a relation to that monad which we call *the soul,* which is, as it were, the centre of the whole.

As the universe is completely filled with monads without any chasm or void, and thereby every body acts upon every other body, according to its vicinity or distance, and is mutually reacted upon by every other body, it follows, says Leibnitz, that every monad is a kind of living mirror, which reflects the whole universe, according to its point of view, and represents the whole more or less distinctly.

I cannot undertake to reconcile this part of the system with what was before mentioned, — to wit, that every change in a monad is the evolution of its own original powers, and would have happened though no other substance had been created. But to proceed.

There are different orders of monads, some higher, and others lower. The higher orders he calls dominant; such is the human soul. The monads that compose the organized bodies of men, animals, and plants, are of a lower order, and subservient to the dominant monads. But every monad, of whatever order, is a complete substance in itself, — indivisible, having no parts; indestructible, because, having no parts, it can-

8*

not perish by any kind of decomposition. It can only perish by annihilation, and we have no reason to believe that God will ever annihilate any of the beings which he has made.

The monads of a lower order may, by a regular evolution of their powers, rise to a higher order. They may successively be joined to organized bodies, of various forms and different degrees of perception; but they never die, nor cease to be in some degree active and percipient.

This philosopher makes a distinction between perception and what he calls *apperception.* The first is common to all monads, the last proper to the higher orders, among which are human souls.

By apperception he understands that degree of perception which reflects, as it were, upon itself; by which we are conscious of our own existence, and conscious of our perceptions; by which we can reflect upon the operations of our own minds, and can comprehend abstract truths. The mind, in many operations, he thinks, particularly in sleep, and in many actions common to us with the brutes, has not this apperception, although it is still filled with a multitude of obscure and indistinct perceptions, of which we are not conscious.

He conceives that our bodies and minds are united in such a manner, that neither has any physical influence upon the other. Each performs all its operations by its own internal springs and powers; yet the operations of one correspond exactly with those of the other, by *a preëstablished harmony,* just as one clock may be so adjusted as to keep time with another, although each has its own moving power, and neither receives any part of its motion from the other. So that according to this system all our perceptions of external objects would be the same, though external things had never existed; our perception of them would continue, although, by the power of God, they should this moment be annihilated. We do not perceive external things because they exist, but because the soul was originally so constituted as to produce in itself all its successive changes, and all its successive perceptions, independently of the external objects.

Every perception or apperception, every operation, in a word, of the soul, is a *necessary* consequence of the state of it immediately preceding that operation; and this state is the *necessary* consequence of the state preceding it; and so backwards, until you come to its first formation and constitution, which produces successively, and by *necessary* consequence, all its successive states to the end of its existence: so that in this respect the soul, and every monad, may be compared to a watch wound up, which, having the spring of its motion in itself, by the gradual evolution of its own spring produces all the successive motions we observe in it.

In this account of Leibnitz's system concerning monads, and the preëstablished harmony, I have kept as nearly as I could to his own expressions, in his *New System of the Nature and Communication of Substances, and of the Union of Soul and Body,* and in the several illustrations of that new system which he afterwards published, and in his *Principles of Nature and Grace founded in Reason.* I shall now make a few remarks upon this system.

1. To pass over the *irresistible necessity* of all human actions, which makes a part of this system, and which will be considered in another place, I observe first, that *the distinction made between perception and apperception is obscure and unphilosophical.* As far as we can discover, every operation of our mind is attended with consciousness, and particularly that which we call the perception of external objects; and to speak of a perception of which we are not conscious, is to speak without any meaning.

As consciousness is the only power by which we discern the operations of our own minds, or can form any notion of them, an operation of mind of which we are not conscious is we know not what; and to call such an operation by the name of *perception* is an abuse of language. No man can perceive an object, without being conscious that he perceives it. No man can think, without being conscious that he thinks. **What** men are not conscious of cannot, therefore, without impropriety, be called either *perception* or *thought* of any kind. And if we will suppose operations of mind of which we are not conscious, and give a name to such creatures of our imagination, that name must signify what we know nothing about.*

2. To suppose bodies organized or unorganized to be made up of *indivisible* monads which have no parts, *is contrary to all that we know of body.* It is essential to a body to have parts; and every part of a body is a body, and has parts also. No number of parts, *without extension or figure,* not even an infinite number, if we may use that expression, can, by being put together, make a whole that has extension and figure, which all bodies have.

3. It is contrary to all that we know of bodies to ascribe to the monads, of which they are supposed to be compounded, *perception and active force.* If a philosopher thinks proper to say, that a clod of earth both perceives and has active force, let him bring his proofs. But he ought not to expect that men who have understanding will so far give it up as to receive without proof whatever his imagination may suggest.

4. This system *overturns all authority of our senses, and leaves not the least ground to believe the existence of the objects of sense, or the existence of any thing which depends upon the authority of our senses;* for our perception of objects, according to this system, has no dependence upon any thing external, and would be the same as it is supposing external objects had never existed, or that they were from this moment annihilated. It is remarkable that Leibnitz's system, that of Malebranche, and the common system of ideas, or images

---

* The language in which Leibnitz expresses his doctrine of latent modifications of mind, which, though out of consciousness, manifest their existence in their effects, is objectionable; the doctrine itself is not only true, but of the very highest importance in psychology, although it has never yet been appreciated, or even understood, by any writer on philosophy in this island. — H.

of external objects in the mind, do all agree in over-
turning all the authority of our senses; and this one
thing, as long as men retain their senses, will always
make all these systems truly ridiculous.

5. The last observation I shall make upon this system, which indeed is equally applicable to all the systems of perception I have mentioned, is, that *it is all
hypothesis, made up of conjectures and suppositions, without proof.* The Peripatetics supposed sensible *species*
to be sent forth by the objects of sense. The moderns
suppose *ideas* in the brain, or in the mind. Malebranche supposed, that we perceive *the ideas of the
Divine mind.* Leibnitz supposed *monads and a pre-
established harmony;* and these monads being creatures
of his own making, he is at liberty to give them what
properties and powers his fancy may suggest.* Such
suppositions, while there is no proof of them offered,
are nothing but the fictions of human fancy; and if
they were true, would solve no difficulty, but raise
many new ones. It is therefore more agreeable to good
sense, and to sound philosophy, to rest satisfied with
what our consciousness and attentive reflection discover
to us of the nature of perception, than, by inventing
hypotheses, to attempt to explain things which are
above the reach of human understanding.†

---

* It is a disputed point whether Leibnitz was serious in his monadology
and proëstablished harmony. — H.

† *God. Guil. Leibnitii Opera Philosophica quæ extant Latina Gallica Ger-
manica omnia,* edited by Erdmann (royal 8vo, Berlin, 1840), is the best
edition of Leibnitz's metaphysical writings. Most of them are also included in *Œuvres de Leibnitz,* published, with an introduction, by M.
Jacques (2 vols., 12mo, Paris, 1842). The best life of this philosopher is
in German, — *Gottfried Wilhelm Freiherr von Leibnitz, Eine Biographie, von
Dr. G. E. Guhrauer* (2 vols., 12mo, Breslau, 1842). A life in English on
the basis of this work, but much abridged, has been published by John M.
Mackie (12mo, Boston, 1845). For an exposition of his system, see
Feuerbach, *Darstellung und Kritik der Leibnitzichen Philosophie;* Buhle, *Histoire de la Philosophie Moderne,* Tome IV. Chap. III.; *Biographie Uni-
verselle,* Art *Leibnitz;* Stewart's *Dissertation,* Part II. Sect. II.

The ashes of Leibnitz repose under the court church of Hanover, with
no other inscription to mark the spot than these two words: — OSSA
LEIBNITII. But, as Mr. Stewart observes, "the best *éloge* of Leibnitz is
furnished by the literary history of the eighteenth century. Whoever
takes the pains to compare it with his works, and with his epistolary cor-

VII. *Locke's Theory.*] The reputation which Locke's *Essay concerning Human Understanding* had at home from the beginning, and which it has gradually acquired abroad, is a sufficient testimony of its merit.* There is perhaps no book of the metaphysical kind that has been so generally read by those who understand the language, or that is more adapted to teach men to think with precision,† and to inspire them with that candor and love of truth which is the genuine spirit of philosophy. He gave, I believe, the first example in the English language of writing on such abstract subjects with a remarkable degree of simplicity and perspicuity; and in this he has been happily imitated by others that came after him. No author has more successfully pointed out the danger of ambiguous words, and the importance of having distinct and determinate notions in judging and reasoning. His observations on the various powers of the human understanding, on the use and abuse of words, and on the extent and limits of human knowledge, are drawn from attentive reflection on the operations of his own mind, the true source of all real knowledge on these subjects, and show an uncommon degree of penetration and judgment. But he needs no panegyric of mine; and I mention these things only that, when I have occasion to differ from him, I may not be thought insensible of the merit of an author whom I highly respect, and to whom I owe my first lights in those studies, as well as my attachment to them.‡

---

respondence, will find reason to doubt, whether, at the singular era when he appeared, he could have more accelerated the advancement of knowledge by the concentration of his studies, than he has actually done by the universality of his aims; and whether he does not afford one of the few instances to which the words of the poet may literally be applied : —

'Si non errâsset, fecerat ille minus.'"

—Ed.

* John Locke was born at Wrington, near Bristol, August 29, 1632, and died at the house of his friend, Sir Francis Masham, at Oates, in Essex, October 28, 1704, where he had passed the last twelve years of his life. —Ed.

† To praise Locke for *precision* is rather too much. — H.

‡ Sir James Mackintosh has said : — " The *Treatise on the Law of War*

He sets out in his essay with a full conviction, common to him with other philosophers, that ideas in the mind are the objects of all our thoughts in every operation of the understanding. This leads him to use the word *idea** so very frequently, beyond what was usual in the English language, that he thought it necessary in his introduction to make this apology: — " It being that term," says he, " which, I think, serves best to stand for whatsoever is the object of the understanding, when a man thinks, I have used it to express whatever is meant by *phantasm, notion, species*, or whatever it is which the mind can be employed about in thinking; and I could not avoid frequently using it. I presume it will be granted me, that there are such ideas in men's minds; every man is conscious of them in himself, and men's words and actions will satisfy him that they are in others."

Speaking of the reality of our knowledge, he says, — " It is evident *the mind knows not things immediately*, but only by the intervention of the ideas it has of them. Our knowledge, therefore, is real, only so far as there is a conformity between our ideas and the reality of things. But what shall be here the criterion? How shall the mind, when it perceives nothing but its own ideas, know that they agree with things themselves? This, though it seems not to want difficulty, yet I think there be two sorts of ideas that we may be assured agree with things."

We see that Mr. Locke was aware, no less than Descartes, that the doctrine of ideas made it necessary, and at the same time difficult, to prove the existence of *a material world* without us; because the mind, according to that doctrine, perceives nothing but a world of

---

and Peace, the *Essay concerning Human Understanding*, the *Spirit of Laws*, and the *Inquiry into the Causes of the Wealth of Nations*, are the works which have most directly influenced the general opinion of Europe during the last two centuries." — *Edinburgh Review*, Vol. XXXVI. p. 240. The *Essay concerning Human Understanding* was first printed in 1690. — ED.

* Locke may be said to have first naturalized the word in English philosophical language, in its Cartesian extension. — H.

ideas in itself. Not only Descartes, but Malebranche and Arnauld, had perceived this difficulty, and attempted to remove it with little success. Mr. Locke attempts the same thing; but his arguments are feeble. He even seems to be conscious of this; for he concludes his reasoning with this observation, — "That we have evidence sufficient to direct us in attaining the good and avoiding the evil caused by external objects, and that this is the important concern we have in being made acquainted with them." This, indeed, is saying no more than will be granted by those who deny the existence of a material world.

As there is no material difference between Locke and Descartes with regard to the perception of objects by the senses, there is the less occasion, in this place, to take notice of all their differences in other points. They differed about the origin of our ideas. Descartes thought some of them were *innate;* * the other maintained, that there are no innate ideas, and that they are all derived from two sources, — to wit, *sensation* and *reflection;* meaning by sensation the operations of our external senses, and by reflection that attention which we are capable of giving to the operations of our own minds.†

They differed with regard to the *essence* both of matter and of mind: the British philosopher holding, that the real essence of both is beyond the reach of human knowledge; the other conceiving, that the very essence

---

* The doctrine of Descartes, in relation to *innate ideas*, has been very generally misunderstood; and by no one more than by Locke. What it really amounted to is clearly stated in his strictures on the *Program* of Regius. Justice has latterly been done him, among others, by Mr. Stewart, in his *Dissertation*, and by M. Laromiguiere, in his *Cours*. See also the old controversy of De Vries with Röell on this point. — H.

† That Locke did not (as even Mr. Stewart supposes) introduce *reflection*, either name or thing, into the philosophy of mind, see Note I. Nor was he even the first explicitly to enunciate *sense* and *reflection* as the two sources of our knowledge; for I can show that this had been done in a far more philosophical manner by some of the schoolmen; reflection with them not being merely, as with Locke, a source of *adventitious, empirical,* or *a posteriori* knowledge, but the mean by which we disclose also the *native* or *a priori* cognitions which the intellect itself contains. — H.

of mind consists in thought, and that of matter in extension, by which he made matter and space not to differ in reality, and no part of space to be void of matter.

Mr. Locke explained, more distinctly than had been done before, the operations of the mind in classing the various objects of thought, and reducing them to *genera* and *species*.   He was the first, I think, who distinguished in substances what he calls the *nominal* essence, which is only the notion we form of a genus or species, and which we express by a definition, from the *real* essence or internal constitution of the thing, which makes it to be what it is.*   Without this distinction, the subtile disputes which tortured the schoolmen for so many ages, in the controversy between the nominalists and realists, could never be brought to an issue. He shows distinctly how we form abstract and general notions, and the use and necessity of them in reasoning.   And as (according to the received principles of philosophers) every notion of our mind must have for its object an idea in the mind itself, he thinks that we form abstract ideas by leaving out of the idea of an individual every thing wherein it differs from other individuals of the same species or genus; and that this power of forming abstract ideas is that which chiefly distinguishes us from brute animals, in whom he could see no evidence of any abstract ideas.

Since the time of Descartes, philosophers have differed much with regard to the share they ascribe to the mind itself in the fabrication of those representative beings called *ideas*, and the manner in which this work is carried on.

Of the authors I have met with, Dr. Robert Hook is the most explicit.   He was one of the most ingenious and active members of the Royal Society of London at its first institution, and frequently read lectures to the Society, which were published among his posthumous works.   In his *Lectures upon Light*, § 7, he makes

---

* Locke has no originality in this respect. — H.

ideas to be material substances; and thinks that the brain is furnished with a proper kind of matter for fabricating the ideas of each sense. The ideas of sight, he thinks, are formed of a kind of matter resembling the Bononian stone, or some kind of phosphorus; that the ideas of sound are formed of some matter resembling the chords or glasses which take a sound from the vibrations of the air; and so of the rest.

The soul, he thinks, may fabricate some hundreds of those ideas in a day; and that, as they are formed, they are pushed farther off from the centre of the brain, where the soul resides. By this means, they make a continued chain of ideas, coiled up in the brain, the first end of which is farthest removed from the centre or seat of the soul, and the other end is always at the centre, being the last idea formed, which is always present the moment when considered; and therefore, according as there is a greater number of ideas between the present sensation or thought in the centre and any other, the soul is apprehensive of a larger portion of time interposed.

Mr. Locke has not entered into so minute a detail of this manufacture of ideas; but he ascribes to the mind a very considerable hand in forming its own ideas. With regard to our sensations, the mind is passive, "they being produced in us only by different degrees and modes of motion in our animal spirits, variously agitated by external objects." These, however, cease to be, as soon as they cease to be perceived; but, by the faculties of memory and imagination, "the mind has an ability, when it wills, to revive them again, and, as it were, to paint them anew upon itself, though some with more, some with less difficulty."

As to the ideas of reflection, he ascribes them to no other cause but to that attention which the mind is capable of giving to its own operations: these, therefore, are formed by the mind itself. He ascribes likewise to the mind the power of compounding its simple ideas into complex ones of various forms; of repeating them, and adding the repetitions together; of dividing and classing them; of comparing them, and, from that comparison, of forming the ideas of their relation; nay, of forming a general idea of a species or genus, by taking from the idea of an individual every thing by which it is distinguished from other individuals of the kind, till at last it becomes an abstract general idea, common to all the individuals of the kind.

The ideas we have of the various qualities of bodies are not all, as Mr. Locke thinks, of the same kind. Some of them are images or resemblances of what is really in the body; others are not. There are certain qualities inseparable from matter; such as extension, solidity, figure, mobility. Our ideas of these are *real resemblances of the qualities in the body;* and these he calls *primary qualities:* but color, sound, taste, smell, heat, and cold he calls *secondary qualities,* and thinks that they are only powers in bodies of producing certain sensations in us; which sensations *have nothing resembling them,* though they are commonly thought to be exact resemblances of something in the body.*
" Thus," says he, " the ideas of heat or light, which we receive, by our eye or touch, from the sun, are commonly thought real qualities existing in the sun, and something more than mere powers in it."

Perhaps it was unfortunate for Mr. Locke that he used the word *idea* so very frequently as to make it very difficult to give the attention necessary to put it always to the same meaning. And it appears evident, that, in many places, he means nothing more by it than the notion or conception we have of any object of thought; that is, the *act of the mind* in conceiving it, and not the *object* conceived.†

---

* Locke only gave a new meaning to old terms. The *first* and *second,* or the *primary* and *secondary* qualities of Aristotle, denoted a distinction similar to, but not identical with, that in question. Locke distinguished nothing which had not been more precisely discriminated by Aristotle and the Cartesians. — H.

† When we contemplate a triangle, we may consider it either as a complement of three sides or of three angles; not that the three sides and the three angles are possible except through each other, but because we may in thought view the figure — *qua* triangle, in reality one and indivisible —

In explaining this word, he says that he uses it for whatever is meant by *phantasm, notion, species.* Here are three synonymes to the word *idea.* The first and last are very proper to express the philosophical meaning of the word, being terms of art in the Peripatetic philosophy, and signifying images of external things in the mind, which, according to that philosophy, are objects of thought. But the word *notion* is a word in common language, whose meaning agrees exactly with the popular meaning of the word *idea,* but not with the philosophical.

When these two different meanings of the word *idea* are confounded in a studied explication of it, there is little reason to expect that they should be carefully distinguished in the frequent use of it. There are many passages in the essay, in which, to make them intelligible, the word *idea* must be taken in one of those senses, and many others, in which it must be taken in the other. It seems probable that the author, not attending to this ambiguity of the word, used it in the one sense or the other, as the subject-matter required; and the far greater part of his readers have done the same.

There is a third sense in which he uses the word not unfrequently, — to signify *objects of thought* that are not

---

in different relations. In like manner, we may consider a representative act of knowledge in two relations, — 1st, as an act representative of something, and, 2d, as an act cognitive of that representation, although, in truth, these are both only one indivisible energy, — the representation only existing as known, the cognition being only possible in a representation. Thus, e. g., in the imagination of a Centaur, the Centaur represented is the Centaur known, the Centaur known is the Centaur represented. It is one act under two relations, — a relation to the subject knowing, a relation to the object represented. But to a cognitive act considered in these several relations we may give either different names, or we may confound them under one, or we may do both: and this is actually done; some words expressing only one relation, others both or either, and others properly one, but abusively also the other. Thus *idea* properly denotes an act of thought considered in relation to an external something beyond the sphere of consciousness, — *a representation ;* but some philosophers, as Locke, abuse it to comprehend the thought also, viewed as cognitive of this representation. Again, *perception, notion, conception, &c., (concept* is, unfortunately, obsolete,) comprehend both, or may be used to denote either of the relations; and it is only by the context that we can ever vaguely discover in which application they are intended. This is unfortunate ; but so it is. — H.

in the mind, but external.   Of this he seems to be sensible, and somewhere makes an apology for it.   When he affirms, as he does in innumerable places, that all human knowledge consists in the perception of the agreement or disagreement of our ideas, it is impossible to put a meaning upon this, consistent with his principles, unless he means by ideas every object of human thought, whether mediate or immediate; every thing, in a word, that can be signified by the subject or by the predicate of a proposition.

Thus we see that the word *idea* has three different meanings in the essay; and the author seems to have used it sometimes in one, sometimes in another, without being aware of any change in the meaning.   The reader slides easily into the same fallacy, that meaning occurring most readily to his mind which gives the best sense to what he reads.   I have met with persons professing no slight acquaintance with the *Essay concerning Human Understanding*, who maintained that the word *idea*, wherever it occurs, means nothing more than *thought*; and that where the author speaks of ideas as images in the mind, and as objects of thought, he is not to be understood as speaking properly, but figuratively or analogically: and, indeed, I apprehend that it would be no small advantage to many passages in the book, if they could admit of this interpretation.

It is not the fault of this philosopher alone to have given too little attention to the distinction between the *operations* of the mind, and the *objects* of those operations.   Although this distinction be familiar to the vulgar, and found in the structure of all languages, philosophers, when they speak of ideas, often confound the two together; and their theory concerning ideas has led them to do so; for ideas, being supposed to be a shadowy kind of beings, intermediate between the thought and the object of thought, sometimes seem to coalesce with the thought, sometimes with the object of thought, and sometimes to have a distinct existence of their own.

The same philosophical theory of ideas has led phi-

9*

losophers to confound the different operations of **the**
understanding, and to call them all by the name **of**
*perception.** Mr. Locke, though not free from **this**
fault, is not so often chargeable with it as some **who**
came after him. The vulgar give the name of *percep-*
tion to that immediate knowledge of external **objects**
which we have by our external senses. This is **its**
proper meaning in our language, though sometimes **it**
may be applied to other things metaphorically or analogically. When I think of any thing that does **not**
exist, as of the republic of Oceana, I do not *perceive*
it; I only *conceive* or *imagine* it.† When I think **of**
what happened to me yesterday, I do not *perceive*, **but**
remember it. When I am pained with the gout, it **is**
not proper to say I *perceive* the pain; I *feel* it, or *am*
conscious of it.‡ It is not an object of perception, **but**
of sensation and of consciousness. So far, the **vulgar**
distinguish very properly the different operations of **the**
mind, and never confound the names of things so different in their nature. But the theory of ideas **leads**
philosophers to conceive all those operations to be **of**
one nature, and to give them one name. They are **all,**
according to that theory, the perception of ideas in **the**
mind. Perceiving, remembering, imagining, being conscious, are all perceiving ideas in the mind, and **are**

---

* No more than by calling them all by the name of *cognitions*, or *acts of*
consciousness. There was no reason, either from etymology or usage, why
perception should not signify the energy of immediately apprehending, *in*
general; and until Reid limited the word to *our apprehension of an external*
world, it was, in fact, employed by philosophers as tantamount to an act of
consciousness. We were in need of a word to express our *sensitive cog-*
nitions as distinct from our *sensitive feelings,* (for the term *sensation* involved
both,) and therefore Reid's restriction should be adopted; but his criticism of other philosophers for their employment of the term in a wider
meaning is wholly groundless. — H.

† And why? Simply because we do not, by such an act, *know* or *appre-*
hend such an object to exist, which is what *perception,* in its wider acceptation, was used to denote; we *merely represent* the object. We could say,
however, that we *perceived* (as we could say that we were *conscious of*) the
republic of Oceana, *as imagined by us, after Harrington.* — H.

‡ Because the feeling of pain, though only possible through consciousness, is not *an act of knowledge.* But it could have been properly said,
I perceive a feeling of pain. At any rate, the expression *I perceive a pain*
is as correct as *I am conscious of a pain.* — H.

called *perceptions.* Hence it is that philosophers speak
of the perceptions of memory and the perceptions of
imagination. They make sensation to be a perception,
and every thing we perceive by our senses to be an
idea of sensation. Sometimes they say, that they are
conscious of the ideas in their own minds; sometimes,
that they perceive them.

However improbable it may appear .that philosophers, who have taken pains to study the operations
of their own minds, should express them less properly
and less distinctly than the vulgar, it seems really to be
the case; and the only account that can be given of
this strange phenomenon I take to be this: that the
vulgar seek no theory to account for the operations of
their minds; they know that they see, and hear, and
remember, and imagine; and those who think distinctly will express these operations distinctly, as their consciousness represents them to the mind. But philosophers think they ought to know, not only that there are
such operations, but *how* they are performed; how they
see, and hear, and remember, and imagine; and, having invented a theory to explain these operations by
ideas or images in the mind, they suit their expressions
to their theory; and, as a false comment throws a cloud
upon the text, so a false theory darkens the phenomena
which it attempts to explain.*

---

* An authentic and ample, but ill-digested and unsatisfactory *Life of
John Locke, with Extracts from his Correspondence, Journals, and Commonplace Books,* was published by Lord King (2d ed., 2 vols., 8vo, London,
1830). The best and most complete edition of his works is that in 10
vols., 8vo, London, 1801, and again in 1810. The criticisms and polemics
to which his writings have given rise are innumerable, of which the following may be referred to as being among the most recent and remarkable : — De Maistre, *Les Soirées de Saint-Petersbourge,* Sixième Entretien.
Cousin, *Histoire de la Philosophie du XVIIIᵉ Siècle,* Tome II.; of this we
have an English translation by Professor Henry, *Elements of Psychology :
included in a Critical Examination of Locke's Essay on the Human Understanding* (3d ed., 12mo, New York, 1842). Tennemann's *Abh. über den
Empirismus in der Philosophie, vorzüglich den Lockischen,* inserted in the
third volume of his German translation of Locke's Essay. Hallam's *Literature of Europe,* from 1650 to 1700, Chap. III. Morell's *Hist. and Crit.
View of Speculative Philosophy,* Part I. Chap. I. Sect. II. Compare what
Stewart says of Locke, in the first of his *Philosophical Essays,* with what
he says of him in his *Dissertation,* Part II. Sect. I. and II. — ED.

VIII. *Berkeley's Theory.*] George Berkeley,* afterwards Bishop of Cloyne, published his *New Theory of Vision* in 1709; his *Treatise concerning the Principles of Human Knowledge*, in 1710; and his *Dialogues between Hylas and Philonous*, in 1713; being then a Fellow of Trinity College, Dublin. He is acknowledged universally to have great merit, as an excellent writer, and a very acute and clear reasoner on the most abstract subjects, not to speak of his virtues as a man, which were very conspicuous; yet the doctrine chiefly held forth in the treatises above mentioned, especially in the last two, has generally been thought so very absurd, that few can be brought to think, either that he believed it himself, or that he seriously meant to persuade others of its truth.

He maintains, and thinks he has demonstrated, by a variety of arguments, grounded on principles of philosophy universally received, that there is no such thing as matter in the universe; that sun and moon, earth and sea, our own bodies, and those of our friends, are nothing but ideas in the minds of those who think of them, and that they have no existence when they are not the objects of thought; that all that is in the universe may be reduced to two categories, — to wit, *minds*, and *ideas in the mind.*

But however absurd this doctrine might appear to the unlearned, who consider the existence of the objects of sense as the most evident of all truths, and what no man in his senses can doubt, the philosophers, who had been accustomed to consider ideas as the immediate objects of all thought, had no title to view this doctrine of Berkeley in so unfavorable a light.

They were taught by Descartes, and by all that came after him, that the existence of the objects of sense is not self-evident, but requires to* be proved by arguments; and although Descartes, and many others, had

---

* Born at Kilerin, in the county of Kilkenny, March 12, 1684, and died at Oxford, January 14, 1753, whither he had repaired a few months before to superintend the education of one of his sons. — ED.

labored to find arguments for this purpose, there did not appear to be that force and clearness in them which might have been expected in a matter of such importance. Mr. Norris had declared, that, after all the arguments that had been offered, the existence of an external world is only probable, but by no means certain. Malebranche thought it rested upon the authority of revelation, and that the arguments drawn from reason were not perfectly conclusive. Others thought, that the argument from revelation was a mere sophism, because revelation comes to us by our senses, and must rest upon their authority.

Thus we see that the new philosophy had been making gradual approaches towards Berkeley's opinion; and, whatever others might do, the philosophers had no title to look upon it as absurd, or unworthy of a fair examination. Several authors attempted to answer his arguments, but with little success, and others acknowledged that they could neither answer them nor assent to them. It is probable the Bishop made but few converts to his doctrine; but it is certain he made some; and that he himself continued, to the end of his life, firmly persuaded, not only of its truth, but of its great importance for the improvement of human knowledge, and especially for the defence of religion. *Dial. Pref.* "If the principles which I here endeavour to propagate are admitted for true, the consequences which I think evidently flow from thence are, that atheism and skepticism will be utterly destroyed, many intricate points made plain, great difficulties solved, several useless parts of science retrenched, speculation referred to practice, and men reduced from paradoxes to common sense."

In the *Theory of Vision* he goes no farther than to assert, that the objects of sight are nothing but ideas in the mind, granting, or at least not denying, that there is a *tangible* world, which is really external, and which exists whether we perceive it or not. Whether the reason of this was, that his system had not, at that time, wholly opened to his own mind, or whether he

thought it prudent to let it into the minds of his readers by degrees, I cannot say. I think he insinuates the
last as the reason in the *Principles of Human Knowledge.*

The *Theory of Vision*, however, taken by itself, and
without relation to the main branch of his system,
contains very important discoveries, and marks of great
genius. He distinguishes, more accurately than any
that went before him, between the immediate objects
of sight, and those of the other senses which are early
associated with them: he shows, that distance, of itself, and immediately, is not seen; but that we learn to
judge of it by certain sensations and perceptions which
are connected with it. This is a very important observation, and I believe was first made by this author.*
It gives much new light to the operations of our senses,
and serves to account for many phenomena in optics,
of which the greatest adepts in that science had always
either given a false account, or acknowledged that they
could give none at all.

We may observe by the way, that the ingenious
author seems not to have attended to a distinction by
which his general assertion ought to have been limited.
It is true that the distance of an object from the eye is
not immediately seen; but there is a certain kind of
distance of one object from another which we see immediately. The author acknowledges that there are
a visible extension and visible figures, which are proper
objects of sight; there must therefore be a visible distance. Astronomers call it *angular* distance; and
although they measure it by the angle which is made
by two lines drawn from the eye to the two distinct
objects, yet it is immediately perceived by sight, even
by those who never thought of that angle.

He led the way in showing how we learn to perceive
the distance of an object from the eye, though this
speculation was carried farther by others who came
after him. He made the distinction between that ex-

---

* This last statement is inaccurate. — H.

tension and figure which we perceive by sight only, and that which we perceive by touch; calling the first *visible*, the last, *tangible* extension and figure. He showed, likewise, that tangible extension, and not visible, is the object of geometry, although mathematicians commonly use visible diagrams in their demonstrations.*

The notion of extension and figure which we get from sight only, and that which we get from touch, have been so constantly conjoined from our infancy in all the judgments we form of the objects of sense, that it required great abilities to distinguish them accurately, and to assign to each sense what truly belongs to it; " so difficult a thing it is," as Berkeley justly observes, " to dissolve a union so early begun, and confirmed by so long a habit." This point he has labored, through the whole of the essay on vision, with that uncommon penetration and judgment which he possessed, and with as great success as could be expected in a first attempt upon so abstruse a subject.

In the new philosophy, the pillars by which the existence of a material world was supported were so feeble, that it did not require the force of a Samson to bring them down; and in this we have not so much reason to admire the strength of Berkeley's genius, as his boldness in publishing to the world an opinion, which the unlearned would be apt to interpret as the sign of a crazy intellect. A man who was firmly persuaded of the doctrine universally received by philosophers concerning ideas, if he could but take courage to call in question the existence of a material world, would easily find unanswerable arguments in that doctrine. " Some truths there are," says Berkeley, " so near and obvious to the mind, that a man need only open his eyes to see them. Such," he adds, " I take this important one to be, that all the choir of heaven,

---

* Properly speaking, it is neither *tangible* nor *visible* extension which is the object of geometry, but *intelligible, pure*, or *a priori* extension. But of this distinction more hereafter. — H.

and furniture of the earth; in a word, all those bodies which compose the mighty frame of the world; have not any subsistence without a mind." — *Princ.*, Sect. VI.

The principle from which this important conclusion is obviously deduced, is laid down in the first sentence of his *Principles of Knowledge* as evident: and, indeed, it had always been acknowledged by philosophers. " It is evident," says he, " to any one who takes a survey of the objects of human knowledge, that they are either ideas actually imprinted on the senses, or else such as are perceived by attending to the passions and operations of the mind; or, lastly, ideas formed by help of memory and imagination, either compounding, dividing, or barely representing those originally perceived in the foresaid ways."

This is the foundation on which the whole system rests. If this be true, then, indeed, the existence of a material world must be a dream that has imposed upon all mankind from the beginning of the world.

The foundation on which such a fabric rests ought to be very solid, and well established; yet Berkeley says nothing more for it than that " it is evident." If he means that it is *self-evident*, this, indeed, might be a good reason for not offering any direct argument in proof of it. But I apprehend this cannot justly be said. Self-evident propositions are those which appear evident to every man of sound understanding, who apprehends the meaning of them distinctly, and attends to them without prejudice. Can this be said of this proposition, that all the objects of our knowledge are *ideas in our own minds?* * I believe, that, to any man

---

* To the idealist, it is of perfect indifference whether this proposition, in Reid's sense of the expression *ideas*, be admitted, or whether it be held that we are conscious of nothing but of *the modifications of our own minds*. For on the supposition that we can know the *non-ego* only in and through the *ego*, it follows, (since we can know nothing immediately of which we are not conscious, and it being allowed that we are conscious only of mind,) that it is contradictory to suppose aught, as known, (i. e. any object of knowledge,) to be known otherwise than as a phenomenon of mind. — H.

In another connection, Sir W. Hamilton had said, that we might give

uninstructed in philosophy, this proposition will appear very improbable, if not absurd. However scanty his knowledge may be, he considers the sun and moon, the earth and sea, as objects of it: and it will be difficult to persuade him, that those objects of his knowledge are ideas in his own mind, and have no existence when he does not think of them. If I may presume to speak my own sentiments, I once believed this doctrine of ideas so firmly, as to embrace the whole of Berkeley's system in consequence of it; till, finding other consequences to follow from it which gave me more uneasiness than the want of a material world, it came into my mind, more than forty years ago, to put the question, What evidence have I for this doctrine, that all the objects of my knowledge are ideas in my own mind? From that time to the present, I have been

---

up the supposition of the existence of ideas as *tertia quædam*, distinct at once from the material object and the immaterial subject, and yet be unable to confute the modern doctrine of egoistical idealism, which is founded on the doctrine, "that all our knowledge is merely *subjective*, or of the mind itself; that the *ego* has no immediate cognizance of a *non-ego* as existing, but that the *non-ego* is only represented to us in a *modification* of the self-conscious *ego*. This doctrine being admitted, the idealist has only to show that the supposition of a *non-ego*, or external world really existent, is a groundless and unnecessary assumption; for, while the *law of parcimony* prohibits the multiplication of substances or causes beyond what the phenomena require, we have manifestly no right to postulate for the *non-ego* the dignity of an independent substance beyond the *ego*, seeing that this *non-ego* is, *ex hypothesi*, known to us, consequently exists for us, only as a phenomenon of the *ego*." Hence he argues that the Scotch philosophers, including Reid, did not go far enough; for their doctrine respecting the mere *suggestion* of extension, on occasion of certain sensations, involves the very groundwork on which modern idealism reposes. "All our knowledge of the *non-ego* is thus rendered merely *ideal* and *mediate*; we have no knowledge of any really objective reality, except through a subjective representation or notion; in other words, we are only immediately cognizant of certain modes of our own minds, and, in and through them, mediately warned of the phenomena of the material universe." Taking this position, even the argument from common sense against idealism becomes unavailing; "for the common sense of mankind only assures us of the existence of an external and extended world, in assuring us that we are *conscious*, not merely of the phenomena of mind in relation to matter, but of the phenomena of matter in relation to mind, — in other words, that we are *immediately percipient* of extended things." Reid himself, he says, seems to have become obscurely aware of this condition, and to have accommodated his later views to it. — ED.

10

candidly and impartially, as I think, seeking for the evidence of this principle, but can find none, excepting the authority of philosophers.

Berkeley foresaw the opposition that would be made to his system, from two different quarters: *first*, from the philosophers; and, *secondly*, from the vulgar, who are led by the plain dictates of nature. The first he had the courage to oppose openly and avowedly; the second he dreaded much more, and therefore takes a great deal of pains, and, I think, uses some art, to court into his party. This is particularly observable in his *Dialogues.* He sets out with a declaration, *Dial.* 1, " That, of late, he had quitted several of the sublime notions he had got in the schools of the philosophers for vulgar opinions," and assures Hylas, his fellow-dialogist, " That, since this revolt from metaphysical notions to the plain dictates of nature and common sense, he found his understanding strangely enlightened; so that he could now easily comprehend a great many things, which before were all mystery and riddle." Pref. to *Dial.* " If his principles are admitted for true, men will be reduced from paradoxes to common sense." At the same time, he acknowledges, " That they carry with them a great opposition to the prejudices of philosophers, which have so far prevailed against the common sense and natural notions of mankind."

When Hylas objects to him, *Dial.* 3, " You can never persuade me, Philonous, that the denying of matter or corporeal substance is not repugnant to the universal sense of mankind "; he answers, " I wish both our opinions were fairly stated, and submitted to the judgment of men who had plain common sense, without the prejudices of a learned education. Let me be represented as one who trusts his senses, who thinks he knows the things he sees and feels, and entertains no doubt of their existence. If by material substance is meant only *sensible body*, that *which is seen and felt,* (and the unphilosophical part of the world, I dare say, mean no more,) then I am more certain of matter's existence than you or any other philosopher pretend to be. If there be any thing which makes the generality of mankind averse from the notions I espouse, it is a misapprehension that I deny the reality of sensible things : but as it is you who are guilty of that, and not I, it follows, that, in truth, their aversion is against your notions, and not mine. I am content to appeal to the common sense of the world for the truth of my notion. I am of a vulgar cast, simple enough to believe my senses, and to leave things as I find them. I cannot, for my life, help thinking that snow is white, and fire hot."

When Hylas is at last entirely converted, he observes to Philonous, " After all, the controversy about matter, in the strict acceptation of it, lies altogether between you and the philosophers, whose principles, I acknowledge, are not near so natural, or so agreeable to the common sense of mankind, and Holy Scripture, as yours." Philonous observes in the end, " That he does not pretend to be a setter up of new notions ; his endeavours tend only to unite, and to place in a clearer light, that truth which was before shared between the vulgar and the philosophers ; the former being of opinion, that those things they immediately perceive are the *real things*, and the latter, that the things immediately perceived are *ideas which exist only in the mind;* which two things put together do, in effect, constitute the substance of what he advances." And he concludes by observing, " That those principles which at first view lead to skepticism, pursued to a certain point, bring men back to common sense."

These passages show sufficiently the author's concern to reconcile his system to the plain dictates of nature and common sense, while he expresses no concern to reconcile it to the received doctrines of philosophers. He is fond of taking part with the vulgar against the philosophers, and of vindicating common sense against their innovations. What pity is it that he did not carry this suspicion of the doctrine of philosophers so far as to doubt of that philosophical tenet on which his whole system is built, — to wit, that the things immediately perceived by the senses are ideas which exist only in the mind!

After all, it seems no easy matter to make the vulgar opinion and that of Berkeley to meet. And to accomplish this, he seems to me to draw each out of its line towards the other, not without some straining. The vulgar opinion he reduces to this, that the very things which we *perceive by our senses* do really exist. This he grants. For these things, says he, are *ideas in our minds, or complexions of ideas, to which we give one name, and consider as one thing;* these are the immediate objects of sense, and these *do really exist.* As to the notion, that those things have an *absolute external existence,* independent of being perceived by any mind, he thinks that this is no notion of the vulgar, but a refinement of philosophers; and that the notion of material substance, as a *substratum* or support of that collection of sensible qualities to which we give the name of an apple or a melon, is likewise an invention of philosophers, and is not found with the vulgar till they are instructed by philosophers. The substance not being an *object of sense,* the vulgar never think of it; or, if they are taught the use of the word, they mean no more by it but *that collection of sensible qualities* which they, from finding them *conjoined in nature,* have been accustomed to call by *one name,* and to consider as *one thing.*

Thus he draws the vulgar opinion near to his own; and, that he may meet it half way, he acknowledges that material things have a real existence out of the mind *of this or that person;* but the question, says he, between the materialist and me is, Whether they have an absolute existence distinct from their being perceived by *God,* and exterior to *all* minds? This, indeed, he says, some heathens and philosophers have affirmed; but whoever entertains notions of the Deity suitable to the Holy Scripture will be of another opinion.

But here an objection occurs, which it required all his ingenuity to answer. It is this. The ideas in my mind cannot be the same with the ideas of any other mind; therefore, if the objects I perceive be *only ideas*, it is impossible that the objects I perceive can exist *anywhere* when I do not perceive them; and it is impossible that two or more minds can perceive *the same object.*

To this Berkeley answers, that this objection presses no less the opinion of the materialist *philosopher* than his. But the difficulty is, to make his opinion coincide with the notions of the *vulgar*, who are firmly persuaded that the very identical objects which they perceive continue to exist when they do not perceive them; and who are no less firmly persuaded, that, when ten men look at the sun or the moon, they all see the same individual object.

To reconcile this repugnancy, he observes, *Dial.* 3, "That if the term *same* be taken in the vulgar acceptation, it is certain, (and not at all repugnant to the principles he maintains,) that different persons may perceive the same thing; or the same thing or idea exist in different minds. Words are of arbitrary imposition; and since men are used to apply the word *same* where no distinction or variety *is perceived*, and he does not pretend to alter their *perceptions*, it follows, that, as men have said before, *Several saw the same thing*, so they may, upon like occasions, still continue to use the same phrase, without any deviation either from propriety of language or the truth of things. But if the term *same* be used in the acceptation of philosophers, who pretend to an abstract notion of identity, then, according to their sundry definitions of this term, (for it is not yet agreed wherein that philosophic identity consists,) it may or may not be possible for divers persons to perceive the same thing; but whether philosophers shall think fit to call a thing the *same* or no, is, I conceive, of small importance. Men may dispute about identity and diversity, without any real difference in their thoughts and opinions, abstracted from names."

Upon the whole, I apprehend that Berkeley has carried this attempt to reconcile his system to the vulgar opinion farther than reason supports him: and he was no doubt tempted to do so from a just apprehension that, in a controversy of this kind, the common sense of mankind is the most formidable antagonist.

Berkeley has employed much pains and ingenuity to show that his system, if received and believed, would not be attended with those bad consequences in the conduct of life which superficial thinkers may be apt to impute to it. His system does not take away, or make any alteration in, our pleasures or our pains: our sensations, whether agreeable or disagreeable, are the same upon his system as upon any other. These are real things, and the only things that interest us. They are produced in us according to certain laws of nature, by which our conduct will be directed in attaining the one, and avoiding the other: and it is of no moment to us whether they are produced immediately by the operation of some powerful intelligent being upon our minds, or by the mediation of some inanimate being which we call *matter*.

The evidence of an All-governing Mind, so far from being weakened, seems to appear even in a more striking light upon his hypothesis than upon the common one. The powers which inanimate matter is supposed to possess have always been the stronghold of atheists, to which they had recourse in defence of their system. This fortress of atheism must be most effectually overturned, *if there is no such thing as matter in the universe.* In all this the Bishop reasons justly and acutely. But there is one uncomfortable consequence of his system which he seems not to have attended to, and from which it will be found difficult, if at all possible, to guard it.

The consequence I mean is this, — that, although it leaves us sufficient evidence of *a supreme intelligent Mind*, it seems to take away all the evidence we have of other intelligent beings *like ourselves*. What I call *a father, a brother*, or *a friend*, is only a parcel of ideas in my own mind; and being ideas in my mind, they cannot possibly have that relation to another mind

which they have to mine, any more than the pain felt
by me can be the individual pain felt by another. I
can find no principle in Berkeley's system which affords
me even probable ground to conclude that there are
other intelligent beings, like myself, in the relations of
father, brother, friend, or fellow-citizen. I am left alone,
as the only creature of God in the universe, in that for-
lorn state of *egoism* into which it is said some of the
disciples of Descartes were brought by his philosophy.

But I must take notice of another part of Berkeley's
system, wherein he seems to have deviated from the
common opinion about ideas, as regards our evidence
of the existence of other *minds*.

Though he sets out in his *Principles of Knowledge*
by telling us that it is evident the objects of human
knowledge are ideas, and builds his whole system upon
this principle; yet, in the progress of it, he finds that
there are certain objects of human knowledge *that are
not ideas*, but things which have a permanent existence.
The objects of knowledge, of which we have no ideas,
are our own minds, and their various operations, other
finite minds, and the Supreme Mind. The reason why
there can be no ideas of spirits and their operations,
the author informs us, is this, — that ideas are passive,
inert, unthinking beings; they cannot, therefore, be the
image or *likeness* of things that have thought, and will,
and active power; we have *notions* of minds, and of .
their operations, but not ideas. We know what we
mean by thinking, willing, and perceiving; we can
reason about beings endowed with those powers, but
we have no ideas of them. A spirit or mind is the
only substance or support wherein the unthinking beings or ideas can exist; but that this substance which
supports or perceives ideas should itself be an idea, or
like an idea, is evidently absurd.

Berkeley foresaw that this might give rise to an objection to his system, and puts it in the mouth of
Hylas, in the following words (*Dial.* 3) : — " If you can
conceive the mind of God, without having an idea of
it, why may not I be allowed to conceive the existence

of matter, notwithstanding that I have no idea of it?"
The answer of Philonous is, — " You neither perceive
matter *objectively*, as you do an inactive being or idea,
nor know it, as you do yourself, by a *reflex act*, neither
do you immediately *apprehend it* by *similitude* of the
one or the other, nor yet collect it by *reasoning* from that
which you know immediately.   All which makes the
case of matter widely different from that of the Deity."

Though Hylas declares himself satisfied with this
answer, I confess I am not; because, if I may trust the
faculties that God has given me, I do perceive matter
objectively; that is, something which is extended and
solid, which may be measured and weighed, is the immediate object of my touch and sight.   And this object
I take to be matter, and not an idea.   And though I
have been taught by philosophers that what I immediately touch is an idea, and not matter, yet I have never
been able to discover this by the most accurate attention to my own perceptions.

Of all the opinions that have ever been advanced by
philosophers, this of Bishop Berkeley, that there is no
material world, seems the strangest and the most apt
to bring philosophy into ridicule with plain men, who
are guided by the dictates of nature and common
sense.   And it will not, I apprehend, be deemed improper to have traced this progeny of the doctrine of
ideas from its origin, and to have observed its gradual
progress, till it acquired such strength, that a pious and
learned bishop had the boldness to usher it into the
world, as demonstrable from the principles of philosophy universally received, and as an admirable expedient for the advancement of knowledge, and for the
defence of religion.*

* *The Works of George Berkeley, D. D., late Bishop of Cloyne, in Ireland.
To which is added, An Account of his Life; and several of his Letters to
Thomas Prior, Esq., Dean Gervais, Mr. Pope, &c.* (3 vols., 8vo, London,
1820). Some additional particulars respecting him are given under his
name in Kippis's edition of the *Biographia Britannica.* Eschenbach published (in 8vo, Rostock, 1756) a German translation of the principal works
written to disprove the existence of the material world (including Berke-

We ought not, in this historical sketch, to omit an author of far inferior name, Arthur Collier, rector of Langford Magna, near Sarum. He published a book in 1713, which he calls *Clavis Universalis; or, a New Inquiry after Truth; being a Demonstration of the Non-existence or Impossibility of an External World.* His arguments are the same in substance with Berkeley's; and he appears to understand the whole strength of his cause. Though he is not deficient in metaphysical acuteness, his style is disagreeable, being full of conceits, of new-coined words, scholastic terms, and perplexed sentences. He appears to be well acquainted with Descartes, Malebranche, and Norris, as well as with Aristotle and the schoolmen; but, what is very strange, it does not appear that he had ever heard of Locke's *Essay,* which had been published twenty-four years, or of Berkeley's *Principles of Knowledge,* which had been published three years.

He says, he had been ten years firmly convinced of the non-existence of an external world, before he ventured to publish his book. He is far from thinking, as Berkeley does, that the vulgar are of his opinion. If his book should make any converts to his system, (of which he expresses little hope, though he has supported it by " nine *demonstrations,*") he takes pains to show that his disciples, notwithstanding their opinion, may, with the unenlightened, speak of material things in the common style. He himself had scruples of conscience about this for some time; and if he had not got over them, he must have shut his lips for ever: but he considered, that God himself has used this style in speaking to men in the Holy Scripture, and has thereby

---

ley's *Dialogues* and Collier's *Clavis Universalis*), with notes and a supplement in refutation of the same. See, also, *A Review of Berkeley's Theory of Vision, designed to show the Unsoundness of that celebrated Speculation. By Samuel Bailey.* (8vo, London, 1842.) The *Westminster Review,* for October, 1842, contains an earnest vindication of Berkeley. Two very ingenious articles on the same subject, and the philosophy of sensation generally, may be found in *Blackwood's Magazine,* in the numbers for June, 1842, and June, 1843. There is also a valuable paper *On the Idealism of Berkeley,* in Stewart's *Philosophical Essays.* — ED.

sanctified it to all the faithful; and that to the pure all
things are pure. He thinks his opinion may be of
great use, especially in religion; and applies it, in particular, to put an end to the controversy about Christ's
presence in the sacrament.

I have taken the liberty to give this short account of
Collier's book, because I believe it is rare, and little
known. I have only seen one copy of it, which is in
the University library of Glasgow.*

IX. *Hume's Theory.*] Two volumes of the *Treatise
of Human Nature* † were published in 1739, and the
third in 1740. The doctrine contained in this treatise
was published anew, in a more popular form, in Mr.
Hume's *Philosophical Essays,* of which there have been
various editions. What other authors, from the time
of Descartes, had called *ideas,* this author distinguished
into two kinds, — to wit, *impressions* and *ideas;* com-
prehending under the first all our sensations, passions,
and emotions; and under the last, *the faint images* of
these, when we remember or imagine them.

He sets out with this as a principle that needs no
proof, and of which, therefore, he offers none, — that

---

* This work, though of extreme rarity, and long absolutely unknown
to the philosophers of this country, had excited, from the first, the attention of the German metaphysicians. A long analysis of it was given in
the *Acta Eruditorum;* it is found quoted by Bilfinger, and other Leibnitzians, and was subsequently translated into German, with controversial
notes, by Professor Eschenbach, of Rostock, in his *Collection of the Principal Writers who deny the Reality of their own Body and of the whole Corporeal
World* [mentioned in the last note]. — H.

A small edition of the *Clavis* was published in Edinburgh in 1836, and
another in a collection of *Metaphysical Tracts, by English Philosophers of the
Eighteenth Century: prepared for the Press by the late Rev. Samuel Parr,
D. D.* (8vo, London, 1837). The work is now, therefore, easily accessible
to English readers. We also have *Memoirs of the Life and Writings of the
Rev. Arthur Collier. By Robert Benson.* (8vo, London, 1837.) Collier
was born at Langford Magna, in the county of Wilts, October 12, 1680,
and died, as he had been born, in the rectory of that place, which had been
nearly a century and a quarter in the family. The precise day of his
death is not known; but he was buried in Langford church, September 9,
1732 — Ed

† The author, David Hume, was born at Edinburgh, April 26, 1711, and
died in the same city, August 25, 1776. — Ed.

all the perceptions of the human mind resolve themselves into these two kinds, *impressions* and *ideas.*   As this proposition is the foundation upon which the whole of Mr. Hume's system rests, and from which it is raised with great acuteness indeed, and ingenuity, it were to be wished that he had told us upon what authority this fundamental proposition rests.   But we are left to guess whether it is held forth as a first principle, which has its evidence in itself, or whether it is to be received upon the authority of philosophers.

Mr. Locke had taught us, that all the immediate objects of human knowledge are ideas in the mind. Bishop Berkeley, proceeding upon this foundation, demonstrated very easily, that there is no material world.   And he thought, that, for the purposes both of philosophy and religion, we should find no loss, but great benefit, in the want of it.   But the Bishop, as became his order, was unwilling to give up the world of spirits.   He saw very well, that ideas are as unfit to represent spirits as they are to represent bodies. Perhaps he saw, that, if we perceive only the ideas of spirits, we shall find the same difficulty in inferring their real existence from the existence of their ideas, as we find in inferring the existence of matter from the idea of it ; and therefore, while he gives up the material world in favor of the system of ideas, he gives up one half of that system in favor of the world of spirits ; and maintains that we can, without ideas, think, and speak, and reason intelligibly about spirits, and what belongs to them.

Mr. Hume shows no such partiality in favor of the world of spirits.   He adopts the theory of ideas in its full extent ; and, in consequence, shows that there is neither matter nor mind in the universe ; nothing but impressions and ideas.   What we call a *body* is only a bundle of sensations ; and what we call the *mind* is only a bundle of thoughts, passions, and emotions, *without any subject.**

---

* Dr. Reid had said, in another connection, — " The author of the *Trea-*

Some ages hence, it will perhaps be looked upon as a curious anecdote, that two philosophers of the eigh-

---

tise of Human Nature appears to me to be but a half-skeptic. He has not followed his principles so far as they lead him; but, after having, with unparalleled intrepidity and success combated vulgar prejudices, when he ha£ but one blow to strike, his courage fails him; he fairly lays down his arms, and yields himself a captive to the most common of all vulgar prejudices, — I mean, the belief of the existence of his own impressions and ideas. I beg, therefore, to have the honor of making an addition to the skeptical system, without which I conceive it cannot hang together. I affirm, that the belief of the existence of impressions and ideas is as little supported by reason, as that of the existence of minds and bodies."
— *Inquiry into the Human Mind,* Chap. V. Sect. VII.

But to this Sir W. Hamilton replies: — "In Reid's strictures upon Hume, he confounds two opposite things. He reproaches that philosopher with inconsequence, in holding to 'the belief of the existence of his own impressions and ideas.' Now, if, by *the existence of impressions and ideas,* Reid meant their existence as mere phenomena of consciousness, his criticism is inept; for a disbelief of their existence, as such phenomena, would have been a suicidal act in the skeptic. Of consciousness the skeptic cannot doubt, because such doubt, being itself an act of consciousness, would contradict, and consequently annihilate, itself. If, again, he meant by *impressions* and *ideas* the hypothesis of representative *entities* different from the mind and its modifications, in that case, the objection is equally invalid. Hume was a skeptic; that is, he *accepted* the premises afforded him by the dogmatist, and carried these premises to their legitimate consequences. To blame Hume, therefore, for not having doubted of his borrowed principles, is to blame the skeptic for not performing a part altogether inconsistent with his vocation. But, in point of fact, the hypothesis of such *entities* is of no value to the idealist or the skeptic. *Impressions* and *ideas,* viewed as *mental modes,* would have answered Hume's purpose not a whit worse than *impressions* and *ideas,* viewed as objects, but *not* as *affections of mind.* The most consistent scheme of idealism known in the history of philosophy is that of Fichte; and Fichte's idealism is founded on a basis which excludes that crude hypothesis of ideas on which alone Reid imagined any doctrine of idealism could possibly be established. And is the acknowledged result of the Fichtean dogmatism less a ñihilism than the skepticism of Hume? 'The sum total,' says Fichte, 'is this: — There is absolutely nothing permanent, either without me or within me, but only an unceasing change I know absolutely nothing of any existence, not even of my own. I myself know nothing, and am nothing. Images (*Bilder*) there are: they constitute all that apparently exists, and what they know of themselves is after the manner of images; images that pass and vanish without there being aught to witness their transition, — that consist, in fact, of the images of images, without significance and without an aim. I myself am one of these images; nay, I am not even thus much, but only a confused image of images. All reality is converted into a marvellous dream, without a life to dream of, and without a mind to dream, — into a dream made up only of a dream of itself. Perception is a dream; thought — the source of all the existence and all the reality which I imagine to myself of *my* existence, of my power, of my destination — is the dream of that dream.'" — ED.

teenth century, of very distinguished rank, were led by a philosophical hypothesis, the one to disbelieve the existence of matter, and the other to disbelieve the existence both of matter and of mind. Such an anecdote may not be uninstructive, if it prove a warning to philosophers to beware of hypotheses, especially when they lead to conclusions which contradict the principles upon which all men of common sense must act in common life.

The *Egoists*, whom we mentioned before, were left far behind by Mr. Hume; for they believed their own existence, and perhaps also the existence of a Deity. But Mr. Hume's system does not even leave him a *self* to claim the property of his impressions and ideas.

A system of consequences, however absurd, acutely and justly drawn from a few principles, in very abstract matters, is of real utility in science, and may be made subservient to real knowledge. This merit Mr. Hume's metaphysical writings have in a great degree.

We had occasion before to observe, that, since the time of Descartes, philosophers, in treating of the powers of the mind, have in many instances confounded things which the common sense of mankind has always led them to distinguish, and which have different names in all languages. Thus, in the perception of an external object, all languages distinguish three things, the *mind* that perceives, the operation of that mind, which is called *perception*, and the *object* perceived. Nothing appears more evident to a mind untutored by philosophy, than that these three are distinct things, which, though related, ought never to be confounded. The structure of all languages supposes this distinction, and is built upon it. Philosophers have introduced a fourth thing in this process, which they call the *idea* of the object, and which is supposed to be an *image* or *representative* of the object, and is said to be the *immediate* object. The vulgar know nothing about this idea; it is a creature of philosophy, introduced to account for, and explain, the manner of our perceiving external objects.

It is pleasant to observe, that while philosophers, for

11

more than a century, have been laboring, by means of ideas, to explain perception and the other operations of the mind, those ideas have by degrees usurped the place of perception, object, and even of the mind itself, and have supplanted those very things they were brought to explain.   Descartes reduced all the operations of the understanding to perception; and what can be more natural to those who believe that they are only different modes of perceiving ideas in our own minds?   Locke confounds ideas, sometimes with the perception of an external object, sometimes with the external object itself.   In Berkeley's system, the idea is the only object, and yet is often confounded with the perception of it. But in Hume's, the idea or the impression, which is only a more lively idea, is mind, perception, and object, all in one: so that by the term *perception*, in Mr. Hume's system, we must understand the mind itself, all its operations, both of understanding and will, and all the objects of these operations.   Perception taken in this sense he divides into our more lively perceptions, which he calls *impressions*,* and the less lively, which he calls *ideas*.

" We may divide," says Mr. Hume,† " all the perceptions of the human mind into two classes or species, which are distinguished by their different degrees of force and vivacity.   The less lively and forcible are commonly denominated *thoughts*, or *ideas*.   The other species want a name in our language, and in most others; let us therefore use a little freedom, and call them *impressions*.   By the term *impressions*, then, I mean all our *more lively perceptions*, when we hear, or

---

* Mr. Stewart (*Elements, Addenda* to Vol. I.) seems to think that the word *impression* was first introduced, as a *technical* term, into the philosophy of mind, by Mr. Hume.   This is not altogether correct.   For, besides the instances which Mr. Stewart himself adduces of the illustration attempted of the phenomena of memory from the analogy of an *impress* and a *trace*, words corresponding to *impression* were among the ancients familiarly applied to the processes of external perception, imagination, &c., in the Atomistic, the Platonic, the Aristotelian, and the Stoical philosophies; while among modern psychologists (as Descartes and Gassendi), the term was likewise in common use. — H.

† *Inquiry concerning Human Understanding*, Sect. II.

see, or feel, or love, or hate, or desire, or will. *Ideas* are
the *less lively perceptions,* of which we are conscious
when we reflect on any of those sensations or movements above mentioned."

When Mr. Hume says, *that we may divide all the
perceptions of the human mind into two classes or species,
which are distinguished by their degrees of force and vivacity,* the manner of expression is loose and unphilosophical.   To differ in *species* is one thing; to differ in
degree is another.   Things which differ in degree only
must be of the same species.   It is a maxim of common
sense, admitted by all men, that *greater* and *less* do not
make a change of species.   The same man may differ
in the degree of his force and vivacity in the morning
and at night, in health and in sickness; but this is so
far from making him a different species, that it does not
so much as make him a different individual.   To say,
therefore, that two different classes or species of perceptions are distinguished by the degrees of their force and
vivacity, is to confound a difference of *degree* with a
difference of *species,* which every man of understanding
knows how to distinguish.

Again, we may object, that this author, having given
the general name of *perceptions* to all the operations of
the mind, and distinguished them into two classes or
species, which differ only in degree of force and vivacity,
tells us, that he gives the name of *impressions* to all our
more lively perceptions, — to wit, when we hear, or see,
or feel, or love, or hate, or desire, or will.   There is great
confusion in this account of the meaning of the word
impression.   When I see, this ,is an *impression.*   But
why has not the author told us whether he gives the
name of *impression* to the object seen, or to that act of
my mind by which I see it?   When I see the full moon,
the full moon is one thing, my perceiving it is another
thing.   Which of these two things does he call an impression?   We are left to guess this; nor does all that
this author writes about impressions clear this point.
Every thing he says tends to darken it, and to lead
us to think that the full moon which I see, and my

seeing it, are not two things, but one and the same thing.*

The same observation may be applied to every other instance the author gives to illustrate the meaning of the word *impression.* " When we hear, when we feel, when we love, when we hate, when we desire, when we will." In all these acts of the mind, there must be an *object,* which is heard, or felt, or loved, or hated, or desired, or willed. Thus, for instance, I love my country. This, says Mr. Hume, is an *impression.* But what is the *impression?* Is it my country, or is it the affection I bear to it? I ask the philosopher this question; but I find no answer to it. And when I read all that he has written on this subject, I find this word *impression* sometimes used to signify an *operation* of the mind, sometimes the *object* of the operation; but, for the most part, it is a vague and indetermined word that signifies both.

I know not whether it may be considered as an apology for such abuse of words, in an author who understood the language so well, and used it with so great propriety in writing on other subjects, that Mr. Hume's system with regard to the mind required a language of a different structure from the common, or, if expressed in plain English, would have been too shocking to the common sense of mankind. To give an instance or two of this. If a man receive a present on which he puts a high value, if he see and handle it, and put it in

---

* This objection is easily answered. The thing (Hume would say) as *unknown,* as *unperceived,* as *beyond the sphere of my consciousness,* is to me as zero; to that, therefore, I could not refer. As *perceived,* as *known,* it must be *within the sphere of my consciousness;* but, as philosophers concur in maintaining that I can only be conscious of my mind and its contents, the object, as perceived, must be either *a mode of,* or *something contained within,* my mind, and to that *internal object, as perceived,* I give the name of *impression.* Nor can the act of perception (he would add) be really distinguished from the object perceived. Both are only relatives, mutually constituent of the same indivisible relation of knowledge; and to that relation and these relatives I give the name of *impression,* precisely as, in different points of view, the term *perception* is applied to the mind perceiving, to the object perceived, and to the act of which these are the inseparable constituents. This likewise has reference to what follows. — H.

his pocket, this, says Mr. Hume, is an *impression*. If the man only dream that he received such a present, this is an *idea*. Wherein lies the difference between this impression and this idea, — between the dream and the reality? They are different classes or species, says Mr. Hume. So far all men will agree with him. But he adds, that they are distinguished only by different degrees of force and vivacity. Here he insinuates a tenet of his own, in contradiction to the common sense of mankind. Common sense convinces every man, that a lively dream is no nearer to a reality than a faint one; and that if a man should dream that he had all the wealth of Crœsus, it would not put one farthing in his pocket.

Philosophers have also differed very much with regard to the *origin* of our ideas, or the *sources whence they are derived*. The Peripatetics held, that all knowledge is derived originally from the senses; and this ancient doctrine seems to be revived by some late French philosophers, and by Dr. Hartley and Dr. Priestley among the British. Descartes maintained, that many of our ideas are *innate*. Locke opposed the doctrine of innate ideas with much zeal, and employs the whole first book of his *Essay* against it. But he admits two different sources of ideas: the operations of our external senses, which he calls *sensation*, by which we get all our ideas of body, and its attributes; and *reflection* upon the operations of our minds, by which we get the ideas of every thing belonging to the mind. The main design of the second book of Locke's *Essay* is to show that all our simple ideas, without exception, are derived from the one or the other, or both, of these sources. In doing this, the author is led into some paradoxes, although, in general, he is not fond of paradoxes; and had he foreseen all the consequences that may be drawn from his account of the origin of our ideas, he would probably have examined it more carefully.

Mr. Hume adopts Locke's account of the origin of our ideas, and *from that principle infers*, that we have no idea of *substance* corporeal or spiritual, no idea of

11*

power, no other idea of a *cause* than that it is something antecedent, and constantly conjoined to that which we call its *effect;* and, in a word, that we can have no idea of any thing but our sensations, and the operations of mind we are conscious of.

This author leaves no power to the mind in framing its ideas and impressions; and no wonder, since he holds that we have no idea of *power*, and that *the mind* is nothing but the succession of impressions and ideas of which we are intimately conscious. He thinks, therefore, that our impressions arise from unknown causes, and that the impressions are the causes of their corresponding ideas. By this he means no more than that they always go before the ideas; for this is all that is necessary to constitute the relation of cause and effect.

As to the *order and succession* of our ideas, he holds it to be determined by *three laws of attraction or association*, which he takes to be original properties of the ideas, by which they attract, as it were, or associate themselves with other ideas, which either *resemble* them, or which have been *contiguous* to them in time and place, or to which they have the relations of *cause and effect*. We may here observe, by the way, that the last of these three laws seems to be included in the second, since causation, according to him, implies no more than contiguity in time and place.

It is not my design at present to show how Mr. Hume, upon the principles he has borrowed from Locke and Berkeley, has, with great acuteness, reared a system of absolute skepticism, which leaves no rational ground to believe any one proposition rather than its contrary: my intention in this place being only to give a detail of the sentiments of philosophers concerning ideas since they became an object of speculation, and concerning the manner of our perceiving external objects by their means.* ·

---

* We have a full, authentic, and interesting *Life and Correspondence of David Hume. By John Hill Burton.* (2 vols., 8vo, Edinburgh, 1846.) There is also an excellent edition of *The Philosophical Works of David Hume* (4 vols., 8vo, Edinburgh, 1826). Some interesting notices are given

CHAPTER VI.

REFLECTIONS ON THE COMMON THEORY OF IDEAS.

I. *Statement of the Question.*]   After so long a detail of the sentiments of philosophers, ancient and modern, concerning ideas, it may seem presumptuous to call in question their existence.   But no philosophical opinion, however ancient, however generally received, ought to rest upon authority.   There is no presumption in requiring evidence for it, or in regulating our belief by the evidence we can find.

To prevent mistakes, the reader must again be reminded, that if by ideas are meant only the *acts* or *operations of our minds* in perceiving, remembering, or imagining objects, I am far from calling in question the existence of those acts.   We are conscious of them every day and every hour of life; and I believe no man of a sound mind ever doubted of the real existence of the operations of mind, of which he is conscious.   Nor is it to be doubted, that, by the faculties which God has given us, we can conceive things that are absent, as well as perceive those that are within the reach of our senses; and that such conceptions may be more or less distinct, and more or less lively and strong.   We have reason to ascribe to the all-knowing and all-perfect Being distinct conceptions of all things existent and possible, and of all their relations; and if these conceptions are called his *eternal ideas*, there ought to be no dispute among philosophers about a word.   The ideas, of whose existence I require the proof, are not the operations of any mind, but *supposed objects* of

---

of Hume and his philosophy by Stewart, in his *Dissertation*, Part II. Sect. VIII.   Jacobi's *David Hume, über den Glauben, oder Idealismus und Realismus* (8vo, Breslau, 1787).   Kant's *Prolegomena;* which has been translated, professedly, into English by Richardson (8vo, London, 1819).

For a statement of Sir W. Hamilton's theory of perception, see Appendix. — ED.

those operations.   They are not perception, remembrance, or conception, but things that are said to be perceived, or remembered, or imagined.

Nor do I dispute the existence of what the vulgar call *the objects of perception.*   These, by all who acknowledge their existence, are called *real things*, not *ideas.*   But philosophers maintain, that, besides these, there are immediate objects of perception in the mind itself: that, for instance, we do not see the sun immediately, but an *idea*, or, as Mr. Hume calls it, an *impression*, in our own minds.   This idea is said to be the image, the resemblance, the representative of the sun, if there be a sun.   It is from the existence of the idea that we must infer the existence of the sun.   But the idea being immediately perceived, there can be no doubt, as philosophers think, of its existence.

In like manner, when I remember or when I imagine any thing, all men acknowledge that there must be something that is remembered, or that is imagined; that is, some *object* of those operations.   The object remembered must be something that did exist in time past.   The object imagined may be something that never existed.   But, say the philosophers, besides these objects which all men acknowledge, there is *a more immediate object* which really exists in the mind at the same time we remember or imagine.   This object is an idea or image of the thing remembered or imagined.

II. *The Common Theory of Ideas opposed by the Common Sense of Mankind.*]   The *first* reflection I would make on this philosophical opinion is, that it is *directly contrary to the universal sense of men who have not been instructed in philosophy.*

There is the less need of any further proof of this, that it is very amply acknowledged by Mr. Hume, in his *Essay on the Academical or Skeptical Philosophy.*[*]   " It seems evident," says he, " that men are carried by a natural instinct, or prepossession, to repose faith in

---

* *Inquiry concerning Human Understanding*, Sect. XII. Part I.

their senses; and that without any reasoning, or even almost before the use of reason, we always suppose an external universe, which depends not on our perception, but would exist though we and every sensible creature were absent or annihilated. Even the animal creation are governed by a like opinion, and preserve this belief of external objects in all their thoughts, designs, and actions.

" It seems also evident, that, when men follow this blind and powerful instinct of nature, they always suppose the very images presented by the senses to be the external objects, and never entertain any suspicion, that the one are nothing but representations of the other. This very table which we see white, and feel hard, is believed to exist independent of our perception, and to be something external to the mind which perceives it. Our presence bestows not being upon it; our absence annihilates it not: it preserves its existence uniform and entire, independent of the situation of intelligent beings who perceive or contemplate it.

" But this universal and primary notion of all men is soon destroyed by the slightest philosophy, which teaches us, that nothing can ever be present to the mind but an image or perception; and that the senses are only the inlets through which these images are received, without being ever able to produce any immediate intercourse between the mind and the object."

It is therefore acknowledged by this philosopher to be a natural instinct or prepossession, a universal and primary opinion of all men, a primary instinct of nature, that the objects which we immediately perceive by our senses are not images in our minds, but external objects, and that their existence is independent of us and our perception.

In this acknowledgment, Mr. Hume, indeed, seems to me more generous, and even more ingenuous, than Bishop Berkeley, who would persuade us, that his opinion does not oppose the vulgar opinion, but only that of the philosophers; and that the external existence of a material world is a philosophical hypothesis, and not the natural dictate of our perceptive powers. The Bishop shows a timidity of engaging such an adversary as a primary and universal opinion of all men. He is rather fond to court its patronage. But the philosopher intrepidly gives a defiance to this antagonist, and seems to glory in a conflict that is worthy of his arm.

" Optat aprum aut fulvum descendere monte leonem."

After all, I suspect that a philosopher who wages war with this adversary will find himself in the same condition as a mathematician who should undertake to demonstrate that there is no truth in the axioms of mathematics.

III. *The Common Theory of Ideas unsupported by Evidence.*] A *second* reflection upon this subject is, *that the authors who have treated of ideas have generally taken their existence for granted, as a thing that could not be called in question; and such arguments as they have mentioned incidentally, in order to prove it, seem too weak to support the conclusion.*

Mr. Norris is the only author I have met with, who professedly puts the question, whether material things can be perceived by us *immediately.* He has offered four arguments to show that they *cannot. First,* " Material objects are without the mind, and therefore there can be no union between the object and the percipient." *Answer,* This argument is lame, until it is shown to be necessary that in perception there should be a union between the object and the percipient. *Second,* " Material objects are disproportioned to the mind, and removed from it by the whole diameter of being." This argument I cannot answer, because I do not understand it.* *Third,* " Because, if material objects were

---

* This confession would, of itself, prove how superficially Reid was versed in the *literature* of philosophy. Norris's second argument is only the statement of a principle generally assumed by philosophers, — that the relation of knowledge infers a correspondence of nature between the subject knowing and the object known. This principle has, perhaps, ex-

immediate objects of perception, there could be no physical science; things necessary and immutable being the only object of science." *Answer*, Although things

---

erted a more extensive influence on speculation than any other; and yet it has not been proved,— nay, is contradicted by the evidence of consciousness itself. To trace the influence of this assumption would be, in fact, in a certain sort, to write the history of philosophy; for, though this influence has never yet been historically developed, it would be easy to show that the belief, explicit or implicit, that what knows and what is immediately known must be of an analogous nature, lies at the root of almost every theory of cognition, from the very earliest to the very latest speculations.

In the more ancient philosophy of Greece, three philosophers (Anaxagoras, Heraclitus, and Alcmæon) are found, who professed the *opposite* doctrine, — that the condition of knowledge lies in the *contrariety*, in the natural antithesis, of subject and object. Aristotle, likewise, in his treatise *On the Soul*, expressly condemns the prevalent opinion, that the similar is only cognizable by the similar; but, in his *Nicomachean Ethics*, he reverts to the doctrine which, in the former work, he had rejected. With these exceptions, no principle, since the time of Empedocles, by whom it seems first to have been explicitly announced, has been more universally received than this, — that the *relation of knowledge* infers an *analogy of existence*. This analogy may be of two degrees. *What knows* and *what is known* may be either *similar* or *the same;* and if the principle itself be admitted, the latter alternative is the more philosophical.

Without entering on details, I may here notice some of the more remarkable results of this principle, in both its degrees. The general principle, not, indeed, exclusively, but mainly, determined the admission of a *representative* perception, by disallowing the possibility of any consciousness, or immediate knowledge, of matter by a nature so different from it as mind; and, in its two degrees, it determined the various hypotheses by which it was attempted to explain the possibility of a representative or mediate perception of the external world. To this principle, in its lower potence, — that what knows must be *similar* in nature to what is immediately known, — we owe the *intentional species* of the Aristotelians, and the *ideas* of Malebranche and Berkeley. From this principle, in its higher potence, — that what knows must be *identical* in nature with what is immediately known, — there flow the *gnostic reasons* of the Platonists, the *preëxisting forms* or *species* of Theophrastus and Themistius, of Adelandus and Avicenna, the (mental) *ideas* of Descartes and Arnauld, the *representations, sensual ideas*, &c. of Leibnitz and Wolf, the *phenomena* of Kant, the *states* of Brown, and (shall we say?) the vacillating doctrine of perception held by Reid himself. Mediately, this principle was the origin of many other famous theories: — of the hierarchical gradation of souls or faculties of the Aristotelians; of the vehicular media of the Platonists; of the hypotheses of a common intellect of Alexander, Themistius, Averroes, Cajetanus, and Zabarella; of the vision in the Deity of Malebranche; and of the Cartesian and Leibnitzian doctrines of assistance and preëstablished harmony. Finally, to this principle is to be ascribed the refusal of the evidence of consciousness to the primary fact, the duality of its perception; and the unitarian schemes of *absolute identity*, *materialism*, and *idealism* are the results. — H.

necessary and immutable be not the immediate objects of perception, they may be immediate objects of other powers of the mind. *Fourth,* " If material things were perceived by themselves, they would be a true light to our minds, as being the intelligible form of our understandings, and consequently perfective of them, and indeed superior to them." If I comprehend any thing of this mysterious argument, it follows from it, that the Deity perceives nothing at all, because nothing can be superior to his understanding, or perfective of it.

There is an argument which is hinted at by Malebranche, and by several other authors, which deserves to be more seriously considered. As I find it most clearly expressed and most fully urged by Dr. Samuel Clarke, I shall give it in his words, in his second reply to Leibnitz, § 4 : — " The soul, without being present to the images of the things perceived, could not possibly perceive them. A living substance can only there perceive where it is present, either to the things themselves, (as the omnipresent God is to the whole universe,) or to the images of things, as the soul is in its proper *sensorium.*"

That nothing can act immediately where it is not, I think, must be admitted; for I agree with Sir Isaac Newton, that power without substance is inconceivable. It is a consequence of this, that nothing can be acted upon immediately where the agent is not present. Let this, therefore, be granted. To make the reasoning conclusive, it is further necessary, that, when we perceive objects, *either they act upon us, or we act upon them.* This does not appear self-evident, nor have I ever met with any proof of it. I shall briefly offer the reasons why I think it ought not to be admitted.

When we say that one being acts upon another, we mean that some power or force is exerted by the agent, which produces, or has a tendency to produce, a change in the thing acted upon. If this be the meaning of the phrase, as I conceive it is, there appears no reason for asserting, that, in perception, either the object acts upon the mind, or the mind upon the object.

An object, in being perceived, does not act at all. I perceive the walls of the room where I sit; but they are perfectly inactive, and therefore act not upon the mind. To be perceived is what logicians call *an exter-* ∨ *nal denomination, which implies neither action nor quality in the object perceived.* Nor could men ever have gone into this notion, that perception is owing to some action of the object upon the mind, were it not that we are so prone to form our notions of the mind from some similitude we conceive between it and body. Thought in the mind is conceived to have some analogy to motion in a body; and as a body is put in motion ∨ by being acted upon by some other body, so we are apt to think the mind is made to perceive by some impulse it receives from the object. But reasonings drawn from such analogies ought never to be trusted. They are, indeed, the cause of most of our errors with regard to the mind. And we might as well conclude, that minds may be measured by feet and inches, or weighed by ounces and drams, because bodies have those properties.*

I see as little reason, in the second place, to believe that in perception the mind acts upon the object. To perceive an object is one thing; to act upon it is an- ∨ other. Nor is the last at all included in the first. To

---

* This reasoning, which is not original with Reid, (see Note S,) is not clearly or precisely expressed. In asserting that "an object, in being perceived, does not act at all," our author cannot mean that it does not act upon the organ of sense; for this would not only be absurd in itself, but in contradiction to his own doctrine, — "it being," he says, "a law of our nature that we perceive not external objects unless certain *impressions be made on the nerves and brain.*" The assertion, — "I perceive the walls of the room where I sit, but they are perfectly inactive, and therefore act not upon the mind," is equally incorrect in statement. *The walls of the room,* strictly so called, assuredly do not act on the mind, or on the eye; but the walls of the room, in this sense, are, in fact, no object of (visual) perception at all. What we see in this instance, and what we loosely call *the walls of the room,* is only the light reflected from their surface in its relation to the organ of sight, i. e. color; but it cannot be affirmed that the rays of light do not act on and affect the retina, optic nerve, and brain. What Aristotle distinguished as the concomitants of sensation — as *extension, motion, position,* &c. — are, indeed, perceived without any relative passion of the sense. But, whatever may be Reid's meaning, it is, at best, vague and inexplicit. — H.

12

say, that I act upon the wall by looking at it, is an abuse of language, and has no meaning. Logicians distinguish two kinds of operations of mind; the first kind produces no effect without the mind; the last does. The first they call *immanent acts;* the second *transitive.* All intellectual operations belong to the first class; they produce no effect upon any external object. But, without having recourse to logical distinctions, every man of common sense knows, that to think of an object and to act upon it are very different things.

As we have, therefore, no evidence that, in perception, the mind acts upon the object, or the object upon the mind, but strong reasons to the contrary, Dr. Clarke's argument against our perceiving external objects immediately, falls to the ground.

This notion, that, in perception, the object must be contiguous to the percipient, seems, with many other prejudices, to be borrowed from analogy. In all the external senses, there must, as has been before observed, be some impression made upon the organ of sense by the object, or by something coming from the object. An impression supposes contiguity. Hence we are led by analogy to conceive something similar in the operations of the mind. Many philosophers resolve almost every operation of mind into impressions and feelings, words manifestly borrowed from the sense of touch. And it is very natural to conceive contiguity necessary between that which makes the impression and that which receives it, between that which feels and that which is felt. And though no philosopher will now pretend to justify such analogical reasoning as this, yet it has a powerful influence upon the judgment, while we contemplate the operations of our minds only as they appear through the deceitful medium of such analogical notions and expressions.*

---

* It is self-evident, that, if a thing is to be an object *immediately* known, it must be known *as it exists.* Now a body must exist in some definite part of space, — in a certain *place;* it cannot, therefore, be immediately known *as existing,* except it be known *in its place.* But this supposes the mind to be immediately present to it in space. — H.

IV. *Hume's Argument stated and refuted.*] There remains only one other argument that I have been able to find urged against our perceiving external objects immediately. It is proposed by Mr. Hume, who, in the essay already quoted, after acknowledging that it is a universal and primary opinion of all men that we perceive external objects immediately, subjoins what follows : —

" But this universal and primary opinion of all men is soon destroyed by the slightest philosophy, which teaches us that nothing can ever be present to the mind but an image or perception; and that the senses are only the inlets through which these images are received, without being ever able to produce any immediate intercourse between the mind and the object. The table which we see seems to diminish as we remove farther from it; but the real table, which exists independent of us, suffers no alteration. It was, therefore, nothing but its image which was present to the mind. These are the obvious dictates of reason; and no man who reflects ever doubted that the existences which we consider, when we say *this house*, and *that tree*, are nothing but perceptions in the mind, and fleeting copies and representations of other existences which remain uniform and independent. So far, then, we are necessitated by reasoning to depart from the primary instincts of nature, and to embrace a new system with regard to the evidence of our senses."

We have here a remarkable conflict between two contradictory ,opinions, wherein all mankind are engaged. On the one side stand all the vulgar, who are unpractised in philosophical researches, and guided by the uncorrupted primary instincts of nature. On the other side stand all the philosophers, ancient and modern, — every man without exception who reflects. In this division, to my great humiliation, I find myself classed with the vulgar.

The passage now quoted is all I have found in Mr. Hume's writings upon this point; and, indeed, there is more reasoning in it than I have found in any other author; I shall therefore examine it minutely.

First, he tells us, that " this universal and primary
opinion of all men is soon destroyed by the slightest
philosophy, which teaches us that nothing can ever be
present to the mind but *an image* or *perception.*"

The phrase of being *present to the mind* has some
obscurity; but I conceive he means being an immediate
object of thought, — an immediate object, for instance,
of perception, of memory, or of imagination. If this
be the meaning (and it is the only pertinent one I can
think of), there is no more in this passage than an assertion of the proposition to be proved, and an assertion that philosophy teaches it. If this be so, I beg
leave to dissent from philosophy till she gives me reason for what she teaches. For though common sense
and my external senses demand my assent to their dictates upon their own authority, yet philosophy is not
entitled to this privilege. But that I may not dissent
from so grave a personage without giving a reason, I
give this as the reason of my dissent. I see the sun
when he shines; I remember the battle of Culloden;
and neither of these objects is an image or perception.

He tells us, in the *next* place, " That the senses are
only the inlets through which these images are received."

Mr. Hume surely did not seriously believe that an
image of *sound* is let in by the ear, an *image* of *smell*
by the nose, an *image* of *hardness* and *softness*, of *solidity* and *resistance*, by the touch. For, besides the absurdity of the thing, which has often been shown, Mr.
Hume and all modern philosophers maintain that the
images which are the immediate objects of perception
have no existence when they are not perceived; whereas, if they were let in by the senses, they must be before they are perceived, and have a separate existence.

Hitherto I see nothing that can be called an argument. Perhaps it was intended only for illustration.
The argument, the only argument, follows : —

" The table which we see seems to diminish as we
remove farther from it; but the real table, which exists
independent of us, suffers no alteration. It was, there-

fore, nothing but its image which was presented to the mind. These are the obvious dictates of reason."

To judge of the strength of this argument, it is necessary to attend to a distinction which is familiar to those who are conversant with the mathematical sciences; I mean the distinction between *real* and *apparent magnitude*. The real magnitude of a line is measured by some known measure of length, as inches, feet, or miles: the real magnitude of a surface or solid, by known measures of surface or of capacity. This magnitude is an object of touch only, and not of sight; nor could we even have had any conception of it, without the sense of touch; and Bishop Berkeley, on that account, calls it *tangible magnitude.** *Apparent* magnitude is measured by the angle which an object subtends at the eye. Supposing two right lines drawn from the eye to the extremities of the object, making an angle of which the object is the subtense, the apparent magnitude is measured by this angle. This apparent magnitude is an object of sight, and not of touch. Bishop Berkeley calls it *visible magnitude*.

If it is asked, What is the apparent magnitude of the sun's diameter? the answer is, that it is about thirty-one minutes of a degree. But if it is asked, What is the real magnitude of the sun's diameter? the answer must be, So many thousand miles, or so many diameters of the earth. From which it is evident, that real magnitude and apparent magnitude are things of a different nature, though the name of magnitude is

---

* The doctrine of Reid — that *real* magnitude or extension is the object of touch and of touch alone — is altogether untenable. For, in the *first* place, magnitude appears greater or less in proportion to the different size of the tactile organ in different subjects; thus, an apple is larger to the hand of a child than to the hand of an adult. Touch, therefore, can, at best, afford a knowledge of the *relation* of magnitudes in proportion to the organ of this or that individual. But, in the *second* place, even in the same individual, the same object appears greater or less, according as it is touched by one part of the body or by another. On this subject, see Weber's *Annotationes de Pulsu, Resorptione, Auditu, et Tactu.* Leipsic, 1834. — H.

Compare Bailey's *Review of Berkeley's Theory of Vision,* Chap. III. — ED.

given to both. The first has three dimensions, the last
only two. The first is measured by a line, the last by
an angle.

From what has been said, it is evident that the *real*
magnitude of a body must continue unchanged while
the body is unchangéd. This we grant. But is it likewise evident that the *apparent* magnitude must continue the same while the body is unchanged? So far
otherwise, that every man who knows any thing of
mathematics can easily demonstrate, that the same
individual object, remaining in the same place, and unchanged, must necessarily vary in its apparent magnitude, according as the point from which it is seen is
more or less distant; and that its apparent length or
breadth will be nearly in a reciprocal proportion to the
distance of the spectator. This is as certain as the
principles of geometry.*

We must likewise attend to this, that though the real
magnitude of a body is not originally an object of
sight, but of touch, yet we learn by experience to judge
of the real magnitude in many cases by sight. We
learn by experience to judge of the distance of a body
from the eye, within certain limits; and from its distance and apparent magnitude taken together, we learn
to judge of its real magnitude. And this kind of
judgment, by being repeated every hour, and almost
every minute, of our lives, becomes, when we are grown
up, so ready and so habitual, that it very much resembles the original perceptions of our senses, and may not
improperly be called *acquired perception.*

Whether we call it *judgment* or *acquired perception*
is a verbal difference. But it is evident, that, by means
of it, we often discover by one sense things which are

---

* The whole confusion and difficulty in this matter arise from not determining what is the *true object* in visual perception. This is not any
distant thing, but merely the rays of light in immediate relation to the
organ. We therefore see a *different object* at every movement, by which
a different complement of rays is reflected to the eye. The things from
which these rays are reflected are not, in truth, *perceived* at all; and to
conceive them as objects of perception is, therefore, erroneous, and produc-
tive of error. — H.

properly and naturally the objects of another. Thus I can say without impropriety, I hear a drum, I hear a great bell, or I hear a small bell; though it is certain that the figure or size of the sounding body is not originally an object of hearing. In like manner, we learn by experience how a body of such a real magnitude, and at such a distance, appears to the eye: but neither its real magnitude, nor its distance from the eye, is *properly an object of sight*, any more than the form of a drum, or the size of a bell, is properly an object of hearing.

If these things be considered, it will appear that Mr. Hume's argument has no force to support his conclusion, nay, that it leads to a contrary conclusion. The argument is this:— The table we see seems to diminish as we remove farther from it; that is, its *apparent* magnitude is diminished; but the real table suffers no alteration, to wit, in its *real* magnitude; therefore it is not the real table we see. I admit both the premises in this syllogism, but I deny the conclusion. The syllogism has what the logicians call two middle terms: *apparent magnitude* is the middle term in the first premise; *real magnitude* in the second. Therefore, according to the rules of logic, the conclusion is not justly drawn from the premises. But, laying aside the rules of logic, let us examine it by the light of common sense.

Let us suppose, for a moment, that it is the real table we see. Must not this real table seem to diminish as we remove farther from it? It is demonstrable that it must. How, then, can this apparent diminution be an argument that it is not the real table? When that which must happen to the real table, as we remove farther from it, does actually happen to the table we see, it is absurd to conclude from this that it is not the real table we see. It is evident, therefore, that this ingenious author has imposed upon himself by confounding real magnitude with apparent magnitude, and that his argument is a mere sophism.

Thus I have considered every argument I have found advanced to prove the existence of ideas, or images of external things, in the mind: and if no better arguments can be found, I cannot help thinking that the whole history of philosophy has never furnished an instance of an opinion so unanimously entertained by philosophers upon so slight grounds.

CHAPTER VII.

OF SENSATION.

I. *The Names of many of our Sensations Ambiguous.*] Having finished what I intend, with regard to that act of mind which we call the perception of an external object, I proceed to consider another, which, by our constitution, is conjoined with perception, and not with perception only, but with many other acts of our minds; and that is *sensation.*

Sensation is a name given by philosophers to an act of mind, which may be distinguished from all others by this, that *it has no object distinct from itself.** Pain of every kind is an uneasy sensation. When I am pained, I cannot say that the pain I feel is one thing, and that my feeling it is another thing. They are one and the same thing, and cannot be disjoined even in imagination. Pain, when it is not felt, has no existence. It can be neither greater or less in degree or duration, nor any thing else in kind, than it is felt to be. It cannot exist by itself, nor in any subject but a sentient being. No quality of an inanimate, insentient being can have the least resemblance to it.

Almost all our perceptions have corresponding sensations which constantly accompany them, and, on that

---

* But sensation, in the language of philosophers, has been generally employed to denote the whole process of sensitive cognition, including *perception proper* and *sensation proper.* On this distinction, see Note D*. — H.

account, are very apt to be confounded with them.
Neither ought we to expect that the sensation and its
corresponding perception should be distinguished in
common language, because the purposes of common
life do not require it. Language is made to serve the
purposes of ordinary conversation; and we have no reason to expect that it should make distinctions that are
not of common use. Hence it happens, that a *quality
perceived*, and the *sensation* corresponding to that perception, often go under the same name.

This makes the names of most of our sensations ambiguous, and this ambiguity has very much perplexed
philosophers. It will be necessary to give some instances, to illustrate the distinction between our sensations and the objects of perception.

When I smell a rose, there is in this operation both
sensation and perception. The agreeable odor I feel,
considered by itself, without relation to any external
object, is merely a sensation. It affects the mind in a
certain way; and this affection of the mind may be
conceived, without a thought of the rose, or any other
object. This sensation can be nothing else than it is
felt to be. Its very essence consists in being felt; and
when it is not felt, it is not. There is no difference between the sensation and the feeling of it; they are one
and the same thing. It is for this reason that we before observed, that in sensation there is no object distinct from that act of the mind by which it is felt; and
this holds true with regard to all sensations.

Let us next attend to the perception which we have
in smelling a rose. Perception has always an external
object; and the object of my perception, in this case, is
that quality in the rose which I discern by the sense of
smell. Observing that the agreeable sensation is raised
when the rose is near, and ceases when it is removed, I
am led by my nature to conclude some quality to be
in the rose which is the cause of this sensation. This
quality in the rose is the object perceived; and that act
of my mind by which I have the conviction and belief
of this quality, is what in this case I call perception.

But it is here to be observed, that the sensation I feel, and the quality in the rose which I perceive, are both called by the same name. *The smell of a rose* is the name given to both : so that this name has two meanings; and the distinguishing its different meanings removes all perplexity, and enables us to give clear and distinct answers to questions about which philosophers have held much dispute.*

Thus, if it is asked whether the smell be in the rose, or in the mind that feels it, the answer is obvious; — that there are two different things signified by the smell of a rose; one of which is *in the mind,* and can be in nothing but in a sentient being; the other is truly and properly *in the rose.* The sensation which I feel is in my mind. The mind is the sentient being; and as the rose is insentient, there can be no sensation, nor any thing resembling sensation, in it. But this sensation in my mind is occasioned by a certain quality in the rose, which is called by the same name with the sensation, *not on account of any similitude,* but because of their *constant concomitancy.*

All the names we have for smells, tastes, sounds, and for the various degrees of heat and cold, have a like ambiguity; and what has been said of the smell of a rose may be applied to them. They signify both a sensation and a quality perceived by means of that sensation. The first is the sign, the last the thing signified. As both are conjoined by nature, and as the purposes of common life do not require them to be disjoined in our thoughts, they are both expressed by the same name; and this ambiguity is to be found in all languages, because the reason of it extends to all.

---

* In reference to this and the following paragraphs, I may observe, that the distinction of *subjective* and *objective* qualities, here vaguely attempted, had been already precisely accomplished by Aristotle, in his discrimination of παθητικαὶ ποιότητες (*qualitates patibiles*) and πάθη (*passiones*). In regard to the Cartesian distinction, which is equally precise, but of which Reid is unaware, it will suffice to say that they called color, as a sensation in the mind, *formal* color; color, as a quality in bodies capable of producing the sensation, *primitive* or *radical* color. — H.

The same ambiguity is found in the names of such diseases as are indicated by a particular painful sensation, such as the toothache or the headache. The toothache signifies a painful sensation, which can only be in a sentient being; but it signifies also a disorder in the body, which has no similitude to a sensation, but is naturally connected with it.

Pressing my hand with force against the table, I feel pain, and I feel the table to be hard. The pain is a sensation of the mind, and there is nothing that resembles it in the table. The hardness is in the table, nor is there any thing resembling it in the mind. Feeling is applied to both, but in a different sense; being a word common to the act of sensation, and to that of perceiving by the sense of touch.

I touch the table gently with my hand, and I feel it to be smooth, hard, and cold. These are qualities of the table perceived by touch; but I perceive them by means of a sensation which indicates them. This sensation not being painful, I commonly give no attention to it. It carries my thought immediately to the thing signified by it, and is itself forgot, as if it had never been. But by repeating it, and turning my attention to it, and abstracting my thought from the thing signified by it, I find it to be merely a sensation, and that it has no similitude to the hardness, smoothness, or coldness of the table which is signified by it.

It is indeed difficult, at first, to disjoin things in our attention which have always been conjoined, and to make that an object of reflection which never was so before; but some pains and practice will overcome this difficulty in those who have got the habit of reflecting on the operations of their own minds.

Although the present subject leads us only to consider the sensations which we have by means of our external senses, yet it will serve to illustrate what has been said, and I apprehend is of importance in itself, to observe, that many operations of mind, to which we give one name, and which we always consider as one thing, are complex in their nature, and made up of several more simple ingredients; and of these ingredients sensation very often makes one. Of this we shall give some instances.

The appetite of hunger includes an uneasy sensation, and a desire of food. Sensation and desire are different acts of mind. The last, from its nature, must have an object; the first has no object. These two ingredients may always be separated in thought; perhaps they sometimes are, in reality; but hunger includes both.

Benevolence towards our fellow-creatures includes an agreeable feeling; but it includes also a desire of the happiness of others. The ancients commonly called it desire. Many moderns choose rather to call it a feeling. Both are right; and they only err who exclude either of the ingredients. Whether these two ingredients are necessarily connected is perhaps difficult for us to determine, there being many necessary connections which we do not perceive to be necessary; but we can disjoin them in thought. They are different acts of the mind.

An uneasy feeling, and a desire, are in like manner the ingredients of malevolent affections; such as malice, envy, revenge. The passion of fear includes an uneasy sensation or feeling, and an opinion of danger; and hope is made up of the contrary ingredients. When we hear of a heroic action, the sentiment which it raises in our mind is made up of various ingredients. There is in it an agreeable feeling, a benevolent affection to the person, and a judgment or opinion of his merit.

If we thus analyze the various operations of our minds, we shall find that many of them which we consider as perfectly simple, because we have been accustomed to call them by one name, are compounded of more simple ingredients; and that sensation, or *feeling*, which is only *a more refined kind of sensation*, makes one ingredient, not only in the perception of external objects, but in most operations of the mind.

II. *Variety and Distribution of our Sensations.*] A small degree of reflection may satisfy us, that the num-

ber and variety of our sensations and feelings are prodigious. For, to omit all those which accompany our
appetites, passions, and affections, our moral sentiments,
and sentiments of taste, even our external senses furnish
a great variety of sensations differing in kind, and almost in every kind an endless variety of degrees. Every
variety we discern, with regard to taste, smell, sound,
color, heat and cold, and in the tangible qualities of
bodies, is indicated by a sensation corresponding to it.*

The most general and the most important division
of our sensations and feelings is into the *agreeable*, the
disagreeable, and the *indifferent*. Every thing we call
pleasure, happiness, or enjoyment, on the one hand, and,
on the other, every thing we call misery, pain, or uneasiness, is sensation or feeling. For no man can for
the present be more happy, or more miserable, than he
feels himself to be. He cannot be deceived with regard
to the enjoyment or suffering of the present moment.
But I apprehend, that, besides the sensations that are
either agreeable or disagreeable, there is still a greater

---

* It has been commonly held by philosophers, both in ancient and modern times, that the division of the senses into five is altogether inadequate;
and psychologists, though not at one in regard to the distribution, are now
generally agreed, that under *touch* — or *feeling* in the strictest signification
of the term — are comprised perceptions which are, at least, as well entitled
to be opposed in species as those of taste and smell.— H.

Mill says, — " A sense of something on the skin, and perhaps also on
the interior parts of the body, taken purely by itself, seems alone *the feeling
of touch*." It is " the feeling which we have when something, without being
seen, comes gently into contact with our skin, in such a way that we cannot say whether it is hard or soft, rough or smooth, or what figure it is, or
of what size." To these he adds as distinct sensations, though commonly
reckoned under the head of touch, — the *sensations of heat and cold*, resembling the ordinary sensations of touch in nothing but this, that the organ
of them is diffused over the whole body; *sensations of disorganization, or of
the approach to disorganization*, in any part of the body, as in lacerations,
burnings, internal inflammations, itchings, &c.; *muscular sensations*, or those
feelings which accompany the action of the muscles, necessary to our idea
of resistance, and manifesting themselves confusedly in a sense of fatigue
or of restlessness; and, finally, *sensations in the alimentary canal*, such as
hunger, sea-sickness, the exhilarating effects of opium, the sense of wretch-
edness attending indigestion, and the like. *Analysis of the Phenomena of
the Human Mind*, Chap. I. Sect. V. - VIII. Compare Brown's *Philosophy
of the Human Mind*, Sect. XXI. - XXIV., and Tissot, *Anthropologie*, Iere
Partie, Lib. I. Sect. III. § 1. — ED.

13

number that are indifferent.* To these we give so little attention, that they have no name, and are immediately forgot, as if they had never been; and it requires attention to the operations of our minds to be convinced of their existence.

For this end, we may observe, that to a good ear every human voice is distinguishable from all others. Some voices are pleasant, some disagreeable; but the far greater part can be said to be neither the one nor the other. The same thing may be said of other sounds, and no less of tastes, smells, and colors; and if we consider that our senses are in continual exercise while we are awake, that some sensation attends every object they present to us, and that familiar objects seldom raise any emotion, pleasant or painful, we shall see reason, besides the agreeable and disagreeable, to admit a third class of sensations, that may be called indifferent.

The sensations that are indifferent are far from being useless. They serve as signs to distinguish things that differ; and the information we have concerning things external comes by their means. Thus, if a man had no ear to receive pleasure from the harmony or melody of sounds, he would still find the sense of hearing of great utility. Though sounds gave him neither pleasure nor pain of themselves, they would give him much useful information; and the like may be said of the sensations we have by all the other senses.

As to the sensations and feelings that are agreeable or disagreeable, they differ much, not only in degree, but in kind and in dignity. Some belong to the animal part of our nature, and are common to us with the brutes. Others belong to the rational and moral part. The first are more properly called *sensations*, the last *feelings*. The French word *sentiment* is common to both.†

---

* This is a point in dispute among philosophers. — H.
† Some French philosophers, since Reid, have attempted the distinction of *sentiment* and *sensation*. — H.

The intention of nature in them is for the most part obvious, and well deserving our notice. It has been beautifully illustrated by a very elegant French writer, in his *Theorie des Sentiments Agréables.*

The Author of nature, in the distribution of agreeable and painful feelings, has wisely and benevolently consulted the good of the human species, and has even shown us, by the same means, what tenor of conduct we ought to hold. For, *first,* The painful sensations of the animal kind are admonitions to avoid what would hurt us;† and the agreeable sensations of this kind in-

---

* Levesque de Pouilly. — H.

† On the uses, or the final cause, of *pain,* see Sir C. Bell's Bridgewater Treatise *On the Hand, its Mechanism, and Vital Endowments, as evincing Design,* Chap. VII. With great force and beauty, this author illustrates the doctrine, that sensibility to pain is a wise and beneficent provision, evidently *intended* to protect us against more serious harm. Accordingly he shows, that, where pain is of use, it is found; where, from any cause, it would not be of use, the part is insensible. Thus, as he says, the skin, by its exquisite sensibility, is made a better safeguard to the delicate textures which are contained within "than if our bodies were covered with the hide of the rhinoceros." Quoting from a lecture which he had delivered before the College of Surgeons, he puts the argument in another form: — "Without meaning to impute to you inattention or restlessness, I may request you to observe how every one occasionally changes his position, and shifts the pressure of the weight of his body: were you constrained to retain one position during the whole hour, you would rise stiff and lame. The sensibility of the skin is here guiding you to that which, if neglected, would be followed even by the death of the part."

"In pursuing the inquiry, we learn with much interest, that, when the bones, joints, and all the membranes and ligaments which cover them, are exposed, they may be cut, pricked, or even burned, without the patient or the animal suffering the slightest pain." The reason is, that the pain is not needed, since no *such* injuries can reach the parts referred to, or never without warning being received through the sensibility of the skin. The only injuries to which the bones, joints, and sinews are liable, without the sensibility of the skin being first excited, are sprains, ruptures, concussions, and the like. In such cases, therefore, our doctrine would lead us to expect that these inward parts would be sensible to pain, that we might be warned, in the only way we could be effectually, of the presence of the evil; and so in fact it is.

"How consistent, then, and beautiful, is the distribution of this quality of life! The sensibility to pain varies with the function of the part. The skin is endowed with sensibility to every possible injurious impression which may be made upon it. But had this kind and degree of sensibility been made universal, we should have been racked with pain in the common motions of the body: the mere weight of one part on another, or the motion of the joint, would have been attended with that degree of suffering which we experience in using or walking with an inflamed limb. But, on

vite us to those actions that are necessary to the preservation of the individual, or of the kind. *Secondly*, By
the same means nature invites us to moderate bodily
exercise, and admonishes us to avoid idleness and inac-
tivity on the one hand, and excessive labor and fatigue
on the other. *Thirdly*, The moderate exercise of all our
rational powers gives pleasure. *Fourthly*, Every species
of beauty is beheld with pleasure, and every species of
deformity with disgust; and we shall find all that we
call beautiful to be something estimable or useful in
itself, or a sign of something that is estimable or useful. *Fifthly*, The benevolent affections are all accompanied with an agreeable feeling, the malevolent with
the contrary. And, *sixthly*, The highest, the noblest,
and most durable pleasure is that of doing well, and
acting the part that becomes us; and the most bitter
and painful sentiment, the anguish and remorse of a
guilty conscience. These observations, with regard to
the economy of nature in the distribution of our painful and agreeable sensations and feelings, are illustrated
by the author last mentioned so elegantly and judiciously, that I shall not attempt to say any thing
upon them after him.

I shall conclude this chapter by observing, that, as

---

the other hand, had the deeper parts possessed no sensibility, we should
have had no guide in our exertions. They have a sensibility limited to
the kind of injury which it is possible may reach them, and which teaches
us what we can do with impunity.

"To contrast still more strongly the sensibility of the surface with the
property of internal parts, to show how very different sensibility is in reality from what is suggested by first experience, and how admirably it is
varied and accommodated to the functions, we shall add one other fact.
The brain is insensible, — that part of the brain which, if disturbed or dis-
eased, takes away consciousness, is as insensible as the leather of our shoe!
That the brain may be touched, or a portion cut off, without interrupting
the patient in the sentence that he is uttering, is a surprising circumstance!"
The reason he supposes to be, that the safety of the brain is otherwise provided for by its strong osseous integuments, so that sensibility here would
only have the effect to expose man to superfluous suffering. "Reason on
it, however, as we may, the fact is so; — the brain, through which every
impression must be conveyed before it is perceived, is itself insensible.
This informs us that sensibility is not a necessary attendant on the delicate
texture of a living part, but that it must have an *appropriate organ*, and
that it is an *especial provision*." — ED.

the confounding our sensations with that perception of
external objects which is constantly conjoined with
them has been the occasion of most of the errors and
false theories of philosophers with regard to the senses,
so the distinguishing these operations seems to me to
be the key that leads to a right understanding of both.

The purposes of life, as was before observed, do not
require them to be distinguished. It is the philosopher
alone who has occasion to distinguish them, when he
would analyze the operation compounded of them.
But philosophers, as well as the vulgar, have been accustomed to comprehend both sensation and perception
under one name, and to consider them as one uncom-
pounded operation. Philosophers, even more than the
vulgar, have generally given the name of *sensation* to
the whole operation of the senses; and all the notions
we have of material things have been called *ideas of
sensation*. This led Bishop Berkeley to take one ingredient of a complex operation for the whole; and having
clearly discovered the nature of sensation, taking it for
granted that all that the senses present to the mind
is sensation, which can have no resemblance to any
thing material, he concluded that there is no material
world.

If the senses furnish us with no materials of thought
but sensations, his conclusion must be just; for no sensation can give us the conception of material things, far
less any argument to prove their existence. But if it
is true that by our senses we have not only a variety
of sensations, but likewise a conception and an immediate natural conviction of external objects, he reasons
from a false supposition, and his arguments fall to the
ground.*

---

* In his *Supplementary Dissertations*, Note D*, Sir W. Hamilton says of
" *sensation proper* and *perception proper*, in correlation ": — " In *perception
proper* there is a higher energy of intelligence than in *sensation proper*.
For though the latter be the apprehension of an affection of the *ego*, and
therefore, in a certain sort, the apprehension of an immaterial quality, still
it is only the apprehension of the *fact* of an organic passion; whereas the
former, though supposing sensation as its condition, and though only the
apprehension of the attributes of a material *non-ego*, is, however, itself

CHAPTER VIII.

OF THE OBJECTS OF PERCEPTION.

I. (1.) *Primary and Secondary Qualities of Body.*] The *objects of perception* are the various *qualities of* bodies. Intending to treat of these only in general, and chiefly with a view to explain the notions which our senses give us of them, I begin with the distinction between *primary* and *secondary* qualities. These were distinguished very early. The Peripatetic system confounded them, and left no difference. The distinction was again revived by Descartes and Locke, and a second time abolished by Berkeley and Hume.* If the

---

without corporeal passion, and, at the same time, the recognition not merely of a fact, but of *relations.*

"*Sensation proper* is the *conditio sine qua non* of a *perception proper* of the primary qualities. For we are only aware of the existence of our organism in being sentient of it, as thus or thus affected ; and are only aware of it being the subject of extension, figure, division, motion, &c., in being percipient of its affections, as like or as unlike, and as out of, or locally external to, each other.

"Every *perception proper* has a *sensation proper* as its condition ; but every *sensation* has not a *perception proper* as its conditionate, — unless, what I think ought to be done, we view the general consciousness of the *locality* of a sensorial affection as a *perception proper.* In this case, the two apprehensions will be always coexistent.

"But though the fact of *sensation proper* and the fact of *perception proper* imply each other, this is all ; for the two cognitions, though coexistent, are not proportionally coexistent. On the contrary, although we can only take note of, that is, *perceive*, the special relations of sensations, on the hypothesis that these sensations exist; a sensation, in proportion as it rises above a low degree of intensity, interferes with the perception of its relations, by concentrating consciousness on its absolute affection alone. It may accordingly be stated as a general rule, *That, above a certain point, the stronger the sensation, the weaker the perception ; and the distincter the perception, the less obtrusive the sensation :* in other words, *Though perception proper and sensation proper exist only as they coexist, in the degree or intensity of their existence they are always found in an inverse ratio to each other.*" — ED.

* For the history of this distinction, see Sir W. Hamilton's *Supplementary Dissertations,* Note D, § 1. Here, as in many other places, by " the Peripatetic system " we must understand the system as held by some of the followers of Aristotle, and not as held by himself. "Aristotle," says Hamilton, " does not abolish the distinction ; — nay, I am confident of

real foundation of this distinction can be pointed out, it will enable us to account for the various revolutions in the sentiments of philosophers concerning it.

Every one knows that *extension, divisibility, figure, motion, solidity, hardness, softness,* and *fluidity* were by Mr. Locke called *primary qualities of body;* and that *sound, color, taste, smell,* and *heat* or *cold* were called *secondary qualities.* Is there a just foundation for this distinction? Is there any thing common to the primary which belongs not to the secondary? And what is it?

I answer, that there appears to me to be a real foundation for the distinction, and it is this: that our senses give us a *direct* and *distinct* notion of the primary qualities, and inform us what they are in themselves; but of the secondary qualities, our senses give us only a *relative* and *obscure* notion.* They inform us only, that they are qualities that affect us in a certain manner, that is, produce in us a certain sensation; but as to what they are in themselves, our senses leave us in the dark.†

Every man capable of reflection may easily satisfy himself, that he has a perfectly *clear* and *distinct* notion of extension, divisibility, figure, and motion. The so-

---

showing, that, to whatever merit modern philosophers may pretend in this analysis, all and each of their observations are to be found, clearly stated, in the writings of the Stagirite." He also says of Locke: — " His doctrine in regard to the attributes of bodies, in so far as these have power to produce sensations and perceptions, or simple ideas, in us, contains absolutely nothing new." — ED.

* By the expression, "*what they are in themselves,*" in reference to the primary qualities, and of "*relative notion,*" in reference to the secondary, Reid cannot mean that the former are known to us *absolutely and in themselves,* — that is, *out of relation* to our cognitive faculties; for he elsewhere admits that *all* our knowledge is relative. Further, if "our senses give us a *direct and distinct notion* of the primary qualities, and *inform us what they are in themselves,*" these qualities, as known, must *resemble,* or be *identical with,* these qualities as existing. — H.

† The distinctions of perception and sensation, and of primary and secondary qualities, may be reduced to *one* higher principle. Knowledge is partly *objective* and partly *subjective: both* these elements are essential to *every* cognition, but in every cognition they are always in the inverse ratio of each other. In *perception* and the *primary* qualities, the objective element preponderates; whereas the subjective element preponderates in *sensation* and the *secondary* qualities. — H.

lidity of a body means no more than that it excludes
other bodies from occupying the same place at the
same time. Hardness, softness, and fluidity are different degrees of cohesion in the parts of a body. It is
fluid when it has no sensible cohesion, soft when the
cohesion is weak, and hard when it is strong. Of the
cause of this cohesion we are ignorant, but the thing
itself we understand perfectly, being immediately informed of it by the sense of touch. It is evident, therefore, that of the primary qualities we have a clear and
distinct notion; we know what they are, though we
may be ignorant of their causes.

I observe, further, that the notion we have of primary qualities is *direct*, and not *relative* only. A relative notion of a thing is, strictly speaking, no notion
of a thing at all, but only of some relation which it
bears to something else.

Thus gravity sometimes signifies the *tendency* of
bodies towards the earth; sometimes it signifies the
cause of that tendency. When it means the first, I
have a direct and distinct notion of gravity: I see it,
and feel it, and know perfectly what it is; but this tendency must have a cause. We give the same name to
the cause; and that cause has been an object of thought
and of speculation. Now what notion have we of this
cause when we think and reason about it? It is evident
we think of it as an unknown cause of a known effect.
This is a relative notion, and it must be obscure, because it gives us no conception of what the thing is,
but of what relation it bears to something else. Every
relation which a thing unknown bears to something
that is known, may give a relative notion of it; and
there are many objects of thought, and of discourse, of
which our faculties can give no better than a relative
notion.

Having premised these things to explain what is
meant by a relative notion, it is evident that our notion
of primary qualities is not of this kind; we know what
they are, and not barely what relation they bear to
something else.

It is otherwise with secondary qualities. If you ask me, what is that quality or modification in a rose which I call its smell, I am at a loss to answer directly. Up-on reflection, I find that I have a distinct notion of the sensation which it produces in my mind. But there can be nothing like to this sensation in the rose, because it is insentient. The quality in the rose is something which occasions the sensation in me; but what that something is, I know not. My senses give me no information upon this point. The only notion, therefore, my senses give is this, that smell in the rose is an unknown quality or modification, which is the cause or occasion of a sensation which I know well. The relation which this unknown quality bears to the sensation with which nature has connected it, is all I learn from the sense of smelling; but this is evidently a *relative* notion. The same reasoning will apply to every secondary quality.

Thus I think it appears that there is a real foundation for the distinction of primary from secondary qualities, and that they are distinguished by this: that of the primary we have by our senses a *direct and distinct* notion; but of the secondary only a *relative* notion, which must, because it is only relative, be *obscure;* they are conceived only as the unknown causes or occasions of certain sensations with which we are well acquainted.

II. *Remarks on the Distinction between Primary and Secondary Qualities.*] The account I have given of this distinction is founded upon no hypothesis. Whether our notions of primary qualities are direct and distinct, those of the secondary relative and obscure, is a matter of fact, of which every man may have certain knowledge by attentive reflection upon them. To this reflection I appeal, as the proper test of what has been advanced, and proceed to make some remarks on the subject.

1. The *primary qualities* are neither *sensations*, nor are they *resemblances* of sensations. This appears to

me self-evident. I have a clear and distinct notion of
each of the primary qualities. I have a clear and distinct notion of sensation. I can compare the one with
the other; and when I do so, I am not able to discern
a resembling feature. Sensation is the act, or the feeling, (I dispute not which,) of a sentient being. Figure,
divisibility, solidity, are neither acts nor feelings. Sensation supposes a sentient being as its subject; for a
sensation that is not felt by some sentient being is an
absurdity. Figure and divisibility suppose a subject
that is figured and divisible, but not a subject that is
sentient.

2. We have no reason to think that the *sensations* by
which we have notice of secondary qualities *resemble
any quality of body.* The absurdity of this notion has
been clearly shown by Descartes, Locke, and many
modern philosophers. It was a tenet of the ancient
philosophy, and is still by many imputed to the vulgar,
but only as a vulgar error. It is too evident to need
proof, that the vibrations of a sounding body do not
resemble the sensation of sound, nor the effluvia of an
odorous body the sensation of smell.

3. The *distinctness* of our notions of primary qualities
prevents all *questions and disputes* about their nature.
There are no different opinions about the nature of extension, figure, or motion, or the nature of any primary
quality. Their nature is manifest to our senses, and
cannot be unknown to any man, or mistaken by him,
though their causes may admit of dispute.

The primary qualities are the objects of the mathematical sciences; and the distinctness of our notions
of them enables us to reason demonstratively about
them to a great extent. Their various modifications
are precisely defined in the imagination, and thereby
capable of being compared, and their relations determined with precision and certainty.

It is not so with secondary qualities. Their nature,
not being manifest to the sense, may be a subject of
dispute. Our feeling informs us that the fire is hot;
but it does not inform us what that heat of the fire is.

But does it not appear a contradiction to say we know
that the fire is hot, but we know not what that heat is?
I answer, There is the same appearance of contradiction in many things, that must be granted. We know
that wine has an inebriating quality; but we know not
what that quality is. It is true, indeed, that, if we had
not some notion of what is meant by the heat of fire,
and by an inebriating quality, we could affirm nothing
of either with understanding. We have a notion of
both; but it is only a relative notion. We know that
they are the causes of certain known effects.

4. The nature of *secondary qualities* is a proper subject of *philosophical disquisition;* and in this philosophy
has made some progress. It has been discovered, that
the sensation of smell is occasioned by the effluvia of
bodies; that of sound by their vibration. The disposition of bodies to reflect a particular kind of light
occasions the sensation of color. Very curious discoveries have been made of the nature of heat, and an
ample field of discovery in these subjects remains.

5. We may see why the sensations belonging to *secondary qualities* are *an object of our attention,* while
those which belong to the *primary* are *not.*

The first are not only signs of the object perceived,
but they bear a capital part in the notion we form of
it. We conceive it only as that which occasions such
a sensation, and therefore cannot reflect upon it without thinking of the sensation which it occasions: we
have no other mark whereby to distinguish it. The
thought of a secondary quality, therefore, always carries
us back to the sensation which it produces. We give
the same name to both, and are apt to confound them
together. But having a clear and distinct conception
of primary qualities, we have no need when we think
of them to recall their sensations. When a primary
quality is perceived, the sensation immediately leads
our thought to the quality signified by it, and is itself
forgot. We have no occasion afterwards to reflect
upon it; and so we come to be as little acquainted
with it as if we had never felt it. This is the case

with the sensations of all primary qualities, when they are not so painful or pleasant as to draw our attention.

When a man moves his hand rudely against a pointed hard body, he feels pain, and may easily be persuaded that this pain is a sensation, and that there is nothing resembling it in the hard body; at the same time he perceives the body to be hard and pointed, and he knows that these qualities belong to the body only. In this case, it is easy to distinguish what he *feels* from what he *perceives.* Let him again touch the pointed body gently, so as to give him no pain; and now you can hardly persuade him that he feels any thing but the figure and hardness of the body; so difficult it is to attend to the sensations belonging to primary qualities, when they are neither pleasant nor painful. They carry the thought to the external object, and immediately disappear and are forgot. Nature intended them only as signs; and when they have served that purpose, they vanish.

6. We are now to consider a supposed contradiction between the vulgar and the philosophers upon this subject. As to the former, it is not to be expected that they should make distinctions which have no connection with the common affairs of life; they do not, therefore, distinguish the primary from the secondary qualities, but speak of both as being equally qualities of the external object. Of the primary qualities they have a distinct notion, as they are immediately and distinctly perceived by the senses; of the secondary, their notions, as I apprehend, are confused and indistinct, rather than erroneous. A secondary quality is the unknown cause or occasion of a well-known effect; and the same name is common to the cause and the effect. Now, to distinguish clearly the different ingredients of a complex notion, and, at the same time, the different meanings of an ambiguous word, is the work of a philosopher; and is not to be expected of the vulgar, when their occasions do not require it.

I grant, therefore, that the notion which the vulgar have of secondary qualities is indistinct and inaccurate. But there *seems* to be a *contradiction* between the vulgar and the philosopher upon this subject, and each charges the other with a gross absurdity. The vulgar say, that fire is hot, and snow cold, and sugar sweet; and that to deny this is a gross absurdity, and contradicts the testimony of our senses. The philosopher says, that heat and cold and sweetness are nothing but sensations in our minds; and it is absurd to conceive that these sensations are in the fire, or in the snow, or in the sugar.

I believe this contradiction between the vulgar and the philosopher is more apparent than real; and that it is owing to *an abuse of language* on the part of the philosopher, and to *indistinct notions* on the part of the vulgar. The philosopher says, there is no heat in the fire, meaning that the fire has not the sensation of heat. His meaning is just; and the vulgar will agree with him, as soon as they understand his meaning: but his language is improper; for there is really a quality in the fire, of which the proper name is *heat;* and the name of *heat* is given to this *quality*, both by philosophers and by the vulgar, much more frequently than to the *sensation* of heat. This speech of the philosopher, therefore, is meant by him in one sense; it is taken by the vulgar in another sense. In the sense in which they take it, it is indeed absurd, and so they hold it to be. In the sense in which he means it, it is true; and the vulgar, as soon as they are made to understand that sense, will acknowledge it to be true. They know as well as the philosopher, that the fire does not feel heat; and this is all that he means by saying there is no heat in the fire.[*]

---

* On the subject of Primary and Secondary Qualities, compare Stewart, *Philosophical Essays*, Essay II. Chap. II. Sect. II. Royer-Collard, *Fragments*, in Jouffroy's *Œuvres de Reid*, Tome III. p. 426 *et seq.* Garnier, *Critique de la Philosophie de Thomas Reid*, p. 73 *et seq.* Rémusat, *Essais de Philosophie*, Essai IX. Brown, *Philosophy of the Human Mind*, Lect. XXV. Sir W. Hamilton, in his *Supplementary Dissertations*, Note D.

Hamilton divides the qualities of body or matter into *primary, secundo-primary,* and *secondary.*

Starting with the simple *datum*, body considered as *substance occupying*

14

III. *Other Objects of Perception.* (2.) *Local Affections in our own Bodies.*] Besides primary and secondary qualities of bodies, there are many other immediate objects of perception. Without pretending to a
complete enumeration, I think they mostly fall under
one or other of the following classes : — *First*, Certain
states or conditions of our own bodies. *Second*, Mechanical powers or forces. ~*Third*, Chemical powers.
Fourth, Medical powers or virtues. *Fifth*, Vegetable
and animal powers.

That we perceive certain disorders in our own bodies
by means of uneasy sensations, which nature has conjoined with them, will not be disputed. Of this kind
are toothache, headache, gout, and every distemper and
hurt which we feel. The notions which our sense
gives of these have a strong analogy to our notions of
secondary qualities. Both are similarly compounded,
and may be similarly resolved, and they give light to
each other.

In the toothache, for instance, there is, *first*, a pain-

---

space, he deduces *a priori*, as necessary to the very conception, its *primary*
qualities, which are the following : — 1. Extension; 2. Divisibility; 3. Size;
4. Density, or Rarity; 5. Figure; 6. Incompressibility absolute; 7. Mobility; 8. Situation.

The *secundo-primary* qualities are modifications, but *contingent* modifications, of the primary. They suppose the primary, but the primary do not
suppose them, and hence they are not conceived by us as *necessary* properties of matter. They are the following, with their various modifications :
— 1. Gravity; 2. Cohesion; 3. Inertia; 4. Repulsion.

The *secondary* qualities, as manifested to us, are not, in propriety, qualities of *body* at all. "As apprehended, they are," he says, "only subjective
affections, and belong to bodies in so far only as these are supposed furnished with the powers capable of specifically determining the various
parts of our nervous apparatus to the peculiar action, or rather passion, of
which they are susceptible; which determined action or passion is the
quality of which alone we are immediately cognizant, the external con-
cause of that internal effect remaining to perception altogether unknown."
He adds : — "Of the secondary qualities, in this relation, there are various
kinds; the variety principally depending on the differences of the different
parts of our nervous apparatus. Such are the proper sensibles, the idio-
pathic affections of our several organs of sense, as color, sound, flavor,
savor, and tactual sensation; such are the feelings from heat, electricity
galvanism, &c.; nor need it be added, such are the muscular and cutaneous
sensations which accompany the perception of the secundo-primary qualities. Such, though less directly the result of foreign causes, are titillation,
sneezing, horripilation, shuddering, the feeling of what is called setting-

ful feeling; and, *secondly*, a conception and belief of some disorder in the tooth, which is believed to be the cause of the uneasy feeling. The first of these is a sensation, the second is a perception;[*] for it includes a conception and belief of an external object. But these two things, though of different natures, are so constantly conjoined in our experience and in our imagination, that we consider them as one. We give the same name to both; for the toothache is the proper name of the pain we feel; and it is the proper name of the disorder in the tooth which causes that pain. If it should be made a question, whether the toothache be in the mind that feels it, or in the tooth that is affected, much might be said on both sides, while it is not observed that the word has two meanings. But a little reflection satisfies us, that the pain is in the mind, and the disorder in the tooth. If some philosopher should pretend to have made a discovery, that the toothache, the gout, the headache, are only sensations in the mind, and that it is a vulgar error to conceive that they are

---

the-teeth-on-edge, &c., &c.; such, in fine, are all the various sensations of bodily pleasure and pain determined by the action of external stimuli."

To mark the difference between the three classes of qualities, he observes:—" The *primary*, being thought as *essential* to the notion of body, are distinguished from the *secundo-primary* and *secondary as accidental;* while the *primary* and *secundo-primary*, being thought as *manifest* or *conceivable in their own nature*, are distinguished from the *secondary* as *in their own nature occult and inconceivable.*" And again:—" Using the terms strictly, the apprehensions of the *primary* are perceptions, not sensations; of the *secondary*, sensations, not perceptions; of the *secundo-primary*, perceptions *and* sensations together." Still further:—" In the apprehension of the *primary* qualities, the mind is primarily and principally *active;* it feels only as it knows [because it only feels, i. e. is conscious, that it knows]. In that of the *secondary*, the mind is primarily and principally *passive;* it knows only as it feels [because it only knows, i. e. is conscious, that it feels]. In that of the *secundo-primary*, the mind is equally and at once *active* and *passive;* in one respect it feels as it knows, in another, it knows as it feels." To illustrate the last statement he adduces the example of the secundo-primary quality of *hardness*, a modification of *cohesion;* which consists of two parts, — *pressure*, which is *felt* in the *subject*, and *resistance*, which is *perceived* to belong to the *object*. — ED.

[*] There is no such "perception," *properly* so called. The cognition is merely an *inference* from the feeling; and its object, at least, only some hypothetical representation of a really *ignotum quid*. Here the *subjective* element preponderates so greatly as almost to extinguish the *objective*. — H.

distempers of the body, he might defend his system in the same manner as those who affirm that there is no sound nor color nor taste in bodies defend that paradox. But both these systems, like most paradoxes, will be found to be only an abuse of words.

We say that we *feel* the toothache, not that we perceive it. On the other hand, we say that we *perceive* the color of a body, not that we feel it. Can any reason be given for this difference of phraseology? In answer to this question, I apprehend, that, both when we feel the toothache and when we see a colored body, there is sensation and perception conjoined. But in the toothache, the sensation, being very painful, engrosses the attention; and therefore we speak of it as if it were felt only, and not perceived: whereas, in seeing a colored body, the sensation is indifferent, and draws no attention. The *quality in the body* which we call its *color* is *the only object of attention;* and therefore we speak of it as if it were perceived, and not felt. Though all philosophers agree that in seeing color there is sensation, it is not easy to persuade the vulgar, that, in seeing a colored body, when the light is not too strong, nor the eye inflamed, they have any sensation or feeling at all.

There are some sensations, which, though they are very often felt, are never attended to, nor reflected upon. We have no conception of them; and therefore, in language, there is neither any name for them, nor any form of speech that supposes their existence. Such are the sensations of color, and of all primary qualities; and therefore those qualities are said to be perceived, but not to be felt. Taste and smell, and heat and cold, have sensations that are often agreeable or disagreeable, in such a degree as to draw our attention; and they are sometimes said to be felt, and sometimes to be perceived. When disorders of the body occasion very acute pain, the uneasy sensation engrosses the attention, and they are said to be felt, not to be perceived.*

---

* As already repeatedly observed, the *objective* element (perception) and

There is another question relating to phraseology, which this subject suggests. A man says, he feels pain in such a particular part of his body, — in his toe, for instance. Now, reason assures us, that pain, being a sensation, can only be in the sentient being as its subject, that is, in the mind. And though philosophers have disputed much about the place of the mind, yet none of them ever placed it in the toe.* What shall we say, then, in this case? Do our senses really deceive us, and make us believe a thing which our reason determines to be impossible? I answer, *first*, that, when a man says he has a pain in his toe, he is perfectly understood, both by himself and those who hear him. This is all that he intends. He really feels what he and all men call a pain in the toe; and there is no deception in the matter. Whether, therefore, there be any impropriety in the phrase or not, is of no consequence in common life. It answers all the ends of speech, both to the speaker and the hearers.

In all languages, there are phrases which have a distinct meaning; while, at the same time, there may be something in the structure of them that disagrees with the analogy of grammar, or with the principles of philosophy. And the reason is, because language is not made either by grammarians or philosophers. Thus we speak of feeling pain, as if pain was something distinct from the feeling of it. We speak of a pain coming and going, and removing from one place to another. Such phrases are meant by those who use them in a

---

the *subjective* element (feeling, sensation) are always in the inverse ratio of each other. This is a law of which Reid and the philosophers were not aware. — H.

* Not in the toe *exclusively*. But, both in ancient and modern times, the opinion has been held that the mind has as much a local presence in the toe as in the head. The doctrine, indeed, long generally maintained was, that, in relation to the body, *the soul is all in the whole, and all in every part.* On the question of the seat of the soul, which has been marvellously perplexed, I cannot enter. I shall only say, in general, that the first condition of the possibility of an immediate, intuitive, or real perception of external things, which our consciousness assures that we possess, is the immediate connection of the cognitive principle with every part of the corporeal organism. — H.

14 *

sense that is neither obscure nor false. But the philosopher puts them into his alembic, reduces them to their first principles, draws out of them a sense that was never meant, and so imagines that he has discovered an error of the vulgar.

† I observe, *secondly*, that, when we consider the sensation of pain by itself, without any respect to its cause, we cannot say with propriety that the toe is either the place or the subject of it. But it ought to be remembered, that, when we speak of pain in the toe, the sensation is combined in our thought with the *cause* of it, which really is in the toe. The cause and the effect are combined in one complex notion, and the same name serves for both. It is the business of the philosopher to analyze this complex notion, and to give different names to its different ingredients. He gives the name of *pain* to the sensation only, and the name of *disorder* to the unknown cause of it. Then it is evident that the disorder only is in the toe, and that it would be an error to think that the pain is in it. But we ought not to ascribe this error to the vulgar, who never made the distinction, and who under the name of pain comprehend both the sensation and its cause.*

Cases sometimes happen, which give occasion even to the vulgar to distinguish the painful sensation from the disorder which is the cause of it. A man who has had his leg cut off, many years after feels pain in a toe of that leg. The toe has now no existence; and he perceives easily, that the toe can neither be the place nor the subject of the pain which he feels: yet it is the same feeling he used to have from a hurt in the toe; and if he did not know that his leg was cut off, it would give him the same immediate conviction of some hurt or disorder in the toe.†

---

* That the pain is where it is felt is, however, the doctrine of common sense. We only feel inasmuch as we have a body and a soul; we only feel pain in the toe inasmuch as we have such a member, and inasmuch as the mind, or sentient principle, pervades it. We just as much *feel* in the toe as we *think* in the head. If (but only if) the latter be a *vitium subreptionis*, as Kant thinks, so is the former. — H.

† This illustration is Descartes's. If correct, it only shows that the con-

The same phenomenon may lead the philosopher, in all cases, to distinguish sensation from perception. We say, that the man had a deceitful feeling, when he felt a pain in his toe after the leg was cut off; and we have a true meaning in saying so. But, if we will speak accurately, our *sensations* cannot be deceitful; they must be what we feel them to be, and can be nothing else. Where, then, lies the deceit? I answer, it lies not in the *sensation*, which is real, but in the *seeming perception* he had of a disorder in his toe. This perception, which nature had conjoined with the sensation, was in this instance fallacious.

The same reasoning may be applied to every phenomenon that can, with propriety, be called a deception of sense. As when one who has the jaundice sees a body yellow which is really white; or when a man sees an object double, because his eyes are not both directed to it; in these, and other like cases, the sensations we have are real, and the deception is only in the perception which nature has annexed to them.

Nature has connected our perception of external objects with certain sensations. If the sensation is produced, the corresponding perception follows even when there is no object, and in this case is apt to deceive us. In like manner, nature has connected our sensations with certain impressions that are made upon the nerves and brain: and, when the impression is made, from whatever cause, the corresponding sensation and perception immediately follow. Thus, in the man who feels pain in his toe after the leg is cut off, the nerve that went to the toe, part of which was cut off with the leg, had the same impression made upon the remaining part, which, in the natural state of his body, was caused by a hurt in the toe: and immediately this

---

nection of mind with organization extends from the centre to the circumference of the nervous system, and is not limited to any part. — H.

Müller makes the fact, as stated in the text, incontestable. *Physiology*, Vol. I. p. 745. — ED.

impression is followed by the sensation and perception which nature connected with it.*

---

* This is a doctrine which cannot be reconciled with that of an intuition or objective perception. All here is subjective. — H.

In his *Supplementary Dissertations*, Note D, § 2, Sir W. Hamilton returns to this example, modifying somewhat the view he had previously entertained: — " Take, for instance, a man whose leg has been amputated. If now two nervous filaments be irritated, the one of which ran to his great, the other to his little toe, he will experience two pains, as in these two members. Nor is there, in propriety, any deception in such sensations. For his toes, as all his members, are his only as they are to him sentient, as endowed with nerves and distinct nerves. The *nerves* thus constitute alone the *whole sentient organism*. In these circumstances, the peculiar nerves of the several toes, running isolated from centre to periphery, and thus remaining, though curtailed in length, unmutilated in function, will, if irritated at any point, continue to manifest their original sensations; and these being now, as heretofore, manifested *out of each other*, must afford the condition of *a perceived extension*, not less *real* than that which they afforded prior to the amputation.

" The hypothesis of an extended *sensorium commune*, or complex nervous centre, the mind being supposed in proximate connection with each of its constituent nervous terminations or origins, may thus be reconciled to the doctrine of *natural realism*.

" It is, however, I think, more philosophical to consider the nervous system as one whole, with each part of which the animating principle is equally and immediately connected, so long as each part remains in continuity with the centre. As to the question of materialism, this doctrine is indifferent. For the connection of an unextended with an extended substance is equally incomprehensible, whether we contract the place of union to a central point, or whether we leave it coextensive with organization."

Several authorities are referred to in support of this view, among which are the following: — St. Gregory of Nyssa, *De Hom. Opif.*, cc. 12, 14, 15; Tiedemann, *Psychologie*, p. 309 *et seq.*; Berard, *Des Rapports du Phys. et du Mor.*, Chap. I. § 2; R. G. Carus, *Vorles. ueb. Psychologie*, passim; Umbreit, *Psychologie*, c. I., and *Beilage*, passim; F. Fischer, *Ueb. d. Sitz d. Seele*, passim. This theory is also supposed to be in accordance with the doctrine of Aristotle, *De Anima*, Lib. I. Cap. IX. § 4, " that the soul contains the body, rather than the body the soul "; — a doctrine on which was founded the common dogma of the schoolmen, " that the soul is all in the whole body, and all in every of its parts," meaning thereby, that the simple, unextended mind, in some inconceivable manner present to all the organs, is percipient of the peculiar affection which each is adapted to receive, and actuates each in the peculiar function which it is qualified to discharge.

Still the common doctrine, as well with psychologists as with physiologists, would seem to be, that the brain is the *sole* organ of the mind, and that the mind is *peculiarly*, if not exclusively, present to that organ, by means of which it *feels* as well as *thinks*. Compare Descartes, *Les Passions de l'Ame*, Partie I. Art. XXX. *et seq.*; Hartley's *Observations on Man*, Part I. Chap. I. Sect. I.; Haller's *First Lines of Physiology*, Chap. X. § 372; Gall's *Functions of the Brain*, Sect I.; Broussais, *De l'Irritation et*

In like manner, if the same impressions which are made at present upon my optic nerves by the objects before me could be made in the dark, I apprehend that I should have the same sensations, and see the same objects which I now see. The impressions and sensations would in such a case be real, and the perception only fallacious.

IV. (3.) *Powers of Bodies.*] Let us next consider the notions which our senses give us of those attributes of bodies called *powers*. This is the more necessary, because power seems to imply some *activity;* yet we consider body as a dead, *inactive* thing, which does not act, but may be acted upon.

Of the mechanical powers ascribed to bodies, that which is called their *vis insita,* or *vis inertiæ,* may first be considered. By this is meant no more than that bodies never change their state of themselves, either from rest to motion, or from motion to rest, or from one degree of velocity, or one direction, to another. In order to produce any such change, there must be some force impressed upon them; and the change produced is precisely proportioned to the force impressed, and in the direction of that force.

That all bodies have this property is a matter of fact, which we learn from daily observation, as well as from the most accurate experiments. Now it seems plain, that this does not imply any activity in body, but rather the contrary. A power in body to change its state would much rather imply activity than its continuing in the same state: so that, although this property of bodies is called their *vis insita,* or *vis inertiæ,* it implies no proper activity,

If we consider, next, the power of gravity, it is a fact, that all the bodies of our planetary system gravi-

---

de la Folie, Partie I. Chap. VI.; Tissot, *Anthropologie,* Partie II Chap. V.; Müller's *Physiology,* Vol. I. p. 816 *et seq.* Most of them hold, that it is only by experience and association of ideas that we are led to refer the pain which we feel *in the brain* to the part of the body where *the cause* of the pain exists. — ED.

tate towards each other. This has been fully proved
by the great Newton. But this gravitation is not conceived by that philosopher to be a power inherent in
bodies, which they exert of themselves, but a force impressed upon them, to which they must necessarily
yield. Whether this force be impressed by some subtile ether, or whether it be impressed by the power of
the Supreme Being, or of some subordinate spiritual
being, we do not know; but all sound natural philosophy, particularly that of Newton, supposes it to be an
impressed force, and not inherent in bodies.*

So that, when bodies gravitate, they do not properly
act, but are acted upon. They only yield to an impression that is made upon them. It is common in language to express, by active verbs, many changes in
things, wherein they are merely passive. And this way
of speaking is used chiefly *when the cause of the change
is not obvious to sense.* Thus we say that a ship sails,
when every man of common sense knows that she has
no inherent power of motion, and is only driven by
wind and tide. In like manner, when we say that the
planets gravitate towards the sun, we mean no more
than that, by some unknown power, they are drawn or
impelled in that direction.

What has been said of the power of gravitation
may be applied to other mechanical powers, such as
cohesion, magnetism, electricity, and no less to chemical and medical powers. By all these, certain effects
are produced, upon the application of one body to another. Our senses discover the effect; but the power
is latent. We know there must be a cause of the
effect, and we form a relative notion of it from its effect;
and very often the same name is used to signify the
unknown cause and the known effect.

We ascribe to vegetables the powers of drawing
nourishment, growing, and multiplying their kind.
Here, likewise, the effect is manifest, but the cause is

---

* That all *activity* supposes an *immaterial* or *spiritual* agent is an ancient
doctrine. It is, however, only an hypothesis. — H.

latent to sense. These powers, therefore, as well as all the other powers we ascribe to bodies, are unknown causes of certain known effects. It is the business of philosophy to investigate the nature of those powers as far as we are able, but our senses leave us in the dark.

V. *Manifest and Occult Qualities.*] We may observe a great similarity in the notions which our senses give us of *secondary qualities*, of the *disorders we feel in our own bodies*, and of the various *powers of bodies* which we have enumerated. (1.) They are all obscure and relative notions, being a conception of some unknown cause of a known effect. (2.) Their names are, for the most part, common to the effect and to its cause. And (3.) they are a proper subject of philosophical disquisition. They might, therefore, I think, not improperly be called *occult qualities*.

This name, indeed, has fallen into disgrace since the time of Descartes. It is said to have been used by the Peripatetics to cloak their ignorance, and to stop all inquiry into the nature of those qualities called *occult*. Be it so. Let those answer for this abuse of the word who were guilty of it. To call a thing occult, if we attend to the meaning of the word, is rather modestly to confess ignorance than to cloak it. It is to point it out as a proper subject for the investigation of philosophers, whose proper business it is to better the condition of humanity by discovering what was before hid from human knowledge.

Were I, therefore, to make a division of the qualities of bodies as they appear to our senses, I would divide them first into those that are *manifest*, and those that are *occult*. The *manifest* qualities are those which Mr. Locke calls *primary*; such as extension, figure, divisibility, motion, hardness, softness, fluidity. The nature of these is manifest even to sense; and the business of the philosopher with regard to them is not to find out their *nature*, which is well known, but to discover *the effects produced by their various combinations*; and, with regard to those of them which are not essential to matter, to discover *their causes as far as he is able.*

The second class consists of *occult* qualities, which may be subdivided into various kinds; as, *first*, the *secondary qualities; secondly*, the *disorders we feel in our own bodies;* and, *thirdly*, all the qualities which we call *powers of bodies*, whether mechanical, chemical, medical, animal, or vegetable; or if there be any other powers not comprehended under these heads. Of all these the *existence* is manifest to sense, but the *nature* is occult; and here the philosopher has an ample field.

What is necessary for the conduct of our animal life, the bountiful Author of nature has made manifest to all men. But there are many other choice secrets of nature, the discovery of which enlarges the power and exalts the state of man. These are left to be discovered by the proper use of our rational powers. They are hid, not that they may be always concealed from human knowledge, but that we may be excited to search for them. This is the proper business of a philosopher, and it is the glory of a man, and the best reward of his labor, to discover what nature has thus concealed.

CHAPTER IX.

OF MATTER AND SPACE.

I. *Origin and Characteristics of our Notion of Body, or Material Substance.*] The objects of sense we have hitherto considered are *qualities*. But qualities must have a subject. We give the names of *matter, material substance*, and *body* to the subject of sensible qualities: and it may be asked what this *matter* is.

I perceive in a billiard-ball, figure, color, and motion; but the ball is not figure, nor is it color, nor motion, nor all these taken together; it is *something* that *has* figure, and color, and motion. This is a dictate of nature, and the belief of all mankind.

As to the nature of this something, I am afraid we can give little account of it but that it has the qualities which our senses discover.

But how do we know that they are qualities, and cannot exist without a subject? I confess I cannot explain how we know that they cannot exist without a subject, any more than I can explain how we know that they exist. We have the information of nature for their existence; and I think we have the information of nature that they are qualities.

The belief that figure, motion, and color are qualities, and require a subject, must either be a judgment of nature, or it must be discovered by reason, or it must be a prejudice that has no just foundation. There are philosophers who maintain that it is a mere prejudice; that a body is nothing but *a collection of what we call sensible qualities;* and that they neither have nor need any *subject.* This is the opinion of Bishop Berkeley and Mr. Hume; and they were led to it by finding that they had not in their minds any *idea of substance.* It could neither be an idea of sensation nor of reflection, the only sources of original and simple ideas which they recognized. But to me nothing seems more absurd than that there should be extension without any thing extended, or motion without any thing moved; yet I cannot give reasons for my opinion, because it seems to me self-evident, and an immediate dictate of my nature.

And that it is the belief of all mankind appears in the structure of all languages; in which we find adjective nouns used to express sensible qualities. It is well known that every adjective in language must belong to some substantive expressed or understood; that is, every quality must belong to some subject.

Sensible qualities make so great a part of the furniture of our minds, their kinds are so many and their number so great, that if prejudice, and not nature, teach us to ascribe them all to a subject, it must have a great work to perform, which cannot be accomplished in a short time, nor carried on to the same pitch in every

15

individual.   We should find, not individuals only, but
nations and ages differing from each other in the
progress which this prejudice had made in their sentiments; ·but we find no such difference among men.
What one man accounts a quality, all men do, and
ever did.

It seems, therefore, to be a judgment of nature, that
the things immediately perceived are qualities, which
must belong to a subject; and all the information that
our senses give us about this subject is, that it is that
to which such qualities belong.   From this it is evident,
that our notion of body or matter, as distinguished
from its qualities, is a relative notion; * and I am afraid
it must always be obscure until men have other faculties.

The philosopher in this seems to have no advantage
above the vulgar; for as they perceive color and figure
and motion by their senses as well as he does, and both
are equally certain that there is a subject of those qualities, so the notions which both have of this subject are
equally obscure.   When the philosopher calls it *a substratum*, and *a subject of inhesion*, those learned words
convey no meaning but what every man understands
and expresses by saying in common language that it
is a thing extended, and solid, and movable.

The relation which sensible qualities bear to their
subject, that is, to body, is not, however, so dark but
that it is easily distinguished from all other relations.
Every man can distinguish it from the relation of an

---

* That is, our notion of *absolute* body is *relative*. This is incorrectly
expressed. We can know, we can conceive, only what is relative. Our
knowledge of *qualities* or *phenomena* is necessarily relative; for these exist
only as they exist *in relation to our faculties*.   The knowledge, or even the
conception, of a substance in itself, and apart from any qualities in relation
to, and therefore cognizable or conceivable by, our minds, involves a contradiction.   Of such we can form only a *negative* notion; that is, we can
merely *conceive it as inconceivable*.   But to call this negative notion a
relative notion is wrong; — 1st, because all our (positive) notions are relative;
and, 2d, because this is itself a negative notion, — i. e. no notion at all, —
simply because there is *no relation*.   The same improper application of the
term *relative* was also made by Reid when speaking of the secondary qualities. — H.

effect to its cause, of a mean to its end, or of a sign to the thing signified by it.

I think it requires some ripeness of understanding to distinguish the qualities of a body from the body. Perhaps this distinction is not made by brutes, nor by infants; and if any one thinks that this distinction is not made by our senses, but by some other power of the mind, I will not dispute this point, provided it be granted that men, when their faculties are ripe, have a natural conviction that sensible qualities cannot exist by themselves without some subject to which they belong.

I think, indeed, that some of the determinations we form concerning matter cannot be deduced solely from the testimony of sense, but must be referred to some other source.

There seems to be nothing more evident, than that all bodies must consist of parts; and that every part of a body is a body, and a distinct being which may exist without the other parts; and yet I apprehend this conclusion is not deduced solely from the testimony of sense: for besides that it is a necessary truth, and therefore no object of sense,* there is a limit beyond which we cannot perceive any division of a body. The parts become too small to be perceived by our senses; but we cannot believe that it becomes then incapable of being further divided, or that such division would make it not to be a body. We carry on the division and subdivision in our thought far beyond the reach of our senses, and we can find no end to it: nay, I think we plainly discern, that there can be no limit beyond which the division cannot be carried. For if there be any limit to this division, one of two things must necessarily happen. Either we have come by division to a body which is extended, but has no parts,

---

* It is creditable to Reid that he perceived that the quality of *necessity* is the criterion which distinguishes *native* from *adventitious* notions or judgments. He did not, however, always make the proper use of it. Leibnitz has the honor of first explicitly enouncing this criterion, and Kant, of first fully applying it to the phenomena. In none has Kant been more successful than in this under consideration. — H.

and is absolutely indivisible; or this body is divisible, but as soon as it is divided it becomes no body. Both these positions seem to me absurd, and one or the other is the necessary consequence of supposing a limit to the divisibility of matter. On the other hand, if it be admitted that the divisibility of matter has no limit, it will follow that no body can be called one individual substance. You may as well call it two, or twenty, or two hundred. For when it is divided into parts, every part is a being or substance distinct from all the other parts, and was so even before the division: any one part may continue to exist, though all the other parts are annihilated.

There is, indeed, a principle long received as an axiom in metaphysics, which I cannot reconcile to the divisibility of matter. It is, that every being is one, — *Omne ens est unum.* By which, I suppose, is meant, that every thing that exists must either be one indivisible being, or composed of *a determinate number* of indivisible beings. Thus an army may be divided into regiments, a regiment into companies, and a company into men. But here the division has its limit; for you cannot divide a man without destroying him, because he is an individual; and every thing, according to this axiom, must be an individual, or made up of individuals.

That this axiom will hold with regard to an army, and with regard to many other things, must be granted: but I require the evidence of its being applicable to all beings whatsoever. Leibnitz, conceiving that all beings must have this metaphysical unity, was by this led to maintain, that matter, and indeed the whole universe, is made up of *monads*, that is, simple and indivisible substances. Perhaps the same apprehension might lead Boscovich into his hypothesis, which seems much more ingenious; to wit, that matter is composed of a definite number of *mathematical points*, endowed with certain powers of attraction and repulsion.

The divisibility of matter without any limit seems to me more tenable than either of these hypotheses; nor do I lay much stress upon the metaphysical axiom, considering its origin. Metaphysicians thought proper to make the attributes common to all beings the subject of a science. It must be a matter of some difficulty to find out such attributes: and, after racking their invention, they have specified three, to wit, *unity*, *verity*, and *goodness;* and these, I suppse, have been invented to make a number, rather than from any clear evidence of their being universal.

There are other determinations concerning matter, which, I think, are not solely founded upon the testimony of sense; such as, that it is impossible that two bodies should occupy the same place at the same time, or that the same body should be in different places at the same time, or that a body can be moved from one place to another without passing through the intermediate places, either in a straight course or by some circuit. These appear to be necessary truths, and therefore cannot be conclusions of our senses; for our senses testify only what is, and not what must necessarily be.

II. *Origin and Characteristics of our Notions of Extension and Space.*] We are next to consider our notion of *space*. It may be observed, that although space be not perceived by any of our senses when all matter is removed, yet, when we perceive any of the primary qualities, space presents itself as *a necessary concomitant:* for there can neither be extension, nor motion, nor figure, nor division, nor cohesion of parts, without space.

There are only two of our senses by which the notion of space enters into the mind, — to wit, touch and sight. If we suppose a man to have neither of these senses, I do not see how he could ever have any conception of space.* Supposing him to have both, until

* According to Reid, extension (space) is a notion *a posteriori*, the result of experience. According to Kant, it is *a priori;* experience only affording the occasions required by the mind to exert the acts of which the intuition of space is a condition. To the former it is thus a *contingent*, to the

he sees or feels other objects, he can have no notion of
space. It has neither color nor figure to make it an
object of sight; it has no tangible quality to make it
an object of touch. But other objects of sight and
touch *carry the notion of space along with them;* and
not the notion only, but the belief of it: for *a body
could not exist if there were no space to contain it :* it
could not *move* if there were no space : its situation, its
distance, and every relation it has to other bodies, *suppose* space.

But though the notion of space seems not to enter
at first into the mind until it is introduced by the
proper objects of sense, yet, being once introduced, it
remains in our conception and belief, though the objects which introduced it be removed. We see no
absurdity in supposing a body to be annihilated; but
the space that contained it remains, and to suppose
that annihilated seems to be absurd. It is so much

---

latter, a *necessary* mental possession. That the notion of *space* is a necessary condition of thought, and that, *as such*, it is impossible to derive it
from experience, has been cogently demonstrated by Kant. But that we
may, through sense, have *empirically* an *immediate* perception of something
extended, I have yet seen no valid reason to doubt. The *a priori* conception does not exclude the *a posteriori* perception ; and this latter cannot be
rejected without belying the evidence of consciousness, which assures us
that we are immediately cognizant, not only of a *self*, but of a *not-self*, —
not only of *mind*, but of *matter ;* and matter cannot be immediately known,
— that is, known as existing, — except as something extended. In this,
however, I venture a step beyond Reid and Stewart, no less than beyond
Kant ; though I am convinced that the philosophy of the two former
tended to this conclusion, which is, in fact, that of the common sense of
mankind. — H.

In his *Supplementary Dissertations*, Note D, § 1, Sir W. Hamilton retracts
one of the statements in the preceding note. He says : — "I may take
this opportunity of modifying a former statement, that, according to Reid,
space is a notion *a posteriori*, the result of experience. On reconsidering
more carefully his different statements on this subject, I am now inclined
to think that his language implies no more than the *chronological* posteriority of this notion ; and that he really held it to be a native, necessary,
a priori form of thought, requiring only certain prerequisite conditions to
call it from virtual into manifest existence. I am confirmed in this view
by finding it is also that of M. Royer-Collard. Mr. Stewart is, however,
less defensible, when he says, in opposition to Kant's doctrine of *space*, —
'I rather lean to the common theory which supposes our first ideas of
space or extension to be *formed* by *other* qualities of matter.' *Dissertation*,
Notes and Illustrations, Note (S s)." — ED.

allied to nothing or emptiness, that it seems *incapable of annihilation or of creation.*

Space not only retains a firm hold of our belief, even when we suppose all the objects that introduced it to be annihilated, but it swells to immensity. We can set no limits to it, either of extent or of duration. Hence we call it *immense, eternal, immovable, and indestructible.*

But it is only an immense, eternal, immovable, and indestructible void or emptiness. Perhaps we may apply to it what the Peripatetics said of their *first matter,* — that whatever it is, *it is potentially only,* not actually.

When we consider parts of space that have *measure and figure,* there is nothing we understand better, nothing about which we can reason so clearly and to so great extent. Extension and figure are *circumscribed* parts of space, and are the object of geometry, a science in which human reason has the most ample field, and can go deeper and with more certainty than in any other. But when we attempt to comprehend the whole of space, and to trace it to its origin, we lose ourselves in the search. The profound speculations of ingenious men upon this subject differ so widely, as may lead us to suspect that the line of human understanding is too short to reach the bottom of it.

Bishop Berkeley, I think, was the first who observed that the extension, figure, and space of which we speak in common language, and of which geometry treats, are originally perceived by the sense of touch only; but that there is a notion of extension, figure, and space which may be got by sight, without any aid from touch. To distinguish these, he calls the first *tangible* extension, *tangible* figure, and *tangible* space; the last he calls *visible.*

As I think this distinction very important in the philosophy of our senses, I shall adopt the names used by the inventor to express it; remembering what has been already observed, that space, whether tangible or visible, is not so properly an *object of sense* as *a necessary concomitant* of the objects both of sight and touch.

The reader may likewise be pleased to attend to this, that when I use the names of *tangible* and *visible space*, I do not mean to adopt Bishop Berkeley's opinion, so far as to think that they are really different things, and altogether unlike. I take them to be different conceptions of the same thing; the one very partial, and the other more complete, but both distinct and just, as far as they reach.

Thus, when I see a spire at a very great distance, it seems like the point of a bodkin; there appears no vane at the top, no angles. But when I view the same object at a small distance, I see a huge pyramid of several angles with a vane on the top. Neither of these appearances is fallacious. Each of them is what it ought to be, and what it must be, from such an object seen at such different distances. These different appearances of the same object may serve to illustrate the different conceptions of space, according as they are drawn from the information of sight alone, or as they are drawn from the additional information of touch.

Our sight alone, unaided by touch, gives a very partial notion of space, but yet a distinct one. When it is considered according to this partial notion, I call it *visible space*. The sense of touch gives a much more complete notion of space; and when it is considered according to this notion, I call it *tangible space*. Perhaps there may be intelligent beings of a higher order, whose conceptions of space are much more complete than those we have from both senses. Another sense added to those of sight and touch might, for what I know, give us conceptions of space as different from those we can now attain as tangible space is from visible, and might resolve many knotty points concerning it, which, from the imperfection of our faculties, we cannot by any labor untie.*

---

* On the origin of the notion of space and its relation to that of body, compare Cousin, *Elements of Psychology*, Chap. II.

He makes the distinguishing characteristics of space to be as follows: — 1. Space is given us as *necessary*, while body is given as that which

III. *Visible and Tangible Extension.*] . Berkeley acknowledges that there is an exact correspondence between the visible figure and magnitude of objects and the tangible; and that every modification of the one has a modification of the other corresponding. He acknowledges, likewise, that nature has established such a connection between the visible figure and magnitude of an object and the tangible, that we learn by experience to know the tangible figure and magnitude from the visible. And having been accustomed to do so from infancy, we get the habit of doing it with such

---

may or may not exist; 2. Space is given us as *without limits*, while body is given as limited on every side; 3. The idea of space is *a pure and wholly rational conception*, that is, we cannot bring it up before us under any determinate form or image, while the idea of body is always accompanied with an image, a sensible representation.

In tracing these ideas to their origin, he is led to notice two orders of relations among our ideas, which it is important clearly to distinguish in respect not only to space, but to all our *a priori* conceptions.

"Two ideas being given, we may inquire whether the one does not *suppose* the other; whether, the one being admitted, we must not admit the other likewise, or be guilty of a paralogism. This is the *logical order* of ideas. If we regard the question of the origin of ideas under this point of view, let us see what result it will give in respect to the particular inquiry before us. The idea of body and the idea of space being given, *which supposes the other?* Which is the *logical* condition of the admission of the other? Evidently the idea of space is the logical condition of the admission of the idea of body. In fact, take any body you please, and you cannot admit the idea of it but under the condition of admitting, at the same time, the idea of space: otherwise you would admit a body which was *nowhere*, which was in no place, and such a body is inconceivable.

"But this is not the sole order of cognition; the logical relation does not comprise all the relations which ideas mutually sustain. There is still another, that of anterior or posterior, the order of the relative development of ideas in time, — their *chronological order*. And the question of the origin of ideas may be regarded under this point of view. Now the idea of space, we have just seen, is clearly the *logical* condition of all sensible experience. Is it also the *chronological* condition of all experience, and of the idea of body? I believe no such thing. If we take ideas in the order in which they actually evolve themselves in the intelligence, if we investigate only their history and successive appearance, it is not true that the idea of space is antecedent to the idea of body. Indeed, it is so little true that the idea of space chronologically supposes the idea of body, that, in fact, if you had not the idea of body, you would never have the idea of space. Take away sensation, take away the sight and touch, and you have no longer any idea of body, and consequently none of space."

His conclusion is, that our notion of body is *empirical*, — that is to say, derived from experience, or *a posteriori;* but our notion of space, though

facility and quickness, that we think we *see* tangible
figure, magnitude, and distance of bodies, when, in
reality, we only collect those tangible qualities from the
corresponding visible qualities, which are natural signs
of them.

The correspondence and connection which Berkeley
shows to be between the visible figure and magnitude
of objects and their tangible figure and magnitude, is
in some respects very similar to that which we have
observed between our sensations and the primary qualities with which they are connected.   No sooner is the

---

developed *on occasion of* experience, is not derived *from* it, inasmuch as
experience does not *contain* it in any other sense than as, in the view of
reason, it *presupposes* it. Experience does not give the notion of space to
reason, but reason gives it to experience; and hence it is said to be *not*
empirical, but a necessary and *a priori* conception of the reason.

Others still maintain that the notion of space is wholly empirical, being
nothing but one of the sensible qualities of body considered abstractly.
Of these psychologists, the ablest, perhaps, is James Mill, who says, —
" *Concrete* terms are *connotative* terms ; *abstract* terms are *non-connotative*
terms. Concrete terms, along with a certain quality or qualities, which is
their principal meaning, or notation, *connote* the object to which the quality
belongs. Thus the concrete *red* always means, that is, connotes, *something*
red, as a rose. We have already by sufficient examples seen, that the
Abstract formed from the Concrete notes precisely that which is noted by
the Concrete, leaving out the *connotation*. Thus, take away the connotation from *red*, and you have *redness;* from *hot*, take away the connotation,
and you have *heat*. The very same is the distinction between the concrete
extended, and the abstract *extension*. What *extended* is with its connotation,
extension is without that connotation."

According to him, therefore, the word *space*, understood in its most comprehensive sense, or *infinite extension,* " is an abstract, differing from its
concrete, like other abstracts, by dropping the connotation. Much of the
mystery in which the idea has seemed to be involved is owing to this single
circumstance, that the abstract term *space* has not had an appropriate
concrete. We have observed, that in all cases abstract terms can be explained only through their concretes; because they note or name a part of
what the concrete names, leaving out the rest. If we were to make a
concrete term, corresponding to the *abstract* term *space*, it must be a word
equivalent to the terms *infinitely extended*. From the ideas included under
the name *infinitely extended*, leave out *resisting*, and you have all that is
marked by the abstract *space*." — *Analysis of the Human Mind*, Chap. XIV.
Sect. IV.

See also Kant's *Critic of Pure Reason*, Part I. Sect. I. ; Fearn's *First
Lines of the Human Mind*, Chap. V.; Whewell's *Philosophy of the Inductive
Sciences*, Part I. Book II. Chap. I. - VI. ; Brown's *Philosophy of the Human
Mind*, Lect. XXIV.; Ballantyne's *Examination of the Human Mind*, Chap.
I. Sect. I.; Brook Taylor's *Contemplatio Philosophica*, p. 45 *et seq.;* Hic-
kok's *Rational Psychology*, Book II. Part I. Chap. I. — ED.

sensation felt, than immediately we have the conception and belief of the corresponding quality. We give no attention to the sensation; it has not a name; and it is difficult to persuade us that there was any such thing.

In like manner, no sooner are the *visible* figure and magnitude of an object seen, than immediately we have the conception and belief of the corresponding *tangible* figure and magnitude. We give no attention to the visible figure and magnitude. They are immediately forgotten, as if they had never been perceived; they have no name in common language; and, indeed, until Berkeley pointed them out as a subject of specuiation, and gave them a name, they had none among philosophers, excepting in one instance, relating to the heavenly bodies, which are beyond the reach of touch. With regard to them, what Berkeley calls *visible* magnitude was by astronomers called *apparent* magnitude.

There is surely an apparent magnitude and an apparent figure of terrestrial objects, as well as of celestial; and this is what Berkeley calls their visible figure and magnitude. But they were never made an object of thought among philosophers, until that author gave them a name, and observed the correspondence and connection between them and tangible magnitude and figure, and how the mind gets the habit of passing so instantaneously from the visible figure, as a sign, to the tangible figure, as the thing signified by it, that the first is perfectly forgotten, as if it had never been perceived.

Visible figure, extension, and space may be made a subject of mathematical speculation, as well as the tangible. In the visible, we find two dimensions only; in the tangible, three. In the one, magnitude is measured by angles; in the other, by lines. Every part of visible space bears some proportion to the whole; but tangible space being immense, any part of it bears no proportion to the whole.

Such differences in their properties led Bishop Berkeley to think, that visible and tangible magnitude and figure are things totally different and dissimilar, and cannot both belong to the same object. And upon this dissimilitude is grounded one of the strongest arguments by which his system is supported. For it may be said, if there be external objects which have a real extension and figure, it must be either *tangible* extension and figure, or *visible*, or *both*.* The last appears absurd; nor was it ever maintained by any man, that the same object has two kinds of extension and figure, totally dissimilar. There is, then, only one of the two really in the object; and the other must be ideal. But no reason can be assigned why the perceptions of one sense should be real, while those of another are only ideal; and he who is persuaded that the objects of sight are ideas only has equal reason to believe so of the objects of touch.

This argument, however, loses all its force, if it be true, as was formerly hinted, that visible figure and extension are only a partial conception, and the tangible figure and extension a more complete conception of that figure and extension which are really in the object.

It has been proved very fully by Bishop Berkeley, that sight alone, without any aid from the informations of touch, gives us no perception, nor even conception, of the distance of any object from the eye. But he was not aware that this very principle overturns the argument for his system, taken from the difference between visible and tangible extension and figure: for, supposing external objects to exist, and to have that tangible extension and figure which we perceive, it follows demonstrably, from the principle now mentioned, that their visible extension and figure must be just what we see them to be. The rules of perspective, and of the projection of the sphere, which is a branch of

---

* Or *neither*. And this omitted supposition is the true. For neither sight nor touch gives us *full* and *accurate* information in regard to the *real* extension and figure of objects. — H.

perspective, are demonstrable. They suppose the existence of external objects, which have a tangible extension and figure; and, upon that supposition, they demonstrate what must be the visible extension and figure of such objects, when placed in such a position and at such a distance.

Hence it is evident, that the visible figure and extension of objects are so far from being incompatible with the tangible, that the first are *a necessary consequence* from the last, to beings that see as we do. The correspondence between them is not arbitrary, like that between words and the things they signify, as Berkeley thought, but it results necessarily from the nature of the two senses; and this correspondence, being always found in experience to be exactly what the rules of perspective show that it ought to be if the senses give true information, *is an argument for the truth of both.*

CHAPTER X.

OF THE EVIDENCE OF SENSE, AND OF BELIEF IN GENERAL.

I. *On Belief in general, and the Different Kinds of Evidence.*] *Belief, assent, conviction,* are words which I think do not admit of logical definition, because the operation of mind signified by them is perfectly simple, and of its own kind. Nor do they need to be defined, because they are common words, and well understood.

Belief must have an *object.* For he that believes must believe something; and that which he believes is called the object of his belief. Of this object of his belief, he must have some conception, clear or obscure; for although there may be the most clear and distinct conception of an object without any belief of its existence, there can be no belief without conception.

Belief is always expressed in language by a propo-
16

sition, wherein something is *affirmed* or *denied.* This
is the form of speech which in all languages is appropriated to that purpose, and without belief there could
be neither affirmation nor denial, nor should we have
any form of words to express either. Belief admits of
all degrees, from the slightest suspicion to the fullest
assurance. These things are so evident to every man
that reflects, that it would be abusing the reader's patience to dwell upon them.

I proceed to observe, that there are many operations
of mind in which, when we analyze them as far as we
are able, we find belief to be an essential ingredient.
A man cannot be conscious of his own thoughts, without believing that he thinks. He cannot perceive an
object of sense, without believing that it exists.* He
cannot distinctly remember a past event, without believing that it did exist. Belief, therefore, is an ingredient in *consciousness,* in *perception,* and in *remembrance.*

---

* Mr. Stewart, *Elements,* Part I. Chap. III., and *Essays,* II. Chap. II.,
proposes a supplement to this doctrine of Reid, in order to explain why
we believe in the existence of the qualities of external objects when they
are not the objects of our perception. This belief he holds to be the result
of *experience,* in combination with an original principle of our constitution,
whereby we are *determined to believe in the permanence of the laws of nature.*
— H.

Mr. Stewart's words are: — "It has always appeared to me, that something of this sort was necessary to complete Dr. Reid's speculations on
the Berkeleian controversy; for, although he has shown our notions concerning the primary qualities of bodies to be connected, by an original
law of our constitution, with the sensations which they excite in our minds,
he has taken no notice of the grounds of our belief that these qualities
have an existence *independent* of our perceptions. This belief (as I have
elsewhere observed) is plainly the result of *experience;* inasmuch as a
repetition of the perceptive act must have been prior to any judgment, on
our part, with respect to the separate and permanent reality of its object.
Nor does *experience* afford a complete solution of the problem; for, as we
are irresistibly led by our perceptions to ascribe to their objects a *future,*
as well as a present, reality, the question still remains, how are we determined by the experience of *the past* to carry our inferences forward to a
portion of time which is yet to come. To myself, the difficulty appears to
resolve itself, in the simplest and most philosophical manner, into that law
of our constitution to which Turgot, long ago, attempted to trace it, —
into our belief of the continuance of 'the laws of nature'; or, in other
words, into an expectation that, in the same combination of circumstances,
the same event will recur." — ED.

Not only in most of our intellectual operations, but in many of the active principles of the human mind, belief enters as an ingredient. Joy and sorrow, hope and fear, imply a belief of good or ill, either present or in expectation. Esteem, gratitude, pity, and resentment imply a belief of certain qualities in their objects. In every action that is done for an end, there must be a belief of its tendency to that end. So large a share has belief in our intellectual operations, in our active principles, and in our actions themselves, that, as faith in things divine is represented as the mainspring in the life of a Christian, so belief in general is the mainspring in the life of a man.

That men often believe what there is no just ground to believe, and thereby are led into hurtful errors, is too evident to be denied: and, on the other hand, that there are just grounds of belief can as little be doubted by any man who is not a perfect skeptic.

We give the name of *evidence* to whatever is a ground of belief. To believe without evidence is a weakness which every man is concerned to avoid, and which every man wishes to avoid. Nor is it in a man's power to believe any thing longer than he *thinks* he has evidence.

What this evidence is, is more easily felt than described. Those who never reflected upon its nature feel its influence in governing their belief. It is the business of the logician to explain its nature, and to distinguish its various kinds and degrees; but every man of understanding can judge of it, and commonly judges right, when the evidence is fairly laid before him, and his mind is free from prejudice. A man who knows nothing of the theory of vision may have a good eye; and a man who never speculated about evidence in the abstract may have a good judgment.

The common occasions of life lead us to distinguish evidence into different kinds, to which we give names that are well understood; such as the evidence of *sense*, the evidence of *memory*, the evidence of *consciousness*, the evidence of *testimony*, the evidence of *axioms*, the evidence of *reasoning*. All men of common understanding agree, that each of these kinds of evidence may afford just ground of belief, and they agree very generally in the circumstances that strengthen or weaken them.

Philosophers have endeavoured, by analyzing the different sorts of evidence, to find out some common nature wherein they all agree, and thereby to reduce them all to one. This was the aim of the schoolmen in their intricate disputes about *the criterion of truth.* Descartes placed this criterion of truth in *clear and distinct perception,* and laid it down as a maxim, that whatever we clearly and distinctly *perceive* to be true *is* true; but it is difficult to know what he understands by clear and distinct perception in this maxim.* Mr. Locke placed it in *a perception of the agreement or disagreement of our ideas,* which perception is immediate in intuitive knowledge, and by the intervention of other ideas in reasoning.

I confess that, although I have, as I think, a distinct notion of the different kinds of evidence above mentioned, and perhaps of some others, which it is unnecessary here to enumerate, yet I am not able to find any common nature to which they may all be reduced. They seem to me to agree only in this, that they are all *fitted by nature to produce belief in the human mind,* — some of them in the highest degree, which we call *certainty,* others in various degrees according to circumstances.

II. *On the Peculiar Nature of the Evidence of Sense.*] I shall take it for granted, that the evidence of sense, when the proper circumstances concur, is good evidence, and a just ground of belief. My intention in this place is only to compare it with the other kinds that have been mentioned, that we may judge whether

---

* On the purport of this maxim consult Descartes's *Principes de la Philosophie,* Iere Partie, 42–47; *Lettres sur les Instances de Gassendi,* No. 10; and IIIeme et IVeme *Meditations.* — ED.

it be reducible to any of them, or of a nature peculiar to itself.

1. It seems to be quite different from the evidence of *reasoning*. All good evidence is commonly called *reasonable* evidence, and very justly, because it ought to govern our belief as reasonable creatures. And, according to this meaning, I think the evidence of sense no less reasonable than that of demonstration. If nature give us information of things that concern us by other means than by reasoning, reason itself will direct us to receive that information with thankfulness, and to make the best use of it. But when we speak of the evidence of reasoning as a particular kind of evidence, it means the evidence of propositions that are inferred by reasoning from propositions already known and believed. Thus the evidence of the fifth proposition of the first book of Euclid's *Elements* consists in this,— that it is shown to be the necessary consequence of the axioms, and of the preceding propositions. In all reasoning, there must be one or more premises, and a conclusion drawn from them. And the premises are called the *reason* why we must believe the conclusion which we see to follow from them.

That the evidence of sense is of a different kind needs little proof. No man seeks a reason for believing what he sees or feels; and if he did, it would be difficult to find one. But though he can give no reason for believing his senses, his belief remains as firm as if it were grounded on demonstration.

Many eminent philosophers, thinking it unreasonable to believe when they could not show a reason, have labored to furnish us with reasons for believing our senses; but their reasons are very insufficient, and will not bear examination. Other philosophers have shown very clearly the fallacy of these reasons, and have, as they imagine, discovered invincible reasons against this belief; but they have never been able either to shake it in themselves, or to convince others. The statesman continues to plod, the soldier to fight, and the merchant to export and import, without being in

16 *

the least moved by the demonstrations that have been. offered of the non-existence of those things about which they are so seriously employed. And a man may as soon, by reasoning, pull the moon out of her orbit, as destroy the belief of the objects of sense.

2. Shall we say, then, that the evidence of sense is the same with that of *axioms*, or *self-evident truths ?* I answer, *first*, that all modern philosophers seem to agree, that the existence of the objects of sense is not self-evident, because some of them have endeavoured to prove it by subtile reasoning, others to refute it. Neither of these can consider it as self-evident.

Secondly, I would observe, that the word *axiom* is taken by philosophers in such a sense, as that the existence of the objects of sense cannot, with propriety, be called an axiom. They give the name of axiom only to self-evident truths that are *necessary*, and are not limited to time and place, but must be true at all times and in all places. The truths attested by our senses are not of this kind; they are *contingent*, and limited to time and place. Thus, that one is the half of two, is an axiom. It is equally true at all times and in all places. We perceive, by attending to the proposition itself, that it cannot but be true; and therefore it is called an eternal, necessary, and immutable truth. That there is at present a chair on my right hand, and another on my left, is a truth attested by my senses; but it is not necessary, nor eternal, nor immutable. It may not be true next minute; and, therefore, to call it an axiom would, I apprehend, be to deviate from the common use of the word.

Thirdly, If the word *axiom* be put to signify *every truth which is known immediately*, without being deduced from any antecedent truth, then the existence of the objects of sense may be called an axiom. For my senses give me as *immediate* conviction of what they testify, as my understanding gives me of what is commonly called an axiom.

3. There is, no doubt, an analogy between the evidence of *sense* and the evidence of *testimony*. Hence

we find in all languages the analogical expressions of the *testimony of sense*, of giving *credit* to our senses, and the like. But there is a real difference between the two, as well as a similitude. In believing upon testimony, we rely upon the authority of a person who testifies: but we have no such authority for believing our senses.

4. Shall we say, then, that this belief is *the inspiration of the Almighty?* I think this may be said in a good sense; for I take it to be the immediate effect of our constitution, which is the work of the Almighty. But if inspiration be understood to imply a persuasion of its coming from God, our belief of the objects of sense is not inspiration; for a man would believe his senses, though he had no notion of a Deity. He who is persuaded that he is the workmanship of God, and that it is a part of his constitution to believe his senses, may think that a good reason to confirm his belief: but he had the belief before he could give this or any other reason for it.

5. If we compare the evidence of *sense* with that of *memory*, we find a great resemblance, but still some difference. I remember distinctly to have dined yesterday with such a company. What is the meaning of this? It is, that I have a distinct conception and firm belief of this past event; not by reasoning, not by testimony, but immediately from my constitution: and I give the name of *memory* to that part of my constitution by which I have this kind of conviction of past events. I see a chair on my right hand. What is the meaning of this? It is, that I have, by my constitution, a distinct conception and firm belief of the present existence of the chair in such a place, and in such a position; and I give the name of *seeing* to that part of my constitution by which I have this immediate conviction. The two operations agree in the immediate conviction which they give. They agree in this also, that the things believed are not necessary, but contingent, and limited to time and place. But they differ in two respects: — *First*, that memory has something for

its object that did exist in time past; but the object of sight, and of all the senses, must be something which exists at present. And, *secondly*, that I see by my eyes, and only when they are directed to the object, and when it is illuminated. But my memory is not limited by any bodily organ that I know, nor by light and darkness, though it has its limitations of another kind.*

6. As to the opinion, that evidence consists in a perception of the agreement or disagreement of ideas, we may have occasion to consider it more particularly in another place. Here I only observe, that, when taken in the most favorable sense, it may be applied with propriety to the evidence of reasoning, and to the evidence of some axioms. But I cannot see how, in any sense, it can be applied to the evidence of *consciousness*, to the evidence of *memory*, or to that of the *senses*.

When I compare the different kinds of evidence above mentioned, I confess, after all, that the evidence of reasoning, and that of some necessary and self-evident truths, seem to be the least mysterious and the most perfectly comprehended; and therefore I do not think it strange that philosophers should have endeavoured to reduce all kinds of evidence to these.

When I see a proposition to be self-evident and necessary, and that the subject is plainly included in the predicate, there seems to be nothing more that I can desire, in order to understand why I believe it. And when I see a consequence that necessarily follows from one or more self-evident propositions, I want nothing more with regard to my belief of that consequence. The light of truth so fills my mind in these cases, that I can neither conceive nor desire any thing more satisfying.

On the other hand, when I remember distinctly a

---

* There is a more important difference than these omitted. In memory, we cannot possibly be conscious, or immediately cognizant, of any object beyond the modifications of the *ego* itself. In perception (if an *immediate perception* be allowed) we must be conscious, or immediately cognizant, of some phenomenon of the *non-ego*. — H.

past event, or see an object before my eyes, this commands my belief no less than an axiom. But when, as a philosopher, I reflect upon this belief, and want to trace it to its origin, I am not able to resolve it into necessary and self-evident axioms, or conclusions that are necessarily consequent upon them. I seem to want that evidence which I can best comprehend, and which gives perfect satisfaction to an inquisitive mind; yet it is ridiculous to doubt, and I find it is not in my power.[*]

CHAPTER XI.

OF THE IMPROVEMENT OF THE SENSES.

I. *In what Respects our Senses are and are not Improvable.*] Our senses may be considered in two views; *first*, as they afford us agreeable sensations, or subject us to such as are disagreeable; and, *secondly*, as they give us information of things that concern us.

In the *first* view, they neither require nor admit of improvement. Both the painful and the agreeable sensations of our external senses are given by nature for certain ends; and they are given in that degree which is the most proper for their end. By diminishing or increasing them, we should not mend, but mar, the work of nature.

Bodily pains are indications of some disorder or hurt

---

[*] If an immediate knowledge of external things — that is, a consciousness of the qualities of the *non-ego* — be admitted, the belief of their existence follows of course. On this supposition, therefore, such a belief would not be unaccountable; for it would be accounted for by the fact of the knowledge in which it would necessarily be contained. Our belief, in this case, of the existence of external objects, would not be more inexplicable than our belief that $2 + 2 = 4$. In both cases it would be sufficient to say, *We believe because we know;* for belief is only unaccountable when it is not the consequent or concomitant of knowledge. By this, however, I do not, of course, mean to say that knowledge is not in itself marvellous and unaccountable. — H.

of the body, and admonitions to use the best means in our power to prevent or remove their causes. As far as this can be done by temperance, exercise, regimen, or the skill of the physician, every man has sufficient inducement to do it.

When pain cannot be prevented or removed, it is greatly alleviated by patience and fortitude of mind. While the mind is superior to pain, the man is not unhappy, though he may be exercised. It leaves no sting behind it, but rather matter of triumph and agreeable reflection, when borne properly, and in a good cause. The Canadians have taught us, that even savages may acquire a superiority to the most excruciating pains; and, in every region of the earth, instances will be found where a sense of duty, of honor, or even of worldly interest, has triumphed over it.

It is evident, that nature intended for man, in his present state, a life of labor and toil, wherein he may be occasionally exposed to pain and danger: and the happiest man is not he who has felt least of those evils, but he whose mind is fitted to bear them by real magnanimity.

Our *active and perceptive powers are improved and perfected by use and exercise.* This is the constitution of nature. But, with regard to the agreeable and disagreeable sensations we have by our senses, the very contrary is an established constitution of nature: *the frequent repetition of them weakens their force.* Sensations at first very disagreeable by use become tolerable, and at last perfectly indifferent. And those that are at first very agreeable by frequent repetition become insipid, and at last 'perhaps give disgust. Nature has set limits to the pleasures of sense, which we cannot pass; and all studied gratification of them, as it is mean and unworthy of a man, so it is foolish and fruitless.

The man who, in eating and drinking, and in other gratifications of sense, obeys the calls of nature, without affecting delicacies and refinements, has all the enjoyment that the senses can afford. If one could, by a soft and luxurious life, acquire a more delicate sensibility to pleasure, it must be at the expense of a like sensibility to pain, from which he can never promise exemption; and at the expense of cherishing many diseases which produce pain.

The improvement of our external senses, as they are the means of giving us information, is a subject more worthy of our attention: for although they are not the noblest and most exalted powers of our nature, yet they are not the least useful. All that we know or can know of the material world must be grounded upon their information; and the philosopher, as well as the day-laborer, must be indebted to them for the largest part of his knowledge.

II. *Original and Acquired Perceptions.*] Some of our perceptions by the senses may be called *original*, because they require no previous experience or learning; but the far greater part are *acquired*, and the fruit of experience.

Three of our senses — to wit, *smell, taste*, and *hearing* — originally give us only certain sensations, and a conviction that these sensations are occasioned by some external object. We give a name to that quality of the object by which it is fitted to produce such a sensation, and connect that quality with the object and with its other qualities.

Thus we learn, that a certain sensation of smell is produced by a rose; and that quality in the rose, by which it is fitted to produce this sensation, we call the smell of the rose. Here it is evident that the sensation is original. The perception, that the rose has that quality which we call its smell, is acquired. In like manner, we learn all those qualities in bodies which we call their smell, their taste, their sound. These are all secondary qualities, and we give the same name to them which we give to the sensations they produce; not from any similitude between the sensation and the quality of the same name, but because the quality is signified to us by the sensation as its sign, and because our senses give us no other knowledge of the quality than that it is fit to produce such a sensation.

By the other two senses, we have much more ample information. . By *sight,* we learn to distinguish objects by their color, in the same manner as by their sound, taste, and smell. By this sense, we perceive visible objects to have extension in two dimensions, to have visible figure and magnitude, and a certain angular distance from one another. These, I conceive, are the original perceptions of sight.*

By *touch,* we not only perceive the temperature of bodies as to heat and cold,† which are secondary qualities, but we perceive originally their three dimensions, their tangible figure and magnitude, their linear distance from one another, their hardness, softness, or fluidity. These qualities we originally perceive by touch only; but, by experience, we learn to perceive all or most of them by sight.

We learn to perceive, by one sense, what originally could have been perceived only by another, by finding a connection between the objects of the different senses. Hence the original perceptions, or the sensations, of one sense, become signs of whatever has always been found connected with them; and from the *sign* the

---

* In another connection, speaking of the perceptions of sight, Sir W. Hamilton has said: — "It is incorrect to say that 'we see the object,' (meaning the thing from which the rays come by emanation or reflection, *but which is unknown and incognizable by sight,*) and so forth. It would be more correct to describe vision, — a perception, by which we take immediate cognizance of light in relation to our organ, — that is, as diffused and figured upon the retina, under various modifications of degree and kind, (brightness and color,) — and likewise as falling on it in a particular direction. The image on the retina is not itself an object of visual perception. It is only to be regarded as the complement of those points, or of that sensitive surface, on which the rays impinge, and with which they enter into relation. The total object of visual perception is thus neither the rays in themselves, nor the organ in itself, but the rays and the living organ in reciprocity: this organ is not, however, to be viewed as merely the retina, but as the whole tract of nervous fibre pertaining to the sense. In an act of vision, as also in the other sensitive acts, I am thus *conscious,* (the word should not be restricted to *self*-consciousness,) or immediately cognizant, not only of the affections of self, but of the phenomena of something different from self, both, however, always in relation to each other." — ED.

† Whether heat, cold, &c., be objects of touch, or of a different sense, has been considered in a former note. — ED.

mind passes immediately to the conception and belief of the *thing signified:* and although the connection in the mind between the sign and the thing signified by it be the effect of custom, this custom becomes a second nature, and it is difficult to distinguish it from the original power of perception.

Thus, if a sphere of one uniform color be set before me, I perceive evidently by my eye its spherical figure and its three dimensions.   All the world will acknowledge, that by sight only, without touching it, I may be certain that it is a sphere; yet it is no less certain, that, by the original power of sight, I could not perceive it to be a sphere, and to have three dimensions.   The eye originally could only perceive two dimensions, and a gradual variation of color on the different sides of the object.   It is *experience* that teaches me that the variation of color is an effect of spherical convexity, and of the distribution of light and shade.   But so rapid is the progress of the thought from the effect to the cause, that we attend only to the last, and can hardly be persuaded that we do not immediately see the three dimensions of the sphere.   Nay, it may be observed, that, in this case, the acquired perception in a manner *effaces* the original one; for the sphere is seen to be of *one uniform color*, though originally there would have appeared a gradual variation of color : but that apparent variation we learn to interpret as the effect of light and shade falling upon a sphere of one uniform color.

A sphere may be painted upon a plane, so exactly as to be taken for a real sphere, when the eye is at a proper distance, and in the proper point of view.   We say in this case, that the eye is deceived, that the appearance is fallacious; but there is no fallacy in the original perception, but only in that which is acquired by custom.   The variation of color exhibited to the eye by the painter's art is the same which nature exhibits by the different degrees of light falling upon the convex surface of a sphere.

In perception, whether original or acquired, there is
17

something which may be called the sign, and something which is signified to us, or brought to our knowledge, by that sign.

In *original* perception, the signs are the various *sensations* which are produced by the impressions made upon our organs. The things signified are the objects perceived in consequence of those sensations, by the *original constitution of our nature.* Thus, when I grasp an ivory ball in my hand, I have a certain sensation of touch. Although this sensation be in the mind, and have no similitude to any thing material, yet, by the laws of my constitution, it is immediately followed by the conception and belief, that there is in my hand a hard, smooth body, of a spherical figure, and about an inch and a half in diameter. This belief is grounded neither upon reasoning nor upon experience; it is the immediate effect of my constitution, and this I call original perception.

In *acquired* perception, the sign may be either a sensation, or something originally perceived. The thing signified is something which, *by experience,* has been found connected with that sign. Thus, when the ivory ball is placed before my eye, I perceive by sight what I before perceived by touch, that the ball is smooth, spherical, of such a diameter, and at such a distance from the eye; and to this is added the perception of its color. All these things I perceive by sight distinctly, and with certainty; yet it is certain, from principles of philosophy, that, if I had not been accustomed to compare the informations of sight with those of touch, I should not have perceived these things by sight. I should have perceived a circular object, having its color gradually more faint towards the shaded side. But I should not have perceived it to have three dimensions, to be spherical, to be of such a linear magnitude, and at such a distance from the eye. That these last mentioned are not original perceptions of sight, but acquired by experience, is sufficiently evident from the principles of optics, and from the art of painters, in painting objects of three dimensions upon a plane which has only two. And it has been put beyond all doubt, by observations recorded of several persons, who, having, by cataracts in their eyes, been deprived of sight from their infancy, were couched and made to see, after they came to years of understanding.*

---

* The reference on this subject is commonly to Cheselden; though it must be confessed that the mode in which the case of the young man couched by that distinguished surgeon is reported does not merit all the eulogia that have been lavished on it. It is at once imperfect and indistinct. Thus, on the point in question, Cheselden says : — " He (the patient) knew not the shape of any thing, nor any one thing from another, however different in shape and magnitude; but, upon being told what things they were, whose form he before knew from feeling, he would carefully observe, that he might know them again; but, having too many objects to learn at once, he forgot many of them, and (as he said) at first he learned to know, and again forgot, a thousand things in a day. One particular only, though it may appear trifling, I will relate. Having often forgotten which was the cat and which the dog, he was ashamed to ask; but catching the cat, which he knew by feeling, he was observed to look at her steadfastly, and then, setting her down, said, ' So puss! I shall know you another time.' "

Here, when Cheselden says that his patient, when recently couched, " knew not the shape of any thing, nor any one thing from another," &c., this cannot mean that he saw no difference between the objects of different shapes and sizes; for, if this interpretation were adopted, the rest of the statement becomes nonsense. If he had been altogether incapable of apprehending differences, it could not be said that, " being told what things they were, whose form he before knew from feeling, he would carefully observe, that he might know them again "; for observation supposes the power of discrimination, and, in particular, the anecdote of the dog and cat would be inconceivable on that hypothesis. It is plain that Cheselden only meant to say, that the things which the patient could previously distinguish and denominate by *touch*, he could not now identify and refer to their appellations by *sight*. And this is what we might, *a priori*, be assured of. A sphere and a cube would certainly make different impressions on him; but it is probable that he could not assign to each its name, though, in this particular case, there is good ground for holding that the slightest consideration would enable a person, previously acquainted with these figures, and aware that one was a cube and the other a square, to connect them with his anterior experience, and to discriminate them by name. See *Philosophical Transactions*, 1728, No. 402. — H.

In another note, Sir W. Hamilton observes: — " Nothing in the whole compass of inductive reasoning appears more satisfactory than Berkeley's demonstration of the necessity and manner of our learning, by a slow process of observation and comparison alone, the connection between the perceptions of vision and touch, and, in general, all that relates to the distance and real magnitude of external things. But, although the same necessity seems in theory equally incumbent on the lower animals as on man, yet this theory is provokingly — and that by the most manifest experience — found totally at fault with regard to them; for we find that all the animals who possess at birth the power of regulated motion (and

Those who have had their eyesight from infancy acquire such perceptions so early, that they cannot recollect the time when they had them not, and therefore make no distinction between them and their original perceptions; nor can they be easily persuaded that there is any just foundation for such a distinction. In all languages, men speak with equal assurance of their *seeing* objects to be spherical or cubical, as of their *feeling* them to be so; nor do they ever dream that these perceptions of sight were not as early and original as the perceptions they have of the same objects by touch.

From what has been said, I think it appears that our original powers of perceiving objects by our senses receive great improvement by use and habit, and, without this improvement, would be altogether insufficient

---

these are those only through whom the truth of the theory can be brought to the test of a decisive experiment) possess also from birth the whole apprehension of distance, &c., which they are ever known to exhibit. The solution of this difficulty by a resort to *instinct* is unsatisfactory; for instinct is, in fact, an occult principle, — a kind of natural revelation, — and the hypothesis of instinct, therefore, only a confession of our ignorance; and, at the same time, if instinct be allowed in the lower animals, how can we determine whether and how far instinct may not, in like manner, operate to the same result in man? — I have discovered, and, by a wide induction, established, that the power of *regulated* motion at birth is, in all animals, governed by the development, at that period, of the cerebellum, in proportion to the brain proper. Is this law to be extended to the faculty of determining distances, &c., by sight?"

Mr. Bailey, in his *Review of Berkeley's Theory of Vision*, contests strenuously the common doctrine respecting the perception of magnitude, figure, and distance, — maintaining that it is not an *acquired*, but an *original*, perception of sight. In particular, he examines all the accredited reports of persons who have been relieved from early or congenital blindness by surgical operations; — not only the case of Cheselden's patient, mentioned above, but that of a boy seven years old (Master W.), related by Mr. Ware, *Philos. Trans.*, 1801; those of John Salter and William Stiff, related by Sir E. Home, *Philos. Trans.*, 1807; and two cases related by Mr. Wardrop, that of James Mitchell, so much valued by Mr. Stewart, and of which a separate memoir was published, and the still more interesting one of a lady, recorded in the *Philos. Trans.*, 1826. He shows that the evidence afforded by these reports is by no means so decisive in favor of the Berkeleian theory as is generally supposed. In other respects his argument is not so successful. For an answer see the *Westminster Review* for October, 1842. See also Adam Smith's *Essays on Philosophical Subjects*, the last essay, *Of the External Senses*; and Young's *Lectures on Intellectual Philosophy*, Lect. XIII. - XV. — Ed.

for the purposes of life.   The daily occurrences of life
not only add to our stock of knowledge, but give additional perceptive powers to our senses; thus time
gives us the use of our eyes and ears, as well as of our
hands and legs.   This is the greatest and most important improvement of our external senses.   It is to be
found in all men come to years of understanding, but
is various in different persons, according to their different occupations, and the different circumstances in
which they are placed.   Every artist acquires an eye,
as well as a hand, in his own profession: his eye becomes skilled in perceiving, no less than his hand in
executing, what belongs to his employment.

III. *Artificial Means of improving the External Senses, and of extending the Information obtained thereby.*]
Besides this improvement of our senses, which *nature*
produces without our intention, there are various ways
in which they may be improved, or their defects reme-
died, *by art*.   As, *first*, by *a due care of the organs of
sense, that they be in a sound and natural state*.   This
belongs to the department of the medical faculty.

Secondly, by *accurate attention to the objects of sense*.
The effects of such attention in improving our senses
appear in every art.   The artist, by giving more attention to certain objects than others do, by that means
perceives many things in those objects which others do
not.   Those who happen to be deprived of one sense
frequently supply that defect, in a great degree, by giving more accurate attention to the objects of the senses
they have.   The blind have often been known to acquire uncommon acuteness in distinguishing things by
feeling and hearing; and the deaf are uncommonly
quick in reading men's thoughts in their countenance.

A *third* way in which our senses admit of improvement is by *additional organs or instruments contrived by
art*.   By the invention of optical glasses, and the gradual improvement of them, the natural power of vision
is wonderfully improved, and a vast addition made to
the stock of knowledge which we acquire by the eye.

17 *

By speaking-trumpets and ear-trumpets, some improvement has been made in the sense of hearing. Whether by similar inventions the other senses may be improved, seems uncertain.

A *fourth* method by which the information got by our senses may be improved is by *discovering the connection which nature has established between the sensible qualities of objects and their more latent qualities.*

By the sensible qualities of bodies, I understand those that are perceived immediately by the senses, such as their color, figure, feeling, sound, taste, smell. The various modifications and various combinations of these are innumerable; so that there are hardly two individual bodies in nature that may not be distinguished by their sensible qualities. The latent qualities are such as are not immediately discovered by our senses, but discovered, sometimes by accident, sometimes by experiment or observation. The most important part of our knowledge of bodies is the knowledge of the latent qualities of the several species, by which they are adapted to certain purposes, either for food, or medicine, or agriculture, or for the materials or utensils of some art or manufacture. I am taught that certain species of bodies have certain latent qualities; but how shall I know that this individual is of such a species? This must be known by the sensible qualities which characterize the species. I must know that this is bread, and that wine, before I eat the one or drink the other. I must know that this is rhubarb, and that opium, before I use the one or the other for medicine.

It is one branch of human knowledge to know the names of the various species of natural and artificial bodies, and to know the sensible qualities by which they are ascertained to be of such a species, and by which they are distinguished from one another. It is another branch of knowledge to know the latent qualities of the several species, and the uses to which they are subservient. The man who possesses both these branches is informed by his senses of innumerable things of real moment, which are hid from those who possess only one, or neither. This is an improvement in the information got by our senses, which must keep pace with the improvements made in natural history, in natural philosophy, and in the arts.

It would be an improvement still higher, if we were able *to discover any connection between the sensible qualities of bodies and their latent qualities, without knowing the species, or what may have been discovered with regard to it.*

Some philosophers of the first rate have made attempts towards this noble improvement, not without promising hopes of success. Thus the celebrated Linnæus has attempted to point out certain sensible qualities by which a plant may very probably be concluded to be poisonous, without knowing its name or species. He has given several other instances, wherein certain medical and economical virtues of plants are indicated by their external appearances. Sir Isaac Newton has attempted to show, that from the colors of bodies we may form a probable conjecture of the size of their constituent parts, by which the rays of light are reflected.

No man can pretend to set limits to the discoveries that may be made by human genius and industry of such connections between the latent and the sensible qualities of bodies. A wide field here opens to our view, whose boundaries no man can ascertain, of improvements that may hereafter be made in the information conveyed to us by our senses.

CHAPTER XII.

OF THE ALLEGED FALLACY OF THE SENSES.

I. *No Foundation for the common Complaint on this Subject.*] Complaints of the fallacy of the senses have been very common in ancient and in modern times, especially among the philosophers. If we should take for granted all they have said on this subject, the natural conclusion from it might seem to be, that the senses are given to us by some malignant demon on purpose to delude us, rather than that they are formed by the wise and beneficent Author of nature, to give us true information of things necessary to our preservation and happiness.

This complaint they have supported by many commonplace instances ; — such as the crooked appearance of an oar in water ; objects being magnified, and their distance mistaken, in a fog ; the sun and moon appearing about a foot or two in diameter, while they are really thousands of miles ; a square tower being taken at a distance to be round. These, and similar appearances, many among the ancient philosophers thought to be sufficiently accounted for by the fallacy of the senses ; and thus the fallacy of the senses was used as a decent cover to conceal their ignorance of the real causes of such phenomena, and served the same purpose as their occult qualities and substantial forms.

Descartes and his followers joined in the same complaint. Antony le Grand, a philosopher of that sect, in the first chapter of his Logic, expresses the sentiments of the sect as follows : — " Since all our senses are fallacious, and we are frequently deceived by them, common reason advises, that we should not put too much trust in them, nay, that we should suspect falsehood in every thing they represent ; for it is imprudence and temerity to trust to those who have once deceived us ; and if they err at any time, they may be believed always to err. They are given by nature for this purpose only, to warn us of what is useful and what is hurtful to us. The order of nature is perverted when we put them to any other use, and apply them for the knowledge of truth."

When we consider that the active part of mankind, in all ages from the beginning of the world, have rested their most important concerns upon the testimony of sense, it will be very difficult to reconcile their conduct with the speculative opinion so generally entertained of the fallaciousness of the senses. Also it seems to be a very unfavorable account of the workmanship of the Supreme Being, to think that he has given us one faculty to deceive us, — to wit, our senses; and another faculty — to wit, our reason — to detect the fallacy.

It deserves, therefore, to be considered, whether the alleged fallaciousness of our senses be not a common error, which men have been led into from a desire to conceal their ignorance, or to apologize for their mistakes.

There are two powers which we owe to our external senses, *sensation*, and *the perception of external objects*.

It is impossible that there can be any fallacy in *sensation*; for we are conscious of all our sensations, and they can neither be any other in their nature, nor greater or less in their degree, than we feel them. It is impossible that a man should be in pain, when he does not feel pain; and when he feels pain, it is impossible that his pain should not be real, and in its degree what it is felt to be; and the same thing may be said of every sensation whatsoever. An agreeable or an uneasy sensation may be forgotten when it is past, but when it is present, it can be nothing but what we feel.

If, therefore, there be any fallacy in our senses, it must be *in the perception of external objects*, which we shall next consider.

And here I grant that we can conceive powers of perceiving external objects more perfect than ours, which possibly beings of a higher order may enjoy. We can perceive external objects only by means of bodily organs; and these are liable to various disorders, which sometimes affect our powers of perception. So the imagination, the memory, the judging and reasoning powers, are all liable to be hurt, or even destroyed, by disorders of the body, as well as our powers of perception; but we do not on this account call them *fallacious*.

Our senses, our memory, and our reason are all limited and imperfect: this is the lot of humanity: but

they are such as the Author of our being saw to be
best fitted for us in our present state.   Superior natures
may have intellectual powers which we have not, or
such as we have in a more perfect degree, and less
liable to accidental disorders: but we have no reason
to think that God has given *fallacious* powers to any
of his creatures: this would be to think dishonorably
of our Maker, and would lay a foundation for universal
skepticism.

II. *Alleged Fallacies of the Senses reducible to Four
Classes.*]   The appearances commonly imputed to the
fallacy of the senses are many, and of different kinds;
but I think they may be reduced to the four following
classes.

First, Many things called deceptions of the senses
are only *conclusions rashly drawn from the testimony of
the senses*.   In these cases the testimony of the senses
is true, but we rashly draw a conclusion from it which
does not necessarily follow.   We are disposed to impute our errors rather to false information than to inconclusive reasoning, and to blame our senses for the
wrong conclusions we draw from their testimony.

Thus, when a man has taken a counterfeit guinea
for a true one, he says his senses deceived him; but he
lays the blame where it ought not to be laid: for we
may ask him, Did your senses give a false testimony of
the color, or of the figure, or of the impression?   No.
But this is all that they testified, and this they testified
truly: from these premises you concluded that it was
a true guinea, but this conclusion does not follow; you
erred, therefore, not in relying upon the testimony of
sense, but in judging rashly from its testimony.   Not
only are your senses innocent of this error, but it is
only by their information that it can be discovered.   If
you consult them properly, they will inform you that
what you took for a guinea is base metal, or is deficient
in weight, and this can only be known by the testimony of sense.

I remember to have met with a man who thought

the argument used by Protestants against the Popish doctrine of transubstantiation, from the·testimony of our senses, inconclusive; because, said he, instances may be given where several of our senses may deceive us. How do we know, then, that there may not be cases wherein they *all* deceive us, and no sense is left to detect the fallacy? I begged of him to show an instance wherein several of our senses deceive us. "I take," said he, "a piece of soft turf, I cut it into the shape of an apple; with the essence of apples I give it the smell of an apple; and with paint, I can give it the skin and color of an apple. Here, then, is a body, which, if you judge by your eye, by your touch, or by your smell, is an apple."

To this I would answer, that no one of our senses deceives us in this case. My sight and touch testify that it has the shape and color of an apple: this is true. The sense of smelling testifies that it has the smell of an apple: this is likewise true, and is no deception. Where, then, lies the deception? It is evident it lies in this, that because this body has some qualities belonging to an apple, I conclude that it is an apple. This is a fallacy, not of the senses, but of inconclusive reasoning.

Many false judgments that are accounted deceptions of sense arise from our mistaking *relative* motion for *real* or *absolute* motion. These can be no deceptions of sense, because by our senses we perceive only the relative motions of bodies; and it is by reasoning that we infer the real from the relative which we perceive. A little reflection may satisfy us of this.

It was before observed, that we perceive extension to be one sensible quality of bodies, and thence are necessarily led to conceive space, though space be of itself no object of sense. When a body is removed out of its place, the space which it filled remains empty till it is filled by some other body, and would remain if it should never be filled. Before any body existed, the space which bodies now occupy was empty space, capable of receiving bodies; for no body can exist where

there is no space to contain it. There is space, therefore, wherever bodies exist, or can exist. Hence it is
evident that space can have no limits. It is no less
evident that it is immovable. Bodies placed in it are
movable, but the place where they were cannot be
moved; and we can as easily conceive a thing to be
moved from itself, as one part of space brought nearer
to or removed farther from another. This space, therefore, which is unlimited and immovable, is called by
philosophers *absolute space*. Absolute or real motion
is a change of place in absolute space. Our senses do
not testify the absolute motion or absolute rest of any
body. When one body removes from another, this
may be discerned by the senses; but whether any body
keeps the same part of absolute space, we do not perceive by our senses. When one body seems to remove
from another, we can infer with certainty that there is
absolute motion; but whether in the one or the other,
or partly in both, is not discerned by sense.

Of all the prejudices which philosophy contradicts, I
believe there is none so general as that the earth keeps
its place unmoved. This opinion seems to be universal, till it is corrected by instruction, or by philosophical speculation. Those who have any tincture of
education are not now in danger of being held by it,
but they find at first a reluctance to believe that there
are antipodes; that the earth is spherical, and turns
round its axis every day, and round the sun every year:
they can recollect the time when reason struggled with
prejudice upon these points, and prevailed at length,
but not without some effort.

The cause of a prejudice so very general is not unworthy of investigation. But that is not our present
business. It is sufficient to observe, that it cannot
justly be called a fallacy of *sense;* because our senses
testify only the change of situation of one body in
relation to other bodies, and not its change of situation
in absolute space. It is only the *relative* motion of
bodies that we perceive, and that we perceive truly.
It is the province of reason and philosophy, from the

relative motions which we perceive, to collect the real and absolute motions which produce them. All motion must be estimated from some point or place which is supposed to be at rest. We perceive not the points of absolute space, from which real and absolute motion must be reckoned; and there are obvious reasons that lead mankind, in the state of ignorance, to make the earth the fixed place from which they may estimate the various motions they perceive. The custom of doing this from infancy, and of using constantly a language which supposes the earth to be at rest, may perhaps be the cause of the general prejudice in favor of this opinion.

Thus it appears, that, if we distinguish accurately between what our senses *really and naturally testify*, and the *conclusions* which we draw from their testimony *by reasoning*, we shall find many of the errors called fallacies of the senses to be no fallacies of the senses, but rash judgments, which are not to be imputed to our senses.

Secondly, Another class of errors imputed to the fallacy of the senses consists of *those to which we are liable in our acquired perceptions*. Acquired perception is not properly the testimony of those senses which God has given us, but a conclusion drawn from what the senses testify. In our past experience, we have found certain things conjoined with what our senses testify. We are led by our constitution to expect this conjunction in time to come; and when we have often found it in our experience to happen, we acquire a firm belief that the things which we have found thus conjoined are connected in nature, and that one is a sign of the other. The appearance of the sign immediately produces the belief of its usual attendant, and we think we perceive the one as well as the other.

That such conclusions are formed even in infancy, no man can doubt; nor is it less certain that they are confounded with the natural and immediate perceptions of sense, and in all languages are called by the same name. We are, therefore, authorized by language

18

to call them *perceptions*, and must óften do so, or speak unintelligibly. But philosophy teaches us in this, as in many other instances, to distinguish things which the vulgar confound. I have therefore given the name of *acquired perceptions* to such conclusions, to distinguish them from what is naturally, originally, and immediately testified by our senses. Whether this acquired perception is to be resolved into some *process of reasoning*, of which we have lost the remembrance, as some philosophers think, or whether *it results immediately from our constitution*, as I rather believe, does not concern the present subject. If the first of these opinions be true, the errors of acquired perception will fall under the first class before mentioned. If not, it makes a distinct class by itself. But whether the one or the other be true, it must be observed, that the errors of acquired perception are not properly fallacies of our senses.

Thus, when a globe is set before me, I perceive by my eyes that it has three dimensions and a spherical figure. To say that this is not perception, would be to reject the authority of custom in the use of words, which no wise man will do: but that it is not the testimony of my sense of seeing, every philosopher knows. I see only a circular form, having the light and color distributed in a certain way over it. But being accustomed to observe this distribution of light and color only in a spherical body, I immediately, from what I see, believe the object to be spherical, and say that I see or perceive it to be spherical. When a painter, by an exact imitation of that distribution of light and color which I have been accustomed to see only in a real sphere, deceives me, so as to make me take that to be a real sphere which is only a painted one, the testimony of my eye is true, — the color and visible figure of the object are truly what I see them to be: the error lies in the conclusion drawn from what I see, — to wit, that the object has three dimensions and a spherical figure. The conclusion is false in this case; but whatever be the origin of this conclusion, it is not properly the testimony of sense.

To this class we must refer the judgments we are apt to form of the distance and magnitude of the heavenly bodies, and of terrestrial objects seen on high. The mistakes we make of the magnitude and distance of objects seen through optical glasses, or through an atmosphere uncommonly clear or uncommonly foggy, belong likewise to this class.

The errors we are led into in *acquired perception* are very rarely hurtful to us in the conduct of life; they are gradually corrected by a more enlarged experience, and a more perfect knowledge of the laws of nature: and the general laws of our constitution, by which we are sometimes led into them, are of the greatest utility.

We come into the world ignorant of every thing, and by our ignorance exposed to many dangers and to many mistakes. Were we sensible of our condition in that period, and capable of reflecting upon it, we should be like a man in the dark, surrounded with dangers, where every step he takes may be into a pit. Reason would direct him to sit down, and wait till he could see about him. Nature has followed another plan. The child, unapprehensive of danger, is led by instinct to exert all his active powers, to try every thing without the cautious admonitions of reason, and to believe every thing that is told him. Sometimes he suffers by his rashness what reason would have prevented; but his suffering proves a salutary discipline, and makes him for the future avoid the cause of it. Sometimes he is imposed upon by his credulity; but it is of infinite benefit to him upon the whole. His activity and credulity are more useful qualities, and better instructors than reason would be; they teach him more in a day than reason would do in a year; they furnish a stock of materials for reason to work upon; they make him easy and happy in a period of his existence, when reason could only serve to suggest a thousand tormenting anxieties and fears: and he acts agreeably to the constitution and intention of nature, even when he does and believes what reason would not justify. So that the wisdom and goodness of the Author of nature are no less conspicuous in withholding the exercise of our reason in this period, than in bestowing it when we are ripe for it.

A *third* class of errors, ascribed to the fallacy of the senses, proceeds from *ignorance of the laws of nature.*

The laws of nature (I mean not *moral* but *physical* laws) are learned either from our own experience, or the experience of others, who have had occasion to observe the course of nature. Ignorance of those laws, or inattention to them, is apt to occasion false judgments with regard to the objects of sense, especially those of *hearing* and of *sight;* which false judgments are often, without good reason, called fallacies of sense.

Sounds affect the ear differently, according as the sounding body is before or behind us, on the right hand or on the left, near or at a great distance. We learn, by the manner in which the sound affects the ear, on what hand we are to look for the sounding body; and in most cases we judge right. But we are sometimes deceived by echoes, or by whispering-galleries, or speaking-trumpets, which return the sound, or alter its direction, or convey it to a distance without diminution. The deception is still greater, because more uncommon, which is said to be produced by ventriloquists, — that is, persons who have acquired the art of modifying their voice, so that it shall affect the ear of the hearers as if it came from another person, or from the clouds, or from under the earth. Some are also said to have the art of imitating the voice of another so exactly, that in the dark they might be taken for the person whose voice they imitate.

It is, indeed, a wonderful instance of the accuracy as well as of the truth of our senses in things that are of real use in life, that we are able to distinguish all our acquaintance by their countenance, by their voice, and by their handwriting, when at the same time we are often unable to say by what minute difference the distinction is made; and that we are so very rarely deceived in matters of this kind, when we give proper

attention to the informations of sense.   However, if
any case should happen in which sounds produced by
different causes are not distinguishable by the ear, this
may prove that our senses are imperfect, but not that
they are *fallacious.*   The ear may not be able to draw
the just conclusion, but it is only our ignorance of the
laws of sound that leads us to a wrong conclusion.

.Deceptions of *sight,* arising from ignorance of the
laws of nature, are more numerous and more remarkable than those of hearing.

The rays of light, which are the means of seeing,
pass in right lines from the object to the eye, when
they meet with no obstruction ; and we are by nature
led to conceive the visible object to be in the direction
of the rays that come to the eye.   But the rays may
be reflected, refracted, or inflected in their passage from
the object to the eye, according to certain fixed laws of
nature, by which means their direction may be changed,
and consequently the apparent place, figure, or magnitude of the object.   Thus, a child seeing himself in a
mirror thinks he sees another child behind the mirror,
that imitates all his motions.   But even a child soon
gets the better of this deception, and knows that he
sees himself only.

All the deceptions made by telescopes, microscopes,
camera obscuras, or magic lanterns, are of the same
kind, though not so familiar to the vulgar.   The ignorant may be deceived by them; but to those who are
acquainted with the principles of optics, they give just
and true information, and the laws of nature by which
they are produced are of infinite benefit to mankind.

There remains *another* class of errors, commonly
called deceptions of sense, and the only one; as I
apprehend, to which that name can be given with
propriety : I mean such as proceed from *some disorder
or preternatural state, either of the external organ, or of
the nerves and brain, which are internal organs of perception.*

In a delirium or in madness, perception, memory, imagination, and our reasoning powers are strangely dis-

18*

ordered and confounded.   There are likewise disorders
which affect some of our senses, while others are sound.
Thus, a man may feel pain in his toes after the leg is
cut off.   He may feel a little ball double, by crossing
his fingers.   He may see an object double, by not
directing both eyes properly to it.   By pressing the ball
of his eye, he may see colors that are not real.   By the
jaundice in his eyes, he may mistake colors.   These
are more properly deceptions of sense than any of the
classes before mentioned.

· We must acknowledge it to be the lot of human
nature, that all the human faculties are liable, by accidental causes, to be hurt and unfitted for their natural
functions, either wholly or in part; but as this imperfection is common to them *all*, it gives no just ground
for accounting any one of them fallacious more than
another.

I add only one observation to what has been said
upon this subject.   It is, that there seems to be a contradiction between what philosophers teach concerning
ideas, and their doctrine of the fallaciousness of the
senses.   We are taught that the office of the senses is
only to give us the ideas of external objects.   If this
be so, there can be no fallacy in the senses.   Ideas can
neither be true nor false.   If the senses testify nothing,
they cannot give false testimony.   If they are not
judging faculties, no judgment can be imputed to
them, whether false or true.   There is, therefore, a contradiction between the common doctrine concerning
ideas and that of the fallaciousness of the senses.
Both may be false, as I believe they are, but both cannot be true.

ESSAY · III.

OF MEMORY.

CHAPTER I.

OF THE NATURE AND FUNCTIONS OF THIS FACULTY.

I. *Memory distinguished from Sensation and Perception.*] In the gradual progress of man from infancy to maturity, there is a certain order in which his faculties are unfolded, and this seems to be the best order we can follow in treating of them. The external senses appear first; memory soon follows, — which we are now to consider.

It is by memory that we have an immediate knowledge of things past.* The senses give us information of things only as they exist in the present moment; and this information, if it were not preserved by memory, would vanish instantly, and leave us as ignorant as if it had never been.

Every man who remembers must remember something, and that which he remembers is called the object of his remembrance. In this, memory agrees with perception, but differs from sensation, which has no object but the feeling itself. Every man can distinguish the thing remembered from the remembrance of it. We may remember any thing which we have seen, or heard, or known, or done, or suffered; but the re-

---

* An *immediate* knowledge of a *past* thing is a contradiction. For we can only know a thing immediately, if we know it in itself, or *as existing;* but what is past cannot be known in itself, for it is *non-existent.* In this respect memory differs from perception. — H.

membrance of it is a particular act of the mind which now exists, and of which we are conscious. To confound these two is an absurdity, which a thinking man could not be led into, but by some false hypothesis which hinders him from reflecting upon the thing which he would explain by it.

In memory we do not find such a train of operations connected by our constitution as in perception. When we perceive an object by our senses, there is, first, some impression made by the object upon the organ of sense, either immediately or by means of some medium. By this, an impression is made upon the nerves and brain, in consequence of which we feel some sensation, and that sensation is attended by that conception and belief of the external object which we call perception. These operations are so connected in our constitution, that it is difficult to disjoin them in our conceptions, and to attend to each without confounding it with the others. But in the operations of memory we are free from this embarrassment; they are easily distinguished from all other acts of the mind, and the names which denote them are free from all ambiguity. Again, the object of memory, or thing remembered, must be something that is *past;* as the object of perception and of consciousness must be something which is *present.* What now is cannot be an object of memory; neither can that which is past and gone be an object of perception or of consciousness.

Memory is always accompanied with the belief of that which we remember, as perception is accompanied with the belief of that which we perceive, and consciousness with the belief of that whereof we are conscious. Perhaps in infancy, or in a disorder of mind, things remembered may be confounded with those which are merely imagined; but in mature years, and in a sound state of mind, every man feels that he must believe what he distinctly remembers, though he can give no other reason of his belief, but that he remembers the thing distinctly; whereas, when he merely imagines a thing ever so distinctly, he has no belief of it upon that account.

This belief, which we have from distinct memory, we account real knowledge, no less certain than if it was grounded on demonstration; no man in his wits calls it in question, or will hear any argument against it. The testimony of witnesses in causes of life and death depends upon it, and all the knowledge of mankind of past events is built on this foundation. There are cases in which a man's memory is less distinct and determinate, and where he is ready to allow that it may have failed him; but this does not in the least weaken its credit, when it is perfectly distinct.

Things remembered must be things formerly perceived or known. I remember the transit of Venus over the sun in the year 1769. I must therefore have perceived it at the time it happened, otherwise I could not now remember it. Our first acquaintance with any object of thought cannot be by remembrance. Memory can only produce a continuance or renewal of a former acquaintance with the thing remembered. The remembrance of a past event is necessarily accompanied with the conviction of our own existence at the time the event happened. I cannot remember a thing that happened a year ago, without a conviction as strong as memory can give, that I, the same identical person who now remember that event, did then exist.[*]

---

[*] Mr. James Mill thus analyzes a fact of memory: — "I remember to have seen and heard George the Third, when making a speech at the opening of his Parliament. In this remembrance there is, first of all, the mere idea, or simple apprehension — the *conception*, as it is sometimes called — of the objects. There is combined with this, *to make it memory*, my idea of my having seen and heard those objects. And this combination is so close, that it is not in my power to separate them. I cannot have the idea of George the Third, — his person and attitude, the paper he held in his hand, the sound of his voice while reading it, the throne, the apartment, the audience, — without having the other idea along with it, that of my having been a witness of the scene.

"Now in this last-mentioned part of the compound, it is easy to perceive two important elements: *the idea of my present self*, the remembering self; and *the idea of my past self*, the remembered or witnessing self. These two ideas stand at the two ends of a portion of my being; that is, of a series of my states of consciousness. That series consists of the successive states of my consciousness intervening between the moment of perception, or the past moment, and the moment of memory, or the present moment. What happens at the moment of memory? The mind

II. *Distinction between Memory and Reminiscence or Recollection.*] Here it is proper to take notice of a distinction which Aristotle makes between *memory* and *reminiscence*, because the distinction has a real foundation in nature, though in our language I think we do not distinguish them by different names.

Memory is a kind of habit which is not always in exercise with regard to things we remember, but is ready to suggest them when there is occasion. The most perfect degree of this habit is, when *the.thing presents itself to our remembrance spontaneously, and without labor, as often as there is occasion.* A second degree is, when the thing is forgotten for a longer or shorter time, even when there is occasion to remember it, *yet at last some incident brings it to mind without any search.* A third degree is, *when we cast about and search for what we would remember, and so at last find it out.* It is this last, I think, which Aristotle calls *reminiscence*, as distinguished from memory.

Reminiscence, therefore, includes *a will* to recollect something past, and a search for it. But here a difficulty occurs. It may be said, that what we will to remember we must conceive, as there can be no will without a conception of the thing willed. A will to remember a thing, therefore, seems to imply that we remember it already, and have no occasion to search for it. But this difficulty is easily removed. When we will to remember a thing, we must remember *something relating to it,* which gives us a relative conception of it; but we may, at the same time, have no conception what the thing is, but only what relation it bears to something else. Thus, I remember that a friend charged me with a commission to be executed at such a place; but I have forgotten what the commission

runs back from that moment to the moment of perception. That is to say, it runs over the intervening states of consciousness, called up by association. But to run over a number of states of consciousness, called up by association, is but another mode of saying that *we associate them ;* and in this case we associate them so rapidly and closely, that they run, as it were, into a single point of consciousness, to which the name of *memory* is assigned." *Analysis of the Human Mind,* Chap. X. — ED.

was. By applying my thought to what I remember concerning it, that it was given by such a person, upon such an occasion, in consequence of such a conversation, I am led, in a train of thought, to the very thing I had forgotten, and recollect distinctly what the commission was.

Aristotle says, that brutes have not reminiscence, and this I think is probable; but, says he, they have memory. It cannot, indeed, be doubted but they have something very like to it, and in some instances in a very great degree. A dog knows his master after long absence. A horse will trace back a road he has once gone, as accurately as a man; and this is the more strange, that the train of thought which he had in going must be reversed in his return. It is very like to some prodigious memories we read of, where a person, upon hearing a hundred names or unconnected words pronounced, can begin at the last, and go backwards to the first, without losing or misplacing one. Brutes certainly may learn much from experience, which seems to imply memory.

Yet I see no reason to think that brutes measure time as men do, by days, months, or years, or that they have any distinct knowledge of the interval between things which they remember, or of their distance from the present moment. If we could not record transactions according to their dates, human memory would be something very different from what it is, and perhaps resemble more the memory of brutes.

III. *Memory an Original and Ultimate Ground of Belief.*] Memory is an *original* faculty, given us by the Author of our being, of which we can give no account, but that we are so made.*

The knowledge which I have of things past by my

---

* From this most modern psychologists dissent. The Hartleian school resolve memory into the association of ideas. Dr. Brown, *Philosophy of the Human Mind*, Lect. XLI., into "a particular suggestion combined with a feeling of the relation of priority." Even Mr. Stewart, *Elements*, Part I. Chap. VII., resolves "the memory of *events*" into a conception and a judgment. — ED.

memory seems to me as unaccountable as an immediate knowledge would be of things to come,* and I can give no reason why I should have the one and not the other, but that such is the will of my Maker. I find in my mind a distinct conception and a firm belief of a series of past events; but how this is produced I know not. I call it memory, but this is only giving a name to it; it is not an account of its cause. I believe most firmly what I distinctly remember; but I can give no reason of this belief. It is the inspiration of the Almighty that gives me this understanding.

When I believe the truth of a mathematical axiom, or of a mathematical proposition, I see that it must be so. Every man who has the same conception of it sees the same. There is a necessary and an evident connection between the subject and the predicate of the proposition; and I have all the evidence to support my belief which I can possibly conceive.

When I believe that I washed my hands and face this morning, there appears no necessity in the truth of this proposition. It might be, or it might not be. A man may distinctly conceive it without believing it at all. How, then, do I come to believe it? I remember it distinctly. This is all I can say. This remembrance is an act of my mind. Is it impossible that this act should be, if the event had not happened? I confess I do not see any necessary connection between the one and the other. If any man can show such a necessary connection, then I think that belief which we have of what we remember will be fairly accounted for; but if this cannot be done, that belief is unaccountable, and we can say no more than that it is the result of our constitution.

---

* An *immediate* knowledge of *things to come* is equally a contradiction with an *immediate* knowledge of *things past*. See note on p. 211. But if, as Reid himself allows, memory depends upon certain enduring affections of the brain, determined by cognition, it seems a strange assertion, on this as on other accounts, that the possibility of a knowledge of the future is not more inconceivable than of a knowledge of the past. Maupertuis, however, has advanced a similar doctrine; and some, also, of the advocates of animal magnetism. — H.

Perhaps it may be said, that the experience we have had of the fidelity of memory is a good reason for relying upon its testimony. I deny not that this may be a reason to those who have had this experience, and who reflect upon it. But I believe there are few who ever thought of this reason, or who found any need of it. It must be some very rare occasion that leads a man to have recourse to it; and in those who have done so, the testimony of memory was believed *before* the experience of its fidelity, and that belief could not be *caused* by the experience which *came after it.*

We know some *abstract* truths, by comparing the terms of the proposition which expresses them, and perceiving some *necessary* relation or agreement between them. It is thus I know that two and three make five; that the diameters of a circle are all equal. Mr. Locke, having discovered this source of knowledge, too rashly concluded that *all* human knowledge might be derived from it; and in this he has been followed very generally, — by Mr. Hume in particular. But I apprehend that our knowledge of *the existence of things contingent* can never be traced to this source. I know that such a thing exists, or did exist. This knowledge cannot be derived from the perception of a necessary agreement between existence and the thing that exists, because there is no such necessary agreement; and therefore no such agreement can be perceived either immediately, or by a chain of reasoning. The thing does not exist necessarily, but by the will and power of him that made it; and there is no contradiction follows from supposing it not to exist. Whence I think it follows, that our knowledge of the existence of our own thoughts, of the existence of all the material objects about us, and of all past contingencies, must be derived, not from a perception of necessary relations or agreements, but from some other source.

Our Maker has provided other means for giving us the knowledge of these things, — means which perfectly answer their end, and produce the effect intended by them. But in what manner they do this is, I fear,

beyond our skill to explain. We know our own
thoughts, and the operations of our minds, by a power
which we call *consciousness :* but this is only giving a
name to this part of our frame. It does not explain
its fabric, nor how it produces in us an irresistible conviction of its informations. We *perceive* material
objects and their sensible qualities by our senses ; but
how they give us this information, and how they
produce our belief in it, we know not. We know
many past events by *memory;* but how it gives this
information, I believe, is inexplicable.

IV. *Physiological Theories to account for Memory.*]
The theory of the Peripatetics is expressed by Alexander Aphrodisiensis, one of the earliest Greek commentators on Aristotle, in these words, as they are translated
by Mr. Harris, in his *Hermes :* * — " Now what phansy
or imagination is, we may explain as follows :— We
may conceive to be formed within us, from the operations of our senses about sensible objects, some impression, as it were, or picture, in our original sensorium, being *a relic of that motion caused within us by the
external object;* a relic, which, when the external object is no longer present, remains, and is still preserved,
being as it were its image, and which, by being thus
preserved, becomes the cause of our having *memory:*
now such a sort of relict, and, as it were, impression,
they call *phansy* or *imagination."*
Another passage from Alcinous, *Of the Doctrines of
Plato,* Chap. IV., shows the agreement of the ancient
Platonists and Peripatetics in this theory : — " When
the form or type of things is imprinted on the mind by
the organs of the senses, and so imprinted as not to be
deleted by time, but preserved firm and lasting, its preservation is called *memory."*
Upon this principle Aristotle imputes the shortness
of memory in children to this cause, that their brain is
too moist and soft to *retain* impressions made upon it;

---

* Book III. Chap. IV.

and the defect of memory in old men he imputes, on the contrary, to the hardness and rigidity of the brain, which hinders its *receiving* any durable impression.*

This ancient theory of the cause of memory is defective in two respects:—*first*, if the cause assigned did really exist, it by no means accounts for the phenome-

---

* In this whole statement Reid is wrong. In the *first* place Aristotle did not impute the defect of memory in children and old persons to any constitution of the *brain;* for, in his doctrine, the *heart*, and not the brain, is the primary sensorium in which the impression is made. In the *second* place, the term *impression* (τύπος) is used by Aristotle in an analogical, not in a literal, signification. See Note K.—H.

For a full account of Aristotle's doctrine respecting memory and reminiscence, see Barth. St. Hilaire's translation of the *Parva Naturalia*, making the second volume of his *Psychologie d'Aristote.* In the preface, the translator, after reviewing what has been written in modern times on the subject of memory, comes to this conclusion: that Aristotle was the first who studied the faculty scientifically, and that his treatise, after the lapse of twenty-two centuries, is still the most complete and the most exact.

At the same time, we are not to suppose that physiological theories to *explain* and *account for* memory have never been entertained to which the strictures in the text apply. As, for example, to "the decaying sense" of Hobbes, *Leviathan*, Part I. Chap. II. Malebranche pushes his invention still farther.

His words are:—"For the explanation of memory it is necessary to remember what has been repeated so many times,—that all our different perceptions depend upon the changes that happen to those fibres that are in that part of the brain in which the soul more particularly resides. This being supposed, the nature of memory is explained; for even as the branches of a tree, which have continued some time bent in a certain form, still preserve an aptitude to be bent anew after the same manner, so the fibres of the brain, having once received certain impressions by the course of the animal spirits, and by the action of objects, retain a long time some facility to receive these same dispositions. Now the memory consists only in this faculty, since we think on the same things when the brain receives the same impressions."

A little farther on, he thinks to explain how the susceptibilities of the mind in this respect are affected by age:—"The most considerable differences that are found in a man's brain, during the whole course of his life, are in infancy, at his full strength, and in old age. The fibres of the brain in children are soft, flexible, and delicate; a riper age dries, hardens, and strengthens them; but in old age they become wholly inflexible, gross, and sometimes mingled with superfluous humors that the feeble heat of this age cannot dissipate. For as we see the fibres which compose the flesh harden by time, and that the flesh of a young partridge is without dispute more tender than that of an old one, so the fibres of the brain of a child or youth will be much more soft and delicate than those of persons more advanced in years." *Search after Truth*, Book II. Chap. V. and VI.; where there is more to the same purpose.—ED.

non; and, *secondly*, there is no evidence, nor even probability, that that cause exists.

It is probable, that in perception some impression is made upon the brain, as well as upon the organ and nerves, because all the nerves terminate in the brain, and because disorders and hurts of the brain are found to affect our powers of perception when the external organ and nerve are sound; but we are totally ignorant of the nature of this impression upon the brain: it can have no resemblance to the object perceived, nor does it in any degree account for that sensation and perception which are consequent upon it. These things have been argued in the second Essay, and shall now be taken for granted to prevent repetition.

If the impression upon the brain be insufficient to account for the perception of objects that are present, it can as little account for the memory of those that are past. So that if it were certain that the impressions made on the brain in perception remain as long as there is any memory of the object, all that could be inferred from this is, that, by the laws of nature, there is a connection established between that impression and the remembrance of that object. But how the impression contributes to this remembrance, we should be quite ignorant; it being impossible to discover how thought of any kind should be produced by an impression on the brain or upon any part of the body.

To say that this impression *is* memory is absurd, if understood literally. If it is only meant that it is the *cause* of memory, it ought to be shown how it produces this effect, otherwise memory remains as unaccountable as before. If a philosopher should undertake to account for the force of gunpowder in the discharge of a musket, and then tell us gravely that the cause of this phenomenon is the drawing of the trigger, we should not be much wiser by this account. As little are we instructed in the cause of memory, by being told that it is caused by a certain impression on the brain. For, supposing that impression on the brain were as necessary to memory as the drawing of the trigger is to the discharge of the musket, we are still as ignorant as we were how memory is produced; so that if the cause of memory assigned by this theory did really exist, it does not in any degree account for memory.

Another defect in this theory is, that there is no evidence nor probability that the cause assigned does exist; that is, that the impression made upon the brain in perception *remains after the object is removed.*

That impression, whatever be its nature, is caused by the impression made by the object upon the organ of sense and upon the nerve. Philosophers suppose, without any evidence, that when the object is removed, and the impression upon the organ and nerve ceases, the impression upon the brain continues and is permanent; that is, that when the cause is removed, the effect continues. The brain surely does not appear more fitted to retain an impression than the organ and nerve. But granting that the impression upon the brain continues after its cause is removed, its effects ought to continue while it continues; that is, the sensation and perception should be as *permanent* as the impression upon the brain which is supposed to be their cause. But here again the philosopher makes a *second* supposition, with as little evidence, but of a contrary nature, — to wit, that *while the cause remains, the effect ceases.* If this should be granted also, *a third* must be made, — that the *same cause,* which at first produced sensation and perception, does afterwards produce memory, — an operation essentially different both from sensation and perception. Again, a *fourth* supposition must be made, — that this cause, though it be permanent, *does not produce its effect at all times;* it must be like an inscription which is sometimes covered with rubbish, and on other occasions made legible: for the memory of things is often interrupted for a long time, and circumstances bring to our recollection what has been long forgot. After all, many things are remembered *which were never perceived by the senses,* being no objects of sense, and, therefore,

19 *

which could make no impression upon the brain by means of the senses.

Thus, when philosophers have piled one supposition upon another, as the giants piled the mountains in order to scale the heavens, all is to no purpose, memory remains unaccountable; and we know as little how we remember things past as how we are conscious of the present.

But here it is proper to observe, that although impressions upon the brain give no aid in accounting for memory, yet it is very probable, that, in the human frame, memory is dependent on some proper state or temperament of the brain.

Although the furniture of our memory bears no resemblance to any temperament of brain whatsoever, as, indeed, it is impossible it should, yet nature may have subjected us to this law, that a certain constitution or state of the brain is necessary to memory. That this is really the case, many well-known facts lead us to conclude. It is possible, that, by accurate observation, the proper means may be discovered of preserving that temperament of the brain which is favorable to memory, and of remedying the disorders of that temperament. This would be a very noble improvement of the medical art. But if it should ever be attained, it would give no aid to understand how one state of the brain assists memory, and another hurts it.

I know certainly that the impression made upon my hand by the prick of a pin occasions acute pain. But can any philosopher show how this cause produces the effect? The nature of the impression is here perfectly known; but it gives no help to understand how that impression affects the mind; and if we know as distinctly that state of the brain which causes memory, we should still be as ignorant as before how that state contributes to memory. We might have been so constituted, for any thing that I know, that the prick of a pin in the hand, instead of causing pain, should cause remembrance; nor would that constitution be more unaccountable than the present. The body and mind operate on each other, according to fixed laws of nature; and it is the business of a philosopher to discover those laws by observation and experiment. But when he has discovered them, he must rest in them as facts whose cause is inscrutable to the human understanding.*

* One of the most instructive cases of the influence of the state of the body, or more particularly of the nervous system, on the memory, is related by Coleridge in his *Biographia Literaria*, Chap. VI., which we shall give in his own words : — " A case of this kind occurred in a Catholic town in Germany, a year or two before my arrival at Göttingen, and had not then ceased to be a frequent subject of conversation. A young woman of four or five and twenty, who could neither read nor write, was seized with a nervous fever; during which, according to the asseverations of all the priests and monks of the neighbourhood, she became *possessed*, and, as it appeared, by a *learned* devil. She continued incessantly talking Latin, Greek, and Hebrew, in very pompous tones, and with most distinct enunciation. This possession was rendered most probable by the known fact that she was, or had been, a heretic. Voltaire humorously advises the Devil to decline all acquaintance with medical men; and it would have been more to his reputation if he had taken this advice in the present instance. The case had attracted the particular attention of a young physician, and, led by his statement, many eminent physiologists and psychologists visited the town, and cross-examined the case on the spot. Sheets full of her ravings were taken down from her own mouth, and were found to consist of sentences coherent and intelligible each for itself, but with little or no connection with each other. Of the Hebrew, a small portion only could be traced to the Bible; the remainder seemed to be in the rabbinical dialect. All trick or conspiracy was out of the question. Not only had the young woman ever been a harmless simple creature, but she was evidently laboring under a nervous fever. In the town in which she had been resident for many years, as a servant in different families, no solution presented itself. The young physician, however, determined to trace her past life step by step; for the patient herself was incapable of returning a rational answer. He, at length, succeeded in discovering the place where her parents had lived; travelled thither, found *them* dead, but an uncle surviving; and from him learnt that the patient had been charitably taken by an old Protestant pastor at nine years old, and had remained with him some years, even till the old man's death. Of this pastor the uncle knew nothing, but that he was a very good man. With great difficulty, and after much search, our young medical philosopher discovered a niece of the pastor's, who had lived with him as his housekeeper, and had inherited his effects. She remembered the girl; related, that her venerable uncle had been too indulgent, and could not bear to hear the girl scolded; that she was willing to have kept her, but that, after her patron's death, the girl herself refused to stay. Anxious inquiries were then, of course, made concerning the pastor's habits, and the solution of the phenomenon was soon obtained. For it appeared, that it had been the old man's custom for years to walk up and down a passage of his house, into which the kitchen door opened, and to read to himself, with a loud voice, out of his favorite books. A considerable number of these were still in the niece's possession. She

V. *Hume's View of Memory.*] Mr. Hume saw farther into the consequences of the common system concerning *ideas*, than any author had done before him.
He saw the absurdity of making every object of thought
double, and splitting it into a *remote* object, which has
a separate and permanent existence, and an *immediate*
object, called an *idea*, or *impression*, which is an image
of the former, and has no existence but when we are
conscious of it. According to this system, we have
no intercourse with the external world but by means of
the internal world of ideas, which *represents* the other
to the mind.

He saw it was necessary to reject one of these worlds
as a fiction, and the question was, which should be rejected; — whether all mankind, learned and unlearned,
had feigned the existence of the external world without
good reason, or whether philosophers had feigned the
internal world of ideas, in order to account for the intercourse of the mind with the external. Mr. Hume
adopted the first of these opinions, and employed his
reason and eloquence in support of it.

According to his system, therefore, impressions and

---

added that he was a very learned man, and a great Hebraist. Among the
books were found a collection of rabbinical writings, together with several
of the Greek and Latin fathers; and the physician succeeded in identify-
ing so many passages with those taken down at the young woman's bed-
side, that no doubt could remain in any rational mind concerning the true
origin of the impressions made on her nervous system."

From the foregoing the author deduces an important and startling inference: — " This authenticated case furnishes both proof and instance that
relics of sensation may exist, for an indefinite time, *in a latent state*, in the
very same order in which they were originally impressed; and as we cannot rationally suppose the feverish state of the brain to act in any other
way than as a stimulus, this fact (and it would not be difficult to adduce
several of the same kind) contributes to make it even probable that all
thoughts are in themselves *imperishable;* and that if the intelligent faculty
should be rendered more comprehensive, it would require only a different
and apportioned organization, — *the body celestial* instead of *the body terrestrial,* — to bring before every human soul *the collective experience of its whole
past existence.* And this, — this, perchance, is the dread *book of judgment,*
in whose mysterious hieroglyphics every idle word is recorded !"

I would add that Dr. Abercrombie, in his *Inquiries concerning the Intellectual Powers,* is naturally led by his professional experience to dwell more
than is usual with psychologists on memory as affected by peculiar states
of the organization. — ED.

ideas in his own mind are the only things a man can know, or can conceive. Nor are these ideas *representatives*, as they were in the old system. There is nothing else in nature, or at least within the reach of our faculties, to be represented. What the vulgar call the perception of an external object, is nothing but a strong impression upon the mind. What we call the remembrance of a past event, is nothing but a present impression or idea, weaker than the former. And what we call imagination is still a present idea, but weaker than that of memory.

That I may not do him injustice, these are his words in his *Treatise of Human Nature*, Book I. Part I. Sect. III.: — " We find by experience, that, when any impression has been present with the mind, it again makes its appearance there as an idea; and this it may do after two different ways: either when in its new appearance it retains a considerable degree of its first vivacity, and is somewhat intermediate betwixt an impression and an idea; or when it entirely loses that vivacity, and is a perfect idea. The faculty by which we repeat our impressions in the first manner is called the *memory*, and the other the *imagination*."

Upon this account of memory and imagination, I shall make some remarks.

First, I wish to know what we are here to understand by experience. It is said, we find all this by experience; and I conceive nothing can be meant by this experience but memory. Not that memory which our author defines, but memory in the common acceptation of the word. He maintains that memory is nothing but a present idea or impression. But, in defining what he takes memory to be, he takes for granted that kind of memory which he rejects. For can we find by experience, that an impression, after its first appearance to the mind, makes a second, and a third, with different degrees of strength and vivacity, if we have not so distinct a remembrance of its first appearance as enables us to know it upon its second and third, notwithstanding that, in the interval, it has undergone a very considerable change? All experience *supposes* memory; and there can be no such thing as experience, without trusting to our own memory, or that of others: so that it appears from Mr. Hume's account of this matter, that he found himself to have that kind of memory which he acknowledges and defines, by exercising that kind which he rejects.

Secondly, What is it we find by experience or memory? It is, "that, when an impression has been present with the mind, it *again* makes its appearance there as an idea, and that after two different ways."

If experience informs us of this, it certainly deceives us; for the thing is impossible, and the author shows it to be so. Impressions and ideas are fleeting, perishable things, which have no existence but when we are conscious of them. If an impression could make a second and a third appearance to the mind, it must have a continued existence during the interval of these appearances, which Mr. Hume acknowledges to be a gross absurdity. It seems, then, that we find, by experience, a thing which is impossible. We are imposed upon by our experience, and made to believe contradictions.

Perhaps it may be said, that these different appearances of the impression are not to be understood literally, but figuratively; that the impression is personified, and made to appear at different times, and in different habits, when no more is meant but that an impression appears at one time; afterwards a thing of a middle nature, between an impression and an idea, which we call memory; and last of all a perfect idea, which we call imagination: that this figurative meaning agrees best with the last sentence of the period, where we are told that memory and imagination are faculties, whereby we repeat our impressions in a more or less lively manner. To repeat an impression is a figurative way of speaking, which signifies making a new impression *similar* to the former.

If, to avoid the absurdity implied in the literal meaning, we understand the philosopher in this figurative one, then his definitions of memory and imagination, when stripped of the figurative dress, will amount to this, — that memory is the faculty of making a weak impression, and imagination the faculty of making an impression still weaker, after a corresponding strong one. These definitions of memory and imagination labor under two defects: *first,* that they convey no notion of the thing defined; and, *secondly,* that they may be applied to things of a quite different nature from those that are defined.

When we are said to have a faculty of making a weak impression after a corresponding strong one, it would not be easy to conjecture that this faculty is memory. Suppose a man strikes his head smartly against the wall, this is an impression; now he has a faculty by which he can repeat this impression with less force, so as not to hurt him; this, by Mr. Hume's account, must be memory. He has a faculty by which he can just touch the wall with his head, so that the impression entirely loses its vivacity. This surely must be imagination; at least it comes as near to the definition given of it by Mr. Hume as any thing I can conceive.

Thirdly, We may observe, that, when we are told that we have a faculty of repeating our impressions in a more or less lively manner, this implies that *we* are the efficient causes of our ideas of memory and imagination; but this contradicts what the author says a little before, where he proves, by what he calls a convincing argument, that *impressions* are the cause of their corresponding ideas. The argument that proves this had need, indeed, to be very convincing, whether we make the idea to be a second appearance of the impression, or a new impression similar to the former. If the first be true, then the impression is the cause of itself. If the second, then the impression after it has gone, and has no existence, produces the idea.*

---

* To the works already cited as treating of memory, we may add Wolf's *Psychologia Empirica,* Part I. Sect. II. Chap. V.; Beattie's *Dissertations*

CHAPTER II.

THE NATURE AND ORIGIN OF OUR NOTION OF DURATION.

I. *Our Notions of Duration, Extension, and Number.*]
From the principles laid down in the preceding chapter, I think it appears that our notion of duration, as well as our belief of it, is got by the faculty of memory. It is essential to every thing remembered that it be something which is past; and we cannot conceive a thing to be past, without conceiving some duration, more or less, between it and the present. As soon, therefore, as we remember any thing, we must have both a notion and a belief of duration. It is necessarily suggested by every operation of our memory; and to that faculty it ought to be ascribed. This is therefore a proper place to consider what is known concerning it.

Duration, extension, and *number* are the measures of all things subject to mensuration. When we apply them to *finite* things which are measured by them, they seem of all things to be the most distinctly conceived, and most within the reach of human understanding.

Extension, having three dimensions, has an endless variety of modifications, capable of being accurately defined; and their various relations furnish the human mind with its most ample field of demonstrative reasoning. *Duration,* having only one dimension, has fewer modifications; but these are clearly understood; and their relations admit of measure, proportion, and demonstrative reasoning.

Number is called *discrete* quantity, because it is compounded of units, which are all equal and similar, and

---

Moral and Critical, the first being *Of Memory and Imagination;* Stewart's *Elements*, who has given a long chapter to this subject; and Feinagle's *New Art of Memory*, to which is prefixed some account of the principal systems of Artificial Memory. — ED.

it can only be divided into units. This is true, in some
sense, even of fractions of unity, to which we now
commonly give the name of number. For in every
fractional number the unit is supposed to be subdivided
into a certain number of equal parts, which are the
units of that denomination, and the fractions of that
denomination are only divisible into units of the same
denomination. Duration and extension are not discrete, but *continued* quantity. They consist of parts
perfectly similar, *but divisible without end.*

In order to aid our conception of the magnitude and
proportions of the various intervals of duration, we
find it necessary to give a name to some known portion
of it, such as *an hour, a day, a year.* These we consider as units, and by the number of them contained in
a larger interval, we form a distinct conception of its
magnitude. A similar expedient we find necessary to
give us a distinct conception of the magnitudes and
proportions of things extended. Thus, number is found
necessary, as a common measure of extension and duration. But this, perhaps, is owing to the weakness of
our understanding. It has even been discovered by the
sagacity of mathematicians, that this expedient does
not in all cases answer its intention. For there are
proportions of continued quantity, which cannot be
perfectly expressed by numbers; such as that between the diagonal and side of a square, and many
others.

The parts of duration have to other parts of it the
relations of prior and posterior, and to the present they
have the relations of past and future. The notion of
past is immediately suggested by memory, as has been
before observed. And when we have got the notions
of present and past, and of prior and posterior, we can
from these frame a notion of the future; for the future
is that which is posterior to the present. Nearness and
distance are relations equally applicable to time and to
place. Distance in time, and distance in place, are
things so different in their nature, and so like in their
relation, that it is difficult to determine whether the

20

name of distance is applied to both in the same or an analogical sense.

The extension of bodies, which we perceive by our senses, leads us necessarily to the conception and belief of a space which remains immovable when the body is removed. And the duration of events which we remember leads us necessarily to the conception and belief of a duration, which would have gone on uniformly, though the event had never happened.* Without space there can be nothing that is extended. And without time there can be nothing that has duration. This I think undeniable. And yet we find that extension and duration are not more clear and intelligible than space and time are dark and difficult objects of contemplation.

As there must be space wherever any thing extended does or can exist, and time when there is or can be any thing that has duration, we can set no bounds to either, even in our imagination. They defy all limitation. The one swells in our conception to *immensity*, the other to *eternity*.

---

* If *space* and *time* be *necessary generalizations* from experience, this is contrary to Reid's own doctrine, that experience can give us no *necessary* knowledge If, again, they be *necessary and original notions*, the account of their origin here given is incorrect. It should have been said that experience is not the *source* of their existence, but only the *occasion* of their manifestation. On this subject, see, *instar omnium*, Cousin on Locke, in his *Cours de Philosophie*, Tome II. Leçons XVII., XVIII. This admirable work has been well translated into English by an American philosopher, Mr. Henry; but the eloquence and precision of the author can only be properly appreciated by those who study the work in the original language. The reader may, however, consult likewise Stewart's *Philosophical Essays*, Essay II. Chap. II.; and Royer-Collard's *Fragments*, IX. and X. These authors, from their more limited acquaintance with the speculations of the German philosophers, are, however, less on a level with the problem. — H.

There can be no doubt that Reid held space and time to be " necessary and original notions." His language may sometimes be inexact; but we are not aware that he ever makes experience "the source" of our notion of time; when he speaks of experience as necessary to our having this notion, he has in view the *chronological*, and not the *logical*, order of our knowledge. Farther on he says more explicitly, — " I know of no ideas or notions that have a better claim to be accounted *simple and original*, than those of *space* and *time*." And, again, he says of *time*, — " As it is one of the simplest objects of thought, the conception of it must be *purely the effect of our constitution*, and given us by some *original power* of the mind." — ED.

An eternity past is an object which we cannot comprehend; but a beginning of time, unless we take it in a figurative - sense, is a contradiction. By a common figure of speech, we give the name of time to those motions and revolutions by which we measure it, such as days and years. We can conceive a beginning of these sensible measures of time, and say that there was a time when they were not, a time undistinguished by any motion or change; but to say that there was a time before all time is a contradiction.

All limited duration is comprehended in time, and all limited extension in space. These, in their capacious womb, contain all finite existences, but are contained by none. Created things have their particular place in space, and their particular place in time; *but time is everywhere, and space at all times.* They embrace each the other, and have that mysterious union which the schoolmen conceive between soul and body. The whole of each is in every part of the other.

We are at a loss to what *category*, or class of things, we ought to refer them. They are not beings, but rather the *receptacles* of every created being, without which it could not have had the possibility of existence. Philosophers have endeavoured to reduce all the objects of human thought to these three classes, *substances*, *modes*, and *relations*. To which of them shall we refer time, space, and number, the most common objects of thought?

Sir Isaac Newton thought that the Deity, by existing everywhere, and at all times, *constitutes* time and space, immensity and eternity. This probably suggested to his great friend, Dr. Clarke, what he calls the argument *a priori* for the existence of an immense and eternal Being. Space and time, he thought, are only abstract or partial conceptions of an immensity and eternity which force themselves upon our belief. And as immensity and eternity are not substances, they must be the attributes of a Being who is necessarily immense and eternal. These are the speculations of men of superior genius. But whether they be as solid as they are sublime, or whether they be the wanderings of imagination in a region beyond the limits of human understanding, I am unable to determine.

The schoolmen made eternity to be a *nunc stans*, — that is, a moment of time that stands still. This was to put a spoke into the wheel of time, and might give satisfaction to those who are to be satisfied by words without meaning. But I can as easily believe a circle to be a square, as time to stand still.

Such paradoxes and riddles, if I may so call them, men are involuntarily led into when they reason about time and space, and attempt to comprehend their nature. They are probably things of which the human faculties give an imperfect and inadequate conception. Hence difficulties arise which we in vain attempt to overcome, and doubts which wé are unable to resolve. Perhaps some faculty which we possess not is necessary to remove the darkness which hangs over them, and makes us so apt to bewilder ourselves when we reason about them.

II. *Locke's Account of the Origin of Ideas.*] It was a very laudable attempt of Mr. Locke "to inquire into the original of those ideas, notions, or whatever else you please to call them, which a man observes, and is conscious to himself he has in his mind, and the ways whereby the understanding comes to be furnished with them." No man was better qualified for this investigation; and I believe no man ever engaged in it with a more sincere love of truth. His success, though great, would, I apprehend, have been greater, if he had not too early formed a system or hypothesis upon this subject, without all the caution and patient induction which are necessary in drawing general conclusions from facts.

The sum of his doctrine I take to be this: — That all our ideas or notions may be reduced to two classes, the *simple* and the *complex;* that the *simple* are purely the work of nature, the understanding being merely passive in receiving them, that they are all suggested by two powers of the mind, — to wit, *sensation* and *reflection*, — and that they are the materials of all our knowledge; that the other class, consisting of *complex* ideas, are formed by the understanding itself, which, being once stored with simple ideas of sensation and reflection, has the power to repeat, to'compare, and to combine them even to an almost infinite variety, and so can make at pleasure new complex ideas; but that it is not in the power of the most exalted wit, or enlarged understanding, by any quickness or variety of thought, to invent or frame one new simple idea in the mind, not taken in by the two ways before mentioned. As our power over the material world reaches only to the compounding, dividing, and putting together, in various forms, the matter which God has made, but reaches not to the production or annihilation of a single atom, so we may compound, compare, and abstract the original and simple ideas which nature has given us, but are unable to fashion in our understanding any simple idea, not received in by our senses from external objects, or by reflection from the operations of our own mind about them.

Mr. Locke says, that by *reflection* he would be understood to mean " the notice which the mind takes of its own operations, and the manner of them." This, I think, we commonly call *consciousness;* from which, indeed, we derive all the notions we have of the operations of our own minds ; and he often speaks of the operations of our own minds as the only objects of reflection. When reflection is taken in this confined sense, to say that all our ideas are ideas either of sensation or reflection is to say that every thing we can conceive is either some object of sense, or some operation of our own minds; which is far from being true.

But the word *reflection* is commonly used in a much more extensive sense ; it is applied to many operations of the mind with more propriety than to that of consciousness. We reflect, when we remember or call to mind what is past, and survey it with attention. We reflect, when we define, when we distinguish, when

20 *

we judge, when we reason, whether about things material or intellectual. When reflection is taken in this sense, which is more common, and therefore more proper,* than the sense which Mr. Locke has put upon it, it may be justly said to be the only source of all our *distinct and accurate* notions of things. For, although our first notions of material things are got by the external senses, and our first notions of the operations of our own minds by consciousness, these first notions are neither simple nor clear. Our senses and our consciousness are continually shifting from one object to another; their operations are transient and momentary, and leave no distinct notion of their objects, until they are recalled by memory, examined with attention, and compared with other things.

This reflection is not one power of the mind; it comprehends many; such as recollection, attention, distinguishing, comparing, judging. By these powers our minds are furnished, not only with many simple and original notions, but with all our notions which are accurate and well defined, and which alone are the proper materials of reasoning. Many of these are neither notions of the objects of sense, nor of the operations of our own minds, and therefore neither ideas of sensation nor of reflection, in the sense that Mr. Locke gives to reflection. But if any one chooses to call them ideas of reflection, taking the word in the more common and proper sense, I have no objection.

Mr. Locke seems to me to have used the word *reflection* sometimes in that limited sense which he has given to it in the definition before mentioned, and sometimes to have fallen unawares into the common sense of the word; and by this ambiguity his account of the origin of our ideas is darkened and perplexed.

---

* This is not correct; and the employment of *reflection* in another meaning than that of ἐπιστροφὴ πρὸς ἑαυτό, — the reflex knowledge or consciousness which the mind has of its own affections, — is wholly a secondary and less proper signification. See Note I. — H.

On the use of the term *reflection*, see page 25 of this volume. — Ed.

III. *Strictures on Locke's Theory of the Origin of the Idea of Duration.*] Having premised these things in general of Mr. Locke's theory of the origin of our ideas or notions, I proceed to some observations on his account of the idea of duration.

" Reflection," he says, " upon the train of ideas, which appear one after another in our minds, is that which furnishes us with the idea of *succession :* and the distance between any two parts of that succession is that we call *duration.*"

If it be meant that the idea of succession is prior to that of duration, either in time or in the order of nature, this, I think, is impossible, because succession, as Dr. Price justly observes, *presupposes* duration, and can in no sense be prior to it ; and therefore it would be more proper to derive the idea of succession from that of duration.

But how do we *get* the idea of succession? It is, says he, by reflecting " upon the train of ideas, which appear one after another in our minds." Reflecting upon the train of ideas can be nothing but *remembering* it, and giving attention to what our memory testifies concerning it ; for if we did not remember it, we could not have a thought about it. So that it is evident that this reflection includes *remembrance*, without which there could be no reflection on what is past, and consequently no idea of succession.

It may also be observed, that, if we speak strictly and philosophically, no kind of *succession* can be an object either of the senses or of consciousness ; because the operations of both are confined to the present point of time, and there can be no succession in a point of time ; and on that account the motion of a body, which is a successive change of place, could not be observed by the senses alone without the aid of memory.

As this observation seems to contradict the common sense and common language of mankind, when they affirm that they *see* a body move, and hold motion to be an object of the senses, it is proper to take notice, that this contradiction between the philosopher and the vulgar is apparent only, and not real. It arises from this, that philosophers and the vulgar differ in the meaning they put upon what is called *the present time*, and are thereby led to make a different limit between sense and memory.

Philosophers give the name of *present* to that indivisible point of time which divides the future from the past: but the vulgar find it more convenient, in the affairs of life, to give the name of *present* to a portion of time which extends more or less, according to circumstances, into the past or the future. Hence we say, the present hour, the present year, the present century, though one point only of these periods can be present in the philosophical sense.

It has been observed by grammarians, that the present tense in verbs is not confined to an indivisible point of time, but is so far extended as to have a beginning, a middle, and an end; and that, in the most copious and accurate languages, these different parts of the present are distinguished by different forms of the verb.

As the purposes of conversation make it convenient to extend what is called the present, the same reason leads men to extend the province of sense, and to carry its limit as far back as they carry the present. Thus a man may say, I saw such a person just now. It would be ridiculous to find fault with this way of speaking, because it is authorized by custom, and has a distinct meaning: but if we speak philosophically, the senses do not testify what we *saw*, but only what we *see;* what I saw last moment I consider as the testimony of sense, though it is now only the testimony of memory. There is no necessity in common life of dividing accurately the provinces of sense and of memory; and therefore we assign to sense, not an indivisible point of time, but that small portion of time which we call the present, which has a beginning, a middle, and an end.

Hence it is easy to see, that, though in common language we speak with perfect propriety and truth when

we say that we *see* a body move, and that motion
is an object of sense, yet when as philosophers we distinguish accurately the province of sense from that of
memory, we can no more see what is past, though but
a moment ago, than we can remember what is present;
so that, speaking philosophically, it is only by the *aid
of memory* that we discern motion, or any succession
whatsoever. We see the present place of the body;
we remember the successive advance it made to that
place : the first can, then, only give us a conception of
motion, when joined to the last.

Having considered the account given by Mr. Locke ✗
of the idea of *succession*, we shall next consider how,
from the idea of succession, he derives the idea of *duration*.

" The distance," he says, " between any two parts of
that succession, or between the appearance of any two
ideas in our minds, is that we call duration."

To conceive this the more distinctly, let us call the
distance between an idea and that which immediately
succeeds it, one element of duration; the distance between an idea and the second that succeeds it, two
elements, and so on: if ten such elements make duration, then one must make duration, otherwise duration
must be made up of parts that have no duration, which
is impossible. For, suppose a succession of as many
ideas as you please, if none of these ideas have duration, nor any interval of duration be between one and
another, then it is perfectly evident there can be no interval of duration between the first and the last, how
great soever their number be. I conclude, therefore,
that there must be duration in every single interval or
element of which the whole duration is made up.
Nothing, indeed, is more certain, than that every elementary part of duration must have duration, as every
elementary part of extension must have extension.

Now it must be observed, that in these elements of
duration, or single intervals of successive ideas, there
is no succession of ideas ; yet we must conceive them
to have duration: whence we may conclude with cer-

tainty, that there is a conception of duration where there is no succession of ideas in the mind.

We may *measure* duration by the succession of thoughts in the mind, as we measure length by inches or feet: but the *notion* or *idea* of duration must be antecedent to the mensuration of it, as the notion of length is antecedent to its being measured.

Mr. Locke draws some conclusions from his account of the idea of duration, which may serve as a touchstone to discover how far it is genuine.

One is, that if it were possible for a waking man to keep only one idea in his mind without variation, or the succession of others, he would have no perception of duration at all; and the moment he began to have this idea would seem to have no distance from the moment he ceased to have it. Now, that one idea should seem to have no duration, and that a multiplication of that *no duration* should seem to have duration, appears to me as impossible, as that the multiplication of nothing should produce something.

Another conclusion which the author draws from this theory is, that the same period of duration appears long to us, when the succession of ideas in our mind is quick, and short when the succession is slow.

There can be no doubt that the same length of duration appears in some circumstances much longer than in others. The time appears long when a man is impatient under any pain or distress, or when he is eager in the expectation of some happiness: on the other hand, when he is pleased and happy in agreeable conversation, or delighted with a variety of agreeable objects that strike his senses or his imagination, time flies away, and appears short. According to Mr. Locke's theory, in the first of these cases the succession of ideas is very quick, and in the last very slow. I am rather inclined to think that the very contrary is the truth. When a man is racked with pain, or with expectation, he can hardly think of any thing but his distress; and the more his mind is occupied by that *sole* object, the longer the time appears. On the other hand, when he

is entertained with cheerful music, with lively conversation, and brisk sallies of wit, there seems to be the
quickest succession of ideas, but the time appears *shortest.* I have heard a military officer, a man of candor
and observation, say, that the time he was engaged in
hot action always appeared to him much shorter than
it really was. Yet I think it cannot be supposed, that
the succession of ideas was then slower than usual.*

If the idea of duration were got merely by the succession of ideas in our minds, that succession must to
ourselves appear equally quick at all times, because the
only measure of duration would be the *number* of succeeding ideas; but I believe every man capable of reflection will be sensible, that at one time his thoughts
come slowly and heavily, and at another time have a
much quicker and livelier motion.

I know of no ideas or notions that have a better
claim to be accounted *simple* and *original*, than those
of space and time. It is essential both to space and
time to be made up of parts, but every part is similar
to the whole, and of the same nature. Different parts
of space, as it has three dimensions, may differ both in
figure and in *magnitude;* but time having only one
dimension, its parts can differ only in *magnitude;* and
as it is one of the simplest objects of thought, the conception of it must be purely the effect of our constitution, and given us by some *original power of the
mind.*

The sense of seeing, by itself, gives us the conception
and belief of only two dimensions of extension, but the
sense of touch discovers three; and reason, from the
contemplation of finite extended things, leads us necessarily to the belief of an immensity that contains them.
In like manner, memory gives us the conception and
belief of finite intervals of duration. From the contemplation of these, reason leads us necessarily to the
belief of an eternity, which comprehends all things

* In travelling, the time seems very short while passing; very long in
retrospect. The cause is obvious. — H.

that have a beginning and end. Our conceptions, both of space and time, are probably partial and inadequate,* and therefore we are apt to lose ourselves, and to be embarrassed in our reasonings about them.†

---

* They are not *probably*, but *necessarily*, partial and inadequate. For we are unable positively to conceive *time* or *space* either as infinite (i. e. without limits) or as not infinite (i. e. as limited). — H.

† Cousin's account of the origin of the idea of time is precise and luminous. "Here, again," he tells us, "we are to distinguish the order of the acquisition of our ideas from their logical order. In the *logical* order of ideas, the idea of any succession of events presupposes that of time. There could not be any succession but upon condition of a continuous duration, to the different points of which the several members of the succession may be attached. Take away the continuity of time, and you take away the possibility of the succession of the events ; just as, the continuity of space being taken away, the possibility of the juxtaposition and coexistence of bodies is destroyed.

"But in the *chronological* order, on the contrary, it is the idea of a succession of events which precedes the idea of time as including them. I do not mean to say in regard to time, any more than in regard to space, that we have a clear, distinct, and complete idea of a succession, and that then the idea of time, as including this series or succession, springs up. I merely say, it is clearly necessary that we should have a perception of some events, in order to conceive that these events are in time, [and in order along with, and by occasion of, those events to have the idea of time awakened in the mind]. Time is the place of events, just as space is the place of bodies ; whoever had no idea of any event [no perception or consciousness of any succession] would have no idea of time. If, then, the logical condition of the idea of succession lies in the idea of time, the chronological condition of the idea of time is the idea of succession.

"Now every idea of *succession* is undeniably an acquisition of experience. It remains to ascertain of what experience. Is it inward or outward experience? The first idea of succession, — is it given in the spectacle of outward events, or in the consciousness of the events that pass within us?

"Take a succession of outward events. In order that these events may be successive, it is necessary that there should be a first event, a second, a third, &c. But if, when you see the second event, you do not remember the first, it would not be the second ; there could be for you no succession. You would always remain fixed at the first event, which would not even have the character of first to you, because there would be no second. The intervention of *memory* is necessary, then, in order to conceive of any succession whatever. Now memory has for its objects nothing external ; it relates not to things, but to ourselves ; we have no memory but of ourselves. When we say, we remember such a person, we remember such a place, — it means nothing more than that we remember to have been seeing such a place, or we remember to have been hearing or seeing such a person. There is no memory but of ourselves, because there is no memory but where there is consciousness. If consciousness, then, is the condition of memory, and memory the condition of time, it follows that the first succession is given us in ourselves, in consciousness, in the proper

CHAPTER III.

OF THE NATURE AND ORIGIN OF OUR NOTION OF PERSONAL IDENTITY.

I. *Of Identity in General.*] The conviction which every man has of his identity, as far back as his memory reaches, needs no aid of philosophy to strengthen it ; and no philosophy can weaken it, without first producing some degree of insanity.

The philosopher, however, may very properly consider this conviction as a phenomenon of human nature worthy of his attention. If he can discover its cause, an addition is made to his stock of knowledge ; if not, it must be held as a part of our original constitution, or an effect of that constitution produced in a manner unknown to us.

That we may form as distinct a notion as we are able of this phenomenon of the human mind, it is proper to consider what is meant by identity in general, what by our own personal identity, and how we are led into that invincible belief and conviction which every man has of his own personal identity, as far as his memory reaches.

Identity in general I take to be a relation between a thing which is known to exist at one time, and a thing which is known to have existed at another time.* If you ask whether they are one and the same, or two different things, every man of common sense under-

---

objects and phenomena of consciousness, — in our thoughts, in our ideas."
— *Elements of Psychology*, Chap. III.

Compare Kant, *Critic of Pure Reason*, Transcendental Æsthetic, Part I. Sect. II. ; Whewell's *Philosophy of the Inductive Sciences*, Part I. Book II. Chap. VI. - IX.; Ballantyne's *Examination of the Human Mind*, Chap. I. Sect. II.; Mill's *Analysis of the Human Mind*, Chap. XIV. Sect. V. — Ed.

* Identity is a relation between our cognitions of a thing, and not between things themselves. It would, therefore, have been better in this sentence to have said, " a relation between a thing *as known* to exist at one time, and a thing *as known* to exist at another time." — H.

21

stands the meaning of your question perfectly. Whence we may infer with certainty, that every man of common sense has a clear and distinct notion of identity.

If you ask a definition of identity, I confess I can give none; it is too simple a notion to admit of logical definition: I can say it is a relation, but I cannot find words to express the specific difference between this and other relations, though I am in no danger of confounding it with any other. I can say that diversity is a contrary relation, and that similitude and dissimilitude are another couple of contrary relations, which every man easily distinguishes in his conception from identity and diversity.

I see evidently that identity supposes *an uninterrupted continuance of existence.* That which has ceased to exist cannot be the same with that which afterwards begins to exist; for this would be to suppose a being to exist after it ceased to exist, and to have had existence before it was produced, which are manifest contradictions. Continued uninterrupted existence is therefore necessarily implied in identity. Hence we may infer, that identity cannot, in its proper sense, be applied to our pains, our pleasures, our thoughts, or any operation of our minds. The pain felt this day is not the same individual pain which I felt yesterday, though they may be *similar* in kind and degree, and have the same cause. The same may be said of every feeling, and of every operation of mind. They are all successive in their nature, like time itself, no two moments of which can be the same moment. It is otherwise with the parts of absolute space. They always are, and were, and will be the same. So far, I think, we proceed upon clear ground in fixing the notion of identity in general.

II. *Nature and Origin of our Idea of Personal Identity.*] It is perhaps more difficult to ascertain with precision the meaning of *personality;* but it is not necessary in the present subject: it is sufficient for our purpose to observe, that all mankind place their personality in something that *cannot be divided, or consist of parts.* A part of a person is a manifest absurdity. When a man loses his estate, his health, his strength, he is still the same person, and has lost nothing of his personality. If he has a leg or an arm cut off, he is the same person he was before. The amputated member is no part of his person, otherwise it would have a right to a part of his estate, and be liable for a part of his engagements. It would be entitled to a share of his merit and demerit, which is manifestly absurd. A person is something indivisible, and is what Leibnitz calls a *monad.*

My personal identity, therefore, implies the continued existence of that indivisible thing which I call *myself.* Whatever this self may be, it is something which thinks, and deliberates, and resolves, and acts, and suffers. I am not thought, I am not action, I am not feeling; I am something that thinks, and acts, and suffers. My thoughts, and actions, and feelings, change every moment; they have no continued, but a successive, existence; but that *self,* or *I,* to which they belong, is permanent, and has the same relation to all the succeeding thoughts, actions, and feelings which I call mine.

Such are the notions that I have of my personal identity. But perhaps it may be said, this may all be fancy without reality. How do you know, — what evidence have you, — that there is such a permanent self which has a claim to all the thoughts, actions, and feelings which you call yours?

To this I answer, that the proper evidence I have of all this is *remembrance.* I remember that twenty years ago I conversed with such a person; I remember several things that passed in that conversation : my memory testifies, not only that this was done, but that it was done by me who now remember it. If it was done by me, I must have existed at that time, and continued to exist from that time to the present: if the identical person whom I call myself had not a part in that conversation, my memory is fallacious; it gives a distinct and positive testimony of what is not true. Every man in his senses believes what he distinctly remembers, and every thing he remembers convinces him that he existed at the time remembered.

Although memory gives the most irresistible evidence of my being the identical person that did such a thing, at such a time, I may have other good evidence of things which befell me, and which I do not remember: I know who bare me, and suckled me, but I do not remember these events.

It may here be observed, (though the observation would have been unnecessary, if some great philosophers had not contradicted it,) that it is not my remembering any action of mine that *makes* me to be the person who did it. This remembrance makes me to *know* assuredly that I did it; *but I might have done it, though I did not remember it.* That relation to me, which is expressed by saying that *I did it,* would be the same, though I had not the least remembrance of it. To say that my remembering that I did such a thing, or, as some choose to express it, my being conscious that I did it, makes me to have done it, appears to me as great an absurdity as it would be to say, that my belief that the world was created made it to be created.

When we pass judgment on the identity of other persons than ourselves, we proceed upon other grounds, and determine from a variety of circumstances, which sometimes produce the firmest assurance, and sometimes leave room for doubt. The identity of persons has often furnished matter of serious litigation before tribunals of justice. But no man of a sound mind ever doubted of his own identity, as far as he distinctly remembered.

The identity of a person is a perfect identity: wherever it is real, it admits of no degrees; and it is impossible that a person should be in part the same, and in part different; because a person is a *monad,* and is not divisible into parts. The evidence of identity in other persons than ourselves does indeed admit of all degrees, from what we account certainty, to the least degree of probability. But still it is true, that the same person is perfectly the same, and cannot be so in part, or in some degree only.

For this cause, I have first considered personal identity, as that which is perfect in its kind, and the natural measure of that which is imperfect.

We probably at first derive our notion of identity from that natural conviction which every man has from the dawn of reason of *his own* identity and continued existence. The operations of our minds are all successive, and have no continued existence. But the thinking being has a continued existence, and we have an invincible belief, that it remains the same when all its thoughts and operations change.

Our judgments of the identity of objects of sense seem to be formed much upon the same grounds as our judgments of the identity of *other persons* than ourselves. Wherever we observe great *similarity*, we are apt to presume identity, if no reason appears to the contrary. Two objects ever so like, when they are perceived at the same time, cannot be the same; but if they are presented to our senses at different times, we are apt to think them the same, merely from their similarity.

Whether this be a natural prejudice, or from whatever cause it proceeds, it certainly appears in children from infancy; and when we grow up, it is confirmed in most instances by experience: for we rarely find two individuals of the same species that are not distinguishable by obvious differences. A man challenges a thief whom he finds in possession of his horse or his watch, only on similarity. When the watchmaker swears that he sold this watch to such a person, his testimony is grounded on similarity. The testimony of witnesses to the identity of a person is commonly grounded on no other evidence.

Thus it appears, that the evidence we have of our own identity, as far back as we remember, is totally of a different kind from the evidence we have of the identity of other persons, or of objects of sense. The first is grounded on *memory*, and gives undoubted certainty.

21

The last is grounded on *similarity*, and on other circumstances, which in many cases are not so decisive as to
leave no room for doubt.

It may likewise be observed, that the identity of
objects of sense is never perfect. All bodies, as they
consist of innumerable parts that may be disjoined
from them by a great variety of causes, are subject to
continual changes of their substance, increasing, diminishing, changing insensibly. When such alterations
are gradual, because language could not afford a different name for every different state of such a changeable
being, it retains the same name, and is considered as
the same thing. Thus we say of an old regiment, that
it did such a thing a century ago, though there now is
not a man alive who then belonged to it. We say
a tree is the same in the seed-bed and in the forest.
A ship of war, which has successively changed her an-
chors, her tackle, her sails, her masts, her planks, and her
timbers, while she keeps the same name, is the same.

The identity, therefore, which we ascribe to bodies,
whether natural or artificial, is not perfect identity; it
is rather something which, for the conveniency of
speech, we call identity. It admits of a great change
of the subject, providing the change be *gradual;* sometimes, even of a total change. And the changes which
in common language are made consistent with identity
differ from those that are thought to destroy it, not in
kind, but in *number* and *degree*. It has no fixed nature
when applied to bodies; and questions about the identity of a body are very often questions about words.
But identity, when applied to persons, has no ambiguity, and admits not of degrees, or of more and less.
It is the foundation of all rights and obligations, and
of all accountableness; and the notion of it is fixed
and precise.

III. *Strictures on Locke's Account of Personal Identity.*] In a long chapter, *Of Identity and Diversity*, Mr.
Locke has made many ingenious and just observations,
and some which I think cannot be defended. I shall

only take notice of the account he gives of our own personal identity. His doctrine upon this subject has been censured by Bishop Butler, in a short essay subjoined to his *Analogy*, with whose sentiments I perfectly agree.

Identity, as has been observed, supposes the continued existence of the being of which it is affirmed, and therefore can be applied only to things which have a continued existence. While any being continues to exist, it is the same being; but two beings which have a different beginning or a different ending of their existence cannot possibly be the same. To this, I think, Mr. Locke agrees.

He observes, very justly, that, to know what is meant by the same person, we must consider what the word *person* stands for; and he defines a person to be an intelligent being, endowed with reason and with consciousness, which last he thinks inseparable from thought. From this definition of a person, it must necessarily follow, that, while the intelligent being continues to exist and to be intelligent, it must be the *same* person. To say that the intelligent being is the person, and yet that the person ceases to exist while the intelligent being continues, or that the person continues while the intelligent being ceases to exist, is to my apprehension a manifest contradiction.

One would think that the definition of a person should perfectly ascertain the *nature* of personal identity, or wherein it consists, though it might still be a question how we come *to know and be assured of* our personal identity.

Mr. Locke tells us, however, " that personal identity, that is, the sameness of a rational being, *consists in consciousness alone*, and, as far as this consciousness can be extended backwards to any past action or thought, so far reaches the identity of that person. So that whatever has the consciousness of present and past actions is the same person to whom they belong." *

* See *Essay*, Book II. Chap. XXVII, – XXIX. The passage given as

This doctrine has some strange consequences, which the author was aware of. (1.) Such as, that if the same consciousness can be transferred from one intelligent being to another, which he thinks we cannot show to be impossible, *then two or twenty intelligent beings may be the same person.* (2.) And if the intelligent being may lose the consciousness of the actions done by him, which surely is possible, then he is not the person that did those actions; so that *one intelligent being may be two or twenty different persons,* if he shall so often lose the consciousness of his former actions.

(3.) There is another consequence of this doctrine, which follows no less necessarily, though Mr. Locke probably did not see it. It is, *that a man may be, and at the same time not be, the person that did a particular action.* Suppose a brave officer to have been flogged when a boy at school for robbing an orchard, to have taken a standard from the enemy in his first campaign, and to have been made a general in advanced life;

---

a quotation in the text is the sum of Locke's doctrine, but not exactly in his words. Long before Butler, to whom the merit is usually ascribed, Locke's doctrine of *personal identity* had been attacked and refuted. This was done even by his earliest critic, John Sergeant, whose words, as he is an author wholly unknown to all historians of philosophy, and his works of the rarest, I shall quote. He thus argues:— "But to speak to the point. Consciousness of any action or other accident we have now, or have had, is nothing but our knowledge that it belonged to us; and since we both agree that we have no *innate* knowledges, it follows that all both actual and habitual knowledges which we have are *acquired* or *accidental* to the subject or *knower.* Wherefore the man, or that thing which is to be the knower, must have had individuality or personality from *other* principles *antecedently* to this knowledge called *consciousness;* and consequently, he will *retain* his identity, or continue the same man, or (which is equivalent) the *same person,* as long as he has those individuating principles. What those individuating principles are which constitute the *man,* or this knowing *individuum,* I have shown above. It being, then, most evident, that a man must *be* the same, ere he can *know* or *be conscious* that he is the same, all his (Locke's) laborious descants and extravagant consequences, which are built on this supposition that consciousness *individuates* the person, can need no farther reflection." — *Solid Philosophy Asserted,* Reflection XIV. § 14.

The same objection was also made by Leibnitz in his strictures on Locke's *Essay.* See *Nouveaux Essais,* Liv. II. Chap. XXVII. For the best criticism of Locke's doctrine of personal identity, I may refer the reader to M. Cousin's *Cours de Philosophie,* Tome II. Leçon XVIII. [*Elements of Psychology,* Chap. III.] — H.

suppose, also, which must be admitted to be possible, that, when he took the standard, he was conscious of his having been flogged at school, and that, when made a general, he was conscious of his taking the standard, but had absolutely lost the consciousness of his flogging. These things being supposed, it follows, from Mr. Locke's doctrine, that he who was flogged at school is the same person who took the standard, and that he who took the standard is the same person who was made a general. Whence it follows, if there be any truth in logic, that the general is the same person with him who was flogged at school. But the general's consciousness does not reach so far back as his flogging; therefore, according to Mr. Locke's doctrine, he is not the person who was flogged. Therefore the general is, and at the same time is not, the same person with him who was flogged at school.*

Leaving the consequences of this doctrine to those who have leisure to trace them, we may observe, with regard to the doctrine itself, —

First, that Mr. Locke attributes to consciousness the conviction we have of our past actions, as if a man may now be conscious of what he did twenty years ago. It is impossible to understand the meaning of this, unless by *consciousness* be meant *memory*, the only faculty by which we have an immediate knowledge of our past actions.†

Sometimes, in popular discourse, a man says he is conscious that he did such a thing, meaning that he distinctly remembers that he did it. It is unnecessary, in common discourse, to fix accurately the limits between consciousness and memory. This was formerly shown to be the case with regard to sense and memory: and therefore distinct remembrance is sometimes called sense, sometimes consciousness, without any in-

---

* Compare Buffier's *Traité des Premières Vérités*, § 505, who makes a similar criticism. — H.

† Locke, it will be remembered, does not, like Reid, view consciousness as a coördinate faculty with memory; but under consciousness he properly comprehends the various faculties as so many special modifications. — H.

convenience. But this ought to be avoided in philosophy, otherwise we confound the different powers of the mind, and ascribe to one what really belongs to another. If a man can be conscious of what he did twenty years or twenty minutes ago, there is no use for memory, nor ought we to allow that there is any such faculty. The faculties of consciousness and memory are chiefly distinguished by this, that the first is an immediate knowledge of the present, the second an immediate knowledge of the past.*

When, therefore, Mr. Locke's notion of personal identity is properly expressed, it is, that personal identity *consists in distinct remembrance;* for, even in the popular sense, to say that I am conscious of a past action means nothing else than that I distinctly remember that I did it.

Secondly, it may be observed, that, in this doctrine, not only is consciousness confounded with memory, but, which is still more strange, *personal identity* is confounded with *the evidence which we have of our personal identity.*

It is very true, that my remembrance that I did such a thing is the evidence I have that I am the identical person who did it. And this, I am apt to think, Mr. Locke meant. But to say that my remembrance that

---

* As already stated, all *immediate* knowledge of the *past* is contradictory. This observation I cannot again repeat. See Note B. — H.

We copy a passage from the Note referred to, though it is little more than a repetition of what was said before : — "As not *now present in time,* an immediate knowledge of the *past* is impossible. The past is only mediately cognizable in and through a present modification relative to, and representative of, it, as having been. To speak of an immediate knowledge of the past involves a contradiction *in adjecto.* For to know the past immediately, it must be known *in itself;* — and to be known in itself, it must be known as *now existing.* But the past is just a negation of the now existent: its very notion, therefore, excludes the possibility of its being immediately known." It is probable that, by an immediate knowledge of the past, Reid meant "a knowledge effected not through the supposed intervention of a vicarious object, *numerically different from the object existing and the mind knowing,* but through a representation of the past or real object, *in and by the mind;* in other words, that by mediate knowledge in this connection he denoted a *non-egoistical,* by *immediate* knowledge an *egoistical* representation " — ED.

I did such a thing, or my consciousness, *makes* me the person who did it, is, in my apprehension, an absurdity too gross to be entertained by any man who attends to the meaning of it; for it is to attribute to memory or consciousness a strange magical power of producing its object, though that object must have existed before the memory or consciousness which produced it. Consciousness is the testimony of one faculty; memory is the testimony of another faculty; and to say that the testimony is the cause of the thing testified, this surely is absurd, if any thing be, and could not have been said by Mr. Locke, if he had not confounded the testimony with the thing testified.

When a horse that was stolen is found and claimed by the owner, the only evidence he can have, or that a judge or witnesses can have, that this is the very identical horse which was his property, is similitude. But would it not be ridiculous from this to infer that the identity of a horse *consists* in similitude only? The only *evidence* I have that I am the identical person who did such actions is, that I remember distinctly I did them; or, as Mr. Locke expresses it, I am conscious I did them. To infer from this, that personal identity consists in consciousness, is an argument which, if it had any force, would prove the identity of a stolen horse to consist solely in similitude.

Thirdly, is it not strange that the sameness or identity of a person should consist in a thing *which is continually changing*, and is not any two minutes the same?

Our consciousness, our memory, and every operation of the mind, are still flowing like the water of a river, or like time itself. The consciousness I have this moment can no more be the same consciousness I had last moment, than this moment can be the last moment. Identity can only be affirmed of things which have a continued existence. Consciousness, and every kind of thought, are transient and momentary, and have no continued existence; and, therefore, if personal identity consisted in consciousness, it would certainly follow, that *no man is the same person any two moments of his life*; and as the right and justice of reward and punishment are founded on personal identity, no man could be responsible for his actions.

But though I take this to be the unavoidable consequence of Mr. Locke's doctrine concerning personal identity, and though some persons may have liked the doctrine the better on this account, I am far from imputing any thing of this kind to Mr. Locke. He was too good a man not to have rejected with abhorrence a doctrine which he believed to draw this consequence after it.

Fourthly, there are many expressions used by Mr. Locke, in speaking of personal identity, which to me are altogether unintelligible, unless we suppose that he confounded that sameness or identity which we ascribe to an individual with the identity which, in common discourse, is often ascribed to many individuals of the same species.

When we say that pain and pleasure, consciousness and memory, are the same in all men, this sameness can only mean similarity, or sameness *of kind*. That the pain of one man can be the same individual pain with that of another man is no less impossible, than that one man should be another man: the pain felt by me yesterday can no more be the pain I feel to-day, than yesterday can be this day; and the same thing may be said of every passion and of every operation of the mind. The same kind or species of operation may be in different men, or in the same man at different times; but it is impossible that the same individual operation should be in different men, or in the same man at different times.

When Mr. Locke, therefore, speaks of "the same consciousness being continued through a succession of different substances"; when he speaks of "repeating the idea of a past action, with the same consciousness we had of it at the first," and of "the same consciousness extending to actions past and to come"; these expressions are to me unintelligible, unless he means not the same individual consciousness, but a consciousness that is similar, or of the same kind. If our personal identity consists in consciousness, as this consciousness cannot be the same individually any two moments, but only of the *same kind*, it would follow, that we are not for any two moments the same individual persons, but the same *kind* of persons. As our consciousness sometimes ceases to exist, as in sound sleep, our personal identity must cease with it. Mr. Locke allows, that the same thing cannot have two beginnings of existence, so that our identity would be irrecoverably gone every time we ceased to think, if it was but for a moment.*

* In addition to the works already cited or referred to on the subjects of personality and personal identity, consult Bouchitté, *Persistance de la Personnalité après la Mort*, published in the *Mémoires* of the Moral Section of the French Academy, *Recueil des Savants Etrangers*, Tome II.; Broussais, *De l'Irritation*, Part I. Chap. V. Sect. IV.; Mill's *Analysis*, Chap. XIV. Sect. VII.; Young's *Intellectual Philosophy*, Lect. XLIII., XLIV.; Leroux, *De l'Humanité*, Introduction. — Ed.

ESSAY IV.

OF CONCEPTION.

CHAPTER I.

OF CONCEPTION, OR SIMPLE APPREHENSION IN GENERAL.

I. *Definition of the Term, with its Synonymes.*] *Conceiving, imagining,*[*] *apprehending, understanding, having a notion of a thing*, are common words used to express that operation of the understanding which the logicians call *simple apprehension*. The *having an idea of a thing* is, in common language, used in the same sense, chiefly I think since Mr. Locke's time.[†]

Logicians define simple apprehension to be *the bare conception of a thing without any judgment or belief about it*. If this were intended for a strictly logical

---

[*] *Imagining* should not be confounded with *conceiving*, &c.; though some philosophers, as Gassendi, have not attended to the distinction. The words *conception, concept, notion*, should be limited to the thought of what cannot be represented in the imagination, — as the thought suggested by a general term. The Leibnitzians call this *symbolical*, in contrast to *intuitive* knowledge. This is the sense in which *conceptio* and *conceptus* have been usually and correctly employed. Mr. Stewart, on the other hand, arbitrarily limits *conception* to the reproduction, in imagination, of an object of sense as actually perceived. See *Elements*, Part I. Chap. III. The discrimination in question is best made in the German language of philosophy, where the term *Begriffe* (conceptions) is strongly contrasted with *Anschauungen* (intuitions), *Bilden* (images), &c. — H.

[†] *In this country* should have been added. Locke only introduced into *English* philosophy the term *idea* in its Cartesian universality. Prior to him, the word was only used with us in its Platonic signification. *Before* Descartes, David Buchanan, a Scotch philosopher, who sojourned in France, had, however, employed *idea* in an equal latitude. See Note G. — H.

definition, it might be a just objection to it, that conception and apprehension are only synonymous words; and that we may as well define conception by apprehension, as apprehension by conception; but it ought to be remembered, that the most simple operations of the mind cannot be logically defined. To have a distinct notion of them, we must attend to them as we feel them in our own minds. He that would have a distinct notion of a scarlet color will never attain it by a definition; he must set it before his eye, attend to it, compare it with the colors that come nearest to it, and observe the specific difference, which he will in vain attempt to express.

Every man is conscious that he can *conceive* a thousand things, of which he *believes* nothing at all; as a horse with wings, a mountain of gold; but although conception may be without any degree of belief, even the weakest belief cannot be without conception. He that believes must have some conception of what he believes.

Without attempting a definition of this operation of the mind, I shall endeavour to explain some of its properties; consider the theories about it; and take notice of some mistakes of philosophers concerning it.

II. *Characteristic Properties of Conception.*] 1. It may be observed, that conception *enters as an ingredient in every operation of the mind.* Our senses cannot give us the belief of any object, without giving some conception of it at the same time. No man can either remember or reason about things of which he has no conception. When we will to exert any of our active powers, there must be some conception of what we will to do. There can be no desire nor aversion, love nor hatred, without some conception of the object. We cannot feel pain without conceiving it, though we can conceive it without feeling it. These things are self-evident.

In every operation of the mind, therefore, in every thing we call thought, there must be conception.

When we analyze the various operations either of the understanding or of the will, we shall always find this at the bottom, like the *caput mortuum* of the chemists, or the *materia prima* of the Peripatetics; but though there is no operation of mind without conception, yet it may be found naked, detached from all others, and then it is called *simple apprehension*, or the bare conception of a thing.

As all the operations of our mind are expressed by language, every one knows that it is one thing to understand what is said, to conceive or apprehend its meaning, whether it be a word, a sentence, or a discourse; it is another thing to judge of it, to assent or dissent, to be persuaded or moved. The first is simple apprehension, and may be without the last, but the last cannot be without the first.

2. In bare conception *there can neither be truth nor falsehood, because it neither affirms nor denies.* Every judgment, and every proposition by which judgment is expressed, must be true or false; and the qualities of true and false, in their proper sense, can belong to nothing but to judgments, or to propositions which express judgment. In the bare conception of a thing there is no judgment, opinion, or belief included, and therefore it cannot be either true or false.

But it may be said, Is there any thing more certain than that men may have true or false conceptions, true or false apprehensions, of things? I answer, that such ways of speaking are indeed so common, and so well authorized by custom, the arbiter of language, that it would be presumption to censure them. It is hardly possible to avoid using them. But we ought to be upon our guard that we be not misled by them to confound things which, though often expressed by the same words, are really different. We must therefore remember, that all the words by which we signify the *bare conception* of a thing are likewise used to signify our *opinions* when we wish to express them with modesty and diffidence. Thus, instead of saying, " This is my opinion," or " This is my judgment," which has the air of dogmaticalness, we say, " I *conceive* it to be thus," which is understood as a modest declaration of our judgment. In like manner, when any thing is said which we take to be impossible, we say, " We cannot *conceive* it," meaning that we cannot believe it. And we shall always find, that, when we speak of true or false conceptions, we mean true or false opinions. An opinion, though ever so wavering, or ever so modestly expressed, must be either true or false; but a bare conception, which expresses no opinion or judgment, can be neither.

If we analyze those speeches in which men attribute truth or falsehood to our conceptions of things, we shall find, in every case, that there is some opinion or judgment implied in what they call conception. A child conceives the moon to be flat, and a foot or two broad; that is, this is his opinion: and when we say it is a false notion, or a false conception, we mean that it is a false opinion. He conceives the city of London to be like his country village; that is, he believes it to be so till he is better instructed. He conceives a lion to have horns; that is, he believes that the animal which men call a lion has horns. Such opinions language authorizes us to call conceptions; and they may be true or false. But bare conception, or what the logicians call *simple apprehension*, implies no opinion, however slight, and therefore can neither be true nor false.

3. *Of all the analogies between the operations of body and those of the mind, there is none so strong and so obvious to all mankind as that which there is between painting, or other plastic arts, and the power of conceiving objects in the mind.* Hence, in all languages, the words by which this power of the mind and its various modifications are expressed are analogical, and borrowed from those arts. We consider this power of the mind as a plastic power, by which we form to ourselves images of the objects of thought.

In vain should we attempt to avoid this analogical language, for we have no other language upon the sub-

22 *

ject; yet it is dangerous, and apt to mislead. All analogical and figurative words have a double meaning;
and, if we are not very much upon our guard, we slide
insensibly from the borrowed and figurative meaning
into the primitive. We are prone to carry the parallel
between the things compared farther than it will hold,
and thus very naturally to fall into error.

To avoid this as far as possible in the present subject, it is proper to attend to the dissimilitude between
conceiving a thing in the mind, and painting it to the
eye, as well as to their similitude. The similitude
strikes and gives pleasure. The dissimilitude we are
less disposed to observe. But the philosopher ought to
attend to it, and to carry it always in mind, in his reasonings on this subject, as a monitor, to warn him
against the errors into which the analogical language
is apt to draw him.

When a man *paints*, there is some work done, which
remains when his hand is taken off, and continues to
exist though he should think no more of it. Every
stroke of his pencil produces an effect, and this effect
is different from his action in making it; for it remains
and continues to exist when the action ceases. The
action of painting is one thing, the picture produced is
another thing. The first is the cause, the second is the
effect. Let us next consider what is done when he only
conceives this picture. He must have conceived it before he painted it: for this is a maxim universally admitted, that every work of art must first be conceived
in the mind of the operator. What is this conception?
It is an act of the mind, a kind of thought. This cannot be denied. But does it produce any effect besides
the act itself? Surely common sense answers this
question in the negative: for every one knows that it is
one thing to conceive, another thing to bring forth into
effect. It is one thing to project, another to execute.
A man may think for a long time what he is to do, and
after all do nothing. Conceiving, as well as projecting
or resolving, is what the schoolmen call an *immanent*
act of the mind, which produces nothing beyond itself.

But painting is a *transitive* act, which produces an effect distinct from the operation, and this effect is the picture. Let this, therefore, be always remembered, that what is commonly called the image of a thing in the mind is no more than the act or operation of the mind in conceiving it.

That this is the common sense of men who are untutored by philosophy, appears from their language. If one ignorant of the language should ask, What is meant by *conceiving a thing?* we should very naturally answer, that it is *having an image of it in the mind;* and perhaps we could not explain the word better. This shows that conception, and the image of a thing in the mind, are synonymous expressions. The image in the mind, therefore, is not the object of conception, nor is it any effect produced by conception as a cause. It is the conception itself. That very mode of thinking which we call conception is by another name called an image in the mind.*

Nothing more readily gives the conception of a thing than the seeing an image of it. Hence, by a figure common in language, conception is called an image of the thing conceived. But to show that it is not a real but a metaphorical image, it is called an image *in the` mind.* We know nothing that is properly in the mind but thought; and when any thing else is said to be in the mind, the expression must be figurative, and signify some kind of thought.

4. Taking along with us what is said in the last article, to guard us against the seduction of the analogical language used on this subject, *we may observe a very strong analogy, not only between conceiving and painting in general, but between the different kinds of our conceptions, and the different works of the painter.* He either makes fancy pictures, or he copies from the

---

* We ought, however, to distinguish *imagination* and *image, conception* and *concept*. *Imagination* and *conception* ought to be employed in speaking of the mental modification, one and indivisible, considered as an act; *image* and *concept*, in speaking of it considered as a product or immediate object. — H.

painting of others, or he paints from the life, that is, from real objects of art or nature which he has seen. I think our conceptions admit of a division very similar.

First, there are conceptions which may be called *fancy pictures*. They are commonly called creatures of fancy, or of imagination. They are not the copies of any original that exists, but are originals themselves. Such was the conception which Swift formed of the island of Laputa and of the country of the Lilliputians; Cervantes, of Don Quixote and his Squire; Harrington, of the Government of Oceana; and Sir Thomas More, of that of Utopia. We can give names to such creatures of imagination, conceive them distinctly, and reason consequentially concerning them, though they never had an existence. They were *conceived* by their creators, and may be *conceived* by others, but they never *existed*. We do not ascribe the qualities of true or false to them, because they are not accompanied with any belief, nor do they imply any affirmation or negation.

Setting aside those creatures of imagination, there are other conceptions, which may be called *copies*, because they have an original or archetype to which they refer, and with which they are believed to agree; and we call them *true* or *false* conceptions, according as they agree or disagree with the standard to which they are referred. These are of two kinds, which have different standards or originals.

The *first* kind is analogous to pictures *taken from the life*. We have conceptions of individual things that really exist, such as the city of London, or the government of Venice. Here the things conceived are the originals; and our conceptions are called *true* when they agree with the thing conceived. Thus, my conception of the city of London is true when I conceive it to be what it really is.

Individual things which really exist being the creatures of God (though some of them may receive their outward form from man), he only who made them knows their whole nature; we know them but in part, and therefore our conceptions of them must in all cases be *imperfect* and *inadequate;* yet they may be true and just, as far as they reach.

The *second* kind is analogous to the copies which the painter makes *from pictures done before.* Such, I think, are the conceptions we have of what the ancients called *universals;* that is, of things which belong or may belong to many individuals. These are kinds and species of things; — such as man, or elephant, which are species of substances; wisdom, or courage, which are species of qualities; equality, or similitude, which are species of relations.*

It may be asked, From what original are these con-⟩ ceptions formed? and When are they said to be true or false?

It appears to me that the original from which they are copied, that is, the thing conceived, is the conception or meaning which other men who understand the language affix to the same words. Things are parcelled into *kinds* and *sorts*, not by nature, but by men. The individual things we are connected with are so many, that to give a proper name to every individual would be impossible. We could never attain the knowledge of them that is necessary, nor converse and reason about them, without sorting them according to their different attributes. Those that agree in certain attributes are thrown into one parcel, and have a general name given them, which belongs equally to every individual in that parcel. This common name must, therefore, signify those attributes which have been observed to be common to every individual in that parcel, and nothing else.

That such *general words* may answer their intention, all that is necessary is that those who use them should affix the same meaning or notion, that is, the same conception, to them. The *common meaning* is the stand-

---

* Of all such we can have no adequate *imagination.* A *universal,* when represented in imagination, is no longer adequate, no longer a universal. We cannot have an *image* of "horse," but only of some individual of that species. *We may, however, have a notion or conception of it.* — H.

ard by which such conceptions are formed, and they are said to be *true* or *false*, according as they agree or disagree with it. Thus, my conception of *felony* is true and just when it agrees with the meaning of that word in the laws relating to it, and in authors who understand the law. The meaning of the word is the thing conceived; and that meaning is the conception affixed to it by those who best understand the language.   •   .

If all the general words of a language had a precise meaning, and were perfectly understood, as mathematical terms are, all verbal disputes would be at an end, and men would never seem to differ in opinion but when they differed in reality; but this is far from being the case. The meaning of most general words is not learned like that of mathematical terms, by an accurate definition, but by the experience we happen to have, by hearing them used in conversation. From such experience we collect their meaning by a kind of induction; and as this induction is for the most part lame and imperfect, it happens that different persons join different conceptions to the same general word; and though we intend to give them the meaning which use, the arbiter of language, has put upon them, this is difficult to find, and apt to be mistaken, even by the candid and attentive. Hence, in innumerable disputes, men do not really differ in their judgments, but in the way of expressing them.

5. Our conception of things *may be strong and lively, or it may be faint and languid in all degrees.* These are qualities which properly belong to our conceptions, though we have no names for them but such as are analogical. Every man is conscious of such a difference in his conceptions, and finds his lively conceptions most agreeable, when the object is not of such a nature as to give pain.

It seems easier to form a lively conception of objects that are familiar, than of those that are not. Our conceptions of *visible* objects are commonly the most lively, when other circumstances are equal: hence poets not only delight in the description of visible objects, but find means, by metaphor, analogy, and allusion, to clothe every object they describe with visible qualities. The lively conception of these makes the object appear, as it were, before our eyes. Lord Kames, in his *Elements of Criticism*, has shown of what importance it is in works of taste to give to objects described what he calls *ideal presence*. To produce this in the mind is indeed the capital aim of poetical and rhetorical description. It carries the man, as it were, out of himself, and makes him a spectator of the scene described. This ideal presence seems to me to be nothing else but a lively conception of the appearance which the object would make if really present to the eye. It may also be observed, that our conceptions of visible objects become more lively by giving them motion, and more still by giving them life and intellectual qualities. Hence, in poetry, the whole creation is animated and endowed with sense and reflection.

Abstract and general conceptions are never *lively*, though they may be *distinct;* and therefore, however necessary in philosophy, seldom enter into poetical description without being particularized or clothed in some visible dress.*

6. Our conceptions of things *may be clear, distinct, and steady; or they may be obscure, indistinct, and wavering.* The liveliness of our conceptions gives pleasure, but it is their distinctness and steadiness that enable us to judge right, and to express our sentiments with perspicuity.

If we inquire into the cause why, among persons speaking or writing on the same subject, we find in one so much darkness, in another so much perspicuity, I believe the chief cause will be found to be, that one had a distinct and steady conception of what he said

---

* They thus cease to be aught *abstract* and *general*, and become merely individual representations. In precise language, they are no longer νοήματα, but φαντασμάτα; no longer *Begriffe*, but *Anschauungen;* no longer *notions* or *concepts*, but *images*. The word "*particularized*" ought to have been *individualized*. — H.

or wrote, and the other had not: men generally find means to express distinctly what they have conceived distinctly.* Horace observes, that proper words spontaneously follow distinct conceptions, — *Verbaque provisam rem non invita sequuntur.*

Some persons find it difficult to enter into a mathematical demonstration. I believe we shall always find the reason to be, that *they do not distinctly apprehend it.* A man cannot be convinced by what he does not understand. On the other hand, I think a man cannot understand a demonstration without seeing the force of it. I speak of such demonstrations as those of Euclid, where every step is set down, and nothing left to be supplied by the reader. Sometimes one who has got through the first four books of Euclid's *Elements,* and sees the force of the demonstrations, finds difficulty in the fifth. What is the reason of this? You may find, by a little conversation with him, that he has not a clear and steady *conception* of ratios and of the terms relating to them. When the terms used in the fifth book have become familiar, and readily excite in his mind a clear and steady conception of their meaning, you may venture to affirm that he will be able to understand the demonstrations of that book, and to see the force of them.

If this be really the case, as it seems to be, it leads us to think that men are very much upon a level with regard to mere judgment, when we take that faculty apart from the apprehension or conception of the things about which we judge; so that a sound judgment seems to be the inseparable companion of a clear and steady apprehension: and we ought not to consider these two as talents, of which the one may fall to the lot of one man, and the other to the lot of another, but as talents which always go together.

It may, however, be observed, that some of our conceptions may be more subservient to reasoning than

* For several just and discriminating remarks on this subject, see Stewart's *Elements,* Part I. Chap. II.— ED.

others which are equally clear and distinct. It was before observed, that some of our conceptions are of *individual* things, others of things *general and abstract.* It may happen, that a man who has very clear conceptions of things individual is not so happy in those of things general and abstract. And this I take to be the reason why we find men who have good judgment in matters of common life, and perhaps good talents for poetical or rhetorical composition, who find it very difficult to enter into abstract reasoning.

7. It has been observed by many authors, that, when we barely conceive any object, the ingredients of that conception *must either be things with which we were before acquainted by some other original power of the mind, or they must be parts or attributes of such things.* Thus, a man cannot conceive colors, if he never saw, nor sounds, if he never heard. If a man had not a conscience, he could not conceive what is meant by moral obligation, or by right and wrong in conduct.

Fancy may combine things that never were combined in reality. It may enlarge or diminish, multiply or divide, compound and fashion the objects which nature presents; but it cannot, by the utmost effort of that creative power which we ascribe to it, bring any one simple ingredient into its productions which nature has not framed, and brought to our knowledge by some other faculty. This Mr. Locke has expressed as beautifully as justly. " The dominion of man, in this little world of his own understanding, is much the same as in the great world of visible things; wherein his power, however managed by art and skill, reaches no farther than to compound and divide the materials that are made to his hand, but can do nothing towards making the least particle of matter, or destroying one atom that is already in being. The same inability will every one find in himself to fashion in his understanding any simple idea not received by the powers which God has given him."

I think all philosophers agree in this sentiment. Mr. Hume, indeed, after acknowledging the truth of the
23

principle in general, mentions what he thinks a single exception to it;—that a man, who had seen all the shades of a particular color except one, might frame in his mind a conception of that shade which he never saw. I think this is not an exception; because a particular shade of a color differs not *specifically*, but only in *degree*, from other shades of the same color.

It is proper to observe, that our most simple conceptions are not those which nature immediately presents to us. When we come to years of understanding, we have the power of analyzing the objects of nature, of distinguishing their several attributes and relations, of conceiving them one by one, and of giving a name to each, whose meaning extends only to that single attribute or relation: and thus our most simple conceptions are not those of any object in nature, but of some single attribute or relation of such objects. Thus nature presents to our senses bodies that are extended in three dimensions, and solid. By analyzing the notion we have of body from our senses, we form to ourselves the conceptions of extension, solidity, space, a point, a line, a surface; all which are more simple conceptions than that of a body. But they are the elements, as it were, of which our conception of a body is made up, and into which it may be analyzed.

8. Though our conceptions must be confined to the ingredients mentioned in the last article, *we are unconfined with regard to the arrangement of those ingredients.* Here we may pick and choose, and form an endless variety of combinations and compositions, which we call creatures of the imagination. These may be clearly conceived, though they never existed: and, indeed, every thing that is made must have been conceived before it was made. Every work of human art, and every plan of conduct, whether in public or in private life, must have been conceived before it is brought to execution. And we cannot avoid thinking, that the Almighty, before he created the universe by his power, had a distinct conception of the whole and of every part, and saw it to be good, and agreeable to his intention.

It is the business of man, as a rational creature, to employ this unlimited power of conception for planning his conduct and enlarging his knowledge. It seems to be peculiar to beings endowed with reason *to act by a preconceived plan.* Brute animals seem either to want this power, or to have it in a very low degree. They are moved by instinct, habit, appetite, or natural affection, according as these principles are stirred by the present occasion. But I see no reason to think that they can propose to themselves a connected plan of life, or form general rules of conduct. Indeed, we see that many of the human species, to whom God has given this power, make little use of it. They act without a plan, as the passion or appetite which is strongest at the time leads them.

9. The last property I shall mention of this faculty is that which essentially distinguishes it from every other power of the mind; and it is, *that it is not employed solely about things which have existence.* I can conceive a winged horse or a centaur, as easily and as distinctly as I can conceive a man whom I have seen. Nor does this distinct conception incline my judgment in the least to the belief, that a winged horse or a centaur ever existed.

It is not so with the other operations of our minds. They are employed about real existences, and carry with them the belief of their objects. When I feel pain, I am compelled to believe that the pain that I feel has a real existence. When I perceive any external object, my belief of the real existence of the object is irresistible. When I distinctly remember any event, though that event may not now exist, I can have no doubt but it did exist. That consciousness which we have of the operations of our own minds implies a belief of the real existence of those operations.

Thus we see that the powers of sensation, of perception, of memory, and of consciousness are all employed solely about objects that do exist, or have existed. But conception is often employed about objects that neither do, nor did, nor will exist. This is the very nature of this faculty, that its object, though distinctly conceived, may have no existence. Such an object we call a creature of imagination; but this creature never was created.

That we may not impose upon ourselves in this matter, we must distinguish between that act or operation of the mind which we call conceiving an object, and the object which we conceive. When we conceive any thing, there is a real act or operation of the mind; of this we are conscious, and can have no doubt of its existence: but every such act must have an object; for he that conceives must conceive something. Suppose he conceives a centaur, he may have a distinct conception of this object, though no centaur ever existed.

The philosopher will say, I cannot conceive a centaur without having *an idea of it in my mind.* But I am at a loss to understand what he means. He surely does not mean that I cannot conceive it without conceiving it. This would make me no wiser. What then is this idea? Is it an animal, half horse and half man? No. Then I am certain it is not the thing I conceive. Perhaps he will say, that the idea is an *image* of the animal, and is the immediate object of my conception, and that the animal is the mediate or remote object.

To this I answer: — *First,* I am certain there are not *two* objects of this conception, but one only; which is as immediate an object of my conception as any can be. *Secondly,* this one object which I conceive is not the *image* of an animal, it is an animal. I know what it is to conceive an image of an animal, and what it is to conceive an animal; and I can distinguish the one of these from the other without any danger of mistake. The thing I conceive is a body of a certain figure and color, having life and spontaneous motion. The philosopher says that the idea is an image of the animal, but that it has neither body, nor color, nor life, nor spontaneous motion. This I am not able to comprehend. *Thirdly,* I wish to know how this idea comes to be an object of my thought, when I cannot even conceive what it means; and if I did conceive it, this would be no evidence of its existence, any more than my conception of a centaur is of its existence.*

But may not a man who conceives a centaur say, that *he has a distinct image of it in his mind?* I think he may. And if he means by this way of speaking what the vulgar mean, who never heard of the philosophical theory of ideas, I find no fault with it. By a distinct image in the mind, the vulgar mean a distinct conception: and it is natural to call it so, on account of the analogy between an image of a thing and the conception of it. On account of this analogy, obvious to all mankind, this operation is called *imagination,* and " an image in the mind" is only a periphrasis for imagination. But to infer from this that there is really an image in the mind, *distinct from the operation of con-*

---

* Sir W. Hamilton, in his *Supplementary Dissertations*, Note B, § 2, remarks as follows on this puzzle of Dr. Reid's : — " Reid maintains that in our cognitions there must be an *object* (real or imaginary) *distinct from the operation of the mind* conversant about it; for the *act* is one thing, and the *object of the act* another. This is erroneous, — at least, it is erroneously expressed. Take an *imaginary* object, and Reid's own instance, — a centaur. Here he says, 'The sole object of conception (imagination) is an animal which I believe never existed.' It 'never existed'; that is, never really, never in nature, never externally, existed. But it is 'an object of imagination.' It is not, therefore, a mere non-existence; for if it had no kind of existence, it could not possibly be the positive object of any kind of thought. For were it an absolute nothing, it could have no qualities (*non-entis nulla sunt attributa*); but the object we are conscious of, as a centaur, has qualities, — qualities which constitute it a determinate something, and distinguish it from every other entity whatsoever. We must, therefore, perforce, allow it some sort of imaginary, ideal representative, or (in the older meaning of the word) *objective* existence in the mind. Now this existence can only be one or other of two sorts; for such object in the mind either *is*, or *is not, a mode of mind.* Of these alternatives the latter cannot be supposed; for this would be an affirmation of the crudest kind of non-egoistical representation, — the very hypothesis against which Reid so strenuously contends. The former alternative remains, — that it is *a mode of the imagining mind;* that it is in fact the plastic act of imagination considered as representing to itself a certain possible form, — a centaur. But then Reid's assertion, that there is always an object distinct from the operation of the mind conversant about it, the act being one thing, the object of the act another, must be surrendered. For the *object* and the *act* are here only one and the same thing in two several relations. Reid's error consists in mistaking a logical for a metaphysical difference, — a distinction of relation for a distinction of entity Or is the error only from the vagueness and ambiguity of expression?" — ED.

23 *

ceiving the object, is to be misled by an analogical expression; as if, from the phrases of deliberating and balancing things in the mind, we should infer that there is really a balance existing in the mind for weighing motives and arguments.

III. *Distinction between Conception and Imagination.*] I take imagination, in its most proper sense, to signify *a lively conception of objects of sight.* This is a talent of importance to poets and orators, and deserves a proper name, on account of its connection with those arts. According to this strict meaning of the word, imagination is distinguished from conception as a part from the whole. We conceive the objects of the other senses, but it is not so proper to say that we imagine them. We conceive judgment, reasoning, propositions, and arguments; but it is rather improper to say that we imagine these things.

This distinction between imagination and conception may be illustrated by an example, which Descartes uses to illustrate the distinction between imagination and pure intellection. We can imagine a triangle or a square so clearly as to distinguish them from every other figure. But we cannot imagine a figure of a thousand equal sides and angles so clearly. The best eye, by looking at it, could not distinguish it from every figure of more or fewer sides. And that conception of its appearance to the eye, which we properly call *imagination,* cannot be more distinct than the appearance itself; yet we can conceive a figure of a thousand sides, and even can demonstrate the properties which distinguish it from all figures of more or fewer sides. It is not by the eye, but by a superior faculty, that we form the notion of a great number, such as a thousand: and a distinct notion of this number of sides not being to be got by the eye, it is not imagined, but it is distinctly *conceived,* and easily distinguished from every other number.*

---

* It is to be regretted that Reid did not more fully develop the distinc-

IV. *Whether the Conceivability of Things is a Test of their Possibility.*] Writers on logic affirm, that our conception of things is *a test of their possibility;* so that what we can distinctly conceive, we may conclude

---

tion between *imagination* and *conception*, on which he here and elsewhere inadequately touches. *Imagination* is not, though in conformity to the etymology of the term, to be limited to the representation of visible objects. Neither ought the term *conceive* to be used in the extensive sense of *understand.* — H.

On the use of these terms Mr. Stewart expresses himself as follows : — "Dr Reid substitutes the word *conception* instead of the *simple apprehension* of the schools, and employs it in the same extensive signification. I think it may contribute to make our ideas more distinct, to restrict its meaning; and for such a restriction we have the authority of philosophers in a case perfectly analogous. In ordinary language, we apply the same word *perception* to the knowledge which we have by our senses of external objects, and to our knowledge of speculative truth; and yet an author would be justly censured, who should treat of these two operations of mind under the same article of perception. I apprehend there is as wide a difference between the conception of a truth and the conception of an absent object of sense, as between the perception of a tree and the perception of a mathematical theorem. I have therefore taken the liberty to distinguish also the two former operations of the mind; and under the article of *conception* shall confine myself to that faculty whose province it is to enable us to form a notion of our past sensations, or of the objects of sense that we have formerly perceived.

" The business of conception, according to the account I have given of it, is to present us with an exact transcript of what we have felt or perceived. But we have, moreover, a power of *modifying our conceptions,* by combining the parts of different ones together, so as to form *new wholes* of our own creation. I shall employ the word *imagination* to express this power; and I apprehend that this is the proper sense of the word, if imagination be the power which gives birth to the productions of the poet and the painter." — *Elements,* Part I. Chap. III.

He afterwards shows that the province of imagination is not limited to the perceptions of sight, or to the sensible world : — "All the objects of human knowledge supply materials to her forming hand; diversifying infinitely the works she produces, while the mode of her operation remains essentially the same. As it is the same power of reasoning which enables us to carry on our investigations with respect to individual objects, and with respect to classes or genera, so it was by the same processes of analysis and combination that the genius of Milton produced the garden of Eden, that of Harrington the commonwealth of Oceana, and that of Shakspeare the characters of Hamlet and Falstaff." — *Ibid.,* Chap. VII. See, also, Rauch's *Psychology,* Part II. Sect. I. Chap. II.

Mr. Stewart has not been generally followed in the restricted and peculiar sense which he gives to the term *conception.* Sir W. Hamilton, as appears from his note on page 269, limits it to the thought of what *cannot* be represented in the imagination, — as the thought suggested by a general term. So does Dr. Whewell, *Philosophy of the Inductive Sciences,* Part I. Book I. Chap. V. — ED.

to be possible, while of what is impossible we can have no conception.

This opinion has been held by philosophers for more than a hundred years, without contradiction or dissent, as far as I know; and if it be an error, it may be of some use to inquire into its origin, and the causes that it has been so generally received as a maxim whose truth could not be brought into doubt.

One of the fruitless questions agitated among the scholastic philosophers in the dark ages * was, What is the criterion of truth? — as if men could have any other way to distinguish truth from error but by the right use of that power of judging which God has given them.

Descartes endeavoured to put an end to this controversy, by making it a fundamental principle in his system, that *whatever we clearly and distinctly perceive is true.* To understand this principle of Descartes, it must be observed that he gave the name of *perception* to every power of the human understanding; and in explaining this very maxim, he tells us that sense, imagination, and pure intellection are only different modes of perceiving, and so the maxim was understood by all his followers. The learned Dr. Cudworth seems also to have adopted this principle. " The criterion of true knowledge," says he, " is only to be looked for in our knowledge and conceptions themselves: for the entity of all theoretical truth is nothing else but clear intelligibility, and whatever is clearly conceived is an entity and a truth; but that which is false, Divine power itself cannot make it to be clearly and distinctly understood. A falsehood can never be clearly conceived or apprehended to be true." — *Eternal and Immutable Morality,* p. 172.

This Cartesian maxim seems to me to have led the way to that now under consideration, which seems to have been adopted as the proper correction of the

---

* This was more a question with the Greek philosophers than with the schoolmen. — H.

former. When the authority of Descartes declined, men began to see that we may clearly and distinctly conceive what is not true, but thought that our conception, though not in all cases a test of truth, might be a test of possibility. This, indeed, seems to be a necessary consequence of the received doctrine of ideas; it being evident that there can be no distinct image, either in the mind or anywhere else, of that which is impossible. The ambiguity of the word *conceive,* as when we say *we cannot conceive such a thing,* meaning that we think it impossible, might likewise contribute to the reception of this doctrine. ˙

But whatever was the origin of this opinion, it seems to prevail universally, and to be received as a maxim.

" The bare having an idea of the proposition proves the thing not to be impossible; for of an impossible proposition there can be no idea." — DR. SAMUEL CLARKE.

" Of that which neither does nor can exist we can have no idea." — LORD BOLINGBROKE.

" The measure of impossibility to us is inconceivableness; that of which we can have no idea but that, reflecting upon it, it appears to be nothing, we pronounce to be impossible." — ABERNETHY.

" In every idea is implied the possibility of the existence of its object, nothing being clearer than that there can be no idea of an impossibility, or conception of what cannot exist." — DR. PRICE.

" Impossibile est cujus nullam notionem formare possumus; possibile e contra, cui aliqua respondet notio." — WOLFII *Ontologia.**

---

* These are not exactly Wolf's expressions. See *Ontologia,* §§ 102, 103; *Philosophia Rationalis,* §§ 522, 528. The same doctrine is held by Tschirnhausen and others. In so far, however, as it is said that *inconceivability* is the criterion of impossibility, it is manifestly erroneous. Of many contradictories we are able to conceive neither; but, by the law of thought called that of *excluded middle,* one of two contradictories must be admitted, — must be true. For example, we can neither conceive, on the one hand, an ultimate minimum of space or of time; nor can we, on the other, conceive their infinite divisibility. In like manner, we cannot conceive the absolute commencement of time or the utmost limit of space, and are yet equally

" It is an established maxim in metaphysics, that
whatever the mind conceives includes the idea of possible existence, or, in other words, that nothing we imagine is absolutely impossible." — D. HUME.

It were easy to muster up many other respectable
authorities for this maxim, and I have never found one
that called it in question.   If the maxim be true in the
extent which the famous Wolf has given it, in the passage above quoted, we shall have a short road to the
determination of every question about the possibility
or impossibility of things.   We need only look into
our own breast, and that, liké the Urim and Thummim,
will give an infallible answer.   If we can conceive the
thing, it is possible; if not, it is impossible.   And surely
every man may know whether he can conceive what is
affirmed or not.

Other philosophers have been satisfied with one half
of the maxim of Wolf.   They say, that *whatever we
can conceive is possible;* but they do not say, that whatever we cannot conceive is impossible.   I cannot help
thinking even this to be a mistake, which philosophers
have been unwarily led ·into, from the causes before
mentioned.   My reasons are these : —

⸱ 1. Whatever is said to be possible or impossible is
expressed by a proposition.   Now, what is it to conceive a proposition ?   I think it is no more than to *understand distinctly its meaning.**   I know no more that

---

unable to conceive them without any commencement or limit.   The absurdity that would result from the assertion, that all that is inconceivable
is impossible, is thus obvious; and so far Reid's criticism is just, though
not new. — H.

* In this sense of the word *conception,* I make bold to say that there is
no philosopher who ever held an opinion different from that of our author.
The whole dispute arises from Reid's giving a wider signification to this
term than that which it has generally received.   In his view, it has two
meanings; in that of the philosophers whom he attacks, it has only one.
To illustrate this, take the proposition, *A circle is a square.*   Here we easily
understand the meaning of the affirmation, because what is necessary to an
act of judgment is merely that the subject and predicate should be brought
into a *unity of relation.*   A judgment is therefore possible, even where the
two terms are contradictory.   But the philosophers never expressed by
the term *conception* this understanding of the purport of a proposition.
What they meant by *conception* was not the *unity of relation,* but the *unity*

can be meant by simple apprehension or conception, when applied to a proposition. The axiom, therefore, amounts to this: every proposition, of which you understand the meaning distinctly, is possible. I am persuaded that I understand as distinctly the meaning of this proposition, — *Any two sides of a triangle are together equal to the third,* — as of this, — *Any two sides of a triangle are together greater than the third;* yet the first of these is impossible.

Perhaps it will be said, that, though you understand the meaning of the impossible proposition, you cannot *suppose* or *conceive* it to be true.

Here we are to examine the meaning of the phrases of *supposing* and *conceiving a proposition to be true.* I can certainly suppose it to be true, because I can draw consequences from it which I find to be impossible, as well as the proposition itself. If by conceiving it to be true be meant giving some degree of assent to it, however small, this I confess I cannot do. But will it be said, that every proposition to which I can give any degree of assent is possible? This contradicts experience, and therefore the maxim cannot be true in this sense. Sometimes, when we say that we cannot conceive a thing to be true, we mean by that expression, that we judge it to be impossible. In this sense, I cannot, indeed, conceive it to be true that two sides of a triangle are equal to a third. I judge it to be impossible. If, then, we understand in this sense the maxim, that nothing we can conceive is impossible, the meaning will be, that nothing is impossible which we judge

---

of representation; and this unity of representation they made the criterion of logical possibility. To take the example already given, they did not say a circle may possibly be a square, because we can understand the meaning of the proposition, *A circle is square;* but, on the contrary, they said it is impossible that a circle can be square, and the proposition affirming this is necessarily false, because we cannot, in consciousness, bring to a *unity of representation* the repugnant notions, circle and square, — that is, *conceive* the notion of a *square circle.* Reid's mistake in this matter is so palpable, that it is not more surprising that he should have committed it, than that so many should not only have followed him in the opinion, but even have lauded it as the refutation of an important error. — H.

to be possible. But does it not often happen, that what one man judges to be possible, another man judges to be impossible? The maxim, therefore, is not true in this sense.

I am not able to find any other meaning of *conceiving a proposition*, or of *conceiving it to be true*, besides these I have mentioned. I know nothing that can be meant by having the idea of a proposition, but either the understanding its meaning, or the judging of its truth. I can understand a proposition that is false or impossible, as well as one that is true or possible; and I find that men have contradictory judgments about what is possible or impossible, as well as about other things. In what sense, then, can it be said, that the having an idea of a proposition gives certain evidence that it is possible?

If it be said, that the idea of a proposition is an *image* of it in the mind, I think, indeed, there cannot be a distinct image, either in the mind or elsewhere, of that which is impossible; but what is meant by *the image of a proposition* I am not able to comprehend, and I shall be glad to be informed.

2. Every proposition that is necessarily true stands opposed to a *contradictory* proposition that is impossible; and *he that conceives one conceives both:* thus, a man who believes that two and three necessarily make five, must believe it to be impossible that two and three should not make five. He conceives both propositions when he believes one. Every proposition carries its contradictory in its bosom, and both are conceived at the same time. " It is confessed," says Mr. Hume, " that, in all cases where we dissent from any person, we conceive both sides of the question, but we can believe only one." From this it certainly follows, that when we dissent from any person about a necessary proposition, we conceive one that is impossible; yet I know no philosopher who has made so much use of the maxim, that whatever we conceive is possible, as Mr. Hume. A great part of his peculiar tenets are built upon it; and if it is true, they must be true. But

he did not perceive that in the passage now quoted, the truth of which is evident, he contradicts it himself.

3. Mathematicians have, in many cases, proved some things to be possible, and others to be impossible, which, without demonstration, would not have been believed; yet I have never found that any mathematician has attempted to prove a thing to be possible because it can be conceived, or impossible because it cannot be conceived.* Why is not this maxim applied to determine whether it is possible to square the circle? — a point about which very eminent mathematicians have differed. It is easy to conceive, that, in the infinite series of numbers and intermediate fractions, some one number, integral or fractional, may bear the same ratio to another as the side of a square bears to its diagonal; † yet, however conceivable this may be, it may be demonstrated to be impossible.

4. Mathematicians often require us to conceive things that are impossible, in order to prove them to be so. This is the case in all their demonstrations *ad absurdum.* Conceive, says Euclid, a right line drawn from one point of the circumference of a circle to another to fall without the circle; ‡ I conceive this, I reason from it, until I come to a consequence that is manifestly absurd; and from thence conclude that the thing which I conceived is impossible.

Having said so much to show that our power of conceiving a proposition is no criterion of its possibility or impossibility, I shall add a few observations on the extent of our knowledge of this kind.

1. There are many propositions which, by the faculties God has given us, we judge to be necessary as well as true. All mathematical propositions are of this kind, and many others. The contradictories of such

---

* All geometry is, in fact, founded on our intuitions of space; that is, in common language, on our conceptions of space and its relations. — H.

† We are able to conceive nothing infinite; and we may *suppose,* but we cannot *conceive, represent,* or *imagine,* the possibility in question. — H.

‡ Euclid does not require us to *conceive* or imagine any such impossibility. The proposition to which Reid must refer is the second of the third book of the *Elements.* — H.

propositions must be impossible. Our knowledge, therefore, of what is *impossible* must at least be as extensive as our knowledge of *necessary* truth.

2. By our senses, by memory, by testimony, and by other means, we know many things to be true which do not appear to be necessary. But whatever is true is possible. Our knowledge, therefore, of what is *possible* must at least extend as far as our knowledge of *truth.*

3. If a man pretends to determine the possibility or impossibility of things beyond these limits, let him bring proof. I do not say that no such proof can be brought. It has been brought in many cases, particularly in mathematics. But I say, that *his being able to conceive a thing is no proof that it is possible.** Mathematics afford many instances of impossibilities in the nature of things, which no man would have believed if they had not been strictly demonstrated. Perhaps, if we were able to reason demonstratively in other subjects to as great extent as in mathematics, we might find many things to be impossible which we conclude without hesitation to be possible.

It is possible, you say, that God might have made a universe of sensible and rational creatures, into which neither natural nor moral evil should ever enter. It may be so for what I know : but how do you *know* that it is possible ? That you can *conceive* it, I grant ; but this is no proof. I cannot admit as an argument, or even as a pressing difficulty, what is grounded on the supposition that such a thing is possible, when there is no good evidence that it is possible, and, for any thing we know, it may in the nature of things be impossible.

---

* Not, certainly, that it is *really possible*, but that it is *problematically possible ;* that is, involves no contradiction, violates no law of thought. This latter is that possibility alone in question. — H.

CHAPTER II.

OF THE TRAIN OF THOUGHT IN THE MIND; OR MENTAL ASSOCIATION.

I. *Preliminary Observations.*] Every man is conscious of a succession of thoughts which pass in his mind while he is awake, even when they are not excited by external objects.*

This continued succession of thought has, by modern philosophers, been called the *imagination.*† I think it was formerly called the *fancy*, or the *phantasy.*‡ If the old name be laid aside, it were to be wished that it had got a name less ambiguous than that of imagination, a name which had two or three meanings besides.

It is often called the *train of ideas.* This may lead one to think that it is a train of bare conceptions; but this would surely be a mistake. It is made up of many other operations of mind, as well as of conceptions or

---

* Mr. Mill, who follows Hume in the distinction which he makes between *impressions* and *ideas*, begins his chapter on this subject thus: — " Thought succeeds thought, idea follows idea, incessantly. If our senses are awake, we are continually receiving sensations of the eye, the ear, the touch, and so forth; but not sensations alone. After sensations, ideas are perpetually excited of sensations formerly received; after those ideas, other ideas: and during the whole of our lives a series of those two states of consciousness, called *sensations* and *ideas*, is constantly going on. I see a horse: that is a sensation. Immediately I think of his master: that is an idea. The idea of his master makes me think of his office; he is a minister of state: that is another idea. The idea of a minister of state makes me think of public affairs; and I am led into a train of political ideas; when I am summoned to dinner. This is a new sensation, followed by the idea of dinner and of the company with whom I am to partake it. The sight of the company and of the food are other sensations; these suggest ideas without end; other sensations perpetually intervene, suggesting other ideas: and so the process goes on." *Analysis*, Chap. III. — Ed.

† By some only, and that improperly. — H.

‡ The Latin *imaginatio*, with its modifications in the vulgar languages, was employed both in ancient and modern times to express what the Greeks denominated φαντασία. *Phantasy*, of which *phansy* or *fancy* is a corruption, and now employed in a more limited sense, was a common name for *imagination* with the old English writers. — H.

ideas. Memory, judgment, reasoning, passions, affections, and purposes, — in a word, every operation of the mind, *excepting those of sense*, is exerted occasionally in this train of thought, and has its share as an ingredient: so that we must take the word *idea* in a very extensive sense, if we make the train of our thoughts to be only a train of ideas.*

To pass from the name and consider the thing, we may observe that the trains of thought in the mind are of two kinds : they are either such as flow spontaneously, like water from a fountain, without any exertion of a governing principle to arrange them; or they are regulated and directed by an active effort of the mind, with some view and intention.

Before we consider these in their order, it is proper to premise, that these two kinds, however distinct in their nature, are for the most part mixed, in persons awake and come to years of understanding. On the one hand, we are rarely so vacant of all project and design as to let our thoughts take their own course without the least check or direction; or if, at any time, we should be in this state, some object will present itself which is too interesting not to engage the attention and rouse the active or contemplative powers that were at rest. On the other hand, when a man is giving the most intense application to any speculation, or to any scheme of conduct, when he wills to exclude every thought that is foreign to his present purpose, such thoughts will often impertinently intrude upon him, in spite of his endeavours to the contrary, and occupy, by a kind of violence, some part of the time destined to another purpose. One man may have the command of his thoughts more than another man, and the same man more at one time than at another; but I apprehend, in the best-trained mind the thoughts will sometimes be restive, sometimes capricious and self-

---

* Stewart and Mill, after Hartley, have proposed to call this succession of thought, *association of ideas*, and this is now the common name; Dr. Brown would substitute *suggestion* for *association*; Sir W. Hamilton calls it *mental suggestion or association*. — ED.

willed, when we wish to have them most under command.

It has been observed very justly, that we must not ascribe to the mind *the power of calling up any thought at pleasure,* because such a call or volition supposes that thought to be already in the mind; for otherwise, how should it be the object of volition? As this must be granted on the one hand, so it is no less certain, on the other, that a man has a considerable power in regulating and disposing his own thoughts. Of this every man is conscious, and I can no more doubt of it than I can doubt whether I think at all.

We seem to treat the thoughts that present themselves to the fancy, as a great man treats the persons who attend his levee. They are all ambitious of his attention; he goes round the circle, bestowing a bow upon one, a smile upon another, asks a short question of a third, while a fourth is honored with a particular conference, and the greater part have no particular mark of attention, but go as they came. It is true, he can give no mark of his attention to those who were not there, but he has a sufficient number for making a choice and distinction. In like manner, a number of thoughts present themselves to the fancy spontaneously; but if we pay no attention to them, nor hold any conference with them, they pass with the crowd, and are immediately forgotten as if they had never appeared. But those to which we think proper to pay attention may be stopped, examined, and arranged, for any particular purpose we have in view.

It may likewise be observed, that a train of thought, which was at first composed by application and judgment, when it has been often repeated and becomes familiar, will present itself spontaneously. Thus, when a man has composed an air in music, so as to please his own ear, after he has played or sung it often, the notes will range themselves in just order, and it requires no effort to regulate their succession.

Thus we see that the fancy is made up of trains of thinking, some of which are spontaneous, others studied

24 *

and regulated, and the greater part are mixed of both kinds, and take their denomination from that which is most prevalent; and that a train of thought, which at first was studied and composed, may by habit present itself spontaneously.

Having premised these things, let us return to those trains of thought which are spontaneous, which must be first in the order of nature.

II. *Spontaneous Trains of Thought.*] When the work of the day is over, and a man lies down to relax his body and mind, he cannot cease from thinking, though he desires it. Something occurs to his fancy; that is followed by another thing, and so his thoughts are carried on from one object to another until sleep closes the scene.

In this operation* of the mind, it is not one faculty only that is employed; there are many that join together in its production. Sometimes the transactions of the day are brought upon the stage and acted over again, as it were, upon this theatre of the imagination. In this case, memory surely acts the most considerable part, since the scenes exhibited are not fictions, but realities, which we remember; yet in this case the memory does not act alone, — other powers are employed, and attend upon their proper objects. The transactions remembered will be more or less interesting; and we cannot then review our own conduct, nor that of others, without passing some judgment upon it. This we approve, that we disapprove. This elevates, that humbles and depresses us. Persons that are not absolutely indifferent to us can hardly appear, even to the imagination, without some friendly or unfriendly emotion. We judge and reason about things, as well as persons, in such reveries. We remember what a man said and did; from this we pass to his designs and to his general character, and frame some hypothesis to

---

* The word *process* might be here preferable. *Operation* would denote that the mind is active in associating the train of thought. — H.

make the whole consistent. Such trains of thought we may call *historical*.

There are others which we may call *romantic*, in which the plot is formed by the creative power of fancy, without any regard to what did or will happen. In these, also, the powers of judgment, taste, moral sentiment, as well as the passions and affections, come in and take a share in the execution. In these scenes, the man himself commonly acts a very distinguished part, and seldom does any thing which he cannot approve. Here the miser will be generous, the coward brave, and the knave honest. Mr. Addison, in *The Spectator*, calls this play of the fancy *castle-building*.

The young politician, who has turned his thoughts to the affairs of government, becomes in his imagination a minister of state. He examines every spring and wheel of the machine of government with the nicest eye and the most exact judgment. He finds a proper remedy for every disorder of the commonwealth, quickens trade and manufactures by salutary laws, encourages arts and sciences, and makes the nation happy at home and respected abroad. He feels the reward of his good administration in that self-approbation which attends it, and is happy in acquiring, by his wise and patriotic conduct, the blessings of the present age and the praises of those that are to come.

It is probable that, upon the stage of imagination, more great exploits have been performed in every age, than have been upon the stage of life from the beginning of the world. An innate desire of self-approbation is undoubtedly a part of the human constitution. It is a powerful spur to worthy conduct, and is intended as such by the Author of our being. A man cannot be easy or happy unless this desire be in some measure gratified. While he conceives himself worthless and base, he can relish no enjoyment. The humiliating, mortifying sentiment must be removed, and this natural desire of self-approbation will either produce a noble effort to acquire real worth, which is its proper direction, or it will lead into some of those arts of self-deceit which create a false opinion of worth.

A castle-builder, in the fictitious scenes of his fancy, will figure, not according to his real character, but according to the highest opinion he has been able to form of himself, and perhaps far beyond that opinion. For in those imaginary conflicts the passions easily yield to reason, and a man exerts the noblest efforts of virtue and magnanimity with the same ease as, in his dreams, he flies through the air, or plunges to the bottom of the ocean.

The romantic scenes of fancy are most commonly the occupation of young minds, not yet so deeply engaged in life as to have their thoughts taken up by its real cares and business. Those active powers of the mind which are most luxuriant by constitution, or have been most cherished by education, impatient to exert themselves, hurry the thought into scenes that give them play; and the boy commences in imagination, according to the bent of his mind, a general or a statesman, a poet or an orator.

In persons come to maturity there is, even in these spontaneous sallies of fancy, some arrangement of thought; and I conceive that it will be readily allowed, that, in those who have the greatest stock of knowledge and the best natural parts, even the spontaneous movements of fancy will be the most regular and connected. They have an order, connection, and unity, by which they are no less distinguished from the dreams of one asleep, or the ravings of one delirious, on the one hand, than from the finished productions of art, on the other.

III. *How what is regular in these Trains is to be explained.*] How is this regular arrangement brought about? It has all the marks of judgment and reason, yet it seems to go before judgment, and to spring forth spontaneously.

Shall we believe, with Leibnitz, that the mind was originally formed like a watch wound up, and that all its thoughts, purposes, passions, and actions are effected by the gradual evolution of the original spring of the machine, and succeed each other in order as necessarily as the motions and pulsations of a watch? If a child of three or four years were put to account for the phenomena of a watch, he would conceive that there is a little man within the watch, or some other little animal, that beats continually and produces the motion. Whether the hypothesis of this young philosopher in turning the watch-spring into a man, or that of the German philosopher in turning a man into a watch-spring, be the most rational, seems hard to determine.*

To account for the regularity of our thoughts from motions of animal spirits, vibrations of nerves, attractions of ideas, or from any other unthinking cause, whether mechanical or contingent, seems equally irrational.

If we be not able to distinguish the strongest marks of thought and design from the effects of mechanism or contingency, the consequence will be very melancholy; for it must necessarily follow, that we have no evidence of thought in any of our fellow-men, — nay, that we have no evidence of thought or design in the structure and government of the universe. If a good period or sentence was ever produced without having had any judgment previously employed about it, why not an Iliad or Æneid? They differ only in less and more; and we should do injustice to the philosopher of Laputa in laughing at his project of making poems by the turning of a wheel, if a concurrence of unthinking causes may produce a rational train of thought.

It is, therefore, in itself highly probable, to say no more, that whatsoever is regular and rational in a train of thought which presents itself spontaneously to a man's fancy, without any study, *is a copy of what had been before composed by his own rational powers, or those of some other person.*

We certainly judge so in similar cases. Thus, in a book I find a train of thinking, which has the marks of knowledge and judgment. I ask how it was produced?

---

* The theory of our mental associations owes much to the philosophers of the Leibnitzian school. — H.

It is printed in a book. This does not satisfy me, because the book has no knowledge nor reason. I am told that a printer printed it, and a compositor set the types. Neither does this satisfy me. These causes perhaps knew very little of the subject. There must be a prior cause of the composition. It was printed from a manuscript. True. But the manuscript is as ignorant as the printed book. The manuscript was written or dictated by a man of knowledge and judgment. This, and this only, will satisfy a man of common understanding; and it appears to him extremely ridiculous to believe that such a train of thinking could originally be produced by any cause that neither reasons nor thinks.

Whether such a train of thinking be printed in a book, or printed, so to speak, in his mind, and issue spontaneously from his fancy, it must have been composed with judgment by himself or by some other rational being.

This, I think, will be confirmed by tracing the progress of the human fancy as far back as we are able.

Man has undoubtedly *a power* (whether we call it *taste* or *judgment* is not of any consequence in the present argument) whereby he distinguishes between a composition and a heap of materials; between a house, for instance, and a heap of stones; between a sentence and a heap of words; between a picture and a heap of colors. It does not appear to me, that children have any regular trains of thought *until this power begins to operate.* Those who are born such idiots as never to show any signs of this power, show as little any signs of regularity of thought. It seems, therefore, that this power is connected with all regular trains of thought, and may be the cause of them.

Such trains of thought discover themselves in children about two years of age. They can then give attention to the operations of older children in making their little houses and ships, and other such things, in imitation of the works of men. They are then capable of understanding a little of language, which shows both a regular train of thinking and some degree of abstraction. I think we may perceive a distinction between the faculties of children of two or three years of age, and those of the most sagacious brutes. They can then perceive design and regularity in the works of others, especially of older children; their little minds are fired with the discovery; they are eager to imitate them, and never at rest till they can exhibit something of the same kind.

As children grow up, they are delighted with tales, with childish games, with designs and stratagems. Every thing of this kind stores the fancy with a new regular train of thought, which becomes familiar by repetition, so that one part draws the whole after it in the imagination. The imagination of a child, like the hand of a painter, is long employed in copying the works of others before it attempts any invention of its own.

The power of invention is not yet brought forth, but it is coming forward, and, like the bud of a tree, is ready to burst its integuments, when some accident aids its eruption. There is no power of the understanding that gives so much pleasure to the owner as that of invention, whether it be employed in mechanics, in science, in the conduct of life, in poetry, in wit, or in the fine arts. I am aware that the power of invention is distributed among men more unequally than almost any other. When it is able to produce any thing that is interesting to mankind, we call it genius, — a talent which is the lot of very few. But there is perhaps a lower kind or lower degree of invention, that is more common. However this may be, it must be allowed that the power of invention, in those who have it, will produce many new regular trains of thought, and these, being expressed in works of art, in writing, or in discourse, will be copied by others.

Thus, I conceive the minds of children, as soon as they have judgment to distinguish what is regular, orderly, and connected from a mere medley of thought, are furnished with regular trains of thinking by these means. And the condition of man requires a longer infancy and youth than that of other animals ; for this reason, among others, that almost every station in civil society requires a multitude of regular trains of thought to be not only acquired, but to be made so familiar, by frequent repetition, as to present themselves spontaneously when there is occasion for them. The imagination even of men of good parts never serves them readily but in things wherein it has been much exercised. A minister of state holds a conference with a foreign ambassador with no greater emotion than a professor in a college prelects to his audience. The imagination of each presents to him what the occasion requires to be said, and how. Let them change places, and both would find themselves at a loss.

The habits which the human mind is capable of acquiring by exercise are wonderful in many instances ; in none more wonderful than in that versatility of imagination which a well-bred man acquires by being much exercised in the various scenes of life. In the morning he visits a friend in affliction. Here his imagination brings forth from its store every topic of consolation, every thing that is agreeable to the laws of friendship and sympathy, and nothing that is not so. From thence he drives to the minister's levee, where imagination readily suggests what is proper to be said or replied to every man, and in what manner, according to the degree of acquaintance or familiarity, of rank or dependence, of opposition or concurrence of interests, of confidence or distrust, that is between them. Nor does all this employment hinder him from carrying on some design with much artifice, and endeavouring to penetrate into the views of others through the closest disguises. From the levee he goes to the House of Commons, and speaks upon the affairs of the nation ; from thence to a ball or assembly, and entertains the ladies.

When such habits are acquired and perfected, they are exercised without any laborious effort, — like the habit of playing upon an instrument of music. There are innumerable motions of the fingers upon the stops or keys, which must be directed in one particular train or succession. There is only one arrangement of those motions that is right, while there are ten thousand that are wrong, and would spoil the music. The musician thinks not in the least of the arrangement of those motions; he has a distinct idea of the tune, and wills to play it. The motions of the fingers arrange themselves so as to answer his intention.

In like manner, when a man speaks upon a subject with which he is acquainted, there is a certain arrangement of his thoughts and words necessary to make his discourse sensible, pertinent, and grammatical. In every sentence there are more rules of grammar, logic, and rhetoric that may be transgressed, than there are words and letters. He speaks without thinking of any of those rules, and yet observes them all, as if they were all in his eye. This is a habit so similar to that of a player on an instrument, that I think both must be got in the same way, that is, by much practice and the power of habit. When a man speaks well and methodically upon a subject without study, and with perfect ease, I believe we may take it for granted that his thoughts run in a beaten track. There is a mould in his mind, which has been formed by much practice, or by study, for this very subject, or for some other so similar and analogous, that his discourse falls into this mould with ease, and takes its form from it.

Hitherto we have considered the operations of fancy that are either spontaneous, or at least require no laborious effort to guide and direct them, and have endeavoured to account for that degree of regularity and arrangement which is found even in them. (1.) The natural powers of judgment and invention, (2.) the pleasure that always attends the exercise of those powers, (3.) the means we have of improving them by imitation of others, and (4.) the effect of practice and habit, seem to me sufficiently to account for this phenomenon, without supposing any unaccountable attractions of ideas by which they arrange themselves.

25

IV. *Trains of Thought directed and regulated by the Will.*] But we are able to direct our thoughts in a certain course, so as to perform a destined task.

Every work of art has its model framed in the imagination. Here the *Iliad* of Homer, the *Republic* of Plato, the *Principia* of Newton, were fabricated. Shall we believe that those works took the form in which they now appear of themselves? — that the sentiments, the manners, and the passions arranged themselves at once in the mind of Homer so as to form the *Iliad?* Was there no more effort in the composition than there is in telling a well-known tale, or singing a favorite song? This cannot be believed. Granting that some happy thought first suggested the design of singing the wrath of Achilles, yet, surely, it was a matter of judgment and choice where the narration should begin, and where it should end. Granting that the fertility of the poet's imagination suggested a variety of rich materials, was not judgment necessary to select what was proper, to reject what was improper, to arrange the materials into a just composition, and to adapt them to each other and to the design of the whole? No man can believe that Homer's ideas, merely by certain sympathies and antipathies, by certain attractions and repulsions inherent in their natures, arranged themselves according to the most perfect rules of epic poetry, and Newton's according to the rules of mathematical composition. I should sooner believe that the poet, after he invoked his Muse, did nothing at all but listen to the song of the goddess. Poets, indeed, and other artists, must make their works appear natural; but nature is the perfection of art, and there can be no just imitation of nature without art. When the building is finished, the rubbish, the scaffolds, the tools, and engines, are carried out of sight, but we know it could not have been reared without them.

The train of thinking, therefore, is capable of being guided and directed, much in the same manner as the horse we ride.* The horse has his strength, his agility,

---

* Mr. Stewart is obliged to admit that the mind has no *direct* power

and his mettle in himself; he has been taught certain movements, and many useful habits that will make him more subservient to our purposes, and obedient to our will; but to accomplish a journey, he must be directed by the rider.

In like manner, fancy has its original powers, which are very different in different persons; it has likewise more regular motions, to which it has been trained by a long course of discipline and exercise; and by which it may, *extempore*, and without much effort, produce things that have a considerable degree of beauty, regularity, and design. But the most perfect works of design are never extemporary. Our first thoughts are reviewed; we place them at a proper distance; examine every part, and take a complex view of the whole. By our critical faculties, we perceive this part to be redundant, that deficient; here is a want of nerves, there a want of delicacy; this is obscure, that too diffuse. Things are marshalled anew, according to a second and more deliberate judgment; what was deficient is supplied; what was dislocated is put in joint; redundances are lopped off, and the whole polished.

---

over the train of our thoughts; that is, we cannot call up at will a particular thought, as this would be to suppose it already in the mind. But it has a twofold *indirect* power. 1. In the first place, it has the power of singling out at pleasure any one idea in the train, detaining it, and making it a particular object of attention. "By doing so, we not only stop the succession that would otherwise take place, but, in consequence of our bringing to view the less obvious relations among our ideas, we frequently divert the current of our thoughts into a new channel. 2. But the principal power we possess over the train of our ideas is founded on the influence which our habits of thinking have on the laws of association;—an influence which is so great, that we may form a pretty shrewd judgment concerning a man's prevailing turn of thought from the transitions he makes in conversation or in writing. It is well known, too, that by means of habit a particular associating principle may be strengthened to such a degree, as to give us a command of all the different ideas in our mind which have a certain relation to each other; so that, when any one of the class occurs to us, we have almost a certainty that it will suggest the rest. Thus, a man who has an ambition to become a punster seldom or never fails in the attainment of his object; that is, he seldom or never fails in acquiring the power which other men have not, of summoning up, on a particular occasion, a number of words different from each other in meaning, but resembling each other, more or less, in sound." — *Elements*, Part I. Chap. V. Sect. III. — ED.

Though poets, of all artists, make the highest claim to inspiration, yet if we believe Horace, a competent judge, no production in that art can have merit, which has not cost such labor as this in the birth.

> " Vos O !
> Pompilius sanguis, carmen reprehendite quod non
> Multa dies, et multa litura coercuit, atque
> Perfectum decies non castigavit ad unguem."

The conclusion I would draw from all that has been said upon this subject is, that every thing that is regular in that train of thought which we call fancy or imagination, from the little designs and reveries of children to the grandest productions of human genius, was originally the *offspring of judgment or taste, applied with some effort greater or less.* What one person composed with art and judgment is imitated by another with great ease. What a man himself at first composed with pains becomes by habit so familiar, as to offer itself spontaneously to his fancy afterwards. But nothing that is regular was ever at first conceived without design, attention, and care.

V. *Laws or Conditions of Mental Association.*]   I shall now make a few reflections upon a theory which has been applied to account for this successive train of thought in the mind. It was hinted by Mr. Hobbes, but has drawn more attention since it was distinctly explained by Mr. Hume.

That author thinks, that the train of thought in the mind is owing to a kind of attraction which ideas have for other ideas that bear certain relations to them. He thinks the complex ideas, which are the common subjects of our thoughts and reasoning, are owing to the same cause. The relations which produce this attraction of ideas, he thinks, are these three only, — to wit, *causation, contiguity in time* or *place*, and *similitude.* He asserts, that these are the only general principles that unite ideas. And having, in another place, occasion to take notice of *contrariety* as a principle of connection among ideas, in order to reconcile this to his system, he tells us gravely, that contrariety may perhaps be considered as *a mixture of causation and resemblance*. That ideas which have any of these three relations do mutually attract each other, so that, one of them being presented to the fancy, the other is drawn along with it, — this he seems to think an original property of the mind, or rather of the ideas, and therefore inexplicable.*

* The history of the doctrine of association has never yet been at all adequately developed. Some of the most remarkable speculations on this matter are wholly unknown. Mr. Hume says, — "I do not find that any philosopher has attempted to enumerate or class all the principles of association; a subject, however, that seems to me very worthy of curiosity. To me there appear to be only three principles of connection among ideas: *resemblance, contiguity in time* or *place, cause and effect.*" — *Essays,* Vol. II. p. 24. Aristotle, and, after him, many other philosophers, had, however, done this, and with even greater success than Hume himself. Aristotle's reduction is to the four following heads : — *proximity in time, contiguity in place, resemblance, contrast.* This is more correct than Hume's; for Hume's second head ought to be divided into two; while our connecting any *particular* events in the relation of *cause and effect* is itself the result of their observed proximity in time and contiguity in place; nay, to custom and this empirical connection (as observed by Reid) does Hume himself endeavour to reduce *the principle of causality* altogether. — H.

In his *Supplementary Dissertations,* Note D**, Sir W. Hamilton returns to the subject, reaffirming that all the attempts which have been made under the name of *Histories of the Association of Ideas* are fragmentary contributions, and meagre and inaccurate as far as they go. "These inadequate attempts," he also says, "have been limited to Germany; and in Germany to the treatises of three authors; for the historical notices on this doctrine, found in the works of other German psychologists, are wholly borrowed from them. I refer to the *Geschichte* of Hissmann (1777); to the *Paralipomena* and *Beytræge* of Maass (1787, 1792); and to the *Vestigia* of Goerenz (1791). In England, indeed, we have a chapter in Mr. Coleridge's *Biographia Literaria.* entitled. *On the Law of Association,* — *its History traced from Aristotle to Hartley ;* but this, in so far as it is of any value, is a plagiarism, and a blundering plagiarism, from Maass ; — the whole chapter exhibiting, in fact, more mistakes than paragraphs. We may judge of Mr. Coleridge's competence to speak of Aristotle, the great philosopher of ancient times, when we find him referring to the *De Anima* for his speculations on the associative principle; opposing the *De Memoria* and *Parva Naturalia* as distinct works; and attributing to Aquinas what belongs exclusively and notoriously to the Stagirite. We may judge of his competence to speak of Descartes, the great philosopher of modern times, when telling us, that *idea,* in the Cartesian philosophy, denotes merely a configuration of the brain; the term. he adds. being first extended by Locke to denote the immediate object of the mind's attention in consciousness. . . . . . Sir James Mackintosh, again, founding on his own research, affirms that Aristotle and his disciples, among whom Vives is specified, confine the application of the law of association ' *exclusively to the phenomena*

First, I observe with regard to this theory, that, although it is true that the thought of any object is apt to lead us to the thought of its cause or effect, of things contiguous to it in time or place, or of things resembling it, yet this enumeration of the relations of things which are apt to lead us from one object to another is very inaccurate.

The enumeration is too large upon his own principles; but it is by far too scanty in reality. Causation, according to his philosophy, implies nothing more than a constant conjunction observed between the cause and the effect, and therefore contiguity must include causation, and his three principles of attraction are reduced to two. But when we take all the three, the enumeration is in reality very incomplete. *Every relation of things has a tendency, more or less, to lead the thought, in a thinking mind, from one to the other;* and not only every relation, but *every kind of contrariety and opposition.** What Mr. Hume says, — that contrariety may perhaps be considered as a mixture " of causation and

---

of recollection, without any glimpse of a more general operation extending to all the connections of *thought and feeling'*; while the enouncement of a general theory of association, thus denied to the genius of Aristotle, is all, and more than all, accorded to the sagacity of Hobbes. The truth, however, is, that in his whole doctrine upon this subject, name and thing, Hobbes is simply a silent follower of the Stagirite; inferior to his master in the comprehension and accuracy of his general views, and not superior, even on the special points selected, either to Aristotle or to Vives." — ED.

* Still something may be gained by a judicious *classification* of the conditions and relations on which mental association depends. Dr. Brown, who has bestowed much attention on this subject, reduces the *primary laws* of association or suggestion to three : *resemblance, contrast, nearness in time* or *place.* These correspond to the four of Aristotle, the third being divisible into two. Again, Dr. Brown thinks that the influence of the three primary laws is modified, in different persons and under different circumstances, by nine *secondary laws.* The latter are : — 1. The longer or shorter continuance of the attention which was given to the associated ideas when in connection. 2. Vividness of the coexistent emotions. 3. Frequency of repetition. 4. Lapse of time. 5. The exclusion of all other associations. 6. Original constitutional differences. 7. The state of the mind at the time 8. The state of the body. 9. Professional habits. See his *Physiology of the Mind,* p. 199, and also his *Lectures,* Lect. XXXV.-XXXVII. Compare Ballantyne's *Examination of the Human Mind,* Chap. II.; Mill's *Analysis,* Chap. III.; and Sir W. Hamilton's *Supplementary Dissertations,* Note D***. — ED.

resemblance," — I can as little comprehend, as if he had said that figure may perhaps be considered as a mixture of color and sound.

Our thoughts pass easily from the end to the means; from any truth to the evidence on which it is founded, the consequences that may be drawn from it, or the use that may be made of it. From a part we are easily led to think of the whole, from a subject to its qualities, or from things related to the relation. Such transitions in thinking must have been made thousands of times by every man who thinks and reasons, and thereby become, as it were, beaten tracks for the imagination.

Not only the relations of objects to each other influence our train of thinking, but the relation they bear to the present *temper* and *disposition* of the mind; their relation to the *habits* we have acquired, whether moral or intellectual; to the *company* we have kept, and to the *business* in which we have been chiefly employed. The same event will suggest very different reflections to different persons, and to the same person at different times, according as he is in good or bad humor, as he is lively or dull, angry or pleased, melancholy or cheerful.

Secondly, Let us consider how far this attraction of ideas must be resolved into original qualities of human nature.

I believe the original principles of the mind, of which we can give no account but that such is our constitution, are more in number than is commonly thought. But we ought not to multiply them without necessity. That trains of thinking, which by frequent repetition have become familiar, should spontaneously offer themselves to our fancy, seems to require no other original quality but *the power of habit.** In all rational think-

---

* We can as well explain habit by association, as association by habit. — H.

Better even, according to Mr. Stewart, who says: — "The wonderful effect of practice in the formation of habits has been often and justly taken notice of, as one of the most curious circumstances in the human constitution. A mechanical operation, for example, which we at first performed with the utmost difficulty, comes, in time, to be so familiar to us, that we are able to perform it without the smallest danger of mistake; even while

ing, and in all rational discourse, whether serious or facetious, the thought must have some relation to what
went before. Every man, therefore, from the dawn of
reason, must have been accustomed to a train of related
objects. These please the understanding, and by custom
become like beaten tracks which invite the traveller.

As far as it is in our power to give a direction to our
thoughts (which it is, undoubtedly, in a great degree),
they will be directed by the active principles common
to men, — by our appetites, our passions, our affections,
our reason, and conscience. And that the trains of
thinking in our minds are chiefly governed by these,
according as one or another prevails at the time, every
man will find in his experience. If the mind is at any
time vacant from every passion and desire, there are
still some objects that are more acceptable to us than
others. The facetious man is pleased with surprising
similitudes or contrasts ; the philosopher, with the relations of things that are subservient to reasoning ; the
merchant, with what tends to profit ; and the politician,
with what may mend the state.

Nevertheless, I believe we are originally disposed, in
imagination, to pass from any one object of thought to
others that are contiguous to it in time or place. This
I think may be observed in brutes and in idiots, as well
as in children, before any habit can be acquired that
might account for it. The sight of an object is apt to
suggest to the imagination what has been seen or felt
in conjunction with it, even when the memory of that
conjunction is gone. They expect events in the same
order and succession in which they happened before ;
and by this expectation, their actions and passions, as
well as their thoughts, are regulated. A horse takes

---

the attention appears to be completely engaged with other subjects. The
truth seems to be, that, *in consequence of the association of ideas*, the different
steps of the process present themselves successively to the thoughts, without any recollection on our part, and with a degree of rapidity proportioned
to the length of our experience, so as to save us the trouble of hesitation
and reflection, by giving us every moment a precise and steady notion of
the effect to be produced." — *Elements*, Part I. Chap. II. — ED.

fright at the place where some object frighted him before. We are apt to conclude from this, that he remembers the former accident. But perhaps there is only an association formed in his mind between the place and the passion of fear, without any distinct remembrance.

Mr. Locke has given us a very good chapter upon the association of ideas; and, by the examples he has given to illustrate this doctrine, I think it appears that very strong associations may be formed at once; not of ideas to ideas only, but of ideas to passions and emotions; and that strong associations are never formed at once, but when accompanied by some strong passion or emotion. I believe this must also be resolved into the constitution of our nature.

It will be allowed by every man, that our happiness or misery in life, that our improvement in any art or science which we profess, and that our improvement in real virtue and goodness, depend in a very great degree on the train of thinking that occupies the mind both in our vacant and in our more serious hours. As far, therefore, as the direction of our thoughts is in our power (and that it is so in a great measure cannot be doubted), it is of the last importance to give them that direction which is most subservient to those valuable purposes. How happy is that mind, in which the light of real knowledge dispels the phantoms of superstition; in which the belief and reverence of a perfect all-governing Mind casts out all fear but the fear of acting wrong; in which serenity and cheerfulness, innocence, humanity, and candor, guard the imagination against the entrance of every unhallowed intruder, and invite more amiable and worthier guests to dwell!*

---

* On the doctrine of mental association the student may consult with advantage, in addition to the works already indicated, Dr. Priestley's *Hartley's Theory of the Human Mind, on the Principle of the Association of Ideas; with Essays relating to the Subject of it;* Cardaillac, *Etudes Elémentaires de Philosophie,* Sect. V.; *Systematic Education,* Vol. II. Chap. XIII., by Dr. Lant Carpenter. The important subject of *casual associations,* and their influence on character and happiness, has been treated most fully and satisfactorily by Mr. Stewart, *Elements,* Part I. Chap. V.—ED.

ESSAY V.

OF ABSTRACTION.

CHAPTER I.

OF GENERAL WORDS.

I. *The Distinction between General Words and Proper Names.*] The words we use in language are either *general words* or *proper names.* Proper names are intended to signify one individual only. Such are the names of men, kingdoms, provinces, cities, rivers, and of every other creature of God, or work of man, which we choose to distinguish from all others of the kind by a name appropriated to it. All the other words of language are general words, not appropriated to signify any one individual thing, but equally related to many.

In every language, rude or polished, general words make the greater part, and proper names the less. Grammarians have reduced all words to eight or nine classes, which are called *parts of speech.* Of these there is only one — to wit, that of *nouns* — wherein proper names are found. All *pronouns, verbs, participles, adverbs, articles, prepositions, conjunctions,* and *interjections* are general words. Of *nouns,* all *adjectives* are general words, and the greater part of *substantives.* Every substantive that has a plural number is a general word; for no proper name can have a plural number, because it signifies only one individual. In all the fifteen books of Euclid's *Elements,* there is not one word that is not general; and the same may be said of many large volumes.

At the same time it must be acknowledged, that all the objects we perceive are *individuals.* Every object of sense, of memory, or of consciousness is an individual object. All the good things we enjoy or desire, and all the evils we feel or fear, must come from individuals; and I think we may venture to say, that every creature which God has made, in the heavens above, or in the earth beneath, or in the waters under the earth, is an individual.

II. *Why General Words are so much more numerous.*] How comes it to pass, then, that in all languages general words make the greatest part of the language, and proper names but a very small and inconsiderable part of it? This seemingly strange phenomenon may, I think, be easily accounted for by the following observations.

First, though there be a few individuals that are obvious to the notice of all men, and therefore have proper names in all languages, — such as the sun and moon, the earth and sea, — yet the greatest part of the things to which we think fit to give proper names are *local;* known perhaps to a village or to a neighbourhood, but unknown to the greater part of those who speak the same language, and to all the rest of mankind. The names of such things, being confined to a corner, and having no names answering to them in other languages, *are not accounted a part of the language,* any more than the customs of a particular hamlet are accounted part of the law of the nation.

Secondly, it may be observed, that every individual object that falls within our view has various attributes; and it is by them that it becomes useful or hurtful to us. We know not the essence of any individual object; all the knowledge we can attain of it is the knowledge of its attributes, — its quantity, its various qualities, its various relations to other things, its place, its situation, and motions. It is by such attributes of things only that we can communicate our knowledge of them to others. By their attributes, our hopes or fears from them are regulated; and it is only by attention to their attributes that we can make them subservient to our ends; and therefore we give names to such attributes.

Now all attributes must from their nature be expressed by general words, and are so expressed in all languages. In the ancient philosophy, attributes in general were called by two names which express their nature. They were called *universals*, because they might belong equally to many individuals, and are not confined to one. They were also called *predicables*, because whatever is predicated, that is, affirmed or denied, of one subject may be of more, and therefore is a universal, and expressed by a general word. A predicable, therefore, signifies the same thing as an attribute, with this difference only, that the first is Latin, the last English.* The attributes we find either in the creatures of God, or in the works of men, are common to many individuals. We either *find* it to be so, or *presume* it may be so, and give them the same name in every subject to which they belong.

There are not only attributes belonging to individual subjects, but there are likewise attributes of attributes, which may be called *secondary attributes*. Most attributes are capable of different degrees, and different modifications, which must be expressed by general words. Thus it is an attribute of many bodies to be moved; but motion may be in an endless variety of directions. It may be quick or slow, rectilineal or curvilineal; it may be equable, or accelerated, or retarded.

As all attributes, therefore, whether primary or secondary, are expressed by general words, it follows, that, in every proposition we express in language, what is affirmed or denied of the subject of the proposition must be expressed by general words.

Thirdly, the same faculties by which we distinguish

---

* They are both Latin, or both English. The only difference is, that the one is of technical, the other of popular application, and that the former expresses as potential what the latter does as actual. — H.

the different attributes belonging to the same subject, and give names to them, enable us likewise to observe, that many subjects agree in certain attributes, while they differ in others. By this means we are enabled to reduce individuals, which are infinite, to a limited number of classes, which are called *kinds* and *sorts;* and, in the scholastic language, *genera* and *species.* Observing many individuals to agree in certain attributes, we refer them all to one class, and give a name to the class. This name comprehends in its signification, not one attribute only, but all the attributes which distinguish that class; and by affirming this name of any individual, we affirm it to have all the attributes which characterize the class: thus men, dogs, horses, elephants, are so many different classes of animals. In like manner we marshal other substances, vegetable and inanimate, into classes. Nor is it only substances that we thus form into classes. We do the same with regard to qualities, relations, actions, affections, passions, and all other things.

When a class is very large, it is divided into subordinate classes in the same manner. The higher class is called a *genus* or kind; the lower, a *species* or sort of the higher. Sometimes a species is still subdivided into subordinate species; and this subdivision is carried on as far as is found convenient for the purpose of language, or for the improvement of knowledge.

In this distribution of things into *genera* and *species,* it is evident that the name of the species comprehends more attributes than the name of the genus. The species comprehends all that is in the genus, and those attributes likewise which distinguish that species from others belonging to the same genus; and the more subdivisions we make, the names of the lower become still the more comprehensive in their signification, but the less extensive in their application to individuals.

Hence it is an axiom in logic, that, the *more extensive* any general term is, it is the *less comprehensive;* and, on the contrary, the *more comprehensive,* the *less extensive.* Thus, in the following series of subordinate

26

general terms, — animal, man, Frenchman, Parisian, —
every subsequent term comprehends in its signification
all that is in the preceding, and something more ; and
every antecedent term extends to more individuals than
the subsequent.

Such divisions and subdivisions of things into *genera*
and *species*, with general names, are not confined to
the learned and polished languages ; they are found in
those of the rudest tribes of mankind : from which we
learn, that the invention and the use of general words,
both to signify the attributes of things, and to signify
the *genera* and *species* of things, is not a subtile invention of philosophers, but an operation which all men
perform by the light of common sense. Philosophers
may speculate about this operation, and reduce it to
canons and aphorisms ; but men of common understanding, without knowing any thing of the philosophy
of it, can put it in practice ; in like manner as they can
see objects, and make good use of their eyes, although
they know nothing of the structure of the eye, or of the
theory of vision.*

---

* This is well illustrated by Adam Smith in the following passage, taken
from the beginning of his *Considerations concerning the First Formation of
Languages :* — " The assignation of particular names to denote particular
objects, that is, the institution of nouns substantive, would, probably, be
one of the first steps towards the formation of language. Two savages,
who had never been taught to speak, but had been bred up remote from
the societies of men, would naturally begin to form that language, by which
they would endeavour to make their mutual wants intelligible to each other,
by uttering certain sounds, whenever they meant to denote certain objects.
Those objects only which were most familiar to them, and which they had
most frequent occasion to mention, would have particular names assigned
to them. The particular cave whose covering sheltered them from the
weather, the particular tree whose fruit relieved their hunger, the particular
fountain whose waters allayed their thirst, would first be denominated by
the words *cave, tree, fountain,* or by whatever other appellations they might
think proper, in that primitive jargon, to mark them. Afterwards, when
the more enlarged experience of these savages had led them to observe,
and their necessary occasions obliged them to make mention of, other
caves, and other trees, and other fountains, they would naturally bestow
upon each of those new objects the same name by which they had been
accustomed to express the similar object they were first acquainted with.
And thus those words, which were originally the proper names of individuals, would each of them insensibly become the common name of a
multitude." — ED.

III. *General Words the Signs of General Conceptions.*] As general words are so necessary in language, it is natural to conclude that there must be *general conceptions*, of which they are the signs. Words are empty sounds when they do not signify the thoughts of the speaker; and it is only from their signification that they are denominated general. Every word that is spoken, considered merely as a sound, is an individual sound. · And it can only be called a general word, because that which it signifies is general. Now that which it signifies is conceived by the mind both of the speaker and hearer, if the word have a distinct meaning, and be distinctly understood. It is therefore impossible that words can have a general signification, unless there be conceptions in the mind of the speaker, and of the hearer, of things that are general.

We are therefore here to consider whether we have such general conceptions, and how they are formed.

To begin with the conceptions expressed by general terms, that is, by such general words as may be the subject or the predicate of a proposition. They are either attributes of things, or they are *genera* or *species* of things.

It is evident, with respect to all the individuals we are acquainted with, that we have a more clear and distinct conception of their *attributes*, than of the subject to which those attributes belong.

Take, for instance, any individual body we have access to know, — what conception do we form of it? Every man may know this from his consciousness. He will find that he conceives it as a thing that has length, breadth, and thickness, such a figure, and such a color; that it is hard, or soft, or fluid; that it has such qualities, and is fit for such purposes. If it is a vegetable, he may know where it grew, what is the form of its leaves, and flower, and seed; if an animal, what are its natural instincts, its manner of life, and of rearing its young. Of these attributes belonging to this individual, and numberless others, he may surely have a distinct conception; and he will find words in language by which he can clearly and distinctly express each of them.

Indeed, the attributes of individuals are all that we distinctly conceive about them. It is true, we conceive a *subject* to which the attributes belong; but of this subject, when its attributes are set aside, we have but an obscure and relative conception, whether it be body or mind.

The other class of general terms are those that signify the *genera* and *species* into which we divide and subdivide things. And if we be able to form distinct conceptions of attributes, it cannot surely be denied that we may have distinct conceptions of *genera* and *species;* because they are only *collections of attributes* which we conceive to exist in a subject, and to which we give a general name. If the attributes comprehended under that general name be distinctly conceived, the thing meant by the name must be distinctly conceived. And the name may justly be attributed to every individual which has those attributes.

Thus, I conceive distinctly what it is to have wings, to be covered with feathers, to lay eggs. Suppose, then, that we give the name of *bird* to every animal that has these three attributes. Here, undoubtedly, my conception of a bird is as distinct as my notion of the attributes which are common to this species : and if this be admitted to be the definition of a bird, there is nothing I conceive more distinctly. If I had never seen a bird, and can but be made to understand the definition, I can easily apply it to every individual of the species, without danger of mistake.

When things are divided and subdivided by men of science, and names given to the *genera* and *species,* those names are defined. Thus, the genera and species of plants, and of other natural bodies, are accurately defined by the writers in the various branches of natural history ; so that, to all future generations, the definition will convey a distinct notion of the genus or *species* defined.

There are, without doubt, many words signifying

genera and *species* of things, which have a meaning somewhat vague and indistinct; so that those who speak the same language do not always use them in the same sense. But if we attend to the cause of this indistinctness, we shall find, that it is not owing to their being general terms, but to this, that there is no definition of them that has authority. Their meaning, therefore, has not been learned by a definition, but by a kind of induction, — by observing to what individuals they are applied by those who understand the language. We learn by habit to use them as we see others do, even when we have not a precise meaning annexed to them. A man may know, that to certain individuals they may be applied with propriety; but whether they can be applied to certain other individuals, he may be uncertain, either from want of good authorities, or from having contrary authorities, which leave him in doubt.

Thus, a man may know, that, when he applies the name of *beast* to a lion or tiger, and the name of *bird* to an eagle or a turkey, he speaks properly. But whether a bat be a bird or a beast, he may be uncertain. If there were any accurate definition of a beast and of a bird, that is of sufficient authority, he could be at no loss.

A genus or species, being a collection of attributes, conceived to exist in one subject, a definition is the only way to prevent any addition or diminution of its ingredients in the conception of different persons; and when there is no definition that can be appealed to as a standard, the name will hardly retain the most perfect precision in its signification.

My design at present being only to show that we have general conceptions no less clear and distinct than those of individuals, it is sufficient for this purpose, if this appears with regard to the conceptions expressed by general terms. To conceive the meaning of a general word, and to conceive that which it signifies, is the same thing. We conceive distinctly the meaning of general terms, therefore we conceive distinctly that which they signify. But such terms do not signify any

26 *

individual, but what is common to many individuals; therefore we have a distinct conception of things common to many individuals, that is, we have distinct general conceptions.

We must here beware of the ambiguity of the word *conception*, which sometimes signifies the act of the mind in conceiving, sometimes the thing conceived, which is the object of that act.* If the word be taken in the first sense, I acknowledge that every act of the mind is an individual act; the universality, therefore, is not in the act of the mind, but in the object, or thing conceived. The thing conceived is an attribute common to many subjects, or it is a genus or species common to many individuals.†

CHAPTER II.

OF THE FORMATION OF GENERAL CONCEPTIONS.

I. *Distribution of the Subject.*] We are next to consider the operations of the understanding, by which we are enabled to form general conceptions. These appear to me to be three : —

First, The resolving or analyzing a subject into its known attributes, and giving a name to each attribute, which name shall signify that attribute, and nothing more.

Secondly, The observing one or more such attributes to be common to many subjects.

The first is by philosophers called *abstraction;* the second may be called *generalizing;* but both are commonly included under the name of *abstraction.*

---

* This last should be called *concept*, which was a term in use with the old English philosophers. — H.

† On the whole subject of *names* and *naming*, see James Mill's *Analysis*, Vol. I p. 83 *et seq.;* Whewell's *Philosophy of the Inductive Sciences*, Vol. I., Aphorisms; and J. S. Mill's *System of Logic*, Book I. — Ed.

It is difficult to say which of them goes first, or whether they are not so closely connected that neither can claim the precedence. For, on the one hand, to perceive an agreement between two or more objects in the same attribute, seems to require nothing more than to compare them together. A savage, upon seeing snow and chalk, would find no difficulty in perceiving that they have the same color. Yet, on the other hand, it seems impossible that he should observe this agreement without abstraction,—that is, distinguishing in his conception the color, wherein those two objects agree, from the other qualities wherein they disagree.

It seems, therefore, that we cannot generalize without some degree of abstraction; but I apprehend we may abstract without generalizing. For what hinders me from attending to the whiteness of the paper before me, without applying that color to any other object? The whiteness of this individual object is an *abstract* conception, but not a *general* one, while applied to one individual only. These two operations, however, are subservient to each other; for the more attributes we observe and distinguish in any one individual, the more agreements we shall discover between it and other individuals.

A *third* operation of the understanding, by which we form abstract conceptions, is the *combining into one whole* a certain number of those attributes of which we have formed abstract notions, and *giving a name* to that combination. It is thus we form abstract notions of the *genera* and *species* of things. These three operations we shall consider in order.

II. *General Conceptions formed by Abstraction and Generalization.*] With regard to *abstraction*, strictly so called, I can perceive nothing in it that is difficult either to be understood or practised. What can be more easy than to distinguish the different attributes which we know to belong to a subject? In a man, for instance, to distinguish his size, his complexion, his age, his fortune, his birth, his profession, and twenty other things that belong to him? To think and speak of these things with understanding, is surely within the reach of every man endowed with the human faculties.

There may be distinctions that require nice discernment, or an acquaintance with the subject that is not common. Thus, a critic in painting may discern the style of Raphael or Titian, when another man could not. A lawyer may be acquainted with many distinctions in crimes, and contracts, and actions, which never occurred to a man who has not studied law. One man may excel another in the talent of distinguishing, as he may in memory or in reasoning; but there is a certain degree of this talent, without which a man would have no title to be considered as a reasonable creature.

It ought likewise to be observed, that attributes may with perfect ease be distinguished and disjoined *in our conception*, which cannot be actually separated *in the subject.* Thus, in a body, I can distinguish its solidity from its extension, and its weight from both; in extension, I can distinguish length, breadth, and thickness; yet none of these can be separated from the body, or from one another. One cannot exist without the other, but one can be conceived without the other.

Having considered abstraction, strictly so called, let us next consider the operation of *generalizing*, which is nothing but the observing one or more attributes to be *common to many subjects.*

If any man can doubt whether there be attributes that are really common to many individuals, let him consider whether there be not many men that are above six feet high, and many below it; whether there be not many men that are rich, and many more that are poor; whether there be not many that were born in Britain, and many that were born in France. To multiply instances of this kind would be to affront the reader's understanding. It is certain, therefore, that there are innumerable attributes that are really common to many individuals; and if this be what the schoolmen called *universale a parte rei*, we may affirm with certainty, that there are such universals.

There are some attributes expressed by general words, of which this may seem more doubtful. Such are the qualities which are *inherent in their several subjects*. It may be said that every subject hath its own qualities, and that which is the quality of one subject cannot be the quality of another subject. Thus, the whiteness of the sheet of paper upon which I write cannot be the whiteness of another sheet, though both are called white. The weight of one guinea is not the weight of another guinea, though both are said to have the same weight.

To this I answer, that the whiteness *of this sheet* is one thing, *whiteness* is another; the conceptions signified by these two forms of speech are as different as the expressions. The first signifies an individual quality really existing, and is not a general conception, though it be an *abstract* one; the second signifies a *general* conception, *which implies no existence*, but may be predicated of every thing that is white, and in the same sense. On this account, if one should say, that the whiteness of this sheet is the whiteness of another sheet, every man perceives this to be absurd; but when he says both sheets are white, this is true and perfectly understood. The conception of whiteness implies no existence; it would remain the same, though every thing in the universe that is white were annihilated.

It appears, therefore, that the general names of qualities, as well as of other attributes, are applicable to many individuals in the same sense, which could not be if there were not general conceptions signified by such names.

The ancient philosophers called these UNIVERSALS or PREDICABLES, and endeavoured to reduce them to five classes; to wit, *genus, species, specific difference, properties*, and *accidents*. Perhaps there may be more classes of universals or attributes, for enumerations so very general are seldom complete; but every attribute, common to several individuals, may be expressed by a general term, which is the sign of a general conception.

How prone men are to form general conceptions we

may see from the use of metaphor, and of the other figures of speech grounded on similitude. Similitude is nothing else than an agreement of the objects compared in one or more attributes; and if there be no attribute common to both, there can be no similitude.

The similitudes and analogies between the various objects that nature presents to us are infinite and inexhaustible. They not only please, when displayed by the poet or wit in works of taste, but they are highly useful in the ordinary communication of our thoughts and sentiments by language. In the rude languages of barbarous nations, similitudes and analogies supply the want of proper words to express men's sentiments, so much, that in such languages there is hardly a sentence without a metaphor; and if we examine the most copious and polished languages, we shall find that a great proportion of the words and phrases which are accounted the most proper may be said to be the progeny of metaphor.

As foreigners, who settle in a nation as their home, come at last to be incorporated, and lose the denomination of foreigners, so words and phrases, at first borrowed and figurative, by long use become denizens in the language, and lose the denomination of figures of speech. When we speak of the *extent* of knowledge, the *steadiness* of virtue, the *tenderness* of affection, the *perspicuity* of expression, no man conceives these to be metaphorical expressions; they are as proper as any in the language. Yet it appears upon the very face of them, that they must have been metaphorical in those who used them first; and that it is by use and prescription that they have lost the denomination of figurative, and acquired a right to be considered as proper words. This observation will be found to extend to a great part, perhaps the greater part, of the words of the most perfect languages.

Sometimes the name of an individual is given to a general conception, and thereby the individual in a manner generalized. As when the Jew, in Shakspeare, says, " A Daniel come to judgment; yea, a Daniel!"

In this speech, "a Daniel" is an attribute, or a universal. The character of Daniel, as a man of singular wisdom, is abstracted from his person, and considered as capable of being attributed to other persons.

Upon the whole, these two operations of abstracting and generalizing appear common to all men that have understanding. The practice of them is, and must be, familiar to every man that uses language; but it is one thing to practise them, and another to explain how they are performed; as it is one thing to see, another to explain how we see. The first is the province of all men, and is the natural and easy operation of the faculties which God has given us. The second is the province of philosophers, and, though a matter of no great difficulty in itself, has been much perplexed by the ambiguity of words, and still more by the hypotheses of philosophers.

A mistake which is carried through the whole of Mr. Locke's *Essay* may be here mentioned. It is, that our simplest ideas or conceptions are got immediately by the senses, or by consciousness, and the complex afterwards formed by compounding them. I apprehend it is far otherwise. Nature presents no object to the senses, or to consciousness, that is not complex. Thus, by our senses we perceive bodies of various kinds; but every body is a complex body; it has length, breadth, and thickness; it has figure, and color, and various other sensible qualities, which are blended together in the same subject; and I apprehend that brute animals, who have the same senses that we have, cannot separate the different qualities belonging to the same subject, and have only a complex and confused notion of the whole. Such, also, would be our notions of the objects of sense, if we had not superior powers of understanding, by which we can analyze the complex object, abstract every particular attribute from the rest, and form a distinct conception of it. So that it is not by the senses immediately, but rather by the powers of analyzing and abstraction, that we get the most simple and the most distinct notions even of the objects of sense.

As it is by analyzing a complex object into its several attributes that we acquire our simplest abstract conceptions, it may be proper to compare this analysis with that which a chemist makes of a compounded boby into the ingredients which enter into its composition; for although there be such an analogy between these two operations, that we give to both the name of analysis or resolution, there is at the same time so great a dissimilitude in some respects, that we may be led into error, by applying to one what belongs to the other.

It is obvious, that the chemical analysis is an operation of the hand upon matter, by various material instruments. The analysis we are now explaining is purely an operation of the understanding, which requires no material instrument, and produces no change upon any external thing; we shall therefore call it *intellectual* or *mental analysis.*

In chemical analysis, the compound body, itself is the subject analyzed, — a subject so imperfectly known, that it may be compounded of various ingredients, when to our senses it appears perfectly simple; and even when we are able to analyze it into the different ingredients of which it is composed, we know not how or why the combination of those ingredients produces such a body.

Thus, pure sea-salt is a body, to appearance, as simple as any in nature. Every the least particle of it, discernible by our senses, is perfectly similar to every other particle in all its qualities. The nicest taste, the quickest eye, can discern no mark of its being made up of different ingredients; yet, by the chemical art, it can be analyzed into an acid and an alkali, and can be again produced by the combination of those two ingredients. But how this combination produces sea-salt, no man has been able to discover. The ingredients are both as unlike the compound as any bodies we know. No man could have guessed, before the thing was known, that sea-salt is compounded of those two ingredients; no man could have guessed, that the union of those two ingredients should produce such a compound as sea-salt. Such, in many cases, are the phenomena of the chemical analysis of a compound body.

If we consider the intellectual analysis of an object, it is evident that nothing of this kind can happen; because the thing analyzed is not an external object imperfectly known; it is *a conception of the mind itself.* And to suppose that there can be any thing in a conception that is not conceived, is a contradiction.

The reason of observing the difference between these two kinds of analysis is, that some philosophers, in order to support their systems, have maintained, that a complex idea may have the appearance of the most perfect simplicity, and retain no similitude to any of the simple ideas of which it is compounded; just as a white color may appear perfectly simple, and retain no similitude to any of the seven primary colors of which it is compounded; or as a chemical composition may appear perfectly simple, and retain no similitude to any of the ingredients.

From which those philosophers have drawn this important conclusion, that a cluster of the ideas of sense, properly combined, may make the idea of a mind; and that all the ideas which Mr. Locke calls *ideas of reflection* are only *compositions of the ideas which we have by our five senses.* From this the transition is easy, that if a proper composition of the ideas of matter may make the idea of a mind, then a proper composition of matter itself may make a mind, and that man is only a piece of matter curiously formed.

In this curious system, the whole fabric rests upon this foundation, that a complex idea, which is made up of various simple ideas, may appear to be perfectly simple, and have no marks of composition, because a compound body may appear to our senses to be perfectly simple.

As far as I am able to judge, this, which it is said may be, cannot be. That a complex idea should be made up of simple ideas, so that, to a ripe understanding reflecting upon that idea, there should be no appearance of composition, nothing similar to the simple

27

ideas of which it is compounded, seems to me to involve a contradiction. The idea is a conception of the mind. If any thing more than this is meant by the idea, I know not what it is; and I wish both to know what it is, and to have proof of its existence. Now, that there should be any thing in the conception of an object which is not conceived, appears to me as manifest a contradiction, as that there should be an existence which does not exist, or that a thing should be conceived and not conceived at the same time.

But, say these philosophers, a white color is produced by the composition of the primary colors, and yet has no resemblance to any of them. I grant it. But what can be inferred from this with regard to the composition of *ideas?* To bring this argument home to the point, they must say that, because a white color is compounded of the primary colors, therefore the *idea* of a white color is compounded of the *ideas* of the primary colors. This reasoning, if it was admitted, would lead to innumerable absurdities. An opaque fluid may be compounded of two or more pellucid fluids. Hence we might infer with equal force, that the *idea* of an opaque fluid may be compounded of the *idea* of two or more pellucid fluids.

Nature's way of compounding *bodies*, and our way of compounding *ideas*, are so different in many respects, that we cannot reason from the one to the other, unless it can be found that ideas are combined by fermentations and elective attractions, and may be analyzed in a furnace by the force of fire and of menstruums. Until this discovery be made, we must hold those to be simple ideas, which, upon the most attentive reflection, have no appearance of composition ; and those only to be the ingredients of complex ideas, which, by attentive reflection, can be perceived to be contained in them.

III. *General Conceptions formed by Combination.*] As, by an intellectual analysis of objects, we form general conceptions of single attributes (which, of all conceptions that enter into the human mind, are the most simple), so, by combining several of these into one parcel, and giving a name to that combination, we form general conceptions that may be very complex, and at the same time very distinct.

Thus, one who, by analyzing extended objects, has got the simple notions of a point, a line, straight or curve, an angle, a surface, a solid, can easily conceive a plane surface terminated by four equal straight lines meeting in four points at right angles. To this species of figure he gives the name of *a square*. In like manner, he can conceive a solid terminated by six equal squares, and give it the name of *a cube*. A square, a cube, and every name of a mathematical figure, is a general term expressing a complex general conception, made by a certain combination of the simple elements into which we analyze extended bodies.

Every mathematical figure is accurately defined by enumerating the simple elements of which it is formed, and the manner of their combination. The definition contains the whole essence of it; and every property that belongs to it may be deduced by demonstrative reasoning from its definition. It is not a thing that exists, for then it would be an individual; but it is a thing that is conceived without regard to existence.

A farm, a manor, a parish, a county, a kingdom, are complex general conceptions, formed by various combinations and modifications of inhabited territory, under certain forms of government. Different combinations of military men form the notions of a company, a regiment, an army. The several crimes which are the objects of criminal law, such as theft, murder, robbery, piracy, — what are they but certain combinations of human actions and intentions, which are accurately defined in criminal law, and which it is found convenient to comprehend under one name and consider as one thing?

When we observe that Nature, in her animal, vegetable, and inanimate productions, has formed many individuals that agree in many of their qualities and attributes, we are led by natural instinct to expect their agreement in other qualities which we have not had occasion to perceive.

The physician expects that the rhubarb which has never yet been tried will have like medical virtues with that which he has prescribed on former occasions. Two parcels of rhubarb agree in certain sensible qualities, from which agreement they are both called by the same general name, *rhubarb*. Therefore it is expected that they will agree in their medical virtues. And as experience has discovered certain virtues in one parcel, or in many parcels, we presume, without experience, that the same virtues belong to all parcels of rhubarb that shall be used.

If a traveller meets a horse, an ox, or a sheep which he never saw before, he is under no apprehension, believing these animals to be of a species that is tame and inoffensive. But he dreads a lion or a tiger, because they are of a fierce and ravenous species.

We are capable of receiving innumerable advantages, and are exposed to innumerable dangers, from the various productions of nature, animal, vegetable, and inanimate. The life of man, if a hundred times longer than it is, would be insufficient to learn from experience the useful and hurtful qualities of every individual production of nature, taken singly.

We have, therefore, a strong and rational inducement both to distribute natural substances into classes, *genera* and *species*, under general names, and to do this with all the accuracy and distinctness we are able. For the more accurate our divisions are made, and the more distinctly the several species are defined, the more securely we may rely that the qualities we find in one or in a few individuals will be found in all of the same species.

It may likewise be observed, that the combinations that have names are nearly, though not perfectly, the same in the different languages of civilized nations that have intercourse with one another. Hence it is that the lexicographer, for the most part, can give words in one language answering perfectly, or very nearly, to those of another; and what is written in a simple style in one language can be translated, almost word for word, into another.* From this we may conclude that there are either certain common principles of human nature, or certain common occurrences of human life, which dispose men, out of an infinite number that might be formed, to form certain combinations rather than others.

In the rudest state of society, men must have occasion to form the general notions of man, woman, father, mother, son, daughter, sister, brother, neighbour, friend, enemy, and many others, to express the common relations of one person to another.

If they are employed in hunting, they must have general terms to express the various implements and operations of the chase. Their houses and clothing, however simple, will furnish another set of general terms, to express the materials, the workmanship, and the excellences and defects of those fabrics. If they sail upon rivers or upon the sea, this will give occasion to a great number of general terms, which otherwise would never have occurred to their thoughts.

The same thing may be said of agriculture, of pasturage, of every art they practise, and of every branch of knowledge they attain. The necessity of general terms for communicating our sentiments is obvious, and the invention of them, as far as we find them necessary, requires no other talent than that degree of understanding which is common to men.

New inventions of general use give an easy birth to new complex notions and new names, which spread as far as the invention does. How many new complex notions have been formed, and names for them invented in the languages of Europe, by the modern inventions of printing, of gunpowder, of the mariner's compass, of optical glasses! The simple ideas combined in those complex notions, and the associating qualities of those

---

* This is only strictly true of the words relative to objects of sense. — H.

27 *

ideas, are very ancient, but they never produced those complex notions until there was use for them.

What is peculiar to a nation in its customs, manners, or laws, will give occasion to complex notions and words peculiar to the language of that nation. Hence it is easy to see why *impeachment* and *attainder* in the English language, and *ostracism* in the Greek language, have not names answering to them in other languages.

I apprehend, therefore, that it is *utility*, and not, as some have thought, *the associating qualities of the ideas*, that has led men to form only certain combinations, and to give names to them in language, while they neglect an infinite number that might be formed.

There remains a very large class of complex general terms, on which I shall make some observations; I mean those by which we name the *genera* and *species* of *natural substances.*

It is utility, indeed, that leads us to give general, names to the various species of natural substances; but, in combining the attributes which are included under the specific name, we are more aided and directed by nature, than in forming other combinations of mixed modes and relations. In the last, the ingredients are brought together in the occurrences of life, or in the actions or thoughts of men. But in the first, the ingredients are united by nature in many individual substances which God has made. We form a general notion of those attributes wherein many individuals agree. We give a specific name to this combination, which name is common to all substances having those attributes, which either do or may exist. The specific name comprehends *neither more nor fewer attributes than we find proper to put into its definition.* It comprehends not time, nor place, nor even existence, although there can be no individual without these.

This work of the understanding is absolutely necessary for speaking intelligibly of the productions of nature, and for reaping the benefits we receive, and avoiding the dangers we are exposed to, from them. The individuals are so many, that to give a proper name to each would be beyond the power of language. If a good or bad quality were observed in an individual, of how small use would this be if there were not a species in which the same quality might be expected?

Without some general knowledge of the qualities of natural substances, human life could not be preserved. And there can be no general knowledge of this kind without reducing them to species under specific names. For this reason, among the rudest nations, we find names for fire, water, earth, air, mountains, fountains, rivers; for the kinds of vegetables they use; of animals they hunt or tame, or that are found useful or hurtful. Each of those names signifies in general a substance having a certain combination of attributes. The name, therefore, must be common to all substances in which those attributes are found.

Such general names of substances being found in all vulgar languages, before philosophers began to make accurate divisions and less obvious distinctions, it is not to be expected that their meaning should be more precise than is necessary for the common purposes of life.

As the knowledge of nature advances, more species of natural substances are observed, and their useful qualities discovered. In order that this important part of human knowledge may be communicated, and handed down to future generations, it is not sufficient that the species have names. Such is the fluctuating state of language, that a general name will not always retain the same precise signification, unless it have a definition in which men are disposed to acquiesce.

There was undoubtedly a great fund of natural knowledge among the Greeks and Romans in the time of Pliny. There is a great fund in his *Natural History;* but much of it is lost to us, for this reason, among others, that we know not what species of substance he means by such a name. Nothing could have prevented this loss but an accurate definition of the name, by which the species might have been distinguished from all others, as long as that name and its definition remained. To prevent such loss in future times, modern philosophers have very laudably attempted to give names and accurate definitions of all the known species of substances wherewith the bountiful Creator has enriched our globe.

Nature invites to this work, by having formed things so as to make it both easy and important. For, *first*, we perceive numbers of individual substances so like in their *obvious* qualities that the most unimproved tribes of men consider them as of one species, and give them one common name. *Secondly*, the more *latent* qualities of substances are generally the same in all the individuals of a species; so that what, by observation or experiment, is found in a few individuals of a species, is presumed and commonly found to belong to the whole. By this we are enabled, from particular facts, to draw general conclusions. This kind of induction is indeed the master key to the knowledge of nature, without which we could form no general conclusions in that branch of philosophy. And, *thirdly*, by the very constitution of our nature, we are led, without reasoning, to ascribe to the whole species what we have found to belong to the individuals. It is thus we come to know that fire burns and water drowns, that bodies gravitate and bread nourishes.

The species of two of the kingdoms of nature — to wit, the *animal* and the *vegetable* — seem to be fixed by nature, by the power they have of producing their like. And in these, men in all ages and nations have accounted the parent and the progeny of the same species. The differences among naturalists with regard to the species of these two kingdoms are very inconsiderable, and may be occasioned by the changes produced by soil, climate, and culture, and sometimes by monstrous productions, which are comparatively rare.

In the *inanimate* kingdom we have not the same means of dividing things into species, and therefore the limits of species seem to be more arbitrary; but, from the progress already made, there is ground to hope, that, even in this kingdom, as the knowledge of it advances, the various species may be so well distinguished and defined as to answer every valuable purpose.

———————

CHAPTER III.

OPINIONS OF PHILOSOPHERS ABOUT UNIVERSALS.

I. *Opinions of the Ancients on the Subject.*] In the ancient philosophy, the *doctrine of universals*, that is, of things which we express by general terms, makes a great figure. The *ideas* of the Pythagoreans and Platonists were universals. All science is employed about universals as its object. It was thought that there can be no science unless its object be something real and immutable, and therefore those who paid homage to truth and science maintained that ideas or universals have a real and immutable existence.

To these *ideas* they ascribed the most magnificent attributes. Of man, of a rose, of a circle, and of every species of things, they believed that there is one idea or form which existed from eternity, before any individual of the species was formed; that this idea is the exemplar or pattern according to which the Deity formed the individuals of the species; that every individual of the species participates of this idea, which constitutes its essence; and that this idea is likewise an object of the human intellect, when, by due abstraction, we discern it to be one in all the individuals of the species.

Thus the idea of every species, though one and immutable, might be considered in three different views or respects; *first*, as having an external existence before there was any individual of the species; *secondly*, as existing in every individual of that species, without division or multiplication, and making the essence of the species; and, *thirdly*, as an object of intellect and of science in man.

Such I take to be the doctrine of Plato, as far as I am able to comprehend it. His disciple, Aristotle, rejected the first of these views of ideas as visionary, but differed little from his master with regard to the last two. He did not admit the existence of universal natures antecedent to the existence of individuals; but he held that every individual consists of *matter* and *form*; that the form (which I take to be what Plato calls the idea) is common to all the individuals of the species, and that the human intellect is fitted to receive the forms of things as objects of contemplation.[*] Such profound speculations about the nature of universals we find even in the first ages of philosophy. I wish I could make them more intelligible to myself and to the reader.

II. *Rise of Nominalism and Conceptualism, and their Modern Defenders.*] Near the beginning of the twelfth century, Roscelin, the master of the famous Abelard, introduced a new doctrine, — *that there is nothing universal but words or names.* For this and other heresies he was much persecuted. However, by his eloquence and abilities, and those of his disciple, Abelard, the doctrine spread, and those who followed it were called *Nominalists.*[†] His antagonists, who held that there are

---

[*] Different philosophers have maintained that Aristotle was a Realist, a Conceptualist, and a Nominalist, in the strictest sense. — H.

" Now I venture to think that the interminable contest between Platonist and Aristotelian, Realist and Nominalist, is, at·bottom, not so much a question of what universals are, as of how they shall be treated; not so much a question of metaphysics as of method. Upon the *nature* of general notions there is a large amount of agreement between the parties: the Realist believes, with the Nominalist, that they are in the human mind, whilst, if the Nominalist believes at all that the world was *created by design*, he can scarcely escape from recognizing the Realist position, that such ideas as *animal, right, motion*, must have had their existence from the beginning in the creative mind. Aristotle might have owned that the universal notions in his mind answer to certain ideas in the Divine, whilst his illustrious master might have confessed that, putting revelation out of the question, there is no way to the absolute, — to *knowledge* of the ideas, — except a careful observation of, and reasoning from, the facts before our eyes." — Thomson's *Laws of Thought*, 2d ed., p. 114 *et seq.* Compare Ravaisson, *Métaphysique d'Aristote.* — ED.

† Abelard was not a Nominalist, like Roscelin; but held a doctrine inter-

.things that are really universal, were called *Realists*. The scholastic philosophers, from this time, were divided into these two sects. Some few took a middle road between the contending parties. That universality, which the Realists held to be in things themselves, Nominalists in names only, they held to be neither in things nor in names *only*, but in our conceptions. On this account they were called *Conceptualists;* but, being exposed to the batteries of both the opposite parties, they made no great figure.*

When the sect of Nominalists was like to expire, it received new life and spirit from Occam, the disciple of Scotus, in the fourteenth century. Then the dispute about universals, *a parte rei*, was revived with the greatest animosity in the schools of Britain, France, and Germany, and carried on, not by arguments only, but by bitter reproaches, blows, and bloody affrays, until the doctrines of Luther and the other Reformers turned the attention of the learned world to more important subjects.

After the revival of learning, Mr. Hobbes adopted the opinion of the Nominalists.† *Human Nature*, Chap. V. Sect. 6 : — " It is plain, therefore," says he, " that there is nothing universal but names." And in his *Leviathan*, Part I. Chap. IV., — " There being nothing universal but names, proper names bring to mind one thing only ; universals recall any one of many."

Mr. Locke, according to the division before mentioned, I think, may be accounted a Conceptualist. He does not maintain that there are things that are universal ; but that we have general or universal ideas which we form by abstraction ; and this power of forming abstract and general ideas he conceives to be that

---

mediate between absolute Nominalism and Realism, corresponding to the opinion since called Conceptualism. A flood of light has been thrown upon Abelard's doctrines by M. Cousin's introduction to his recent publication of the unedited works of that illustrious thinker. — H.

* The later Nominalists of the school of Occam were really Conceptualists, in our sense of the term. — H.

† Hobbes is justly said by Leibnitz to have been *ipsis Nominalibus nominalior. They* were really Conceptualists. — H.

which makes the chief distinction in point of understanding between men and brutes.

Mr. Locke's doctrine about abstraction has been combated by two very powerful antagonists, — Bishop Berkeley and Mr. Hume, — who have taken up the opinion of the Nominalists. The former thinks (Introduction to his *Principles of Human Knowledge*), " that the opinion, that the mind has a power of forming abstract ideas, or notions of things, has had a chief part in rendering speculation intricate and perplexed, and has occasioned innumerable errors and difficulties in almost all parts of knowledge." To the same effect Mr. Hume, *Treatise of Human Nature*, Book I. Part I. Sect. 7 : — " A very material question has been started concerning abstract or general ideas, whether they be general or particular in the mind's conception of them ? A great philosopher [be means Dr. Berkeley] has disputed the received opinion in this particular, and has asserted that all general ideas are nothing but particular ones annexed to a certain term, which gives them a more extensive signification, and makes them recall, upon occasion, other individuals which are similar to them. As I look upon this to be one of the greatest and most valuable discoveries that have been made of late years in the republic of letters, I shall here endeavour to confirm it by some arguments, which I hope will put it beyond all doubt and controversy."

I shall make an end of this subject with some reflections on what has been said upon it by these two eminent philosophers.

1. A triangle, in general, or any other universal, might be called an idea by a Platonist; but, in the style of modern philosophy, it is not an idea, nor do we ever ascribe to ideas the properties of triangles. It is never said of any idea, that it has three sides and three angles. We do not speak of equilateral, isosceles, or scalene ideas, nor of right-angled, acute-angled, or obtuse-angled ideas. And if these attributes do not belong to ideas, it follows necessarily that a triangle is not an idea. The same reasoning may be applied to every other universal.

Ideas are said to have a real existence in the mind, at least while we think of them; but universals have no real existence. When we ascribe existence to them, it is not an existence in time or place, but existence in some individual subject; and this existence means no more than that they are truly attributes of such a subject. Their existence is nothing but *predicability,* or *the capacity of being attributed to a subject.* The name of *predicables,* which was given them in ancient philosophy, is that which most properly expresses their nature.[*]

2. I think it must also be granted that universals cannot be the objects of *imagination,* when we take that word in its strict and proper sense. " I find," says Berkeley, " I have a faculty of imagining or representing to myself the ideas of those particular things I have perceived, and of variously compounding and dividing them. I can imagine a man with two heads, or the upper parts of a man joined to the body of a horse. I can imagine the hand, the eye, the nose, each by itself, abstracted or separated from the rest of the body. But then, whatever hand or eye I imagine, it

---

[*] Here M. Cousin makes a distinction and an exception: — " Let us consult the human mind and the truth of internal facts. It is an unquestionable fact, that, when you speak of *book in general,* you do not connect with the idea of book that of real existence. On the contrary, I ask if, when you speak of *space in general,* you do not add to this idea a belief in the reality of space? I ask if it is with space as with book; if you believe, for instance, that there are, without you, nothing but particular spaces, — that there is not a universal space, capable of embracing all possible bodies, a space one and the same with itself, of which different particular spaces are nothing but arbitrary portions and measures? It is certain that, when you speak of *space,* you have the conviction that out of yourself there is something which is space; and also, when you speak of *time,* you have the conviction that there is out of yourself something which is time, although you know neither the nature of time nor space. Different times and different spaces are not the constituent elements of space and time; time and space are not solely for you the collection of different times and different spaces. But you believe that time and space are in themselves; that it is not two or three spaces, two or three ages, which constitute space and time: for every thing derived from experience, whether in respect to space or time, is finite, and the characteristic of space and of time for you is to be infinite, without beginning and without end. Time resolves itself into eternity, and space into immensity." — *Elements of Psychology,* Chap. V. — ED.

must have some particular shape or color. Likewise, the idea of a man that I frame to myself must be either of a white, or a black, or a tawny, a straight or a crooked, a tall, or a low, or a middle-sized man."

I believe every man will find in himself what this ingenious author found, — that he cannot imagine a man without color, or stature, or shape. Imagination, as we before observed, properly signifies a conception of the appearance an object would make to the eye if actually seen. A universal is not an object of any external sense, and therefore cannot be *imagined;* but it may be distinctly *conceived.* When Mr. Pope says,

" The proper study of mankind is *man*,"

I conceive his meaning distinctly, though I neither imagine a black or a white, a crooked or a straight man. The distinction between conception and imagination is real, though it be too often overlooked, and the words taken to be synonymous. I can conceive a thing that is impossible, but I cannot distinctly imagine a thing that is impossible. I can conceive a proposition or a demonstration, but I cannot imagine either. I can conceive understanding and will, virtue and vice, and other attributes of mind, but I cannot imagine them. In like manner, I can distinctly conceive universals, but I cannot imagine them.

3. Berkeley, in his reasoning against abstract general ideas, seems unwillingly or unwarily to grant all that is necessary to support abstract and general conceptions. " A man," he says, " may consider a figure merely as triangular, without attending to the particular qualities of the angles or relations of the sides. So far he may abstract. But this will never prove that he can frame an abstract general inconsistent idea of a triangle."

If a man may consider a figure merely as triangular, he must have some conception of this object of his consideration; for no man can consider a thing which he does not conceive. He has a conception, therefore, of a triangular figure, merely as such. I know no more that is meant by an abstract general conception of a triangle.

He that considers a figure merely as triangular must understand what is meant by the word *triangular*. If to the conception he joins to this word he adds any particular quality of angles or relation of sides, he misunderstands it, and does not consider the figure merely as triangular. Whence I think it is evident, that he who considers a figure merely as triangular must have the conception of a triangle, abstracted from any quality of angles or relation of sides.

4. Let us next consider the Bishop's notion of *generalizing*. He does not absolutely deny that there are general ideas, but only that there are *abstract* general ideas. "An idea," he says, "which, considered in itself, is particular, becomes general by being made to *represent* or stand for all other particular ideas of the *same sort*. To make this plain by an example, suppose a geometrician is demonstrating the method of cutting a line in two equal parts. He draws, for instance, a black line of an inch in length. This, which is in itself a particular line, is nevertheless, with regard to its signification, general; since, as it is there used, it represents all particular lines whatsoever; so that what is demonstrated of it is demonstrated of all lines, or, in other words, of a line in general. And as that particular line becomes general by being made a sign, so the name *line*, which, taken absolutely, is particular, by being a sign is made general."

Here I observe, that when a particular idea is made a sign to represent and stand for all of a sort, this supposes a distinction of things into *sorts* or *species*. To be of a sort, implies having those attributes which characterize the sort and are *common to all the individuals* that belong to it. There cannot, therefore, be a sort without general attributes, nor can there be any conception of a sort without a conception of those general attributes which distinguish it. The conception of a sort, therefore, is an abstract general conception. The particular idea cannot surely be made a sign of a thing of which we have no conception. I do not say that you must have an idea of the sort, but surely you ought to understand or conceive what it means, when you make a particular idea a representative of it, otherwise your particular idea represents you know not what.

When I demonstrate any general property of a triangle, — such as that the three angles are equal to two right-angles, — I must understand or conceive distinctly what is *common to all triangles*. I must distinguish the common attributes of all triangles from those wherein particular triangles may differ. And if I conceive distinctly what is common to all triangles, without confounding it with what is not so, this is to form a general conception of a triangle. And without this, it is impossible to know that the demonstration extends to all triangles.

The Bishop takes particular notice of this argument, and makes this answer to it: — " Though the idea I have in view, whilst I make the demonstration, be, for instance, that of an isosceles rectangular triangle, whose sides are of a determinate length, I may nevertheless be certain that it extends to all other rectilinear triangles, of what sort or bigness soever ; and that because neither the right angle, nor the equality or determinate length of the sides, is at all concerned in the demonstration."

But if he do not, in the idea he has in view, clearly distinguish what is common to all triangles from what is not, it would be impossible to discern whether something that is not common be concerned in the demonstration or not. In order, therefore, to perceive that the demonstration extends to all triangles, it is necessary to have *a distinct conception of what is common to all triangles, excluding from that conception all that is not common.* And this is all I understand by an abstract general conception of a triangle.

5. Having considered the opinions of Bishop Berkeley on this subject, let us next attend to those of Mr. Hume, as they are expressed, Part I. Sect. 7, *Treatise*

of Human Nature. Quantity or quality, according to him, is inconceivable, without a precise notion of its degree; and on this ground, that it is impossible to *distinguish* things that are not *actually separable.* " The precise length of a line is not different or distinguishable from the line."

I have before endeavoured to show that things inseparable in their nature may be distinguished in our conception. And we need go no farther to be convinced of this than the instance here brought to prove the contrary. The precise length of a line, he says, is not distinguishable from the line. When I say, *This is a line*, I say and mean one thing. When I say, *It is a line of three inches*, I say and mean another thing. If this be not to distinguish the precise length of the line from the line, I know not what it is to distinguish.

6. Mr. Hume endeavours to explain how it is that an individual idea, annexed to a general term, may serve all the purposes in reasoning which have been ascribed to abstract general ideas : — " When we have found a resemblance among several objects that often occur to us, we apply the same name to all of them, whatever differences we may observe in the degrees of their quantity and quality, and whatever other differences may appear among them. After we have acquired a custom of this kind, the hearing of that name revives the idea of one of these objects, and makes the imagination conceive it, with all its circumstances and proportions."

He allows that we find a resemblance among several objects, and such a resemblance as leads us to apply the same name to all of them. This concession is sufficient to show that we have general conceptions. There can be no resemblance in objects that have no common attribute; and if there be attributes belonging in common to several objects, and in man a faculty to observe and conceive these and to give names to them, this is to have general conceptions.

7. The author says, — " It is certain that we form the idea of individuals whenever we use any general term.

28 *

The word raises up an individual idea, and makes the imagination conceive it, with all its particular circumstances and proportions."

This fact he takes a great deal of pains to account for from the effect of custom. But the fact should be ascertained before we take pains to account for it. I can see no reason to believe the fact; and I think a farmer can talk of his sheep and his black cattle without conceiving in his imagination one individual, with all its circumstances and proportions. If this be true, the whole of his theory of general ideas falls to the ground. To me it appears that, when a general term is well understood, it is only by accident if it suggest some individual of the kind; but this effect is by no means constant.

I perfectly understand what mathematicians call a line of the fifth order; yet I never conceived in my imagination any one of the kind, in all its circumstances and proportions. Sir Isaac Newton first formed a distinct *general* conception of lines of the third order; and *afterwards,* by great labor and deep penetration, found out and described the particular *species* comprehended under that general term. According to Mr. Hume's theory, he must *first* have been acquainted with the *particulars,* and then have learned by custom to apply one general name to all of them.*

---

* The whole controversy of Nominalism and Conceptualism is founded on the ambiguity of the terms employed. The opposite parties are substantially at one. Had our British philosophers been aware of the Leibnitzian distinction of *intuitive* and *symbolical* knowledge, and had we, like the Germans, different terms, like *Begriff* and *Anschauung,* to denote different kinds of thought, there would have been as little difference of opinion in regard to the nature of general notions in this country as in the Empire. With us, *idea, notion, conception,* &c., are confounded, or applied by different philosophers in different senses.

I must put the reader on his guard against Dr. Thomas Brown's speculations on this subject. His own doctrine of universals, in so far as it is peculiar, is self-contradictory; and nothing can be more erroneous than his statement of the doctrine held by others, especially by the Nominalists. — H.

For a full account of this famous controversy, see the general historians of philosophy, particularly Brucker and Tennemann. Also, Rousselot, *Etudes sur la Philosophie dans le Moyen-Age,* Tome I. p. 126 *et seq.;* Remu-

ESSAY VI.

OF JUDGMENT.

CHAPTER I.

OF JUDGMENT IN GENERAL.

I. *Definition of the Term.*] The definition commonly given of *judgment*, by the more ancient writers in logic, was, that it is *an act of the mind, whereby one thing is affirmed or denied of another.* I believe this is as good a definition of it as can be given. Why I prefer it to some later definitions will afterwards appear. Without pretending to give any other, I shall make two remarks upon it, and then offer some general observations on this subject.

It is true, that it is by affirmation or denial that we express our judgments; but there may be judgment which is not expressed. It is a solitary act of the mind, and the expression of it by affirmation or denial is not at all essential to it. It may be tacit, and not expressed. Nay, it is well known that men may judge contrary to what they affirm or deny; the definition, therefore, must be understood of *mental affirmation or*

---

sat, *Abelard*, Tome I. p. 313 *et seq.*, and Tome II. p. 1 *et seq.*; and, above all, the brilliant Preface by Cousin to his *Ouvrages inédits d'Abelard*, referred to in a former note. Of English works, besides those already mentioned, the following are proper to be consulted:—Stewart's *Elements*, Part I. Chap. IV.; R. E. Scott's *Intellectual Philosophy*, Chap. IV. Sect. 2; Brown's *Philosophy of the Human Mind*, Lect. XLVI., XLVII.; Hazlitt's *Essays on the Principles of Human Action, on the Systems of Hartley and Helvetius, and on Abstract Ideas*; and Hampden's *Scholastic Philosophy considered in Relation to Christian Theology*, Lecture II, and Notes.—ED.

denial, which indeed is only another name for judgment.

Affirmation or denial is very often the expression of testimony, which is a different act of the mind, and ought to be distinguished from judgment. A judge asks of a witness what he knows of such a matter to which he was an eye or ear witness. He answers by affirming or denying something. But his answer does not express his judgment; it is his *testimony.* Again, I ask a man his opinion in a matter of science or of criticism. His answer is not testimony; it is the expression of his *judgment.* Testimony is a social act, and it is essential to it to be *expressed by words or signs.* A tacit testimony is a contradiction: but there is no contradiction in a tacit judgment; it is complete without being expressed. In testimony, a man pledges his veracity for what he affirms; so that a false testimony is a *lie :* but a wrong judgment is not a lie; it is only an *error.*

I believe, in all languages, testimony and judgment are expressed by the same form of speech. A proposition affirmative or negative, with a verb in what is called the indicative mood, expresses both. To distinguish them by the form of speech, it would be necessary that verbs should have two indicative moods, one for testimony, and another to express judgment. I know not that this is found in any language. And the reason is, not surely that the vulgar cannot distinguish the two (for every man knows the difference between a lie and an error of judgment), but that, from the matter and circumstances, we can easily see whether a man intends to give his testimony, or barely to express his judgment.

Although men must have judged in many cases before tribunals of justice were erected, yet it is very probable that there were tribunals before men began to *speculate* about judgment, and that the word may be borrowed from the practice of tribunals. As a judge, after taking the proper evidence, passes sentence in a cause, and that sentence is called his *judgment,* so the mind, with regard to whatever is true or false, passes sentence, or determines according to the evidence that appears. Some kinds of evidence leave no room for doubt. Sentence is passed immediately, without seeking or hearing any contrary evidence, because the thing is certain and notorious. In other cases, there is room for weighing evidence on both sides before sentence is passed. The analogy between a tribunal of justice and this inward tribunal of the mind is too obvious to escape the notice of any man who ever appeared before a judge. And it is probable that the, word *judgment*, as well as many other words we use in speaking of this operation of mind, is grounded on this analogy.

II. *Observations respecting the Nature and Province of Judgment.*] Having premised these things, that it may be clearly understood what I mean by judgment, I proceed to make some general observations concerning it.

First, judgment is an act of the mind *specifically different from simple apprehension,* or the bare conception of a thing. It would be unnecessary to observe this, if some philosophers had not been led by their theories to a contrary opinion. Although there can be no judgment without a conception of the things about which we judge, yet conception may be without any judgment.* Judgment can be expressed by a proposition only, and a proposition is a complete sentence; but simple apprehension may be expressed by a word or words which make no complete sentence. When simple apprehension is employed about a proposition, every man knows that it is one thing to apprehend a proposition, that is, to conceive what it means; but it is quite another thing to judge it to be true or false.

---

* There is no conception possible without a judgment affirming its (ideal) existence, its subjective reality, — an existential judgment. Apprehension is as impossible without judgment, as judgment is impossible without apprehension. The apprehension of a thing, or notion, is only realized in the mental affirmation that the *concept* ideally exists, and this affirmation is a judgment. In fact, all consciousness supposes a judgment, as all consciousness supposes a discrimination. — H.

Secondly, there are notions or ideas that ought to be referred to the faculty of judgment as their source; because, if we had not that faculty, they could not enter into our minds; and to those that have that faculty, and are capable of reflecting upon its operations, they are obvious and familiar.

Among these we may reckon the notion of judgment itself; the notions of a proposition, of its subject, predicate, and copula; of affirmation and negation, of true and false, of knowledge, belief, disbelief, opinion, assent, evidence. From no source could we acquire these notions, but from reflecting upon our judgments. Relations of things make one great class of our notions or ideas; and we cannot have the idea of any relation without some exercise of judgment, as will appear afterwards.

Thirdly, in persons come to years of understanding, *judgment necessarily accompanies all sensation, perception by the senses, consciousness, and memory.*

I restrict this to persons come to the years of understanding, because it may be a question, whether infants, in the first period of life, have any judgment or belief at all. The same question may be put with regard to brutes and some idiots. This question is foreign to the present subject; and I say nothing here about it, but speak only of persons who have the exercise of judgment. In them it is evident, that a man who feels pain judges and believes that he is really pained. The man who perceives an object believes that it exists, and is what he distinctly perceives it to be; nor is it in his power to avoid such judgment. And the like may be said of memory and of consciousness.

Whether judgment ought to be called a necessary concomitant of these operations, or rather a part or ingredient of them, I do not dispute; but it is certain, that all of them are accompanied with a determination that something is true or false, and a consequent belief. If this determination be not judgment, it is an operation that has got no name; for it is not simple apprehension, neither is it reasoning; it is a mental affirmation or negation; it may be expressed by a proposition affirmative or negative, and it is accompanied with the firmest belief. These are the characteristics of judgment; and I must call it judgment, till I can find another name for it.

The judgments we form are either of *things necessary*, or of *things contingent*.

That three times three are nine, that the whole is greater than a part, are judgments about things necessary. Our assent to such necessary propositions is not grounded upon any operation of sense, of memory, or of consciousness, nor does it require their concurrence; it is unaccompanied by any other operation than that of conception, which must accompany all judgment; we may therefore call this judgment of things necessary, *pure judgment.*

Our judgment of things contingent must always rest upon some other operation of the mind, such as sense, or memory, or consciousness, or credit in testimony, which is itself grounded upon sense. That I now write upon a table covered with green cloth, is a contingent event, which I judge to be most undoubtedly true. My judgment is grounded upon my perception, and is a necessary concomitant or ingredient of my perception. That I dined with such a company yesterday, I judge to be true, because I remember it; and my judgment necessarily goes along with this remembrance, or makes a part of it.

There are many forms of speech in common language which show that the senses, memory, and consciousness are considered as judging faculties. We say that a man judges of colors by his eye, of sounds by his ear. We speak of the evidence of sense, the evidence of memory, the evidence of consciousness. But evidence is the ground of judgment, and when we see evidence, it is impossible not to judge.

When we speak of seeing or remembering any thing, we indeed hardly ever add, that we judge it to be true. But the reason of this appears to be, that such addition would be mere superfluity of speech, because every one knows that what I see or remember I must judge to be true, and cannot do otherwise. And for the same reason, in speaking of any thing that is self-evident or strictly demonstrated, we do not say that we judge it to be true. This would be superfluity of speech, because every man knows that we must judge that to be true which we hold self-evident or demonstrated.

There is therefore good reason why, in speaking or writing, judgment should not be expressly mentioned, when all men know it to be necessarily implied; that is, when there can be no doubt. In such cases, we barely mention the evidence. But when the evidence mentioned leaves room for doubt, then, without any superfluity or tautology, we say we judge the thing to be so, because this is not implied in what was said before. A woman with child never says, that, going such a journey, she carried her child along with her. We know that, while it is in her womb, she must carry it along with her. There are some operations of mind that may be said to carry judgment in their womb, and can no more leave it behind them than the pregnant woman can leave her child. Therefore, in speaking of such operations, it is not expressed.

Our judgments of this kind are purely the gift of nature, nor do they admit of improvement by culture. The memory of one man may be more tenacious than that of another; but both rely with equal assurance upon what they distinctly remember. One man's sight may be more acute, or his feeling more delicate, than that of another; but both give equal credit to the distinct testimony of their sight and touch. And as we have this belief by the constitution of our nature, without any effort of our own, so no effort of ours can overturn it. The skeptic may perhaps persuade himself, in general, that he has no ground to believe his senses or his memory; but in particular cases that are interesting, his disbelief vanishes, and he finds himself under a necessity of believing both.

These judgments may, in the strictest sense, be called *judgments of nature.* Nature has subjected us to them whether we will or not. They are neither got, nor can they be lost, by any use or abuse of our faculties; and it is evidently necessary to our preservation that it should be so. For if belief in our senses and in our memory were to be learned by culture, the race of men would perish before they learned this lesson. It is necessary to all men for their being and preservation, and therefore is unconditionally given to all men by the Author of nature.

A *fourth* observation is, that some exercise of *judgment is necessary in the formation of all abstract and general conceptions*, whether more simple or more complex, — *in dividing, in defining*, and, in general, *in forming all clear and distinct conceptions of things, which are the only fit materials of reasoning*.

These operations are allied to each other, and therefore I bring them under one observation. They are more allied to our rational nature than those mentioned in the last observation, and therefore are considered by themselves.

It is impossible to distinguish the different attributes belonging to the same subject, without judging that they are really different and distinguishable, and that they have that relation to the subject which logicians express by saying that they may be *predicated* of it. We cannot generalize, without judging that the same attribute does or may belong to many individuals. It has been shown, that our simplest general notions are formed by these two operations of distinguishing and generalizing; judgment therefore is exercised in forming the *simplest general notions*. In those that are *more complex*, and which have been shown to be formed by combining the more simple, there is another act of the judgment required; for such combinations are not made at rándom, but for an end; and judgment is employed in fitting them to that end. We form complex general notions for conveniency of arranging our thoughts in discourse and reasoning; and therefore, of an infinite number of combinations that might be formed, we *choose* only those that are useful and necessary.

29

That judgment must be employed in *dividing*, as well as in distinguishing, appears evident. It is one thing to divide a subject properly, another to cut it in pieces. *Hoc non est dividere, sed frangere rem*, said Cicero, when he censured an improper division of Epicurus. Reason has discovered rules of division, which have been known to logicians more than two thousand years.

There are rules likewise of *definition* of no less antiquity and authority. A man may no doubt divide or define properly without attending to the rules, or even without knowing them. But this can only be, when he has *judgment* to perceive that to be right in a particular case, which the rule determines to be right in all cases.

I add, in general, that, without *some* degree of judgment, we can form no *accurate and distinct notions* of things; so that one province of judgment is, to aid us in forming clear and distinct conceptions of things, which are *the only fit materials for reasoning*.

This will probably appear to be a paradox to philosophers who have always considered the formation of ideas of every kind as belonging to simple apprehension; and that the sole province of judgment is to put them together in affirmative or negative propositions: and therefore it requires some confirmation.

1. I think it necessarily follows, from what has been already said in this observation. For if, without some degree of judgment, a man can neither distinguish, nor divide, nor define, nor form any general notion, simple or complex, he surely, without some degree of judgment, cannot have in his mind the materials necessary to reasoning.

There cannot be any proposition in language which does not involve some general conception. The proposition, that *I exist*, which Descartes thought the first of all truths, and the foundation of all knowledge, cannot be conceived without the conception of *existence*, one of the most abstract general conceptions.

A man cannot believe his own existence, or the existence of any thing he sees or remembers, until he has so much judgment as to distinguish things that really exist from things which are only conceived. He sees a man six feet high; he conceives a man sixty feet high; he judges the first object to exist, because he sees it; the second he does not judge to exist, because he only conceives it. Now, I would ask whether he can attribute existence to the first object, and not to the second, without knowing what existence means. It is impossible.

In every other proposition, the predicate at least must be a general notion, a *predicable* and a *universal* being one and the same. Besides this, every proposition either affirms or denies. And no man can have a distinct conception of a proposition, who does not understand distinctly the meaning of *affirming* or *denying*: but these are very general conceptions, and, as was before observed, are derived from judgment, as their source and origin.

I am sensible that a strong objection may be made to this reasoning, and that it may seem to lead to an absurdity, or a contradiction. It may be said, that every judgment is a mental affirmation or negation. If, therefore, some previous exercise of judgment be necessary to understand what is meant by affirmation or negation, the exercise of judgment must go before any judgment, which is absurd. In like manner, every judgment may be expressed by a proposition, and a proposition must be conceived before we can judge of it. If, therefore, we cannot conceive the meaning of a proposition without a previous exercise of judgment, it follows that judgment must be previous to the conception of any proposition, and, at the same time, that the conception of a proposition must be previous to all judgment, which is a contradiction.

The reader may please to observe, that I have limited what I have said to "*distinct conception*," and "*some degree of judgment*"; and it is by this means I hope to avoid this labyrinth of absurdity and contradiction. The faculties of conception and judgment have an infancy and a maturity, as man has. What I have said is limited to their mature state. I believe in their infant state they are very weak and indistinct; and that, by imperceptible degrees, they grow to maturity, each giving aid to the other, and receiving aid from it. But which of them first began this friendly intercourse is beyond my ability to determine. It is like the question concerning the bird and the egg. In the present state of things, it is true that every bird comes from an egg, and every egg from a bird; and each may be said to be previous to the other. But if we go back to the origin of things, there must have been some bird that did not come from an egg, or some egg that did not come from any bird.

In like manner, in the mature state of man, distinct conception of a proposition supposes some previous exercise of judgment, and distinct judgment supposes distinct conception. Each may truly be said to come from the other, as the bird from the egg, and the egg from the bird. But if we trace back this succession to its origin, — that is, to the first proposition that was ever conceived by the man, and the first judgment he ever formed, — I determine nothing about them, nor do I know in what order, or how, they were produced.*

---

* On the manner in which the human intellect begins to develop itself, M. Cousin expresses himself thus : — " Primitively nothing is abstract, nothing is general; every thing is particular, every thing is concrete. The understanding does not begin with these formulas : *There is no modification without its subject; There is no body without space.* But a modification being given, it conceives a particular subject of this modification; a body being given, it conceives that this body is in a space; a particular succession being given, it conceives that this particular succession is in a determinate time. It is so with all our primitive conceptions; they are all particular, determined, concrete. Our primitive conceptions, moreover, present two distinct characteristics; some are *contingent,* others are *necessary.* Under the eye of consciousness there may be a sensation of pleasure or of pain, which I perceive as actually existing; but this sensation may vary, change, disappear. Hence very soon may arise the conviction, that this sensible phenomenon which I notice is indeed real, but that it may exist or may not exist, and therefore I may feel it or not feel it. This is a characteristic which philosophers have designated as *contingent.* But when I conceive that a body is in space, if I endeavour to conceive the contrary, — that a body may be without space, — I cannot succeed. This conception of space is a conception which philosophers have designated by the term *necessary.*

21

The necessity of some degree of judgment to *clear and distinct* conceptions of things may, I think, be

---

"But whence do all our conceptions, contingent or necessary, come ? From the faculty of conceiving, which is in us, by whatever name you call this faculty of which we are all conscious, — mind, reason, thought, understanding, or intelligence. The operations of this faculty, our conceptions, are essentially affirmative, — if not orally, yet mentally. To deny, even, is to affirm ; for it is to affirm the contrary of what had been first affirmed. To doubt, also, is to affirm ; for it is to affirm uncertainty. Besides, we evidently do not commence by doubt or negation, but by affirmation. Now to affirm, in any way, is *to judge.* If, then, every intellectual operation resolves itself into an operation of judgment, all our conceptions, whether contingent or necessary, resolve themselves into judgments contingent or necessary ; and all our primitive operations being concrete and synthetic, it follows that all the primitive judgments, supposed by these operations, are also exercised under this form.

" When the mind translates itself into language, the primary expressions of its judgments are, like the judgments themselves, concrete and synthetic. Faithful images of the development of the mind, languages begin, not by *words*, but by *phrases*, by propositions very complex. A primitive proposition is a whole, corresponding to the natural synthesis by which the mind begins. These primitive propositions are by no means abstract propositions, such as these : — *There is no quality without a subject ; There is no body without space containing it ;* and the like : but they are all particular, such as, — *I exist ; This body exists ; Such a body is in that space ; God exists.* These propositions are such as refer to a particular and determinate object, which is either *self*, or *body*, or *God.* But after having expressed its primitive, concrete, and synthetic propositions, the mind operates upon these judgments *by abstraction ;* it neglects that which is concrete in them to consider only the form of them, — for example, the character of necessity with which many of them are invested, and which, when disengaged and developed, gives, instead of the concrete propositions, *I exist ; These bodies are in such a space,* &c., the abstract propositions, *There can be no modification without a subject ; There can be no body without space ; There can be no succession without time,* &c. The general was at first enveloped in the particular ; then, from the complexity of the primitive fact, you disengage the general from the particular and you express it by itself.

" We do not begin by propositions, but by judgments ; the judgments do not come from the propositions, but the propositions come from the judgments, which themselves come from the faculty of judging, which is grounded in the original capacity of the mind. *A fortiori,* then, we do not begin by ideas ; for ideas are given us in the propositions. Take, for example, the idea of space. It is not given us by itself, but in this complete proposition, *There is no body without space,* which proposition is only a form of a judgment. Take away the proposition, which could not be made without the judgment, and you have not the ideas ; but as soon as language permits you to translate your judgments into propositions, then you can consider separately the different elements of these propositions, that is to say, *ideas,* separately from each other.

" To speak strictly, there are in nature no propositions, either concrete or abstract, particular or general, and still less are there ideas in nature. What is there in nature ? Besides bodies there is nothing except minds,

illustrated by this similitude. An artisan, suppose a carpenter, cannot work in his art without tools, and these tools must be made by art. The exercise of the art, therefore, is necessary to make the tools, and the tools are necessary to the exercise of the art. There is the same appearance of contradiction as in what I have advanced concerning the necessity of some degree of judgment in order to form clear and distinct conceptions of things. These are the tools we must use in judging and in reasoning, and without them must make very bungling work; yet these tools cannot be made without some exercise of judgment.

2. The necessity of some degree of judgment in forming accurate and distinct notions of things will further appear, if we consider attentively what notions we can form without any aid of judgment, (1.) of the objects of sense, (2.) of the operations of our own minds, or (3.) of the relations of things.

(1.) To begin with *the objects of sense*. It is acknowledged on all hands, that the first notions we have of sensible objects are got by the external senses only, and probably before judgment is brought forth; but these first notions are neither *simple*, nor are they *accurate and distinct,* — *rudis indigestaque moles*. Before we can have any distinct notion of this mass, it must be analyzed; the heterogeneous parts must be separated in our conception, and the simple elements, which before lay hid in the common mass, must first be distinguished, and then put together into one whole. In this

and among these, that which is *ourselves*, which conceives and knows directly things, — minds and bodies. And in the order of minds what is there *innate?* Nothing but the mind itself, the understanding, the faculty of knowing. *The understanding*, as Leibnitz has profoundly said, *is innate to itself:* the development of the understanding is equally innate, in this sense, that it cannot but take place when the understanding is once given, with the power which is proper to it, and the conditions of its development supplied. There are no innate ideas, any more than innate propositions; but there is a capacity, faculty, or power, innate in the understanding, that acts and projects itself in primitive judgments, which, when language comes in, express themselves in propositions, and these propositions, decomposed by abstraction and analysis, engender distinct ideas." — *Elements of Psychology*, Chap. VII. — ED.

way it is that we form distinct notions even of the objects of sense; but this analysis and composition, by habit, becomes so easy, and is performed so readily, that we are apt to overlook it, and to impute the distinct notion we have formed of the object to the senses alone; and this we are the more prone to do, because, when once we have distinguished the sensible qualities of the object from one another, the sense gives testimony to each of them.

You perceive, for instance, an object white, round, and a foot in diameter: I grant that you perceive all these attributes of the object by sense; but if you had not been able to distinguish the color from the figure, and both from the magnitude, your senses would only have given you one complex and confused notion of all these mingled together. A man who is able to say with understanding, or to determine in his own mind, that this object is white, must have distinguished whiteness from other attributes. If he has not made this distinction, he does not understand what he says.

Suppose a cube of brass to be presented at the same time to a child of a year old and to a man. The regularity of the figure will attract the attention of both; both have the senses of sight and of touch in equal perfection; and therefore, if any thing be discovered in this object by the man which cannot be discovered by the child, it must be owing, not to the senses, but to some other faculty which the child has not yet attained. *First*, then, the man can easily distinguish the body from the surface which terminates it; this the child cannot do. *Secondly*, the man can perceive that this surface is made up of six planes of the same figure and magnitude; the child cannot discover this. *Thirdly*, the man perceives that each of these planes has four equal sides and four equal angles, and that the opposite sides of each plane, and the opposite planes, are parallel.

It will surely be allowed that a man of ordinary judgment may observe all this in a cube which he makes an object of contemplation and takes time to consider;

that he may give the name of a square to a plane
terminated by four equal sides and four equal angles,
and the name of a cube to a solid terminated by six
equal squares; all this is nothing else but analyzing
the figure of the object presented to his senses into its
simplest elements, and again compounding it of those
elements. By this analysis and composition two effects
are produced. 1. From the one complex object which
his senses presented, though one of the most simple
the senses can present, he educes many simple and distinct notions of right lines, angles, plane surface, solid,
equality, parallelism; notions which the child has not
yet faculties to attain. 2. When he considers the cube
as compounded of these elements, put together in a
certain order, he has then, and not before, a distinct
and scientific notion of a cube. The child neither conceives those elements, nor in what order they must be
put together, so as to make a perfect cube; and therefore has no accurate notion of a cube, which can make
it a subject of reasoning.

Hence it is, that when any vehement passion or
emotion *hinders the cool application of judgment,* we
get no distinct notion of an object, even though the
sense be long directed to it. A man who is put into a
panic by thinking he sees a ghost, may stare at it long
without having any distinct notion of it; it is his understanding and not his sense that is disturbed by his
horror. If he can lay that aside, judgment immediately
enters upon its office, and examines the length and
breadth, the color and figure and distance of the object.
Of these, while his panic lasted, he had no distinct
notion, though his eyes were open all the time. When
the eye of sense is open, but that of judgment shut by
a panic, or by any violent emotion that engrosses the
mind, we see things confusedly, and probably much in
the same manner that brutes and perfect idiots do, and
infants before the use of judgment.

There are, therefore, notions of the objects of sense
which are gross and indistinct, and there are others that
are distinct and scientific. The former may be got

from the senses alone, but the latter cannot be obtained without some degree of judgment.

The clear and accurate notions which geometry presents to us of a point, a right line, an angle, a square, a circle, of ratios direct and inverse, and others of that kind, can find no admittance into a mind that has not some degree of judgment. They are not properly ideas of the senses, nor are they got by compounding ideas of the senses; but by analyzing the ideas or notions we get by the senses into their simplest elements, and again combining these elements into various, accurate, and elegant forms, which the senses never did nor can exhibit.

(2.) Having said so much of the notions we get from the senses alone of the objects of sense, let us next consider what notions we can have from *consciousness alone* of *the operations of our minds.*

Mr. Locke very properly calls consciousness an internal sense. It gives the like immediate knowledge of things in the mind, that is, of our own thoughts and feelings, as the senses give us of things external. There is this difference, however, that an external object may be at rest, and the sense may be employed about it for some time. But the objects of consciousness are never at rest; the stream of thought flows like a river, without stopping a moment; the whole train of thought passes in succession under the eye of consciousness, which is always employed about the present. But is it consciousness that analyzes complex operations, distinguishes their different ingredients, and combines them in distinct parcels under general names? This surely is not the work of consciousness, nor can it be performed without reflection, recollecting and judging of what we were conscious of and distinctly remember. This reflection does not appear in children. Of all the powers of the mind, it seems to be of the latest growth, whereas consciousness is coeval with the earliest.

Mr. Locke has restricted the word *reflection* to that which is employed about the operations of our minds,

without any authority, as I think, from custom, the
arbiter of language; for surely I may reflect upon what
I have seen or heard, as well as upon what I have
thought. The word, in its proper and common meaning, is equally applicable to objects of sense and to
objects of consciousness.* He has likewise confounded
reflection with consciousness, and seems not to have
been aware that they are different powers, and appear
at very different periods of life.

(3.) I proposed, in the *third* place, to consider our
notions of the *relations of things :* and here I think,
that, without judgment, we cannot have *any* notion of
relations.

There are two ways in which we get the notion of
relations.

The first is by comparing the related objects, *when
we have before had the conception of both.* By this
comparison, we perceive the relation, either immediately, or by a process of reasoning. That my foot is
longer than my finger, I perceive immediately ; and
that three is the half of six. This immediate perception is immediate and intuitive judgment. That the
angles at the base of an isosceles triangle are equal, I
perceive by a process of reasoning, in which it will be
acknowledged there is judgment.

Another way in which we get the notion of relations
(which seems not to have occurred to Mr. Locke) is,
when, by attention to one of the related objects, we
perceive or judge that it must, from its nature, have a
certain relation to something else, which before, perhaps, we never thought of; and thus our attention to
one of the related objects *produces the notion of its cor-
relate, and of a certain relation between them.* Thus,
when I attend to color, figure, weight, I cannot help
judging these to be qualities which cannot exist with-

---

* Here, as before, Reid errs in what he says of *reflection.* Consciousness and reflection cannot be analyzed into different powers. *Reflection,*
in Locke's meaning of the word (and this is the more correct), is only *consciousness, concentrated by an act of the will on the phenomena of mind,* — i. e.
internal attention; in Reid's, what is it but *attention in general ?* — H.

out a subject; that is, something which is colored, figured, heavy. If I had not perceived such things to be qualities, I should never have had any notion of their subject, or of their relation to it. Also, by attending to the operations of thinking, memory, reasoning, we perceive or judge that there must be something which thinks, remembers, and reasons, which we call *the mind.* When we attend to any change that happens in nature, judgment informs us that there must be a cause of this change, which had power to produce it; and thus we get the notions of *cause* and *effect*, and of *the relation between them.* When we attend to body, we perceive that it cannot exist without space; hence we get the notion of *space* (which is neither an object of sense nor of consciousness), and of the relation which bodies have to a certain portion of unlimited space, as their *place.*

I apprehend, therefore, that all our notions of relation may more properly be ascribed to judgment as their source and origin, than to any other power of the mind. We must first perceive relations by our judgment, before we can conceive them without judging of them; as we must first perceive colors by sight, before we can conceive them without seeing them.

III. *Locke's Distinction between Knowledge and Judgment rejected.*] I take it to be a peculiarity of Mr. Locke, that he makes *knowledge* and *judgment* distinct faculties of the mind. His words are (*Essay,* Book IV. Chap. XIV. §§ 3, 4): — " The faculty which God has given to man to supply the want of clear and certain knowledge, where that cannot be had, is *judgment;* whereby the mind takes its ideas to agree or disagree, or, which is the same, any proposition to be true or false, without perceiving a demonstrative evidence in the proofs. Thus, the mind has two faculties, conversant about truth and falsehood. *First,* Knowledge, whereby it certainly perceives, and is undoubtedly satisfied of the agreement or disagreement of any ideas. *Secondly,* Judgment, which is the putting ideas together, or separating them from one another in the mind, when their certain agreement or disagreement is not perceived, but presumed to be so."

Knowledge, I think, sometimes signifies things known; sometimes that act of the mind by which we know them. And in like manner *opinion* sometimes signifies things believed; sometimes the act of the mind by which we believe them. But *judgment* is the faculty which is exercised in *both* these acts of the mind. In knowledge, we judge without doubting; in opinion, with some mixture of doubt. But I know no authority, besides that of Mr. Locke, for calling knowledge *a faculty*, any more than for calling opinion a faculty. Neither do I think that knowledge is confined within the narrow limits which Mr. Locke assigns to it; because the far greater part of what all men call human knowledge is in things which admit of neither intuitive nor demonstrative proof.

I have all along used the word *judgment* in a more extended sense than Mr. Locke does in the passage above mentioned. I understand by it that operation of mind by which we determine, concerning any thing that may be expressed by a proposition, whether it be true or false. Every proposition is either true or false; so is every judgment. A proposition may be simply conceived without judging of it. But when there is not only a conception of the proposition, but a mental affirmation or negation, an assent or dissent of the understanding, whether weak or strong, that is judgment.

I think that, since the days of Aristotle, logicians, and other writers, for the most part, have taken the word in this sense, though it has other meanings, which there is no danger of confounding with this. We may take the authority of Dr. Watts, as a logician, as a man who understood English, and who had a. just esteem of Mr. Locke's *Essay*. *Logic*, Introduction: —
" Judgment is that operation of the mind, wherein we join two or more ideas together by one affirmation or negation : that is, we either affirm or deny *this* to be

that. So *this tree is high; that horse is not swift; the mind of man is a thinking being; mere matter has no thought belonging to it; God is just; good men are often miserable in this world; a righteous governor will make a difference betwixt the evil and the good;* which sentences are the effect of judgment, and are called propositions." And, Part II. Chap. II. Sect. IX.:— " The evidence of sense is, when we frame a proposition according to the dictate of any of our senses. So we judge, *that grass is green; that a trumpet gives a pleasant sound; that fire burns wood; water is soft; and iron hard.*"

In this meaning, judgment extends to every kind of evidence, *probable* or *certain,* and to every degree of assent or dissent. It extends to all knowledge as well as to all opinion: with this difference only, that in knowledge it is more firm and steady, like a house founded upon a rock; in opinion it stands upon a weaker foundation, and is more liable to be shaken and overturned.

These differences about the meaning of words are not mentioned as if truth were on one side, and error on the other, but as an apology for deviating, in this instance, from the phraseology of Mr. Locke, which is for the most part accurate and distinct; and because attention to the different meanings that are put upon words by different authors is the best way to prevent our mistaking verbal differences for real differences of opinion.

CHAPTER II.

OF COMMON SENSE.

I. *Different Significations of the Term Sense in Philosophical and Popular ·Language.*] The word *sense,* in common language, seems to have a different meaning
30

from that which it has in the writings of philosophers; and those different meanings are apt to be confounded, and to occasion embarrassment and error. Not to go back to ancient philosophy upon this point, modern philosophers consider sense as a power that has nothing to do with judgment. Sense they consider as the power by which we *receive certain ideas or impressions from objects;* and judgment as the power by which we *compare those ideas, and perceive their necessary agreements and disagreements.*

The external senses give us the idea of color, figure, sound, and other qualities of body, primary or secondary. Mr. Locke gave the name of *internal sense* to consciousness, because by it we have the ideas of thought, memory, reasoning, and other operations of our own minds. Dr. Hutcheson, of Glasgow, conceiving that we have simple and original ideas which cannot be imputed either to the external senses or to consciousness, introduced other internal senses; such as the *sense of harmony,* the *sense of beauty,* and the *moral sense.* Ancient philosophers also spoke of internal senses, of which memory was accounted one.

But all these senses, whether external or internal, have been represented by philosophers as the means of furnishing our minds with ideas, without including any kind of judgment. Dr. Hutcheson defines a sense to be " a determination of the mind to receive any idea from the presence of an object independent on our will."

" By this term [*sense*] philosophers in general have denominated those faculties, in consequence of which we are liable to feelings relative to ourselves only, and from which they have not pretended to draw any conclusions concerning the nature of things; whereas truth is not relative, but absolute and real." — Dr. Priestley's *Examination of Dr. Reid,* &c., p. 123.

On the contrary, in common language, sense always implies *judgment.* A man of sense is a man of judgment. Good sense is good judgment. Nonsense is what is evidently contrary to right judgment. Common sense is that degree of judgment which is common to men with whom we can converse and transact business.

Seeing and hearing by philosophers are called senses, because we have ideas by them; by the vulgar they are called senses, because we judge by them. We judge of colors by the eye; of sounds by the ear; of beauty and deformity by taste; of right and wrong in conduct by our moral sense or conscience.

Sometimes philosophers, who represent it as the sole province of sense to furnish us with ideas, fall unawares into the popular opinion, that they are judging faculties. Thus Locke, Book IV. Chap. XI. § 2:— "And of this (that the quality or accident of color really exists, and has a being without me), the greatest assurance I can possibly have, and to which my faculties can attain, is the testimony of my eyes, which are the proper and sole *judges* of this thing."

This popular meaning of the word *sense* is not peculiar to the English language. The corresponding words in Greek, Latin, and I believe in all the European languages, have the same latitude. The Latin words *sentire, sententia, sensa,** sensus,* from the last of which the English word *sense* is borrowed, express judgment or opinion, and are applied indifferently to objects of external sense, of taste, of morals, and of the understanding.

I cannot pretend to assign the reason why a word, which is no term of art, which is familiar in common conversation, should have so different a meaning in philosophical writings. I shall only observe, that the philosophical meaning corresponds perfectly with the account which Mr. Locke and other modern philosophers give of judgment. For if the *sole* province of the senses, external and internal, be to furnish the mind with the ideas about which we judge and reason, it seems to be a natural consequence, that the *sole* prov-

---

* What does *sensa* mean? Is it an *erratum*, or does he refer to *sensa*, — *once* only, I believe, employed by Cicero, and interpreted by Nonius Marcellus as *quæ sentiuntur?* — H.

ince of judgment should be to compare those ideas, and to perceive their necessary relations.

These two opinions seem to be so connected, that one may have been the cause of the other. I apprehend, however, that, if both be true, there is no room left for any knowledge or judgment, either of the real existence of contingent things, or of their contingent relations.

To return to the popular meaning of the word *sense*. I believe it would be much more difficult to find good authors who never use it in that meaning, than to find such as do. We may take Mr. Pope as good authority for the meaning of an English word. He uses it often, and in his Epistle to the Earl of Burlington has made a little descant upon it.

> " Oft have you hinted to your brother peer
> A certain truth, which many buy too dear;
> Something there is more needful than expense,
> And something previous e'en to taste, — 't is sense.
> Good sense, which only is the gift of Heaven;
> And though no science, fairly worth the seven;
> A light, which in yourself you must perceive,
> Jones and Le Nôtre have it not to give."

II. *Meaning of the Term Common Sense.*] This inward light or sense is given by Heaven to different persons in different degrees. There is a certain degree of it which is necessary to our being subjects of law and government, capable of managing our own affairs, and answerable for our conduct towards others: this is called *common sense*, because it is common to all men whom we can transact business with, or call to account for their conduct.

The laws of all civilized nations distinguish those who have this gift of Heaven from those who have it not. The last may have rights which ought not to be violated, but, having no understanding in themselves to direct their actions, the laws appoint them to be guided by the understanding of others. It is easily discerned by its effects in men's actions, in their speeches, and even in their looks; and when it is made a question, whether a man has this natural gift or not, a judge or a jury, upon a short conversation with him, can, for the most part, determine the question with great assurance.

The same degree of understanding which makes a man capable of acting with common prudence in the conduct of life, makes him capable of discovering what is true and what is false in matters that are self-evident, and which he distinctly apprehends. All knowledge, and all science, must be built upon principles that are self-evident; and of such principles, every man who has common sense is a competent judge, when he conceives them distinctly. Hence it is, that disputes very often terminate in an appeal to common sense. While the parties agree in the first principles on which their arguments are grounded, there is room for reasoning; but when one denies what to the other appears too evident to need or to admit of proof, reasoning seems to be at an end; an appeal is made to common sense, and each party is left to enjoy his own opinion.

There seems to be no remedy for this, nor any way left to discuss such appeals, unless the decisions of common sense can be brought into a code, in which all reasonable men shall acquiesce. This, indeed, if it were possible, would be very desirable, and would supply a desideratum in logic; and why should it be thought impossible that reasonable men should agree in things that are self-evident?

All that is intended in this chapter is to explain the meaning of common sense, that it may not be treated, as it has been by some, as a new principle, or as a word without any meaning. I have endeavoured to show, that sense, in its most common, and therefore its most proper meaning, signifies judgment, though philosophers often use it in another meaning. From this it is natural to think, that common sense should mean common judgment; and so it really does.

What the precise limits are which divide common judgment from what is beyond it, on the one hand, and from what falls short of it, on the other, may be difficult to determine; and men may agree in the meaning

of the word who have different opinions about those
limits, or who even never thought of fixing them. This
is as intelligible as that all Englishmen should mean
the same thing by the county of York, though perhaps
not a hundredth part of them can point out its precise
limits. Indeed, it seems to me that *common sense* is as
unambiguous a word, and as well understood, as the
county of York. We find it in innumerable places in
good writers; we hear it on innumerable occasions in
conversation; and, as far as I am able to judge, always
in the same meaning. And this is probably the reason
why it is so seldom defined or explained.

Dr. Johnson, in the authorities he gives to show that
the word *sense* signifies *understanding, soundness of
faculties, strength of natural reason,* quotes Dr. Bentley
for what may be called a definition of common sense,
though probably not intended for that purpose, but
mentioned accidentally: — " God hath endowed mankind with power and abilities, which we call natural
light and reason, and common sense."

It is true, that common sense is a popular, and not
a scholastic word; and by most of those who have
treated systematically of the powers of the understanding, it is only occasionally mentioned, as it is by other
writers. But I recollect two philosophical writers who
are exceptions to this remark. One is Buffier, who
treated largely of common sense, as a principle of
knowledge, above fifty years ago.* The other is Bishop

---

* " Buffier's *Traité des Premières Vérités* was first published in 1717, his
Elemens de Métaphysique in 1724. If we except Lord Herbert's treatise
De Veritate, these works exhibit the first regular and comprehensive
attempt to found philosophy on certain primary truths, given in certain
primary sentiments or feelings." In his *Supplementary Dissertations,* Note
A, § 6, Sir W. Hamilton subjoins a succinct exposition of Buffier's doctrine, and concludes the article by warning his readers against the misrepresentations of the anonymous English translator of the treatise on *First
Truths.* " Not only," as he tells us, " have these never been exposed, but
Mr. Stewart has bestowed on that individual an adventitious importance,
by lauding his 'acuteness and intelligence,' while acquiescing in his 'severe
but just animadversions' on Dr. Beattie. — *Elements,* Part II. Chap. I.
Sect. III.

" The translator to his version, which appeared in 1780, has annexed an
elaborate Preface, the sole object of which is to inveigh against Reid,

Berkeley, who, I think, has laid as much stress upon common sense, in opposition to the doctrines of phi-

---

Beattie, and Oswald, — more especially the last two, — for at once *stealing* and *spoiling* the doctrine of the learned Jesuit.

" In regard to the *spoiling*, the translator is the only culprit. According to him Buffier's ' *common sense* is a disposition of mind not natural, but acquired by age and time.' (pp. iv., xxxiv.) ' Those first truths which are its object require experience and meditation to be conceived, and the judgments thence derived are the result of exercising reason.' (p. v.) ' The use of *reason* is *reasoning* '; and ' *common sense* is that degree of understanding in all things to which the generality of mankind are capable of attaining by the exertion of their rational faculty.' (p. xvii.) In fact, Buffier's *first* truths, on his translator's showing, are *last* truths; for when ' by time we arrive at the knowledge of an infinitude of things, and by the use of reason (i. e. by reasoning) form our judgment on them, *those judgments are then justly to be considered as first truths* ' *!!!* (p. xviii.) But how, it will be asked, does he give any color to so unparalleled a perversion? By the very easy process of, — 1°, throwing out of account, or perverting, what his author does say; — 2°, interpolating what his author not only does not say, but what is in the very teeth of his assertions; and 3°, by founding on these perversions and interpolations as on the authentic words of his author.

" As to the *plagiarism*, I may take this opportunity of putting down, once and for ever, this imputation, although the character of the man might have well exempted Reid from all suspicion of so unworthy an act. It applies only to the *Inquiry*; and there the internal evidence is almost of itself sufficient to prove that Reid could not, prior to that publication, have been acquainted with Buffier's treatise. The strongest, indeed the sole presumption, arises from the employment, by both philosophers, of the term *common sense*, which, strange to say, sounded to many in this country as singular and new; whilst it was even commonly believed, that, before Reid, Buffier was the first, indeed the only philosopher, who had taken notice of this principle, as one of the genuine sources of our knowledge. After the testimonies now adduced, and to be adduced, it would be the apex of absurdity to presume that none but Buffier could have suggested to Reid either the principle or its designation. Here are given *forty-eight* authorities, ancient and modern, for the philosophical employment of the term *common sense, previous to Reid*, and from any of these Reid may be said to have borrowed it with equal justice as from Buffier; but, taken together, they concur in proving that the expression, in the application in question, was one in general use, and free as the air to all and each who chose thus to employ it.

" But, in fact, what has not been noticed, we know, from an incidental statement of Reid himself, — and this, be it noticed, prior to the charge of plagiarism, — that he only became acquainted with the treatise of Buffier after the publication of his own *Inquiry* For in his *Account of Aristotle's Logic*, written and published some ten years subsequently to that work, he says, — ' I have *lately* met with a very judicious treatise written by Father Buffier,' &c., Chap. VI. Sect. II. Compare, also, *Intellectual Powers* [the passage to which this note is appended]. In this last work, however, published *after* the translation of Buffier, though indirectly defending the less manifestly innocent partners in the accusation from the charge advanced, his self-respect prevents him from saying a single word in his own vindication." — ED.

losophers, as any philosopher that has come after
him.

Men rarely ask what common sense is; because
every man believes himself possessed of it, and would
take it for an imputation upon his understanding to be
thought unacquainted with it. Yet I remember two
very eminent authors who have put this question; and
it is not improper to hear their sentiments upon a subject so frequently mentioned, and so rarely canvassed.

It is well known, that Lord Shaftesbury gave to one
of his treatises the title of *Sensus Communis; an Essay
on the Freedom of Wit and Humor, in a Letter to a
Friend;* in which he puts his friend in mind of a free
conversation with some of their friends on the subjects
of morality and religion. Amidst the different opinions
started and maintained with great life and ingenuity,
one or other would every now and then take the liberty
to appeal to common sense. Every one allowed the
appeal; no one would offer to call the authority of the
court in question, till a gentleman, whose good understanding was never yet brought in doubt, desired the
company very gravely that they would tell him what
common sense was.

" If," said he, " by the word *sense,* we were to understand opinion and judgment, and by the word *common,*
the generality, or any considerable part of mankind, it
would be hard to discover where the subject of common sense could lie; for that which was according to
the sense of one part of mankind was against the sense
of another: and if the majority were to determine
common sense, it would change as often as men
changed. That, in religion, common sense was as
hard to determine as *catholic* or *orthodox.* What to
one was absurdity, to another was demonstration. In
policy, if plain British or Dutch sense were right,
Turkish and French must certainly be wrong. And as
mere nonsense as passive obedience seemed, we found
it to be the common sense of a great party amongst
ourselves, a greater party in Europe, and perhaps the
greatest party in all the world besides. As for morals,

the difference was still wider; for even the philosophers could never agree in one and the same system. And some, even of our most admired modern philosophers, had fairly told us, that virtue and vice had no other law or measure than mere fashion and vogue."

This is the substance of the gentleman's speech, which, I apprehend, explains the meaning of the word perfectly, and contains all that has been said, or can be said, against the authority of common sense, and the propriety of appeals to it. As there is no mention of any answer immediately made to this speech, we might be apt to conclude, that the noble author adopted the sentiments of the intelligent gentleman whose speech he recites. But the contrary is manifest, from the title of *Sensus Communis* given to his Essay, from his frequent use of the word, and from the whole tenor of the Essay.

The author appears to have a double intention in that Essay, corresponding to the double title prefixed to it. One intention is, to justify the use of wit, humor, and ridicule, in discussing among friends the gravest subjects. " I can very well suppose," says he, " men may be frighted out of their wits; but I have no apprehension they should be laughed out of them. I can hardly imagine, that, in a pleasant way, they should ever be talked out of their love for society, or reasoned out of humanity and common sense."

The other intention, signified by the title *Sensus Communis*, is carried on hand in hand with the first, and is, to show that common sense is not so vague and uncertain a thing as it is represented to be in the skeptical speech before recited. " I will try," says he, " what certain knowledge or assurance of things may be recovered in that very way (to wit, of humor), by which all certainty, you thought, was lost, and an endless skepticism introduced."

He gives some criticisms upon the expression *sensus communis* in Juvenal, Horace, and Seneca; and after showing, in a facetious way, throughout the treatise, that the fundamental principles of morals, of politics, of criticism, and of every branch of knowledge, are the dictates of common sense, he sums up the whole in these words : — " That some moral and philosophical truths there are so evident in themselves, that it would be easier to imagine half mankind run mad, and joined precisely in the same species of folly, than to admit any thing as truth, which should be advanced against such natural knowledge, fundamental reason, and common sense." And, on taking leave, he adds, — " And now, my friend, should you find I had moralized in any tolerable manner according to common sense, and without canting, I should be satisfied with my performance."

Another eminent writer who has put the question what common sense is, is Fénelon, the famous Archbishop of Cambray. That ingenious and pious author, having had an early prepossession in favor of the Cartesian philosophy, made an attempt to establish, on a sure foundation, the metaphysical arguments which Descartes had invented to prove the being of the Deity. For this purpose, he begins with the Cartesian doubt. He proceeds to find out the truth of his own existence, and then to examine wherein the evidence and certainty of this and other such primary truths consisted. This, according to Cartesian principles, he places in the clearness and distinctness of the ideas. On the contrary, he places the absurdity of the contrary propositions in their being repugnant to his clear and distinct ideas.

To illustrate this, he gives various examples of questions manifestly absurd and ridiculous, which every man of common understanding would at first sight perceive to be so, and then goes on to this purpose : — " What is it that makes these questions ridiculous ? Wherein does this ridicule precisely consist ? It will perhaps be replied, that it consists in this, that they shock common sense. But what is this same *common sense ?* Is it not the *first notions* that all men have equally of the same things ? This common sense, which is always and in all places the same ; which prevents inquiry ; which makes inquiry in some cases ridiculous ;

which, instead of inquiring, makes a man laugh whether he will or not; which puts it out of a man's power to doubt; this sense, which only waits to be consulted, — which shows itself at the first glance, and immediately discovers the evidence or the absurdity of a question, — is not this the same that I call *my ideas?*

"Behold, then, those ideas or general notions, which it is not in my power either to contradict or examine, and by which I examine and decide in every case, insomuch that I laugh instead of answering, as often as any thing is proposed to me which is evidently contrary to what these immutable ideas represent."

I shall only observe upon this passage, that the interpretation it gives of Descartes's criterion of truth, whether just or not, is the most intelligible and the most favorable I have met with.

I beg leave to mention one passage from Cicero, and to add two or three from late writers, which show that this word has not become obsolete, or changed its meaning. *De Oratore*, Lib. III. 50.—" Omnes enim tacito quodam sensu, sine ulla arte aut ratione, in artibus ac rationibus, recta ac prava dijudicant. Idque cum faciant in picturis, et in signis, et in aliis operibus, ad quorum intelligentiam a naturâ minus habent instrumenti, tum multo ostendunt magis in verborum, numerorum, vocumque judicio; quod ea sint in *communibus* infixa *sensibus;* neque earum rerum quemquam funditus natura voluit expertem."

Hume's *Essays and Treatises*, Vol. I. p. 5.—"But a philosopher who proposes only to represent the common sense of mankind in more beautiful and more engaging colors, if by accident he commits a mistake, goes no further, but, renewing his appeal to common sense and the natural sentiments of the mind, returns into the right path, and secures himself from any dangerous illusion."

Hume's *Inquiry concerning the Principles of Morals*, p. 2.—"Those who have refused the reality of moral distinctions may be ranked among the disingenuous disputants. The only way of converting an antagonist

of this kind is to leave him to himself: for, finding that
nobody keeps up the controversy with him, it is probable he will at last, of himself, from mere weariness,
come over to the side of common sense and reason."
Priestley's *Institutes*, Preliminary Essay, Vol. I. p. 27.
— " Because common sense is a sufficient guard against
many errors in religion, it seems to have been taken for
granted, that that common sense is a sufficient instructor also, whereas in fact, without positive instruction, men would naturally have been mere savages with
respect to religion ; as, without similar instruction, they
would be savages with respect to the arts of life and
the sciences.　Common sense can only be compared
to a judge ; but what can a judge do without evidence and proper materials from which to form a judgment ?"
Priestley's *Examination of Dr. Reid*, &c., p. 127. —
" But should we, out of complaisance, admit that what
has hitherto been called judgment may be called sense,
it is making too free with the established signification
of words to call it common sense, which, in common
acceptation, has long been appropriated to a very different thing, viz., to that capacity for judging of common
things that persons of middling capacities are capable
of."　Again, p. 129. — " I should therefore expect, that,
if a man was so totally deprived of common sense as
not to be able to distinguish truth from falsehood in
one case, he would be equally incapable of distinguishing it in another."
From this cloud of testimonies, to which hundreds
might be added, I apprehend that whatever censure is
thrown upon those who have spoken of common sense
as a principle of knowledge, or who have appealed to it
in matters that are self-evident, will fall light, when
there are so many to share in it.　Indeed, the authority
of this tribunal is too sacred and venerable, and has
prescription too long in its favor, to be now wisely
called in question.　Those who are disposed to do
so may remember the shrewd saying of Mr. Hobbes,
— " When reason is against a man, a man will be

against reason." This is equally applicable to common sense.[*]

---

[*] In the fifth section of the same Dissertation referred to in the last note, Sir W. Hamilton defines with clearness and precision the various acceptations of the term *common sense*, only two or three of which need here be noticed. Sometimes " it denotes *the complement of those cognitions or convictions which we receive from nature; which all men profess in common; and by which they test the truth of knowledge and the morality of actions.* This is the meaning in which the expression is now emphatically employed in philosophy, and which may be, therefore, called its *philosophical* signification. As authorities for its use in this relation, Reid has adduced legitimate examples from Bentley, Shaftesbury, Fénelon, Buffier, and Hume. The others which he quotes from Cicero and Priestley can hardly be considered as more than instances of the employment of the words; for the former, in the particular passage quoted, does not seem to mean by *sensus communis* more than the faculty of *apprehending sensible relations* which all possess; and the latter explicitly states, that he uses the words in the meaning which we are hereafter to consider. Mr. Stewart, *Elements*, Part II. Chap. I. Sect. IV., to the examples of Reid adds only a single, and that not an unambiguous instance, from Bayle. It therefore still remains to show that in this signification its employment is not only of authorized usage, but, in fact, one long and universally established. This is done in the series of testimonies I shall adduce in a subsequent part of this note [from Hesiod to De la Mennais, in all one hundred and six witnesses], — principally, indeed, to prove that the *doctrine* of *common sense*, notwithstanding many schismatic aberrations, is the one catholic and perennial philosophy, but which also concur in showing that this, too, is the *name* under which that doctrine has for two thousand years been most familiarly known, at least in the Western world. Of these, Lucretius, Cicero, Horace, Seneca, Tertullian, Arnobius, and St. Augustine exhibit the expression as recognized in the language and philosophy of ancient Rome; while some fifty others prove its scientific and colloquial usage in every country of modern Europe."

According to another acceptation of the term *common sense*, " it denotes *such an ordinary complement of intelligence, that, if a person be deficient therein, he is accounted mad or foolish. Sensus communis* is thus used in Phædrus, Lib. I. 7; but Horace, *Serm.*, Lib. I. 3, and Juvenal, *Sat.* VIII. 73, are erroneously, though usually, interpreted in this signification. In modern Latinity (as in Milton *Contra Salmasium*, Cap. VIII.), and in most of the vulgar languages, the expression in this meaning is so familiar, that it would be idle to adduce examples. Sir James Mackintosh, *Dissertations*, &c., p. 387 of the collected edition, imagines, indeed, that this is the only meaning of *common sense*; and on this ground censures Reid for the adoption of the term; and even Mr. Stewart's objections to it seem to proceed on the supposition, that this is the proper or more accredited signification. See *Elements*, Part II. Chap. I. Sect. II.; and *Life of Reid*, Sect. II. This is wrong; but Reid himself, it must be acknowledged, does not sufficiently distinguish between this and the last-mentioned acceptation; as may be seen from the tenor of his chapter on Common Sense, but especially from the concluding chapter of the *Inquiry*."

Again, when *common sense* is used with emphasis on the substantive and not on the adjective, it often, in popular langr age, " expresses *native prac-*

31

III. *Relation of Reason and Common Sense to each other.*] It is absurd to conceive that there can be any opposition between reason and common sense. It is, indeed, the first-born of reason, and, as they are commonly joined together in speech and in writing, they are inseparable in their nature.

We ascribe to reason two offices, or two degrees. The first is to judge of things self-evident; the second to draw conclusions that are not self-evident from those that are. The first of these is the province, and the sole province, of common sense; and therefore it coincides with reason in its whole extent, and is only another name for *one branch or one degree of reason.* Perhaps it may be said, Why, then, should you give it a particular name, since it is acknowledged to be only a degree of reason? It would be a sufficient answer to this, Why do you abolish a name which is to be found in the language of all civilized nations, and has acquired a right by prescription? Such an attempt is equally foolish and ineffectual. Every wise man will be apt to think, that a name which is found in all languages as far back as we can trace them, is not without some use.

But there is an obvious reason why this degree of reason should have a name appropriated to it; and that is, that *in the greatest part of mankind no other degree of reason is to be found.* It is this degree that entitles them to the denomination of reasonable creatures. It is this degree of reason, and this only, that makes a man capable of managing his own affairs, and answerable for his conduct towards others. There is, therefore, the best reason why it should have a name appropriated to it.

---

tical intelligence, natural prudence, mother wit, tact in behaviour, acuteness in the observation of character, &c., in contrast to habits of acquired learning, or of speculation away from the affairs of life. I recollect no unambiguous examples of the phrase, in this precise acceptation, in any ancient author. In modern languages, and more particularly in French and English, it is of ordinary occurrence. Thus, Voltaire's saying, ' Le sens commun n'est pas si commun ';—which, I may notice, was stolen from Buffier, *Méta-physique,* § 69."—ED.

These two degrees of reason differ in other respects, which would be sufficient to entitle them to *distinct* names.

The first is purely *the gift of Heaven.* And where Heaven has not given it, no education can supply the want. The second is *learned by practice and rules,* when the first is not wanting. A man who has common sense may be taught to reason. But if he has not that gift, no teaching will make him able either to judge of first principles or to reason from them.

I have only this further to observe, that the province of common sense is *more extensive in refutation than in confirmation.* A conclusion drawn by a train of just reasoning from true principles cannot possibly contradict any decision of common sense, because truth will always be consistent with itself. Neither can such a conclusion receive any confirmation from common sense, because it is not within its jurisdiction.

But it is possible, that, by setting out from false principles, or by an error in reasoning, a man may be led to a conclusion that contradicts the decisions of common sense. In this case, the conclusion is within the jurisdiction of common sense, though the reasoning on which it was grounded be not; and a man of common sense may fairly reject the conclusion, without being able to show the error of the reasoning that led to it. Thus, if a mathematician, by a process of intricate demonstration, in which some false step was made, should be brought to this conclusion, that two quantities, which are equal to a third, are not equal to each other, a man of common sense, without pretending to be a judge of the demonstration, is well entitled to reject the conclusion, and to pronounce it absurd.*

---

* In Jouffroy's *Mélanges Philosophiques* there is an article, *De la Philosophie et du Sens Commun* (translated by Mr. Ripley, in his *Philosophical Miscellanies,* Vol. I. p. 305 *et seq.*), in which he marks with some distinctness their relation to each other.

" Before their accession to philosophy, philosophers, in their capacity as men, bore within them the light of common sense ; they made use of it in their judgments and in their conduct; and whatever may be the result of their scientific labors, it is not perceived that they renounce common sense

CHAPTER III.

OF FIRST PRINCIPLES IN GENERAL.

I. *Nature, Necessity, and Use of First Principles.*]
One of the most important distinctions of our judgments is, that some of them are *intuitive*, others *grounded on argument.*

It is not in our power to judge as we will. The judgment is carried along necessarily by the evidence, real or seeming, which appears to us at the time. But in propositions that are submitted to our judgment

---

in the ordinary affairs of life, or that they are any more converted to their own doctrines than the great mass of mankind. They avow in practice, not only the existence, but the superiority, of the solutions of common sense. What, then, do they seek? What is the purpose of their endeavours? Let us attempt to explain it.

" The solutions of common sense *are not established in any explicit manner, and in a positive form,* in the human mind. Ask the first man you meet, what idea he has formed of the Good, or what he thinks concerning the nature of things; — he will not know what you say. If you attempt to explain to him the meaning of those two questions, at least unless you use all the skill of Socrates, he will find it hard to comprehend you. But undertake to call in question, with the Stoics, that pleasure is a good, or to deny, with the spiritualists, the existence of matter; — you will see him laugh at your folly, and exhibit the most unconquerable conviction with regard to those two points. It will be the same with every other question. Common sense, therefore, is an opinion of undoubted reality; but men are governed by it almost unconsciously; its existence is proved by the single fact, that they judge and act as if they possessed it. Taken as a whole, it is obscure; no one can give account of it; but when a particular case occurs, it is manifested at once by a clear and positive application; it then returns into the shade. It is perceived in every judgment, in every determination; but, except in its application, it is as if it were not; *and it is precisely this obscurity which makes it insufficient for thinking men.* Reflection cannot be satisfied with this species of inspiration, the characteristic of which is to be ignorant of itself, and to be satisfied with this ignorance. The *élite* of humanity is not satisfied with these obscure glimpses, these vague persuasions: it seeks to *comprehend* what every body *believes;* it wishes to obtain *clear* solutions of the great questions that concern man; and with it commences *philosophy.* To philosophize is to comprehend; to comprehend is not to know, but to verify what we knew before. How could we wish to comprehend, if we were ignorant of what we wished to comprehend?"

To the same effect, but more pointedly, Sir W. Hamilton, Note A, § 3: — " Nor is it true, that the argument from *common sense* denies the decision to the judgment of philosophers, and accords it to the verdict of the vul-

there is this great difference ; some are of such a nature
that a man of ripe understanding may apprehend them
distinctly, and perfectly understand their meaning without. finding himself under any necessity of believing
them to be true or false, probable or improbable. The
judgment remains in suspense, until it is inclined to
one side or another by reasons or arguments.

But there are other propositions which are no sooner
understood than they are believed. The judgment follows the apprehension of them necessarily, and both
are equally the work of nature, and the result of our
original powers. There is no searching for evidence,
no weighing of arguments ; the proposition is not deduced or inferred from another ; it has the light of truth

---

gar. Nothing can be more erroneous. We admit, nay, we maintain, as
D'Alembert well expresses it, that ' the truth in metaphysics, like the truth
in matters of taste, is a truth of which all minds have the germ within
themselves ; to which, indeed, the greater' number pay no attention, but
which they can recognize the moment it is pointed out to them. But if,
in this sort, we are able to *understand*, all are not able to *instruct*. The
merit of conveying easily to others true and simple notions is much greater
than is commonly supposed ; for experience proves how rarely this is to
be met with. Sound metaphysical ideas are common truths, which every
one apprehends, but which few have the talent to develop. So difficult is
it on any subject to make our own what belongs to every one.' *Mélanges*,
Tome IV. § 6. Or, to employ the words of the ingenious Lichtenberg, —
'Philosophy, twist the matter as we may, is always a sort of chemistry
(Scheidekunst). The peasant employs all the principles of abstract philosophy, only *inveloped*, *latent*, *engaged*, as the men of physical science
express it ; the philosopher exhibits the *pure* principle.' *Hinterlassene
Schriften*, Vol. II. p. 67.

" It must be recollected, also, that, in appealing to the consciousness of
mankind in general, we only appeal to the consciousness of those not dis-
qualified to pronounce a decision. ' In saying (to use the words of Aristotle) simply and without qualification, that this or that *is a known truth*,
we do not mean that it is in fact recognized by *all*, but only by *such as are
of a sound understanding* ; just as, in saying absolutely that a thing is whole-
some, we must be held to mean, to such as are of a hale constitution.'
Top., Lib. VI. Cap. IV. § 7. — We may, in short, say of the true philosopher what Erasmus, in an epistle to Hutton, said of Sir Thomas More : —
' Nemo minus ducitur *vulgi judicio* ; sed rursus nemo minus abest a *sensu
communi*.' " See also the Appendix to this volume.

Compare Beattie's *Essay on the Nature and Immutability of Truth*, Part
I. Chap. II. ; Oswald's *Appeal to Common Sense*, Vol. I. *passim* ; Priestley's
Examination of Dr. Reid's Inquiry, &c. ; Cogan's *Ethical Questions*, Specu-
lation V. ; Galluppi, *Lettere Filosofiche* (translated into French by M.
Peisse, *Lettres Philosophiques*, Paris, 1844), Let. XI. ; *Blackwood's Mag-
azine* for August, 1847. — ED.

in itself, and has no occasion to borrow it from another.

Propositions of the last kind, when they are used in matters of science, have commonly been called *axioms;* and, on whatever occasion they are used, are called *first principles, principles of common sense, common notions, self-evident truths.* Cicero calls them *naturæ judicia, judicia communibus hominum sensibus infixa.* Lord Shaftesbury expresses them by the words, *natural knowledge, fundamental reason,* and *common sense.**

---

* For the nomenclature of first principles, see Sir W. Hamilton's Note A, § 5. His remarks on two or three of the appellations which have recently grown into favor are here given.

"1. *Instinctive beliefs, cognitions, judgments,* &c.

"Priestley (*Examination,* &c., passim) has attempted to ridicule Reid's use of the terms *instinct* and *instinctive,* in this relation, as an innovation, not only in philosophy, but in language; and Sir James Mackintosh (*Dissertations,* p. 388) considers the term *instinct* not less improper than the term *common sense.* As to the impropriety, though, like most other psychological terms, these are not unexceptionable, they are, however, less so than many, nay, than most, others. An *instinct* is an agent which performs blindly and ignorantly a work of intelligence and knowledge. The terms *instinctive belief, instinctive judgment, instinctive cognition,* are therefore expressions not ill adapted to characterize a belief, judgment, cognition, which, as the result of no anterior consciousness, is, like the products of animal instinct, the intelligent effect of (as far as we are concerned) an unknown cause. In like manner, we can hardly find more suitable expressions to indicate those incomprehensible spontaneities themselves, of which the primary facts of consciousness are the manifestations, than *rational* or *intellectual instincts.* In fact, if *reason* can justly be called *a developed feeling,* it may, with no less propriety, be called *an illuminated instinct;* — in the words of Ovid,

　　　　'Et quod nunc ratio, impetus ante fuit.'

As to an innovation either in language or philosophy, this objection only betrays the ignorance of the objector. Mr. Stewart (*Essays,* Ess. II. Chap. II.) adduces Boscovich and D'Alembert as authorities for the employment of the terms *instinct* and *instinctive* in Reid's signification. But, before Reid, he might have found them *thus* applied by Cicero, Scaliger, Bacon, Herbert, Descartes, Rapin, Pascal, Poiret, Barrow, Leibnitz, Musæus, Feuerlin, Hume, Bayer, Kames, Reimarus, and a host of others; while subsequent to the *Inquiry into the Human Mind,* besides Beattie, Oswald, Campbell, Ferguson, among our Scottish philosophers, we have, with Hemsterhuis in Holland, in Germany Tetens, Jacobi, Bouterwek, Neeb, Köppen, Ancillon, and many other metaphysicians who have adopted and defended the expressions.

"2. *A priori truths, principles, cognitions, notions, judgments,* &c.

"The term *a priori,* by the influence of Kant and his school, is now very generally employed to characterize those elements of knowledge which are

I hold it to be certain, and even demonstrable, that *all knowledge got by reasoning must be built upon first principles.*

This is as certain as that every house must have a foundation. The power of reasoning, in this respect, resembles the mechanical powers or engines; it must have a fixed point to rest upon, otherwise it spends its force in the air, and produces no effect.

When we examine, in the way of analysis, the evidence of any proposition, either we find it self-evident,

---

not obtained *a posteriori,* — are not evolved out of experience as factitious generalizations; but which are native to, are potentially in, the mind antecedent to the act of experience, on occasion of which (as constituting its subjective conditions) they are first actually elicited into consciousness. These, like many, indeed most others of his technical expressions, are old words applied in a new signification. Previously to Kant, the terms *a priori* and *a posteriori* were, in a sense which descended from Aristotle, properly and usually employed, the former to denote a reasoning from cause to effect, the latter, a reasoning from effect to cause. The term *a priori* came, however, in modern times, to be extended to any abstract reasoning from a given notion to the conditions which such notion involved; hence, for example, the title *a priori* bestowed on the ontological and cosmological arguments for the existence of the Deity. The latter of these, in fact, starts from experience, — from the observed contingency of the world, — in order to construct the supposed notion on which it founds. Clarke's cosmological demonstration, called *a priori,* is therefore, so far, properly an argument *a posteriori.*

" 3. *Transcendental truths, principles, cognitions, judgments,* &c.

" In the schools, *transcendentalis* and *transcendens* were convertible expressions, employed to mark a term or notion which *transcended,* that is, which rose above, and thus contained under it, the categories, or *summa genera,* of Aristotle. Such, for example, is *being,* of which the ten categories are only subdivisions. Kant, according to his wont, twisted these old terms into a new signification. First of all, he distinguished them from each other. *Transcendent* (*transcendens*) he employed to denote what is wholly beyond experience, being given neither as an *a posteriori* nor *a priori* element of cognition, — what, therefore, transcends every category of thought. *Transcendental* (*transcendentalis*) he applied to signify the *a priori* or necessary cognitions, which, though manifested in, as affording the conditions of, experience, transcend the sphere of that contingent or adventitious knowledge which we acquire by experience. Transcendental is not, therefore, what transcends, but what in fact constitutes, a category of thought. This term, though probably from another quarter, has found favor with Mr. Stewart; who proposes to exchange the expression *principles of common sense,* for, among other names, that of *transcendental truths.*"

The designation by which Mr. Stewart prefers, on the whole, to distinguish primary truths is either *fundamental laws of human belief* or *primary elements of human reason. Elements,* Part II. Chap. I. — ED.

or it rests upon one or more propositions that support
it. The same thing may be said of the propositions
that support it; and of those that support them, as far
back as we can go. But we cannot go back in this
track to infinity. Where, then, must this analysis
stop? It is evident that it must stop only when we
come to propositions which support all that are built
upon them, but are themselves supported by none, that
is, to self-evident propositions.

Let us next consider a synthetical proof of any kind,
where we begin with the premises, and pursue a train
of consequences, until we come to the last conclusion,
or thing to be proved. Here we must begin, either
with self-evident propositions, or with such as have
been already proved. When the last is the case, the
proof of the propositions thus assumed is a part of
our proof; and the proof is deficient without it. Suppose, then, the deficiency supplied, and the proof com-
pleted, is it not evident that it must set out with self-
evident propositions, and that the whole evidence must
rest upon them? So that it appears to be demonstrable, that, *without first principles, analytical reasoning
could have no end, and synthetical reasoning could have
no beginning;* and that every conclusion got by reasoning must rest with its whole weight upon *first principles*, as the building does upon its foundation.

It would doubtless contribute greatly to the stability of human knowledge, and consequently to the improvement of it, if *the first principles upon which the
various parts of it are grounded were pointed out and
ascertained.*

We have ground to think so from facts, as well as
from the nature of the thing. There are two branches
of human knowledge in which this method has been
followed, — to wit, mathematics and natural philosophy: in mathematics, as far back as we have books.
It is in this science only, that, for more than two thousand years since it began to be cultivated, we find no
sects, no contrary systems, and hardly any disputes;
or, if there have been disputes, they have ended as soon

as the animosity of parties subsided, and have never been again revived. The science, once firmly established upon the foundation of a few axioms and definitions, as upon a rock, has grown from age to age, so as to become the loftiest and the most solid fabric that human reason can boast.

Natural philosophy, till less than two hundred years ago, remained in the same fluctuating state with the other sciences. Every new system pulled up the old by the roots. The system-builders, indeed, were always willing to accept of the aid of first principles, when they were of their side; but finding them insufficient to support the fabric which their imagination had raised, they were only brought in as auxiliaries, and so intermixed with conjectures and with lame inductions, that their systems were like Nebuchadnezzar's image, whose feet were partly of iron and partly of clay.

Lord Bacon first delineated the only solid foundation on which natural philosophy can be built: and Sir Isaac Newton reduced the principles laid down by Bacon into three or four axioms, which he calls *regulæ philosophandi*. From these, together with the phenomena observed by the senses, which he likewise lays down as first principles, he deduces, by strict reasoning, the propositions contained in the third book of his *Principia*, and in his *Optics;* and by this means has raised a fabric in those two branches of natural philosophy, which is not liable to be shaken by doubtful disputation, but stands immovable upon the basis of self-evident principles.*

We may observe, by the way, that the reason why logicians have been so unanimous in determining the *rules of reasoning*, from Aristotle down to this day, seems to be, that they were by that great genius raised, in a scientific manner, from a few definitions and axioms. It may further be observed, that when men differ about a deduction, whether it follows from certain premises, this I think is always owing to their dif-

---

* Compare Stewart's *Elements*, Part II. Chap. I.

fering about some first principle. I shall explain this by an example. Suppose that, from a thing having begun to exist, one man infers that it must have had a cause; another man does not admit the inference. Here it is evident that the first takes it for a self-evident principle, that every thing which begins to exist must have a cause. The other does not allow this to be self-evident. Let them settle this point, and the dispute will be at an end.

Thus I think it appears, that in matters of science, if the terms be properly explained, the first principles upon which the reasoning is grounded be laid down and exposed to examination, and the conclusions regularly deduced from them, it might be expected that men of candor and capacity, who love truth, and have patience to examine things coolly, might come to unanimity with regard to the force of the deductions, and that their differences might be reduced to those they may have about first principles.

II. *Means of determining what ought to be admitted as First Principles.*] We are next to consider whether *nature has left us destitute of means whereby the candid and honest part of mankind may be brought to unanimity when they happen to differ about first principles.*

When men differ about things that are taken to be first principles, or self-evident truths, reasoning seems to be at an end. Each party appeals to common sense; and if one man's common sense gives one determination, another man's a contrary determination, there would seem, at first sight, to be no remedy but to leave every man to enjoy his own opinion. It is in vain to reason with a man who denies the first principles on which the reasoning is grounded. Thus, it would be in vain to attempt the proof of a proposition in Euclid to a man who denies the axioms. Indeed, we *ought* never to reason with men who deny first principles *from obstinacy and unwillingness to yield to reason.*

But is it not possible, that *men who really love truth,*

and are open to conviction, may differ about first principles?

I think it is possible, and that it cannot, without great want of charity, be denied to be possible.

When this happens, every man who believes that there is a real distinction between truth and error, and that the faculties which God has given us are not in their nature fallacious, must be convinced that there is a defect, or a perversion of judgment, on the one side or the other. A man of candor and humility will, in such a case, very naturally suspect his own judgment, so far as to be desirous to enter into a serious examination even of what he has long held as a first principle. He will think it not impossible that, although his heart be upright, his judgment may have been perverted, by education, by authority, by party zeal, or by some other of the common causes of error, from the influence of which neither parts nor integrity exempt the human understanding.

In such a state of mind, so amiable, and so becoming every good man, has nature left him destitute of any rational means by which he may be enabled, either to correct his judgment if it be wrong, or to confirm it if it be right?

I hope it is not so. I hope that, by the means which nature has furnished, controversies about first principles may be brought to an issue, and that the real lovers of truth may come to unanimity with regard to them. It is true, that, in other controversies, the process by which the truth of a proposition is discovered, or its falsehood detected, is by showing its necessary connection with first principles, or its repugnancy to them. It is true, likewise, that, when the controversy is whether a proposition be itself a first principle, this process cannot be applied. The truth, therefore, in controversies of this kind, labors under a peculiar disadvantage. But it has advantages of another kind to compensate this.

For, in the *first* place, in such controversies, *every man is a competent judge;* and therefore it is difficult to impose upon mankind.

To judge of first principles requires no more than a sound mind free from prejudice, and a distinct conception of the question. The learned and the unlearned, the philosopher and the day-laborer, are upon a level, and will pass the same judgment, when they are not misled by some bias, or taught to renounce their understanding from some mistaken religious principle.

In matters beyond the reach of common understanding, the many are led by the few, and willingly yield to their authority. But in matters of common sense, the few must yield to the many, when local and temporary prejudices are removed. No man is now moved by the subtile arguments of Zeno against motion, though perhaps he knows not how to answer them.

The ancient skeptical system furnishes a remarkable instance of this truth. That system, of which Pyrrho was reputed the father, was carried down, through a succession of ages, by very able and acute philosophers, who taught men to believe nothing at all, and esteemed it the highest pitch of human wisdom to withhold assent from every proposition whatsoever. It was supported with very great subtilty and learning, as we see from the writings of Sextus Empiricus, the only author of that sect whose writings have come down to our age.

Yet, as this system was an insult upon the common sense of mankind, it died away of itself; and it would be in vain to attempt to revive it. The modern skepticism, I mean that of Mr. Hume, is very different from the ancient, otherwise it would not have been allowed a hearing; and, when it has lost the grace of novelty, it will die away also, though it should never be refuted.

Secondly, we may observe, that opinions which contradict first principles are distinguished from other errors by this, — *that they are not only false, but absurd;* and, to discountenance absurdity, nature has given us a particular emotion, — to wit, that of *ridicule*, — which seems intended for this very purpose of putting out of countenance what is absurd, either in opinion or practice.

This weapon, when properly applied, cuts with as keen an edge as argument. Nature has furnished us with the first to expose absurdity, as with the last to refute error. Both are well fitted for their several offices, and are equally friendly to truth, when properly used. Both may be abused to serve the cause of error; but the same degree of judgment which serves to detect the abuse of argument in false reasoning, serves to detect the abuse of ridicule when it is wrongly directed. Some have from nature a happier talent for ridicule than others; and the same thing holds with regard to the talent of reasoning. But it must be acknowledged, that the emotion of ridicule, even when most natural, may be stifled by an emotion of a contrary nature, and cannot operate till that is removed. Thus, if the notion of sanctity is annexed to an object, it is no longer a laughable matter; and this visor must be pulled off before it appears ridiculous. Hence we see, that notions which appear most ridiculous to all who consider them coolly and indifferently have no such appearance to those who never thought of them but under the impression of religious awe and dread. And even where religion is not concerned, the novelty of an opinion to those who are too fond of novelties; the gravity and solemnity with which it is introduced; the opinion we have entertained of the author; its apparent connection with principles already embraced, or subserviency to interests which we have at heart; and, above all, its being fixed in our minds at that time of life when we receive implicitly what we are taught, — may cover its absurdity, and fascinate the understanding for a time.

But if ever we are able to view it naked, and stripped of those adventitious circumstances from which it borrowed its importance and authority, the natural emotion of ridicule will exert its force. An absurdity can be entertained by men of sense no longer than it wears a mask. When any man is found who has the skill or the boldness to pull off the mask, it can no longer bear the light; it slinks into dark corners for a while, and then is no more heard of but as an object of ridicule.

32

Thus I conceive that first principles, which are really the dictates of common sense, and directly opposed to absurdities in opinion, will always, from the constitution of human nature, support themselves, and gain rather than lose ground among mankind.

It may be observed, *thirdly*, that although it is contrary to the nature of first principles to admit of direct or *apodictical* proof; *yet there are certain ways of reasoning even about them, by which those that are just and solid may be confirmed, and those that are false may be detected.*

It may here be proper to mention some of the topics from which we may reason in matters of this kind.

First. It is a good argument *ad hominem*, if it can be shown, that a first principle which a man rejects stands upon the same footing with others which he admits; for, when this is the case, he must be guilty of an inconsistency who holds the one and rejects the other.

Thus the faculties of consciousness, of memory, of external sense, and of reason, are all equally the gifts of nature. No good reason can be assigned for receiving the testimony of one of them, which is not of equal force with regard to the others. The greatest skeptics admit the testimony of consciousness, and allow that what it testifies is to be held as a first principle. If, therefore, they reject the immediate testimony of sense, or of memory, they are guilty of an inconsistency.

Secondly. A first principle may admit of a proof *ad absurdum.*

In this kind of proof, which is very common in mathematics, we suppose the contradictory proposition to be true. We trace the consequences of that supposition in a train of reasoning; and if we find any of its necessary consequences to be manifestly absurd, we conclude the supposition from which it followed to be false; and therefore its contradictory to be true. There is hardly any proposition, especially of those that may claim the character of first principles, that stands alone and unconnected. It draws many others along with it in a chain that cannot be broken. He that takes it up must bear the burden of all its consequences; and if that is too heavy for him to bear, he must not pretend to take it up.

Thirdly. I conceive that the *consent of ages and nations, of the learned and unlearned,* ought to have great authority with regard to first principles, where every man is a competent judge.

Our ordinary conduct in life is built upon first principles, as well as our speculations in philosophy, and every motive to action supposes some belief. When we find a general agreement among men in principles that concern human life, this must have great authority with every sober mind that loves truth. Still, it will be said, What has authority to do in matters of opinion? Is truth to be determined by most votes? Or is authority to be again raised out of its grave to tyrannize over mankind?

Authority, though a very tyrannical mistress to private judgment, may yet, on some occasions, be a useful handmaid; this is all she is entitled to, and this is all I plead in her behalf. The justice of this plea will appear by putting a case in a science, in which, of all sciences, authority is acknowledged to have least weight.

Suppose a mathematician has made a discovery in that science, which he thinks important; that he has put his demonstration in just order; and, after examining it with an attentive eye, has found no flaw in it. I would ask, Will there not be still in his breast some diffidence, some jealousy lest the ardor of invention may have made him overlook some false step? This must be granted. He commits his demonstration to the examination of a mathematical friend, whom he esteems a competent judge, and waits with impatience the issue of his judgment. Here I would ask again, whether the verdict of his friend, according as it is favorable or unfavorable, will not greatly increase or diminish his confidence in his own judgment. Most certainly it will, and it ought. If the judgment of his friend agree with his own, especially if it be confirmed by two or three able judges, he rests secure of his discovery without further examination; but if it be unfavorable, he is brought back into a kind of suspense, until the part that is suspected undergoes a new and a more rigorous examination.

I hope what is supposed in this case is agreeable to nature, and to the experience of candid and modest men on such occasions; yet here we see a man's judgment, even in a mathematical demonstration, conscious of some feebleness in itself, seeking the aid of authority to support it, greatly strengthened by that authority, and hardly able to stand erect against it, without some new aid.

Now, in a matter of common sense, every man is no less a competent judge, than a mathematician is in a mathematical demonstration; and there must be a great presumption that the judgment of mankind, in such a matter, is the natural issue of those faculties which God has given them. Such a judgment can be erroneous only when *there is some cause of the error, as general as the error is.* When this can be shown to be the case, I acknowledge it ought to have its due weight. But to suppose a general deviation from truth among mankind in things self-evident, of which no cause can be assigned, is highly unreasonable.

Perhaps it may be thought impossible to collect the general opinion of men upon any point whatsoever; and, therefore, that this authority can serve us in no stead in examining first principles. But I apprehend, that, in many cases, this is neither impossible nor difficult.

Who can doubt whether men have universally believed the existence of a material world? Who can doubt whether men have universally believed, that every change that happens in nature must have a cause? Who can doubt whether men have universally believed that there is a right and a wrong in human conduct, — some things that merit blame, and others that are entitled to approbation? The universality of these opinions, and of many such that might be named, is sufficiently evident, from the whole tenor of human conduct, as far as our acquaintance reaches, and from the history of all ages and nations of which we have any records.

There are other opinions that appear to be universal, from what is common in the structure of all languages. Language is the express image and picture of human thoughts; and from the picture we may draw some certain conclusions concerning the original. We find in all languages the same parts of speech; we find nouns, substantive and adjective; verbs, active and passive, in their various tenses, numbers, and moods. Some rules of syntax are the same in all languages.

Now, what is common in the structure of languages indicates a uniformity of opinion in those things upon which that structure is grounded. The distinction between substances and the qualities belonging to them, between thought and the being that thinks, between thought and the objects of thought, is to be found in the structure of all languages; and therefore systems of philosophy, which abolish those distinctions, wage war with the common sense of mankind.

We are apt to imagine, that those who formed languages were no metaphysicians; but the first principles of all sciences are the dictates of common sense, and lie open to all men; and every man, who has considered the structure of language in a philosophical light, will find infallible proofs that those who have framed it, and those who use it with understanding, have the power of making accurate distinctions, and of forming general conceptions, as well as philosophers. Nature has given those powers to all men, and they can use them when their occasions require it; but they leave it to the philosophers to give names to them, and to descant upon their nature. In like manner, nature has given eyes to all men, and they can make good use of them; but the structure of the eye, and the theory of vision, are the business of philosophers.

Fourthly. Opinions that appear so early in the minds

32 *

of men, that they *cannot be the effect of education, or of false reasoning,* have a good claim to be considered as first principles. Thus the belief we have, that the persons about us are living and intelligent beings, is a belief for which, perhaps, we can give some reason, when we are able to reason; but we had this belief before we could reason, and before we could learn it by instruction. It seems, therefore, to be an immediate effect of our constitution.

(Fifthly. The last topic I shall mention is, when an opinion is *so necessary in the conduct of life, that, without the belief of it, a man must be led into a thousand absurdities in practice,* such an opinion, when we can give no other reason for it, may safely be taken for a first principle.

Thus I have endeavoured to show, that, although first principles are not capable of direct proof, yet differences that may happen with regard to them among men of candor are not without remedy; that nature has not left us destitute of means by which we may discover errors of this kind; and that there are ways of reasoning, with regard to first principles, by which those that are truly such may be distinguished from vulgar errors or prejudices.*

---

* On the means of discriminating and determining first principles, which is one of the most difficult points in the philosophy of common sense, Sir W. Hamilton, in Note A, § 4, expresses himself thus: — "These characters, I think, may be reduced to four: — 1°, their *incomprehensibility;* 2°, their *simplicity;* 3°, their *necessity* and *absolute universality;* 4°, their *comparative evidence* and *certainty.*

"1. In reference to the first; — a conviction is incomprehensible when there is merely given us in consciousness *That its object is* (ὅτι ἔστι); and when we are unable to comprehend through a higher notion or belief, *Why, or How it is* (διότι ἔστι). When we are able to comprehend why or how a thing is, the belief of the existence of that thing is not a primary *datum* of consciousness, but a subsumption under the cognition or belief which affords its reason.

"2. As to the second; — it is manifest, if a cognition or belief be made up of, and can be explicated into, a plurality of cognitions or beliefs, that, as a compound, it cannot be original.

"3. Touching the third; — necessity and universality may be regarded as coincident. For when a belief is necessary, it is, *eo ipso,* universal; and that a belief is universal is a certain index that it must be necessary. See Leibnitz, *Nouveaux Essais,* Lib. I. § 4. To prove the necessity, the uni-

III. *Enumeration of the First Principles of Contingent Truths.*] The truths that fall within the compass of human knowledge, whether they be self-evident, or deduced from those that are self-evident, may be re-

---

versality must, however, be absolute; for a relative universality indicates no more than custom and education, howbeit the subjects themselves may deem that they follow only the dictates of nature. As St. Jerome has it, — *Unaquæque gens hoc legem naturæ putat, quod didicit.*

"It is to be observed that the necessity here spoken of is of two kinds. There is one necessity, when we cannot construe it to our minds as possible, that the deliverance of consciousness should not be true. This logical impossibility occurs in the case of what are called necessary truths, — *truths of reason* or *intelligence;* as in *the law of causality, the law of substance,* and still more in *the laws of identity, contradiction,* and *excluded middle.* There is another necessity, when it is not unthinkable that the deliverance of consciousness may possibly be false, but, at the same time, when we cannot but admit that this deliverance is of such or such a purport. This is seen in the case of what are called *contingent truths,* or *truths of fact.* Thus, for example, I can theoretically suppose that the external object I am conscious of in perception may be, in reality, nothing but a mode of mind or self. I am unable, however, to think that it does not appear to me — that consciousness does not compel me to regard it — *as* a mode of matter or not-self. And such being the case, I cannot practically believe the supposition I am able speculatively to maintain. For I cannot believe this supposition without believing that the last ground of all belief is not to be believed; which *is* self-contradictory. 'Nature,' says Pascal, 'confounds the Pyrrhonist'; and, among similar confessions, those of Hume, of Fichte, of Hommel, may suffice for an acknowledgment of the impossibility which the skeptic, the idealist, the fatalist, finds in practically believing the scheme which he views as theoretically demonstrated.

"4. The fourth and last character of our original beliefs is their comparative evidence and certainty. This, along with the third, is well stated by Aristotle, — 'What *appears to all,* that we affirm *to be;* and he who rejects this belief will assuredly advance *nothing better deserving of credence.*' And again : — 'If we know and believe through certain original principles, we must know and believe these with *paramount certainty,* for the very reason that we know and believe all else through them.' And such are the truths in regard to which the Aphrodisian says, — 'Though some men may verbally dissent, all men are in their hearts agreed.' This constitutes the first of Buffier's essential qualities of primary truths, which is, as he expresses it, 'to be so clear, that, if we attempt to prove or to disprove them, this can be done only by propositions which are manifestly *neither more evident nor more certain.*'"

Compare Buffier's *First Truths,* Part I. Chap. VII.; Stewart's *Elements,* Part II. Chap. I ; Coleridge's *Aids to Reflection,* comment on the eighth of his *Aphorisms on Spiritual Religion ;* Jacques, *Sur le Sens Commun, comme Principe et comme Méthode Philosophique,* passim, published in *Mém. de l'Acad. Royale des Sciences Mor. et Pol.,* Tome I., Savants Etrangers; Whewell's *Philosophy of the Inductive Sciences,* Part I. Book I.; Mill's *System of Logic,* Book II. Chap. V. Most of these authorities treat exclusively of the first principles of necessary truths. — ED.

duced to two classes. They are either *necessary and immutable truths,* whose contrary is impossible ; or they are *contingent and mutable,* depending upon some effect of will and power, which had a beginning, and may have an end.

That a cone is the third part of a cylinder of the same base and the same altitude, is a necessary truth. It depends not upon the will and power of any being. It is immutably true, and the contrary impossible. That the sun is the centre, about which the earth, and the other planets of our system, perform their revolutions, is a truth ; but it is not a necessary truth. It depends upon the power and will of that Being who made the sun and all the planets, and who gave them those motions that seemed best to him.

As the minds of men are occupied much more about truths that are contingent than about those that are necessary, I shall first endeavour to point out the principles of the former kind. If the enumeration should appear to some redundant, to others deficient, and to others both ; if things which I conceive to be first principles should to others appear to be vulgar errors, or to be truths which derive their evidence from other truths, and therefore not first principles ; in these things every man must judge for himself.

1. *First,* then, I hold, as a first principle, *the existence of every thing of which I am conscious.*

Consciousness is an operation of the understanding of its own kind, and cannot be logically defined. The objects of it are our present pains, our pleasures, our hopes, our fears, our desires, our doubts, our thoughts of every kind ; in a word, all the passions, and all the actions and operations of our own minds, while they are present. We may remember them when they are past ; but we are conscious of them only while they are present.

When a man is conscious of pain, he is certain of its existence ; when he is conscious that he doubts, or believes, he is certain of the existence of those operations. But the irresistible conviction he has of the reality of those operations is not the effect of reasoning; it is immediate and intuitive. The existence, therefore, of those passions and operations of our minds, of which we are conscious, is a first principle, which Nature requires us to believe upon her authority.

If I am asked to prove that I cannot be deceived by consciousness, — to prove that it is not a fallacious sense, — I can find no proof. I cannot find any antecedent truth from which it is deduced, or upon which its evidence depends. It seems to disdain any such derived authority, and to claim my assent in its own right. If any man could be found so frantic as to deny that he thinks, while he is conscious of it, I may wonder, I may laugh, or I may pity him, but I cannot. reason the matter with him. We have no common principles from which we may reason, and therefore can never join issue in an argument.

This, I think, is the only principle of common sense that has never directly been called in question.* It seems to be so firmly rooted in the minds of men, as to retain its authority with the greatest skeptics. Mr. Hume, after annihilating body and mind, time and space, action and causation, and even his own mind, acknowledges the reality of the thoughts, sensations, and passions of which he is conscious.

No philosopher has attempted by any hypothesis to account for this consciousness of our own thoughts, and the certain knowledge of their real existence which accompanies it. By this they seem to acknowledge, that this at least is an original power of the mind ; a power by which we not only have ideas, but original judgments, and the knowledge of real existence.

I cannot reconcile this immediate knowledge of the operations of our own minds with Mr. Locke's theory, that all knowledge consists in perceiving the agreement and disagreement of ideas. What are the ideas, from

---

* It could not possibly be called in question. For, in doubting the fact of his consciousness, the skeptic must at least affirm the fact of his doubt; but to affirm a doubt is to affirm the *consciousness* of it : the doubt would, therefore, be self-contradictory, — i. e. annihilate itself. — H.

whose comparison the knowledge of our own thoughts results? Or what are the agreements or disagreements which convince a man that he is in pain when he feels it.*

2. Another first principle, I think, is, that *the thoughts of which I am conscious are the thoughts of a being which I call* MYSELF, *my* MIND, *my* PERSON.

The thoughts and feelings of which we are conscious are continually changing, and the thought of this moment is not the thought of the last; but something which I call *myself* remains under this change of thought. This self has the same relation to all the successive thoughts I am conscious of; they are all *my* thoughts; and every thought which is not my thought must be the thought of some other person.

If any man asks a proof of this, I confess I can give none; there is an evidence in the proposition itself which I am unable to resist. Shall I think, that thought can stand by itself without a thinking being? or that ideas can feel pleasure or pain? My nature dictates to me that it is impossible. And that nature has dictated the same to all men appears from the structure of all languages: for in all languages men have expressed thinking, reasoning, willing, loving, hating, by *personal* verbs, which from their nature require a person who thinks, reasons, wills, loves, or hates. From which it appears, that men have been taught by nature to believe that thought requires a thinker, reason a reasoner, and love a lover.†

---

* See M. Cousin's criticism on Locke's theory of knowledge, showing its inadequacy in respect to all immediate or ultimate cognitions, and all cognitions of real existences of whatever kind. *Elements of Psychology,* Chap. VIII. and IX. — ED.

† This is precisely what Descartes intended by his celebrated enthymem, *Cogito, ergo sum,* — so often objected to by Reid and others, and so feebly and hesitatingly defended by Stewart, *Essays,* Ess. I. Chap. I. M. Cousin, in his *Fragments Philosophiques,* 3d ed., Tome I. p. 334 *et seq.*, has set the question in its true light: — "Before Spinoza and Reid, Gassendi had attacked the enthymem of Descartes. 'The proposition, *I think, therefore I am,* supposes,' says Gassendi, 'this *major,* — *That which thinks exists;* and consequently involves a begging of the question.' To this Descartes replies: — 'I do not beg the question, for I do not suppose

Here we must leave Mr. Hume, who conceives it to be a vulgar error, that, besides the thoughts we are conscious of, there is a mind which is the subject of those thoughts. If the mind be any thing else than impressions and ideas, it must be a word without a meaning. The mind, therefore, according to this philosopher, is a word which signifies a bundle of perceptions ; or, when he defines it more accurately, " it is that succession of related ideas and impressions, of which we have an intimate memory and consciousness."

---

any *major*. I maintain that the proposition, *I think, therefore I exist*, is a particular truth which is introduced into the mind without recourse to any more general truth, and independently of any logical deduction. It is not a prejudice, but a natural judgment, which at once and irresistibly strikes the intelligence.' ' The notion of existence,' says he, in reply to the objections, ' is a primitive notion, not obtained by any syllogism, but evident in itself ; and the mind discovers it by intuition.' Reasoning does not logically deduce existence from thought ; but the mind cannot think without knowing itself, because *being* is given in and under thought : — *Cogito, ergo sum.* The certainty of thinking does not go before the certainty of existence ; the former contains and develops the latter ; they are two contemporaneous verities blended in one fundamental verity. The fundamental complex verity is the sole principle of the Cartesian philosophy."

But Reid would still object, " Why not *begin* with some fact of the senses, as well as with some fact of consciousness, inasmuch as both rest on the same evidence ? " — They do not rest on the same evidence ; for, as has been repeatedly intimated before, doubting the consciousness is the *only* doubt which is absolutely self-contradictory, which annihilates itself, and which, therefore, not only cannot be defended, but cannot be entertained. Descartes, following a method of the merits of which we do not now speak, was in quest of some fact or principle which he could not possibly doubt even in speculation, and such a fact or principle he found in the testimony of consciousness *alone*. This, therefore, he not only made his point of departure, but the *point d'appui* of his whole system, professing to accept nothing but the facts of consciousness and what these facts either contain or presuppose. In the same spirit one of the early English followers of Descartes wrote : — " If we reflect but upon our own souls, how manifestly do the *species* [notions] of *reason, freedom, perception,* and the like, offer themselves to us, whereby we may know a thousand times more distinctly what our *souls* are than what our *bodies* are. For the former we know by an immediate converse with ourselves, and a distinct sense of their operations ; whereas all our knowledge of the body is little better than merely historical, which we gather up by scraps and piecemeal from more doubtful and uncertain experiments which we make of them : but the notions which we have of *a mind*, i. e. something within us that thinks, apprehends, reasons, and discourses, are so clear, and distinct from all those notions which we fasten upon a body, that we can easily conceive that, if all *body-being* in the world were destroyed, yet we might then as well subsist as now we do." — Smith's *Select Discourses*, Disc. IV. Chap. VI. — ED.

I am, therefore, that succession of related ideas and impressions of which I have the intimate memory and consciousness. But who is the *I* that has this memory and consciousness of a succession of ideas and impressions? Why, it is nothing but that succession itself. Hence I learn, that this succession of ideas and impressions intimately remembers, and is conscious of itself. I would wish to be further instructed, whether the impressions remember and are conscious of the ideas, or the ideas remember and are conscious of the impressions, or if both remember and are conscious of both? and whether the ideas remember those that come after them, as well as those that were before them? These are questions naturally arising from this system, that have not yet been explained.

This, however, is clear, that this succession of ideas and impressions not only remembers and is conscious, but that it judges, reasons, affirms, denies; nay, that it eats and drinks, and is sometimes merry and sometimes sad. If these things can be ascribed to a succession of ideas and impressions, in a consistency with common sense, I should be very glad to know what is nonsense.

The scholastic philosophers have been wittily ridiculed, by representing them as disputing upon this question, — *Num chimæra bombinans in vacuo possit comedere secundas intentiones?* And I believe the wit of man cannot invent a more ridiculous question. But, if Mr. Hume's philosophy be admitted, this question deserves to be treated more gravely; for if, as we learn from this philosophy, a succession of ideas and impressions may eat, and drink, and be merry, I see no good reason why a chimera, which, if not the same, is of kin to an idea, may not chew the cud upon that kind of food which the schoolmen call *second intentions.**

---

* All this criticism of Hume proceeds on the erroneous hypothesis that he was a *dogmatist*. He was a *skeptic*, — that is, he *accepted* the principles asserted by the prevalent dogmatism; and only showed that such and such conclusions were, on these principles, inevitable. The absurdity was not Hume's, but Locke's. This is the kind of criticism, however, with which Hume is generally assailed. — H.

3. Another first principle I take to be, that *those things did really happen which I distinctly remember.*

This has one of the surest marks of a first principle; for no man ever pretended to prove it, and yet no man in his wits calls it in question. The testimony of memory, like that of consciousness, is immediate; it claims our assent upon its own authority.*

Suppose that a learned counsel, in defence of a client against the concurring testimony of witnesses of credit, should insist upon a new topic to invalidate the testimony. " Admitting," says he, " the integrity of the witnesses, and that they distinctly remember what they have given in evidence, it does not follow that the prisoner is guilty. It has never been proved that the most distinct memory may not be fallacious. Show me any necessary connection between that act of the mind which we call memory, and the past existence of the event remembered. No man has ever offered a shadow of argument to prove such a connection; yet this is one link of the chain of proof against the prisoner; and if it have no strength, the whole proof falls to the ground. Until this, therefore, be made evident, until it can be proved, that we may safely rest upon the testimony of memory for the truth of past events, no judge or jury can justly take away the life of a citizen upon so doubtful a point."

I believe we may take it for granted, that this argument from a learned counsel would have no other effect upon the judge or jury, than to convince them that he was disordered in his judgment. Counsel is allowed to plead every thing for a client that is fit to persuade or to move; yet I believe no counsel ever had the boldness to plead this topic. And for what reason? For no other reason, surely, but because it is absurd. Now, what is absurd at the bar is so in the philosopher's

---

* The *datum* of memory does *not* stand upon the same ground as the *datum* of simple consciousness. In so far as memory is consciousness, it cannot be denied. We cannot, without contradiction, deny the fact of memory as a present consciousness; but we may, without contradiction, suppose that the past given therein is only an illusion of the present. — H.

33

chair. What would be ridiculous, if delivered to a jury of honest, sensible citizens, is no less so when delivered gravely in a philosophical dissertation.

4. Another first principle is *our own personal identity and continued existence, as far back as we remember any thing distinctly.*

This we know immediately, and not by reasoning. It seems, indeed, to be a part of the testimony of memory. Every thing we remember has such a relation to ourselves, as to imply necessarily our existence at the time remembered. And there cannot be a more palpable absurdity than that a man should remember what happened before he existed. He must therefore have existed as far back as he remembers any thing distinctly, if his memory be not fallacious. This principle, therefore, is so connected with the last mentioned, that it may be doubtful whether both ought not to be included in one. Let every one judge of this as he sees reason. The proper notion of identity, and the opinions of Mr. Locke on this subject, have been considered before under the head of Memory.

5. Another first principle, I think, is, that *we have some degree of power over our actions, and the determinations of our will.*

All power must be derived from the Fountain of power and of every good gift. Upon his good pleasure its continuance depends, and it is always subject to his control. Beings to whom God has given any degree of power, and understanding to direct them to the proper use of it, must be accountable to their Maker. But those who are intrusted with no power can have no account to make ; for all good conduct consists in the right use of power ; all bad conduct in the abuse of it. To call to account a being who never was intrusted with any degree of power, is an absurdity no less than it would be to call to an account an inanimate being. We are sure, therefore, if we have any account to make to the Author of our being, that we must have some degree of power, which, as far as it is properly used, entitles us to his approbation ; and, when abused, renders us obnoxious to his displeasure.

It is not easy to say in what way we first get the *notion* or *idea of power*. It is neither an object of sense nor of consciousness. We see events, one succeeding another; but we see not the power by which they are produced. We are conscious of the operations of our minds; but power is not an operation of mind. If we had no notions but such as are furnished by the external senses and by consciousness, it seems to be impossible that we should ever have any conception of power. Accordingly, Mr. Hume, who has reasoned the most accurately upon this hypothesis, denies that we have any idea of power, and clearly refutes the account given by Mr. Locke of the origin of this idea.

But it is in vain to reason from an hypothesis against a fact, the truth of which every man may see by attending to his own thoughts. It is evident, that all men, very early in life, not only have an idea of power, but a conviction that they have some degree of it in themselves; for this conviction is necessarily implied in many operations of mind, which are familiar to every man, and without which no man can act the part of a reasonable being.

First. It is implied *in every act of volition.* " Volition, it is plain," says Mr. Locke, " is an act of the mind, knowingly exerting that dominion which it takes itself to have over any part of the man, by employing it in, or withholding it from, any particular action." Every volition therefore implies a conviction of power to do the action willed. A man may desire to make a visit to the moon, or to the planet Jupiter; but nothing but insanity could make him will to do so. And if even insanity produced this effect, it must be by making him think it to be in his power.

Secondly. This conviction is implied *in all deliberation;* for no man in his wits deliberates whether he shall do what he believes not to be in his power.

Thirdly. The same conviction is implied *in every resolution or purpose formed in consequence of deliberation.* A man may as well form a resolution to pull the moon out of her sphere, as to do the most insignificant action which he believes not to be in his power. The same thing may be said of every promise or contract wherein a man plights his faith; for he is not an honest man who promises what he does not believe he has power to perform.

As these operations imply a belief of some degree of power in ourselves, so there are others equally common and familiar, which imply a like belief with regard to others. When we impute to a man any action or omission, as a ground of approbation or of blame, we must believe he had power to do otherwise. The same is implied in all advice, exhortation, command, and rebuke, and in every case in which we rely upon his fidelity in performing any engagement, or executing any trust.

It is not more evident that mankind have a conviction of the existence of a material world, than that they have the conviction of some degree of power in themselves, and in others, every one over his own actions, and the determinations of his will, — a conviction so early, so general, and so interwoven with the whole of human conduct, that it must be the natural effect of our constitution, and intended by the Author of our being to guide our actions. It resembles our conviction of the existence of a material world in this respect also, that even those who reject it in speculation find themselves under a necessity of being governed by it in their practice; and thus it will always happen when philosophy contradicts first principles.*

6. Another first principle is, that *the natural faculties, by which we distinguish truth from error, are not fallacious.*

If any man should demand a proof of this, it is impossible to satisfy him. For suppose it should be mathematically demonstrated, this would signify nothing in this case; because, to judge of a demonstration,

---

* This subject is discussed by Reid more at length in his *Essays on the Active Powers of Man*, Ess. I. See also Stewart's *Philosophy of the Active and Moral Powers*, Walker's edition, Book II. Chap. VI.; Cousin's *Elements of Psychology*, Chap. IV.; and Bowen's *Lowell Lectures*, Lect. IV. — ED.

a man must trust his faculties, and take for granted the very thing in question. If a man's honesty were called in question, it would be ridiculous to refer it to the man's own word whether he be honest or not. The same absurdity there is in attempting to prove, by any kind of reasoning, probable or demonstrative, that our reason is not fallacious, since the very point in question is whether reasoning may be trusted.

Descartes certainly made a false step in this matter; for having suggested this doubt among others, — that whatever evidence he might have from his consciousness, his senses, his memory, or his reason, yet possibly some malignant being had given him those faculties on purpose to impose upon him; and, therefore, that they are not to be trusted without a proper voucher, — to remove this doubt he endeavours to prove the being of a Deity who is no deceiver: whence he concludes, that the faculties he had given him are true and worthy to be trusted.

It is strange that so acute a reasoner did not perceive, that in this reasoning there is evidently *a begging of the question.* For if our faculties be fallacious, *why may they not deceive us in this reasoning as well as in others?* And if they are to be trusted in this instance without a voucher, why not in others? Every kind of reasoning for the veracity of our faculties amounts to no more than taking their own testimony for their veracity, and this we must do implicitly, until God give us new faculties to sit in judgment upon the old; and the reason why Descartes satisfied himself with so weak an argument for the truth of his faculties most probably was, that he never seriously doubted of it.

If any truth can be said to be prior to all others in the order of nature, this seems to have the best claim; because in every instance of assent, whether upon intuitive, demonstrative, or probable evidence, the truth of our faculties is taken for granted, and is, as it were, one of the premises on which our assent is grounded.*

---

* There is a presumption in favor of the veracity of the primary data

33 *

How, then, come we to be assured of this fundamental truth on which all others rest? Perhaps *evidence*, as in many other respects it resembles *light*, so in this also, — that as light, which is the discoverer of all visible objects, discovers itself at the same time, so evidence, which is the voucher for all truth, vouches for itself at the same time. This, however, is certain, that such is the constitution of the human mind, that evidence discerned by us forces a corresponding degree of assent. And a man who perfectly understood a just syllogism, without believing that the conclusion follows from the premises, would be a greater monster than a man born without hands or feet.

We are born under a necessity of trusting to our reasoning and judging powers; and a real belief of their being fallacious cannot be maintained for any considerable time by the greatest skeptic, because it is doing violence to our constitution. It is like a man's walking upon his hands, a feat which some men upon occasion can exhibit; but no man ever made a long journey in this manner. Cease to admire his dexterity, and he will, like other men, betake himself to his legs.

We may here take notice of a property of the principle under consideration, that seems to be common to it with many other first principles, and which can hardly be found in any principle that is built solely upon reasoning; and that is, that in most men it produces its effect *without ever being attended to, or made an object of thought*. No man ever thinks of this principle, unless when he considers the grounds of skepticism; yet it invariably governs his opinions. When a man in the common course of life gives credit to the testimony of his senses, his memory, or his reason, he does not put the question to himself, whether these faculties may deceive him; yet the trust he reposes in them supposes an inward conviction, that, in that instance at least, they do not deceive him.

---

of consciousness. This can only be rebutted by showing that these facts are contradictory. *Skepticism* attempts to show this on the principles which *dogmatism* postulates. — H.

It is another property of this and of many first principles, that they force assent *in particular instances more powerfully than when they are turned into a general proposition.* Many skeptics have denied every general principle of science, excepting, perhaps, the existence of our present thoughts; yet these men reason, and refute, and prove, they assent and dissent in particular cases. They use reasoning to overturn all reasoning, and judge that they ought to have no judgment, and see clearly that they are blind. Many have in general maintained that the senses are fallacious, yet there never was found a man so skeptical as not to trust his senses in particular instances, when his safety required it; and it may be observed of those who have professed skepticism, that their skepticism lies in generals, while in particulars they are no less dogmatical than others.*

7. Another first principle I take to be, that *certain features of the countenance, sounds of the voice, and gestures of the body, indicate certain thoughts and dispositions of mind.*

That many operations of the mind have their natural signs in the countenance, voice, and gesture, I suppose every man will admit. *Omnis enim motus animi,* says Cicero, *suum quemdam habet a natură vultum, et vocem, et gestum.* The only question is, whether we understand the signification of those signs by the constitution of our nature, by a kind of natural perception similar to the perceptions of sense; or whether we gradually learn the signification of such signs from experience, as we learn that smoke is a sign of fire, or that the freezing of water is a sign of cold. I take the first to be the truth.

It seems to me incredible, that the notions men have of the expression of features, voice, and gesture are entirely the fruit of experience. Children, almost as soon as born, may be frighted and thrown into fits by a threatening or angry tone of voice. I knew a man who

---

* Compare Jouffroy's *Introduction to Ethics,* Lect. IX.; and Javary, *De la Certitude,* passim. — ED.

could make an infant cry, by whistling a melancholy
tune in the same or in the next room; and again, by
altering his key, and the strain of his music, could make
the child leap and dance for joy.

It is not by experience surely that we learn the *expression* of music; for its operation is commonly strongest the first time we hear it. One air expresses mirth
and festivity; so that, when we hear it, it is with difficulty we can forbear to dance. Another is sorrowful
and solemn. One inspires with tenderness and love;
another with rage and fury.

> "Hear how Timotheus' varied lays surprise,
> And bid alternate passions all and rise;
> While, at each change, the son of Lybian Jove
> Now burns with glory, and then melts with love.
> Now his fierce eyes with sparkling fury glow,
> Now sighs steal out, and tears begin to flow.
> Persians and Greeks like turns of nature found,
> And the world's victor stood subdued by sound."

The countenance and gesture have an expression no
less strong and natural than the voice. The first time
one sees a stern and fierce look, a contracted brow, and
a menacing posture, he concludes that the person is inflamed with anger. Shall we say, that, previous to experience, the most hostile countenance has as agreeable
an appearance as the most gentle and benign? This
surely would contradict all experience; for we know
that an angry countenance will fright a child in the
cradle. Who has not observed, that children, very
early, are able to distinguish what is said to them in
jest from what is said in earnest, by the tone of the
voice, and the features of the face? They judge by
these natural signs, even when they seem to contradict
the artificial.

If it were by experience that we learn the meaning
of features, and sound, and gesture, it might be expected that we should recollect the time when we first
learnt those lessons, or at least some of such a multitude. Those who give attention to the operations of
children can easily discover the time when they have
their earliest notices from experience, — such as that

flame will burn, or that knives will cut. But no man is able to recollect in himself, or to observe in others, the time when the expression of the face, voice, and gesture was learned.

Nay, I apprehend that it is impossible that this should be learned from experience. When we see the sign, and see the thing signified always conjoined with it, experience may be the instructor, and teach us how that sign is to be interpreted. But how shall experience instruct us when we see the sign only, — when the thing signified is invisible? Now this is the case here; the thoughts and passions of the mind, as well as the mind itself, are invisible, and therefore their connection with any sensible sign cannot be first discovered by experience; there must be some earlier source of this knowledge.

Nature seems to have given to men a faculty or sense by which this connection is perceived. And the operation of this sense is very analogous to that of the external senses. When I grasp an ivory ball in my hand, I feel a certain sensation of touch. In the sensation there is nothing external, nothing corporeal. The sensation is neither round nor hard; it is an act or feeling of the mind, from which I cannot, by reasoning, infer the existence of any body. But, by the constitution of my nature, the sensation carries along with it the conception and belief of a round, hard body really existing in my hand. In like manner, when I see the features of an expressive face, I see only figure and color variously modified. But by the constitution of my nature, the visible object brings along with it the conception and belief of a certain passion or sentiment in the mind of the person. In the former case, a sensation of touch is the sign, and the hardness and roundness of the body I grasp is signified by that sensation. In the latter case, the features of the person are the sign, and the passion or sentiment is signified by it.

The power of natural signs, to signify the sentiments and passions of the mind, is seen in the signs of *dumb persons*, who can make themselves to be understood in a considerable degree, even by those who are wholly inexperienced in that language.

It is seen in the traffic which has been frequently carried on between people that have *no common acquired language*. They can buy and sell, and ask and refuse, and show a friendly or hostile disposition by natural signs.

It was seen still more in the actors among the ancients, who performed the *gesticulation* upon the stage, while others *recited the words*. To such a pitch was this art carried, that we are told Cicero and Roscius used to contend whether the orator could express any thing by words which the actor could not express in dumb show by gesticulation; and whether the same sentence or thought could not be acted in all the variety of ways in which the orator could express it in words.

But the most surprising exhibition of this kind was that of the *pantomimes* among the Romans, who acted plays, or scenes of plays, without any recitation, and yet could be perfectly understood. And here it deserves our notice, that, although it required much study and practice in the pantomimes to excel in their art, yet it required neither study nor practice in the spectators to understand them. It was *a natural language*, and therefore understood by all men, whether Romans, Greeks, or barbarians, by the learned and the unlearned. Lucian relates, that a king, whose dominions bordered upon the Euxine Sea, happening to be at Rome in the reign of Nero, and having seen a pantomime act, begged him of Nero, that he might use him in his intercourse with all the nations in his neighbourhood. " For," said he, " I am obliged to employ I don't know how many interpreters, in order to keep up a correspondence with neighbours who speak many languages, and do not understand mine; but this fellow will make them all understand him."

For these reasons, I conceive, it must be granted, not only that there is a connection established by nature between certain signs in the countenance, voice, and gesture, and the thoughts and passions of the mind; but also, that, by our constitution, we understand the meaning of those signs, and from the sign conclude the existence of the thing signified.*

8. Another first principle appears to me to be, that *there is a certain regard due to human testimony in matters of fact, and even to human authority in matters of opinion.*

Before we are capable of reasoning about testimony or authority, there are many things which it concerns us to know, for which we can have no other evidence. The wise Author of nature has planted in the human mind a propensity to rely upon this evidence before we can give a reason for doing so. This, indeed, puts our judgment almost entirely in the power of those who are about us in the first period of life; but this is necessary both to our preservation and to our improvement. If children were so framed, as to pay no regard to testimony or to authority, they must, in the literal sense, " perish for lack of kno wledge." It is not more necessary that they should be fed before they can feed themselves, than that they should be instructed in many things before they can discover them by their own judgment.

But when our faculties ripen, we find reason to check that propensity to yield to testimony and to authority, which was so necessary and so natural in the first period of life. We learn to reason about the regard due to them, and see it to be a childish weakness to lay more stress upon them than reason justifies. Yet, I believe, to the end of life, most men are more apt to go into this extreme than into the contrary; and the natural propensity still retains some force.

The natural principles, by which our judgments and opinions are regulated before we come to the use of reason, seem to be no less necessary to such a being as

---

* Compare Condillac, *Essai sur l'Origine des Connoissances Humaines*, II° Partie (translated by Nugent, *An Essay on the Origin of Human Knowledge*). Upham's *Mental Philosophy*, Appendix to Vol. II. Chap. I. — ED.

man, than those natural instincts which the Author of
nature has given us to regulate our actions during that
period.*

9. The last principle of contingent truths I mention
is, that, *in the phenomena of nature, what is to be will
probably be like to what has been in similar circumstances.*

We must have this conviction as soon as we are
capable of learning any thing from experience; for all
experience is grounded upon a belief that the future
will be like the past. Take away this principle, and
the experience of a hundred years makes us no wiser
with regard to what is to come.

This is one of those principles, which, when we grow
up and observe the course of nature, we can *confirm*
by reasoning. We perceive that nature is governed by
fixed laws, and that, if it were not so, there could be
no such thing as prudence in human conduct; there
would be no fitness in any means to promote an end;
and what, on one occasion, promoted it, might as probably, on another occasion, obstruct it. But the principle is necessary for us before we are able to discover
it by reasoning, and therefore is made a part of our
constitution, and produces its effects before the use of
reason.

This principle remains in all its force when we come
to the use of reason; but we learn to be more cautious
in the application of it. We observe more carefully
the circumstances on which the past event depended,
and learn to distinguish them from those which were
accidentally conjoined with it. In order to this, a number of experiments, varied in their circumstances, is
often necessary. Sometimes a single experiment is
thought sufficient to establish a general conclusion.
Thus, when it was once found that, in a certain degree
of cold, quicksilver became a hard and malleable metal,

---

* See more on this topic in Campbell's *Dissertation on Miracles*, Part I.
Sect. I., and Chalmers's *Evidences of the Christian Revelation*, Book I.
Chap. III. — ED.

there was good reason to think, that the same degree of cold would always produce this effect to the end of the world.

I need hardly mention, that the whole fabric of natural philosophy is built upon this principle, and, if it be taken away, must tumble down to the foundation. Therefore the great Newton lays it down as an axiom, or as one of his laws of philosophizing, in these words: — *Effectuum naturalium ejusdem generis easdem esse causas.* This is what every man assents to as soon as he understands it, and no man asks a reason for it. It has therefore the most genuine marks of a first principle.

It is very remarkable, that, although all our expectation of what is to happen in the course of nature is derived from the belief of this principle, yet no man thinks of asking what is the ground of this belief. Mr. Hume, I think, was the first* who put this question; and he has shown clearly and invincibly, that it is neither grounded upon reasoning, nor has that kind of intuitive evidence which mathematical axioms have. It is not a necessary truth.

He has endeavoured to account for it upon his own principles. It is not my business at present to examine the account he has given of this universal belief of mankind; because, whether his account of it be just or not (and I think it is not), yet, as this belief is universal among mankind, and is not grounded upon any antecedent reasoning, but upon the constitution of the mind itself, it must be acknowledged to be a first principle, in the sense in which I use that word.†

IV. *First Principles of Necessary Truths.*] About most of the *first principles of necessary truths* there has

---

* Hume was not the first: but on the various opinions touching the ground of our expectancy, I cannot touch. — H.

† Compare Stewart's *Elements*, Part I. Chap. IV. Sect. 5, and *Essays*, Ess. II. Chap. II.; Brown's *Philosophy of the Mind*, Lect. VI., and *Cause and Effect*, Parts III. and IV.; and Bailey, *On the Pursuit of Truth*, Essay III. — J. S. Mill contends for the empirical origin of this principle, *System of Logic*, Book III. Chap. III. and XXI. — ED.

been no dispute, and therefore it is the less necessary to dwell upon them. It will be sufficient to divide them into different classes; to mention some by way of specimen, in each class; and to make some remarks on those of which the truth has been called in question.

They may, I think, most properly be divided according to the sciences to which they belong.

1. There are some first principles that may be called *grammatical*; such as, that *every adjective in a sentence must belong to some substantive expressed or understood; that every complete sentence must have a verb.*

Those who have attended to the structure of language, and formed distinct notions of the nature and use of the various parts of speech, perceive, without reasoning, that these, and many other such principles, are *necessarily* true.

2. There are *logical* axioms; such as, that *any contexture of words, which does not make a proposition, is neither true nor false; that every proposition is either true or false; that no proposition can be both true and false at the same time; that reasoning in a circle proves nothing; that whatever may be truly affirmed of a genus, may truly be affirmed of all the species and all the individuals belonging to that genus.*

3. Every one knows there are *mathematical* axioms. Mathematicians have, from the days of Euclid, very wisely laid down the axioms or first principles on which they reason. And the effect which this appears to have had upon the stability and happy progress of this science gives no small encouragement to attempt to lay the foundation of other sciences in a similar manner, as far as we are able.*

Mr. Hume has discovered, as he apprehends, a weak side, even in mathematical axioms; and thinks that it is not strictly true, for instance, that *two right lines can cut one another in one point only.* The principle he

---

* On mathematical axioms, see Stewart's *Elements*, Part II. Chap. I. §§ 1, 2; Whewell's *Philosophy of the Inductive Sciences*, Book II. Chap. V.; Mill's *System of Logic*, Book II. Chap. V. and VI. — ED

reasons from is, that every simple idea is a copy of a preceding impression; and therefore, in its precision and accuracy, can never go beyond its original. From which he reasons in this manner:— No man ever saw or felt a line so straight, that it might not cut another, equally straight, in two or more points. Therefore there can be no idea of such a line. The ideas that are most essential to geometry, such as those of equality, of a straight line, and of a square surface, are far, he says, from being distinct and determinate; and the definitions destroy the pretended demonstrations. Thus, mathematical demonstration is found to be a rope of sand.

I agree with this acute author, that, if we could form no notion of points, lines, and surfaces more accurate than those we see and handle, there could be no mathematical demonstration. But every man that has understanding, by analyzing, by abstracting, and compounding the rude materials exhibited by his senses, can fabricate, in his own mind, those elegant and accurate forms of mathematical lines, surfaces, and solids. If a man finds himself incapable of forming a precise and determinate notion of the figure which mathematicians call a cube, he not only is no mathematician, but is incapable of being one. But if he has a precise and determinate notion of that figure, he must perceive that it is terminated by six mathematical surfaces, perfectly square, and perfectly equal. He must perceive that these surfaces are terminated by twelve mathematical lines, perfectly straight, and perfectly equal, and that those lines are terminated by eight mathematical points.

When a man is conscious of having these conceptions distinct and determinate, as every mathematician is, it is in vain to bring metaphysical arguments to convince him that they are not distinct. You may as well bring arguments to convince a man racked with pain that he feels no pain. Every theory that is inconsistent with our having accurate notions of mathematical lines, surfaces, and solids, must be false.

4. I think there are axioms, even in *matters of taste.*

Notwithstanding the variety found among men, in taste, there are, I apprehend, some common principles, even in matters of this kind. I never heard of any man who thought it a beauty in a human face to want a nose, or an eye, or to have the mouth on one side. How many ages have passed since the days of Homer? Yet, in this long tract of ages, there never was found a man who took Thersites for a beauty.

The *Fine Arts* are very properly called the *Arts of Taste*, because the principles of both are the same; and in the fine arts, we find no less agreement among those who practise them than among other artists. No work of taste can be either relished or understood by those who do not agree with the author in the principles of taste. Homer, and Virgil, and Shakspeare, and Milton, had the same taste; and all men who have been acquainted with their writings, and agree in the admiration of them, must have the same taste. The fundamental rules of poetry and music and painting, and dramatic action and eloquence, have been always the same, and will be so to the end of the world.

The variety we find among men in matters of taste is easily accounted for, consistently with what we have advanced. There is a taste that is *acquired*, and a taste that is *natural*. This holds with respect both to the external sense of taste and the internal. Habit and fashion have a powerful influence upon both.

Of tastes that are natural, there are some that may be called *rational*, others that are merely *animal*. Children are delighted with brilliant and gaudy colors, with romping and noisy mirth, with feats of agility, strength, or cunning; and savages have much the same taste as children. But there are tastes that are more intellectual. It is the dictate of our rational nature, that love and admiration are misplaced when there is no intrinsic worth in the object. In those operations of taste which are rational, we judge of the real worth and excellence of the object, and our love or admiration is guided by that judgment. In such operations there is judgment as well as feeling, and the feeling depends upon the judgment we form of the object. I do not maintain that taste, so far as it is acquired, or so far as it is merely animal, can be reduced to principles. But as far as it is founded on judgment, it certainly may. The virtues, the graces, the muses, have a beauty that is intrinsic. It lies not in the feelings of the spectator, but in the real excellence of the object. If we do not perceive their beauty, it is owing to the defect or to the perversion of our faculties.

And as there is an *original* beauty in certain moral and intellectual qualities, so there is a *borrowed* and *derived* beauty in the natural signs and expressions of such qualities. The features of the human face, the modulations of the voice, and the proportions, attitudes, and gestures of the body, are all natural expressions of good or bad qualities of the person, and derive a beauty or a deformity from the qualities which they express. Works of art express some quality of the artist, and often derive an additional beauty from their utility or fitness for their end. Of such things there are some that ought to please, and others that ought to displease. If they do not, it is owing to some defect in the spectator. But what has real excellence will always please those who have a correct judgment and a sound heart.

The sum of what has been said upon this subject is, that, setting aside the tastes which men acquire by habit and fashion, there is a natural taste, which is partly animal and partly rational. With regard to the first, all we can say is, that the Author of nature, for wise reasons, has formed us so as to receive pleasure from the contemplation of certain objects, and disgust from others, before we are capable of perceiving any real excellence in one, or defect in the other. But that taste which we may call *rational,* is that part of our constitution by which we are made to receive pleasure from the contemplation of what we conceive to be excellent in its kind, the pleasure being annexed to this judgment, and regulated by it. This taste may be true or false, according as it is founded on a true or false judgment. And if it may be true or false, it must have first principles.*

5. There are also first principles in *morals*. That *an unjust action has more demerit than an ungenerous one;* that *a generous action has more merit than a merely just one;* that *no man ought to be blamed for what it was not in his power to hinder;* that *we ought not to do to others what we would think unjust or unfair to be done to us in like circumstances:* these are moral axioms, and many others might be named which appear to me to have no less evidence than those of mathematics.

Some perhaps may think, that our determinations, either in matters of taste or in morals, ought not to be accounted necessary truths : that they are grounded upon the constitution of that faculty which we call *taste,* and of that which we call the *moral sense* or *conscience;* which faculties might have been so constituted as to have given determinations different, or even contrary, to those they now give : that, as there is nothing sweet or bitter in itself, but according as it agrees or disagrees with the external sense called taste, so there is nothing beautiful or ugly in itself, but according as it agrees or disagrees with the internal sense, which we also call taste ; and nothing morally good or ill in itself, but according as it agrees or disagrees with our moral sense.

This, indeed, is a system, with regard to morals and taste, which has been supported in modern times by great authorities. And if this system be true, the consequence must be, that there can be no principles, either of taste or of morals, that are necessary truths. For, according to this system, all our determinations, both with regard to matters of taste and with regard to morals, are reduced to *matters of fact,* — to such, I mean, as these, that by our constitution we have on

---

* Compare Kames's *Elements of Criticism*, Chap. XXV. ; Sir Joshua Reynolds's *Discourses*, Disc. VII. ; *Edinburgh Review*, Vol. XVIII. p. 43 *et seq.;* Cousin *Sur le Fondement des Idées Absolues*, Leçons XIX. et XX. (Cousin's Chapters on Beauty have been translated by J. C. Daniel, *The Philosophy of the Beautiful*.) — ED.

such occasions certain agreeable feelings, and on other occasions certain disagreeable feelings.

But I cannot help being of a contrary opinion, being persuaded that a man who determined that polite behaviour has great deformity, and that there is a great beauty in rudeness and ill-breeding, would *judge* wrong, whatever his feelings were. In like manner, I cannot help thinking, that a man who determined that there is more moral worth in cruelty, perfidy, and injustice, than in generosity, justice, prudence, and temperance, would *judge* wrong, whatever his constitution was. And if it be true that there is *judgment* in our determinations of taste and of morals, it must be granted that what is true or false in morals, or in matters of taste, is *necessarily so.* For this reason, I have ranked the first principles of morals and of taste under the class of necessary truths.*

6. The last class of first principles I shall mention, we may call *metaphysical.*

I shall particularly consider three of these, because they have been called in question by Mr. Hume.

(1.) The *first* is, that *the qualities which we perceive by our senses must have a subject, which we call* BODY, *and that the thoughts we are conscious of must have a subject, which we call* MIND.

It is not more evident that two and two make four, than it is that figure cannot exist, unless there be something that is figured, nor motion without something that is moved. I not only perceive figure and motion, but I perceive them to be qualities : they have a necessary relation to something in which they exist as their subject. The difficulty which some philosophers have found in admitting this, is entirely owing to the theory of ideas. A subject of the sensible qualities which we perceive by our senses, is *not an idea either of sensation or of consciousness ;* therefore, say they, we have no

---

* Compare Bentham's *Principles of Morals and Legislation,* Chap. II.; Jouffroy's *Introduction to Ethics,* Lect. XX.; Whewell's *Lectures on Systematic Morality,* Lect. II. and III. — ED.

such idea. Or, in the style of Mr. Hume, From what impression is the idea of substance derived? It is not a copy of any impression; therefore there is no such idea.

The distinction between sensible qualities and the substance to which they belong, and between thought and the mind that thinks, is not the invention of philosophers; it is found in the structure of all languages, and therefore must be common to all men who speak with understanding. And I believe no man, however skeptical he may be in speculation, can talk on the common affairs of life for half an hour, without saying things that imply his belief of the reality of these distinctions.

Mr. Locke acknowledges, " That we cannot conceive how simple ideas of sensible qualities should subsist alone; and therefore we suppose them to exist in, and to be supported by, some common subject." In his *Essay*, indeed, some of his expressions seem to leave it dubious whether this belief that sensible qualities must have a subject be a true judgment, or a vulgar prejudice. But in his first letter to the Bishop of Worcester, he removes this doubt, and quotes many passages of his *Essay*, to show that he neither denied nor doubted of the existence of substances, both thinking and material; and that he believed their existence on the same ground the Bishop did, to wit, " on the repugnancy to our conceptions, that modes and accidents should subsist by themselves." He offers no proof of this repugnancy; nor, I think, can any proof of it be given, because it is a first principle.

It were to be wished that Mr. Locke, who inquired so accurately and laudably into the origin, certainty, and extent of human knowledge, had turned his attention more particularly to the origin of these two opinions which he firmly believed; to wit, that sensible qualities must have a subject which we call body, and that thought must have a subject which we call mind. A due attention to these two opinions, which govern the belief of all men, even of skeptics in the practice of life, would probably have led him to perceive, that sensation and consciousness are *not* the *only* sources of human knowledge; and that there are principles of belief in human nature, of which we can give no other account but that *they necessarily result from the constitution of our faculties;* and that, if it were in our power to throw off their influence upon our practice and conduct, we could neither speak nor act like reasonable men.*

(2.) The *second* metaphysical principle I mention is, that *whatever begins to exist must have a cause which produced it.*

With regard to this point, we must hold one of these three things; either that it is an opinion for which *we have no evidence,* and which men have foolishly taken up without ground; or that it is *capable of direct proof* by argument; or that it is *self-evident, and needs no proof,* but ought to be received as an axiom which cannot by reasonable men be called in question.

The *first* of these suppositions would put an end to all philosophy, to all religion, to all reasoning that would carry us beyond the objects of sense, and to all prudence in the conduct of life.

As to the *second* supposition, that this principle may be proved by direct reasoning, I am afraid we shall find the proof extremely difficult, if not altogether impossible.

I know only of three or four arguments that have been urged by philosophers, in the way of abstract reasoning, to prove that things which begin to exist must have a cause.

One is offered by Mr. Hobbes, another by Dr. Samuel Clarke, another by Mr. Locke. Mr. Hume, in his *Treatise of Human Nature,* Book I. Part III. Sect. III., has examined them all; and, in my opinion, has shown that they take for granted the thing to be proved; a

---

* See Royer-Collard, *Fragments,* VIII., appended to Jouffroy's *Œuvres de Reid,* Tome IV. p. 300; Cousin's *Elements of Psychology,* Chap. III.; Mill's *Analysis,* Chap. XI. — ED.

kind of false reasoning which men are apt to fall into when they attempt to prove what is self-evident.

It has been thought, that, although this principle does not admit of proof from abstract reasoning, it may be proved from experience, and may be justly drawn by *induction from instances that fall within our observations.*

I conceive this method of proof would leave us in great uncertainty, for these three reasons : —

First. Because the proposition to be proved is not a contingent but a *necessary* proposition. It is not, that things which begin to exist commonly have a cause, or even that they always in fact have a cause; but that they must have a cause, and cannot begin to exist without a cause. Propositions of this kind, from their nature, are incapable of proof by induction. *Experience* informs us only of what *is* or *has been*, not of what *must be ;* and the conclusion must be of the same nature with the premises. For this reason, no mathematical proposition can be proved by induction. Though it should be found by experience in a thousand cases that the area of a plane triangle is equal to the rectangle under the altitude and half the base, this would not prove that it must be so in all cases, and cannot be otherwise ; which is what the mathematician affirms. In like manner, though we had the most ample experimental proof that things which have begun to exist had a cause, this would not prove that they must have a cause. Experience may show us what is the established course of nature, but can never show what connections of things are in their nature necessary.

Secondly. General maxims, grounded on experience, have only a degree of probability proportioned to the extent of our experience, and ought always to be understood *so as to leave room for exceptions*, if future experience shall discover any such. The law of gravitation has as full a proof from experience and induction as any principle can be supposed to have. Yet if any philosopher should, by clear experiment, show that there is a kind of matter in some bodies which does not gravitate, the law of gravitation ought to be limited by that exception. Now it is evident that men have never considered the principle of the necessity of causes as a truth of this kind, which may admit of limitation or exception; and therefore it has not been received upon this kind of evidence.

Thirdly. I do not see that experience could satisfy us that every change in nature actually has a cause. In the far greater part of the changes in nature that fall within our observation, *the causes are unknown,* and therefore, from experience, we cannot know whether they have causes or not. Causation is not an object of sense. The only experience we can have of it is in the consciousness we have of exerting some power in ordering our thoughts and actions.* But this experience is surely too narrow a foundation for a general conclusion, that all things that have had or shall have a beginning must have a cause. For these reasons, this principle cannot be drawn from *experience,* any more than from abstract reasoning.

The *third* supposition is, that it is to be admitted as a first or self-evident principle. Two reasons may be urged for this.

First. The *universal consent of mankind,* not of philosophers only, but of the rude and unlearned vulgar.

Mr. Hume, as far as I know, was the first that ever expressed any doubt of this principle.† And when we consider that he has rejected every principle of human knowledge, excepting that of consciousness, and has not even spared the axioms of mathematics, his authority is of small weight.

Setting aside the authority of Mr. Hume, what has philosophy been employed in, since men first began to

---

* From this consciousness, many philosophers have, after Locke, endeavoured to deduce our whole notion of *causality.* The ablest development of this theory is that of M. Maine de Biran [*Examen des Leçons de Philosophie de M. Laromiguière,* § 8, and *Exposition de la Doctrine Philosophique de Leibnitz*]; the ablest refutation of it, that of his friend and editor, M. Cousin [in his Preface to the fourth volume of *Œuvres de Maine de Biran,* and in *Elements of Psychology,* Chap. IV.]. — H.

† Hume was not the first. — H.

philosophize, but in the investigation of the causes of things? This it has always professed, when we trace it to its cradle. It never entered into any man's thought, before the philosopher we have mentioned, to put the previous question, whether things have a cause or not. Had it been thought possible that they might not, it may be presumed, that, in the variety of absurd and contradictory causes assigned, some one would have had recourse to this hypothesis.

They could conceive the world to arise from an egg, — from a struggle between love and strife, between moisture and drought, between heat and cold; but they never supposed that it had no cause. We know not any atheistic sect that ever had recourse to this topic, though by it they might have evaded every argument that could be brought against them, and answered all objections to their system. But rather than adopt such an absurdity, they contrived some imaginary cause — such as chance, a concourse of atoms, or necessity — as the cause of the universe.

The accounts which philosophers have given of particular phenomena, as well as of the universe in general, proceed upon the same principle. That every phenomenon must have a cause, was always taken for granted. *Nil turpius physico*, says Cicero, *quam fieri sine causa quicquam dicere.* Though an Academic, he was dogmatical in this. And Plato, the father of the Academy, was no less so. Πάντι γὰρ ἀδύνατον χωρὶς αἴτιον γένεσιν ἔχειν ("It is impossible that any thing should have its origin without a cause"). — *Timæus.*

Secondly. Another reason why I conceive this to be a first principle is, that mankind not only assent to it in speculation, but that the *practice of life is grounded upon it* in the most important matters, even in cases where experience leaves us doubtful; and it is impossible to act with common prudence if we set it aside.

In great families there are so many bad things done by a certain personage called *Nobody*, that it is proverbial that there is a Nobody about every house who does a great deal of mischief; and even where there is the exactest inspection and government, many events will happen of which no other author can be found : so that, if we trust merely to experience in this matter, Nobody will be found to be a very active person, and to have no inconsiderable share in the management of affairs. But whatever countenance this system may have from experience, it is too shocking to common sense to impose upon the most ignorant. A child knows, that, when his top or any of his playthings are taken away, it must be done by somebody. Perhaps it would not be difficult to persuade him that it was done by some invisible being, but that it should be done by nobody he cannot believe.

Suppose a man's house to be broken open, his money and jewels taken away. Such things have happened times innumerable without any apparent cause; and were he only to reason from experience in such a case, how must he behave? He must put in one scale the instances wherein a cause was found of such an event, and in the other scale the instances where no cause was found, and the preponderant scale must determine whether it be most probable that there was a cause of this event, or that there was none. Would any man of common understanding have recourse to such an expedient to direct his judgment?

Suppose a man to be found dead on the highway, his skull fractured, his body pierced with deadly wounds, his watch and money carried off. The coroner's jury sits upon the body, and the question is put, What was the cause of this man's death, — was it accident, or *felo de se*, or murder by persons unknown? Let us suppose an adept in Mr. Hume's philosophy to make one of the jury, and that he insists upon the previous question, — whether there was any cause of the event, or whether it happened without a cause.

Surely, upon Mr. Hume's principles, a great deal might be said upon this point; and, if the matter is to be determined by past experience, it is dubious on which side the weight of argument might stand. But we may venture to say, that, if Mr. Hume had been of

35

such a jury, he would have laid aside his philosophical principles, and acted according to the dictates of common prudence.*

(3.) The *third* and *last* metaphysical principle I mention, which is opposed by the same author, is, that *design and intelligence in the cause may be inferred, with certainty, from marks or signs of them in the effect.*

Intelligence, design, and skill are not objects of the external senses, nor can we be conscious of them in any person but ourselves. Even in ourselves, we cannot, with propriety, be said to be conscious of the natural or acquired talents we possess. We are conscious only of the operations of mind in which they are exerted. Indeed, a man comes to know his own mental abilities, just as he knows another man's, by the *effects* they produce, when there is occasion to put them to exercise.

A man's wisdom is known to us only by the signs of it in his conduct; his eloquence, by the signs of it in his speech. In the same manner we judge of his virtue, of his fortitude, and of all his talents and qualities of mind. Yet it is to be observed, that we judge of men's talents with as little doubt or hesitation as we judge of the immediate objects of sense. One person, we are sure, is a perfect idiot; another, who feigns idiotism to screen himself from punishment, is found upon trial to have the understanding of a man, and to be accountable for his conduct. We perceive one man to be open, another cunning; one to be ignorant, another very knowing; one to be slow of understanding, another quick. Every man forms such judgments of

---

* As has been intimated more than once, Mr. Hume did not lay down his conclusions as true, as something to be believed, — for he was a *skeptic*, and not a *believer*, — but as following inevitably from the assumptions of the *dogmatists*. It is the triumph of skepticism to show that *speculation* and *practice* are irreconcilable.

On the *principle of causality*, consult Hutton's *Investigation of the Principles of Knowledge*, Part II. Sect. VI.; Scott's *Inquiry into the Limits and Peculiar Objects of Physical and Metaphysical Science*, Chap. III. Sect. I.; Cousin's *Elements of Psychology*, Chap. IV.; Whewell's *Philosophy of the Inductive Sciences*, Part I. Book III. Chap. I.–IV.; Mill's *System of Logic*, Book III. Chap. XXI.; Bowen's *Lowell Lectures*, Lect. IV. and VI.—ED.

those he converses with; and the common affairs of life depend upon such judgments. We can as little avoid them as we can avoid seeing what is before our eyes.

From this it appears, that it is no less a part of the human constitution to judge of men's characters, and of their intellectual powers, from the signs of them in their actions and discourse, than to judge of corporeal objects by our senses; that such judgments are common to the whole human race that are endowed with understanding; and that they are absolutely necessary in the conduct of life.

Now, every judgment of this kind we form is only a particular application of the general principle, that intelligence, wisdom, and other mental qualities in the cause, may be inferred from their marks or signs in the effect. The actions and discourses of men are effects, of which the actors and speakers are the causes. The effects are perceived by our senses; but the causes are behind the scene. We only conclude their existence and their degrees from our observation of the effects. From wise conduct we infer wisdom in the cause; from brave actions we infer courage; and so in other cases.

This inference is made with perfect security by all men. We cannot avoid it; it is necessary in the ordinary conduct of life; it has therefore the strongest marks of being *a first principle.*

Perhaps some may think that this principle may be learned either by *reasoning*, or by *experience*, and therefore that there is no ground to think it a first principle.

If it can be shown to be got by *reasoning*, by all or the greater part of those who are governed by it, I shall very readily acknowledge that it ought not to be esteemed a first principle. But I apprehend the contrary appears from very convincing arguments.

First. The principle is *too universal* to be the effect of reasoning. It is common to philosophers and to the vulgar; to the learned and to the most illiterate; to the civilized and to the savage: and of those who are governed by it, not one in ten thousand can give a reason for it.

Secondly. We find philosophers, ancient and modern, who can reason excellently on subjects that admit of reasoning, when they have occasion to defend this principle, not offering reasons for it, or any *medium* of proof, but appealing to the common sense of mankind; mentioning particular instances, to make the absurdity of the contrary opinion more apparent, and sometimes using the weapons of wit and ridicule, which are very proper weapons for refuting absurdities, but altogether improper in points that are to be determined by reasoning.

To confirm this observation, I shall quote two authors, an ancient and a modern, who have more expressly undertaken the defence of this principle than any others I remember to have met with, and whose good sense and ability to reason, where reasoning is proper, will not be doubted.

The first is Cicero, whose words, Lib. I. Cap. 13, *De Divinatione*, may be thus translated : — " Can any thing done by chance have all the marks of design ? Four dice may, by chance, turn up four aces; but do you think that four hundred dice, thrown by chance, will turn up four hundred aces ? Colors thrown upon canvas without design may have some similitude to a human face; but do you think they might make as beautiful a picture as that of the Coan Venus ? A hog turning up the ground with his nose may make something of the form of the letter A ; but do you think that a hog might describe on the ground the ' Andromache' of Ennius ? Carneades imagined, that in the stone quarries at Chios he found, in a stone that was split, a representation of the head of a little Pan, or sylvan deity. I believe he might find a figure not unlike; but surely not such a one as you would say had been formed by an excellent sculptor like Scopas. For so, verily, the case is, that chance never perfectly imitates design." Thus Cicero.[*]

---

[*] See also his *De Natura Deorum*, Lib. II. Cap. 37. — H.

Now, in all this discourse, I see very good sense, and what is apt to convince every unprejudiced mind; but I see not in the whole a single step of reasoning. It is barely an appeal to every man's common sense.

Let us next see how the same point is handled by the excellent Archbishop Tillotson, *Works*, Vol. I. Sermon I. — " For I appeal to any man of reason, whether any thing can be more unreasonable, than obstinately to impute an effect to chance which carries on the face of it all the arguments and characters of design? Was ever any considerable work, in which there was required a great variety of parts, and an orderly and regular adjustment of these parts, done by chance? Will chance fit means to ends, and that in ten thousand instances, and not fail in any one? How often might a man, after he had jumbled a set of letters in a bag, fling them out upon the ground before they would fall into an exact poem, yea, or so much as make a good discourse in prose? And may not a little book be as easily made as this great volume of the world? How long might a man sprinkle colors upon canvas with a careless hand before they would make the exact picture of a man? And is a man easier made by chance than his picture? How long might twenty thousand blind men, which should be sent out from the remote parts of England, wander up and down before they would all meet upon Salisbury plains, and fall into rank and file in the exact order of an army? And yet this is much more easy to be imagined than how the innumerable blind parts of the matter should rendezvous themselves into a world. A man that sees Henry the Seventh's chapel at Westminster might with as good reason maintain (yea, and much better, considering the vast difference between that little structure and the huge fabric of the world), that it was never contrived or built by any man, but that the stones did by chance grow into those curious figures into which we see them to have been cut and graven; and that upon a time (as tales usually begin), the materials of that building, the stone, mortar, timber, iron, lead, and glass, happily met

35*

together, and very fortunately ranged themselves into that delicate order in which we see them now so close compacted, that it must be a very great chance that parts them again. What would the world think of a man that should advance such an opinion as this, and write a book for it? If they would do him right, they ought to look upon him as mad."

In this passage, the excellent author takes what I conceive to be the proper method of refuting an absurdity, by exposing it in different lights, in which every man of common understanding perceives it to be ridiculous. And although there is much good sense, as well as wit, in the passage I have quoted, I cannot find one *medium* of proof in the whole.

I have met with one or two respectable authors who draw an argument from *the doctrine of chances*, to show how improbable it is that a regular arrangement of parts should be the effect of chance, or that it should not be the effect of design. I do not object to this reasoning; but I would observe, that the doctrine of chances is a branch of mathematics little more than a hundred years old, while the conclusion in question has been held by all men from the beginning of the world. It cannot, therefore, be thought, that men were originally led to this conclusion by that reasoning. Indeed, it may be doubted whether the first principle upon which all the mathematical reasoning about chances is grounded is more self-evident than this conclusion drawn from it, or whether it is not a particular instance of that general conclusion.

We are next to consider whether we may not learn from *experience*, that effects which have all the marks and tokens of design must proceed from a designing cause.

I apprehend that we cannot learn this truth from experience, for two reasons.

First. Because it is a *necessary* truth, not a contingent one. It agrees with the experience of mankind since the beginning of the world, that the area of a triangle is equal to half the rectangle under its base and perpendicular. It agrees no less with experience, that the sun rises in the east and sets in the west. So far as experience goes, these truths are upon an equal footing. But every man perceives this distinction between them, that the first is a necessary truth, and that *it is impossible it should not be true;* but the last is not necessary, but contingent, depending upon the will of Him who made the world. As we cannot learn from experience that twice three must necessarily make six, so neither can we learn from experience that certain effects must proceed from a designing and intelligent cause. Experience informs us only of what *has been*, but never of what *must be*.

Secondly. It may be observed, that experience can show a connection between a sign, and the thing signified by it, in those cases only, where *both the sign and the thing signified* are perceived, and have always been perceived in conjunction. But if there be any case where *the sign only* is perceived, experience can never show its connection with the thing signified. Thus, for example, thought is a sign of a thinking principle or mind. But how do we know that thought cannot be without a mind? If any man should say that he knows this by experience, he deceives himself. It is impossible he can have any experience of this; because, though we have an immediate knowledge of the existence of thought in ourselves by consciousness, yet we have no immediate knowledge of a mind. The mind is not an immediate object either of sense or of consciousness. We may therefore justly conclude, that the necessary connection between thought and a mind, or thinking being, is not learned from experience.

The same reasoning may be applied to the connection between a work excellently fitted for some purpose, and design in the author or cause of that work. One of these — to wit, the work — may be an immediate object of perception. But the design and purpose of the author cannot be an immediate object of perception; and therefore experience can never inform us of any connection between the one and the other, far less of a necessary connection.

Thus I think it appears, that the principle we have been considering — to wit, that, from certain signs or indications in the effect, we may infer that there must have been intelligence, wisdom, or other intellectual or moral qualities in the cause — is a principle which we get neither by reasoning nor by experience; and therefore, if it be a true principle, it must be a first principle. There is in the human understanding a light, by which we see immediately the evidence of it, when there is occasion to apply it.

Of how great importance this principle is in common life, we have already observed. And I need hardly mention its importance in natural theology. The clear marks and signatures of wisdom, power, and goodness, in the constitution and government of the world, is, of all arguments that have been advanced for the being and providence of the Deity, that which in all ages has made the strongest impression upon candid and thinking minds; an argument which has this peculiar advantage, that it gathers strength as human knowledge advances, and is more convincing at present than it was some centuries ago. King Alphonso might say, that he could contrive a better planetary system than that which astronomers held in his day.* That system was not the work of God, but the fiction of men. But since the true system of the sun, moon, and planets has been discovered, no man, however atheistically disposed, has pretended to show how a better could be contrived.

When we attend to the marks of good contrivance which appear in the works of God, every discovery we make in the constitution of the material or intellectual system becomes a hymn of praise to the great Creator and Governor of the world. And a man who is pos-

---

* Alphonso X. of Castile. He flourished in the thirteenth century, — a great mathematician and astronomer. To him we owe the Alphonsine Tables. His saying was not so pious and philosophical as Reid states; but that, " had he been present with God at the creation, he could have supplied some useful hints towards the better ordering of the universe." — H.

sessed of the genuine spirit of philosophy will think it impiety to contaminate the Divine workmanship, by mixing it with those fictions of human fancy called theories and hypotheses, which will always bear the signatures of human folly, no less than the other bears those of Divine wisdom.

I know of no person who ever called in question the principle now under our consideration, when it is applied to the actions and discourses of men: for this would be to deny that we have any means of discerning a wise man from an idiot, or a man that is illiterate in the highest degree from a man of knowledge and learning, which no man has had the effrontery to do. But, in all ages, those who have been unfriendly to the principles of religion have made attempts to weaken the force of the argument for the existence and perfections of the Deity, which is founded on this principle. That argument has got the name of the *Argument from Final Causes;* and, as the meaning of this name is well understood, we shall use it.

The argument from final causes, when reduced to a syllogism, has these two premises : — *First,* that *design and intelligence in the cause may, with certainty, be inferred from marks or signs of them in the effect.* This is the principle we have been considering, and we may call it the *major* proposition of the argument. The *second,* which we call the *minor* proposition, is, that *there are in fact the clearest marks of design and wisdom in the works of nature.* The *conclusion* is, that *the works of nature are the effects of a wise and intelligent cause.* One must either assent to the conclusion, or deny one or other of the premises.

Those among the ancients who denied a God or a providence seem to me to have yielded the *major* proposition, and to have denied the *minor;* conceiving that there are not in the constitution of things such marks of wise contrivance as are sufficient to put the conclusion beyond doubt. This, I think, we may learn from the reasoning of Cotta the Academic, in the third book of Cicero, *Of the Nature of the Gods.*

The gradual advancement made in the knowledge of nature has put this opinion quite out of countenance. When the structure of the human body was much less known than it is now, the famous Galen saw such evident marks of wise contrivance in it, that, though he had been educated an Epicurean, he renounced that system, and wrote his book *Of the Use of the Parts of the Human Body*, on purpose to convince others of what appeared so clear to himself, that it was impossible that such admirable contrivance should be the effect of chance. Those, therefore, of later times, who are dissatisfied with this argument from final causes, have quitted the stronghold of the ancient atheists, which had become untenable, and have chosen rather to make a defence against the *major* proposition.

Descartes seems to have led the way in this, though he was no atheist. But, having invented some new arguments for the being of God, he was perhaps led to disparage those that had been used before, that he might bring more credit to his own.* Or perhaps he

---

* The following succinct statement of Descartes's proofs of a Deity is translated from the *Dictionnaire des Sciences Philosophiques*, Art. *Dieu.*

" The *ontological proof*, as it is called by Kant, has for its principle the *idea* of an absolutely perfect being. It was first adduced in the *Proslogium* of St. Anselm, the argument of which, originally conceived under the form of a prayer, may be stated thus : — All men have the idea of God, — even those who deny it; for they cannot deny that of which they have no idea. The idea of God is the idea of a being absolutely perfect, one whom we cannot imagine to have a superior. Now the idea of such a being necessarily implies *existence ;* otherwise we might imagine another being, who, by the superaddition of *existence* to the perfection of the first, would thereby excel him ; that is to say, excel one who, by supposition, is absolutely perfect. Consequently, we cannot conceive the idea of God without being constrained to believe that he exists. Descartes, evidently without any acquaintance with his predecessor of the eleventh century, fell on the same proof; but, by the manner in which he developed it, he has made it more legitimate, and saved it, in advance, from the formidable objection of Kant. In fact, the philosopher of the Middle Age, and, following in the same steps, Cudworth and Leibnitz, confined themselves wholly to the *idea* of perfection, thinking to make the notion of existence come out of that alone by way of deduction and analysis ; but they did not show how this idea is indissolubly connected with experience, or the perception of reality, that is to say, of facts, and imposed on our mind as the condition even of reality and of facts, as a necessary and irresistible belief, and not as a pure conception, or a supposition invented at pleasure.

was offended with the Peripatetics, because they often mixed final causes with physical, in order to account for the phenomena of nature.

What they failed to do, Descartes has done. Taking for his point of departure an incontestable fact, an immediate verity, our own existence, Descartes ascends to the belief in a being absolutely perfect. The latter belief is not *deduced* from the former ; it is given us, it is *imposed* upon us, immediately and at the same time with the former. The Cartesian argument under its first form, such as we find it in the *Discourse de la Méthode*, may be expressed thus : — As soon as I perceive myself, an imperfect being, to exist, I have the idea of a perfect being, and am under the necessity of admitting that this idea has been imparted to me by a being who is actually perfect, who really possesses all the perfections of which I have some idea, — that is to say, who is God. In another place (3ᵉ *Méditation*) Descartes has combined the idea of perfection with the principle of causality : — I do not exist by myself ; for if I were the cause of my own existence I should have given myself all the perfections of which I have an idea. I exist then by another, and this being by whom I exist is all-perfect ; otherwise I should be able to apply to him the same reasoning which I have just applied to myself. It is the argument of St. Anselm, and not that of Descartes, which Leibnitz has reduced to the form of a regular syllogism, and which has since been attacked by Kant, in his *Critic of Pure Reason*. The syllogism of Leibnitz is as follows : — *A being from whose essence we can conclude existence, exists in fact, if it is possible.* This proposition, as it is an identical axiom, needs no proof. *Now God is such a being that we can infer from his essence his existence.* This, also, as it is the definition of God, stands in no need of proofs. *Therefore, if God is possible, God exists.* — *Nouveaux Essais*, Liv. IV. § 7. Here, however, it is proper to remark that what Leibnitz thought to add to the *Proslogium* had been added before by Cudworth, using nearly the same words. — *Intellectual System*, Chap. V. Sect. I., Harrison's edit., Vol. III. p. 39.

"Another proof, wholly due to Descartes (*Discours de la Méthode*, 4ᵉ Partie, and 3ᵉ *Méditation*), is that which is drawn from the idea of the infinite. It has received from the author of the *Méditations* the same form as the preceding, with which it is blended. It is presented to us, therefore, as an immediate or first principle of reason, of which we have cognizance as soon as we arrive at consciousness of ourselves, and which we can no more call into doubt than our own existence. At the same time, says Descartes, that I perceive myself as a finite being, I have the idea of an infinite being. This idea, from which I cannot withdraw myself, and which is derived from no other idea, comes to me neither from myself nor from any other finite being ; for how could the finite produce the idea of the infinite ? Therefore it has been imparted to me by a being really infinite. Hence we see that the Infinite, such as Descartes conceives it, is not an abstract notion, applicable indiscriminately to all things ; it is the very principle of our ideas, — that is to say, of reason and of thought."

See the same article for a statement of three other forms of the *metaphysical* argument for the Divine existence. This argument is not in favor among English theologians generally ; but those who have adopted it are among the most distinguished, — such as Henry More, Dr. Samuel Clarke, and Bishop Butler. The popular objections chiefly insisted on at the present day are not new. See also L. F. Ancillon, *Judicium de Judiciis*

He maintained, therefore, that *physical* causes only should be assigned for phenomena; that the philosopher has nothing to do with final causes; and that it is presumption in us to pretend to determine for what end any work of nature is framed. Some of those who were great admirers of Descartes, and followed him in many points, differed from him in this, particularly Dr. Henry More and the pious Archbishop Fénelon: but others, after the example of Descartes, have shown a contempt of all reasoning from final causes. Among these, I think, we may reckon Maupertuis and Buffon. But the most direct attack has been made upon this principle by Mr. Hume, who puts an argument in the mouth of an Epicurean, on which he seems to lay great stress.

The argument is, that the universe is a *singular* effect, and therefore we can draw no conclusion from it, whether it may have been made by wisdom or not. If I understand the force of this argument, it amounts to this, — that if we had been accustomed to see worlds produced, *some by wisdom and others without it,* and had observed that such a world as this which we inhabit was always the effect of wisdom, we might then, from past experience, conclude that this world was made by wisdom; but having no such experience, we have no means of forming any conclusion about it.

That this is the strength of the argument appears, because, if the marks of wisdom seen in one world be no evidence of wisdom, the like marks seen in ten thousand will give as little evidence, unless, in time past, we perceived *wisdom itself* conjoined with the tokens of it; and, from their perceived conjunction in time past, conclude, that although, in the present world, we see only one of the two, the other must accompany it.

circa *Argumentum Cartesium pro Existentia Dei;* Bouchitté, *Histoire des Preuves de l'Existence de Dieu,* published in *Mémoires de l'Academie Royale des Sciences Morales et Politiques,* Tome I., Savants Etrangers; Crombie's *Natural Theology,* Chap. I.; Turton's *Natural Theology considered with Reference to Lord Brougham's Discourse on that Subject,* Sect. V. — ED.

Whence it appears, that this reasoning of Mr. Hume is built on the supposition, that our inferring design from the strongest marks of it is entirely owing to *our past experience of having always found these two things conjoined.* But I hope I have made it evident that this is not the case. And indeed it is evident, that, according to this reasoning, we can have no evidence of mind or design in any of our fellow-men.

How do I know that any man of my acquaintance has understanding? I never saw his understanding. I see only certain effects, which my judgment leads me to conclude to be marks and tokens of it.

But, says the skeptical philosopher, you can conclude nothing from these tokens, unless past experience has informed you that such tokens are always joined with understanding. Alas! Sir, it is impossible I can ever have this experience. The understanding of another man is no immediate object of sight, or of any other faculty which God has given me; and unless I can conclude its existence from tokens that are visible, I have no evidence that there is understanding in any man.

It seems, then, that the man who maintains that there is no force in the argument from final causes, must, if he will be consistent, see no evidence of the existence of any intelligent being but himself.*

---

* Compare Kant's *Critic of Pure Reason*, Third Division of the Second Book of Transcendental Dialectic; Lord Brougham's *Discourse on Natural Theology*, Part I.; Baden Powell's *Connection of Natural and Divine Truth*, Sect. III., IV.; Whewell's *Philosophy of the Inductive Sciences*, Part I. Book IX. Chap. VI.; Hume's *Dialogues concerning Natural Religion;* Irons's *Whole Doctrine of Final Causes;* Bowen's *Lowell Lectures*, Lect. IX. See, also, the works by Bouchitté, Crombie, and Turton, referred to in the last note. — ED.

ESSAY VII.

OF REASONING.

CHAPTER I.

OF REASONING IN GENERAL, AND OF DEMONSTRATION.

I. *Of Reasoning in General, as distinguished from Judgment.*] The power of *reasoning* is very nearly allied to that of *judging;* and it is of little consequence in the common affairs of life to distinguish them nicely. On this account, the same name is often given to both. We include both under the name of *reason.** The as-

---

* " *Reason* (λόγος, *ratio, raison,* Vernunft) is a very vague, vacillating, and equivocal word. Throwing aside various accidental significations which it has obtained in particular languages, as in Greek denoting not only the *ratio,* but the *oratio,* of the Latins ; throwing aside its employment, in most languages, for *cause, motive, argument, principle of probation,* or *middle term of a syllogism,* and considering it only as a philosophical word denoting a faculty, or complement of faculties ; — in this relation it is found employed in the following meanings, not only by different individuals, but frequently, to a greater or less extent, by the same philosopher.

"It has, both in ancient and modern times, been very commonly employed, like *understanding* and *intellect,* to denote our intelligent nature in general (λογικὸν μέρος) ; and this usually as distinguished from the lower cognitive faculties, as sense, imagination, memory, — but always, and emphatically, as in contrast to the feelings and desires. In this signification, to follow the Aristotelic division, it comprehends, — 1°, *conception,* or *simple apprehension* (ἔννοια, νόησις τῶν ἀδιαιρέτων, *conceptus, conceptio, apprehensio simplex,* das Begreifen) ; — 2°, the *compositive* and *divisive process, affirmation and negation, judgment* (σύνθεσις καὶ διαίρεσις, ἀπόφανσις, *judicium*) ; — 3°, *reasoning* or the *discursive faculty* (διάνοια, λόγος, λογισμός, τὸ συλλογί-ζεσθαί, *discursus, ratiocinatio*) ; — 4°, *intellect* or *intelligence* proper, either as the intuition, or as the place, of principles or self-evident truths (νοῦς, *intellectus, intelligentia, mens*).

" It has not unfrequently been employed to comprehend the *third* and *fourth* of the special functions above enumerated, — to wit, the *dianoetic*

sent we give to a proposition is called judgment, whether the proposition be self-evident, or derive its evidence by reasoning from other propositions.   Yet there
is a distinction between reasoning and judging.   Reasoning is *the process by which we pass from one judgment to another which is the consequence of it.*   Accord-

---

and *noetic*. In this meaning it is taken by Reid in his *later* works.   Thus,
in the *Intellectual Powers*, he states that *reason*, in its first office or degree
(the noetic), is identical with *common sense*, — in its second (the dianoetic),
with *reasoning*.

"It has very generally, both in ancient and modern philosophy, been
employed for the *third* of the above special functions ; — λόγος and λογισμός,
ratio and *ratiocinatio*, *reason* and *reasoning*, being thus compounded.

"In the ancient systems it was very rarely used exclusively for the *fourth*
special function, the *noetic*, in contrast to the *dianoetic*. Aristotle, indeed
(*Eth. Nic.*, Lib. VI. c. 12 ; *Eth. Eud.*, Lib. V. c. 8), expressly says that
reason is *not* the faculty of principles, that faculty being *intelligence* proper.
Boethius (*De Cons. Phil.*, Lib. V. Pr. 5) states that *reason* or *discursive intellect* belongs to man, while *intelligence* or *intuitive intellect* is the exclusive
attribute of Divinity ; while Porphyry somewhere says that ' we have *intelligence* in common with the gods, and *reason* in common with the brutes.'
Sometimes, however, it was apparently so employed.   Thus St. Augustine
seems to view *reason* as the faculty of intuitive truths, and as opposed to
reasoning (*De Quant. An.*, § 53 ; *De Immort. An.*, §§ 1, 10).   This, however,
is almost a singular exception.

"In modern times, though we frequently meet with *reason*, as a general
faculty, distinguished from *reasoning*, as a particular, yet, until Kant, I am
not aware that *reason* (*Vernunft*) was ever exclusively, or even emphatically,
used in a signification corresponding to the *noetic* faculty, in its strict and
special meaning, and opposed to *understanding* (*Verstand*) viewed as com-
prehending the other functions of thought, — unless Crusius (*Weg*, &c.,
§ 62 *et seq.*) may be regarded as Kant's forerunner in this innovation.   Indeed, the *Vernunft* of Kant, in its special signification (for he also uses it
for *reason* in the first or more general meaning, as indeed nothing can be
more vague and various than his employment of the word), cannot without
considerable qualification be considered analogous to νοῦς, far less to *common sense*; though his usurpation of the term for the *faculty of principles*
probably determined Jacobi (who had originally, like philosophers in general, confounded *Vernunft* with *Verstand*, *reason* with *reasoning*) to appropriate the term *reason* to what he had at first opposed to it, under the name
of *belief* (*Glaube*).

"Kant's abusive employment of the term *reason*, for the faculty of the
Unconditioned, determined also its adoption, under the same signification,
in the philosophy of Fichte, Schelling, and Hegel ; though νοῦς, *intellectus*,
intelligentia, which had been applied by 'the Platonists in a similar sense,
were (through *Verstand*, by which they had been always rendered into
German) the only words suitable to express that cognition of the Absolute,
in which subject and object, knowledge and existence, God and man, are
supposed to be identified."
   Abridged from Sir W. Hamilton's Note A, § 5. — ED.

ingly, our judgments are distinguished into *intuitive*, which are not grounded upon any preceding judgment, and *discursive*, which are deduced from some preceding judgment by reasoning.

In all reasoning, therefore, there must be a proposition inferred, and one or more from which it is inferred. And this power of inferring, or drawing a conclusion, is only another name for reasoning; the proposition inferred being called the *conclusion*, and the proposition or propositions from which it is inferred, the *premises*.

Reasoning may consist of many steps; the first conclusion being a premise to a second, that to a third, and so on, till we come to the last conclusion. A process consisting of many steps of this kind is so easily distinguished from judgment, that it is never called by that name. But when there is only a single step to the conclusion, the distinction is less obvious, and the process is sometimes called judgment, sometimes reasoning.

It is not strange, that, in common discourse, judgment and reasoning should not be very nicely distinguished, since they are in some cases confounded even by logicians. We are taught in logic, that judgment is expressed by one proposition, but that reasoning requires two or three. But so various are the modes of speech, that what in one mode is expressed by two or three propositions may in another mode be expressed by one. Thus I may say, *God is good; therefore good men shall be happy.* This is reasoning, of that kind which logicians call an *enthymem*, consisting of an antecedent proposition, and a conclusion drawn from it. But this reasoning may be expressed by one proposition, thus: *Because God is good, good men shall be happy.* This is what they call a *causal proposition*, and therefore expresses judgment; yet the enthymem, which is reasoning, expresses no more.

Reasoning, as well as judgment, must be true or false; both are grounded upon evidence which may be probable or demonstrative, and both are accompanied with assent or belief.

The power of reasoning is justly accounted one of the prerogatives of human nature; because by it many important truths have been and may be discovered, which without it would be beyond our reach; yet it seems to be only a kind of crutch to a limited under standing. We can conceive an understanding, superior to human, to which that truth appears intuitively which we can only discover by reasoning. For this cause, though we must ascribe judgment to the Almighty, we do not ascribe reasoning to him, because it implies some defect or limitation of understanding. Even among men, to use reasoning in things that are self-evident is trifling; like a man going upon crutches when he can walk upon his legs.

What reasoning is can be understood only by a man who has reasoned, and who is capable of reflecting upon this operation of his own mind. We can define it only by synonymous words or phrases, such as *inferring, drawing a conclusion*, and the like. The very notion of reasoning, therefore, can enter into the mind by no other channel than that of reflecting upon the operation of reasoning in our own minds; and the notions of premises and conclusion, of a syllogism and all its constituent parts, of an enthymem, sorites, demonstration, paralogism, and many others, have the same origin.

The exercise of reasoning on various subjects, not only strengthens the faculty, but furnishes the mind with a store of materials. Every train of reasoning which is familiar becomes a beaten track in the way to many others. It removes many obstacles which lay in our way, and smooths many roads which we may have occasion to travel in future disquisitions. When men of equal natural parts apply their reasoning power to any subject, the man who has reasoned much on the same or on similar subjects has a like advantage over him who has not, as the mechanic who has store of tools for his work has over him who has his tools to make, or even to invent.

In a train of reasoning, the evidence of every step,

36 *

where nothing is left to be supplied by the reader or hearer, must be *immediately discernible to every man of ripe understanding who has a distinct comprehension of the premises and conclusion, and who compares them together.* To be able to comprehend, in one view, a combination of steps of this kind, is more difficult, and seems to require a superior natural ability. In all, it may be much improved by habit.

But the highest talent in reasoning is *the invention of proofs;* by which, truths remote from the premises are brought to light. In all works of understanding, invention has the highest praise; it requires an extensive view of what relates to the subject, and a quickness in discerning those affinities and relations which may be subservient to the purpose.

In all invention there must be some end in view: and sagacity in finding out the road that leads to this end is, I think, what we call *invention.* In this chiefly, as I apprehend, and in clear and distinct conceptions, consists that superiority of understanding which we call *genius.*

In every chain of reasoning, the evidence of the last conclusion can be no greater than that of *the weakest link of the chain,* whatever may be the strength of the rest.

II. *Of Demonstrative Reasoning.*] The most remarkable distinction of reasonings is, that some are *probable,* others *demonstrative.*

In every step of demonstrative reasoning, the inference is necessary, and we perceive it to be impossible that the conclusion should not follow from the premises. In probable reasoning, the connection between the premises and the conclusion is not necessary, nor do we perceive it to be impossible that the first should be true while the last is false.

Hence demonstrative reasoning has no degrees, nor can one demonstration be stronger than another, though, in relation to our faculties, one may be more easily comprehended than another. Every demonstration gives equal strength to the conclusion, and leaves no possibility of its being false.

It was, I think, the opinion of all the ancients, that demonstrative reasoning can be applied only to truths that are necessary, and not to those that are contingent. In this, I believe, they judged right. Of all created things, the existence, the attributes, and consequently the relations resulting from those attributes, are contingent. They depend upon the will and power of him who made them. These are *matters of fact*, and admit not of demonstration.

The field of demonstrative reasoning, therefore, is the various relations of things *abstract*, that is, of things which we conceive, without regard to their existence. Of these, as they are conceived by the mind, and are nothing but what they are conceived to be, we may have a clear and adequate comprehension. Their relations and attributes are necessary and immutable. They are the things to which the Pythagoreans and Platonists gave the name of ideas. I would beg leave to borrow this meaning of the word *idea* from those ancient philosophers, and then I must agree with them, that ideas are the only objects about which we can reason demonstratively.

There are many even of our ideas about which we can carry on no considerable train of reasoning. Though they be ever so well defined and perfectly comprehended, yet their agreements and disagreements are few, and these are discerned at once. We may go a step or two in forming a conclusion with regard to such objects, but can go no farther. There are others, about which we may, by a long train of demonstrative reasoning, arrive at conclusions very remote and unexpected.

The reasonings I have met with that can be called strictly demonstrative may, I think, be reduced to two classes. They are either *metaphysical*, or they are *mathematical.*

In metaphysical reasoning, the process is always short. The conclusion is but a step or two, seldom more, from the first principle or axiom on which it is grounded, and the different conclusions depend not one upon another.

It is otherwise in mathematical reasoning. Here the field has no limits. One proposition leads on to another, that to a third, and so on without end.

If it should be asked, why demonstrative reasoning has so wide a field in mathematics, while, in other abstract subjects, it is confined within very narrow limits, I conceive this is chiefly owing to the nature of *quantity*, the object of mathematics.

Every quantity, as it has magnitude, and is divisible into parts without end, so, in respect of its magnitude, it has a certain ratio to every quantity of the kind. The ratios of quantities are innumerable, such as, a half, a third, a tenth, double, triple. All the powers of number are insufficient to express the variety of ratios. For there are innumerable ratios which cannot be perfectly expressed by numbers, such as the ratio of the side to the diagonal of a square, of the circumference of a circle to the diameter. Of this infinite variety of ratios, every one may be clearly conceived, and distinctly expressed, *so as to be in no danger of being mistaken for any other.* Extended quantities, such as lines, surfaces, solids, besides the variety of relations they have in respect of magnitude, have no less variety in respect of *figure;* and every mathematical figure may be *accurately defined, so as to distinguish it from all others.*

There is nothing of this kind in other objects of abstract reasoning. Some of them have various degrees; but these are *not capable of measure, nor can they be said to have an assignable ratio to others of the kind.* They are either simple, or compounded of a few indivisible parts; and therefore, if we may be allowed the expression, can touch only in few points. But mathematical quantities, being made up of parts without number, can touch in innumerable points, and be compared in innumerable different ways.

There have been attempts made to measure the merit of actions by the ratios of the affections and principles of action from which they proceed. This may, perhaps, in the way of analogy, serve to illustrate what was before known; but I do not think any truth can be discovered in this way. There are, no doubt, degrees of benevolence, self-love, and other affections; but when we apply ratios to them, I apprehend we have no distinct meaning.*

Some demonstrations are called *direct*, others *indirect*. The first kind leads directly to the conclusion to be proved. Of the indirect, some are called demonstrations *ad absurdum*. In these the proposition contradictory to that which is to be proved is demonstrated to be false, or to lead to an absurdity; whence it follows, that its contradictory, that is, the proposition to be proved, is true. This inference is grounded upon an axiom in logic, that, of two contradictory propositions, if one be false, the other must be true.†

---

* Mr. J. S. Mill, in his ingenious chapter, *Of Demonstration and Necessary Truths*, says: — "The opinion of Dugald Stewart respecting the foundations of geometry is, I conceive, substantially correct; — that it is built upon hypotheses; that it owes to this alone the peculiar certainty supposed to distinguish it; and that in any science whatever, by reasoning from a set of hypotheses, we may obtain a body of conclusions as certain as those of geometry, that is, as strictly in accordance with the hypotheses, and as irresistibly compelling assent *on condition* that those hypotheses are true." He allows, however, that the opponents of Stewart have greatly the advantage of him on another important point in the theory of geometrical reasoning, — the necessity of admitting as first principles *axioms* as well as *definitions*. "The axioms," he says, "as well those which are indemonstrable as those which admit of being demonstrated, differ from that other class of fundamental principles which are involved in the definitions, in this, that they are true without any mixture of hypothesis." "It remains to inquire, what is the ground of our belief in axioms? — what is the evidence on which they rest? I answer, they are experimental truths; generalizations from observation. The proposition, *Two straight lines cannot inclose a space*, — or, in other words, *Two straight lines which have once met do not meet again, but continue to diverge*, — is an induction from the evidence of our senses." According to Mill, therefore, all truths, including mathematical truth, are either empirical or hypothetical.

For a brilliant polemic on this whole subject, see Stewart, *Elements*, Part II. Chap. IV.; Whewell's *Mechanical Euclid, to which are added, Remarks on Mathematical Reasoning*, and his *Philosophy of the Inductive Sciences*, Part I. Book II.; *Edinburgh Review*, Vol. LXVII. p. 81 *et seq.*; *Quarterly Review*, Vol. LXVIII. p. 177 *et seq.*; Mill's *Logic*, Book II. Chap. V., VI. — ED.

† This is called *the principle of the excluded middle*, — viz. between two contradictories. — H.

The *lex exclusi medii* reads thus: — "Either a given judgment must be true of any subject, or its contradictory; there is no middle course." — ED.

Another kind of *indirect* demonstration proceeds by enumerating all the suppositions that can possibly be made concerning the proposition to be proved, and then demonstrating that all of them, excepting that which is to be proved, are false; whence it follows, that the excepted supposition is true. Thus one line is proved to be equal to another, by proving first that it cannot be greater, and then that it cannot be less: for it must be either greater, or less, or equal; and two of these suppositions being demonstrated to be false, the third must be true.

All these kinds of demonstration are used in mathematics, and perhaps some others. They have all equal strength. The direct demonstration is preferred where it can be had, for this reason only, as I apprehend, that it is the shortest road to the conclusion. The nature of the evidence and its strength are the same in all: only we are conducted to it by different roads.

III. *How far Morality is capable of Demonstration.*] What has been said of demonstrative reasoning may help us to judge of an opinion of Mr. Locke, advanced in several places of his *Essay;* — to wit, " that *morality* is capable of demonstration as well as mathematics."

In Book III. Chap. XI., having observed that, mixed modes, especially those belonging to morality, being such combinations of ideas as the mind puts together of its own choice, the signification of their names may be perfectly and exactly defined, he adds, § 16: — " Upon this ground it is that I am bold to think, that morality is capable of demonstration as well as mathematics: since the precise real essence of the things moral words stand for may be perfectly known, and so the congruity or incongruity of the things themselves be certainly discovered, in which consists perfect knowledge. Nor let any one object, that the names of substances are often to be made use of in morality, as well as those of modes, from which will arise obscurity; for, as to substances, when concerned in moral discourses, their divers natures are not so much inquired into as supposed : *v. g.*, when we say that *man is subject to law*, we mean nothing by *man* but a corporeal rational creature ; what the real essence or other qualities of that creature are, in this case, is no way considered."

Again, in Book IV. Chap. III. § 18 : — " The idea of a Supreme Being, whose workmanship we are, and the idea of ourselves, being such as are clear in us, would, I suppose, if duly considered and pursued, afford such foundation of our duty and rules of action, as might place morality among the sciences capable of demonstration. The relation of other modes may certainly be perceived, as well as those of number and extension ; and I cannot see why they should not be capable of demonstration, if due methods were thought on to examine or pursue their agreement or disagreement."

He afterwards gives as instances two propositions, as moral propositions of which we may be as certain as of any in mathematics ; and considers at large what may have given the advantage to the ideas of *quantity*, and made them be thought more capable of certainty and demonstration.

Some of his learned correspondents, particularly his friend Mr. Molyneux, urged and importuned him to compose a system of morals according to the idea he had advanced in his *Essay;* and, in his answer to these solicitations, he only pleads other occupations, without suggesting any change of his opinion, or any great difficulty in the execution of what was desired.

Those philosophers who think that our determinations in morals are not real judgments, that right and wrong in human conduct are only certain *feelings* or *sensations* in the person who contemplates the action, must reject Mr. Locke's opinion without examination. For if the principles of morals be not a matter of judgment, but of feeling only, there can be no demonstration of them ; nor can any other reason be given for them, but that men are so constituted by the Author of their being, as to contemplate with pleasure the actions we call virtuous, and with disgust those we call vicious. But if our determinations in morality be *real judg-*

ments, and, like all other judgments, be either *true* or *false*, it is not unimportant to understand upon what *kind of evidence* those judgments rest.

The argument offered by Mr. Locke, to show that morality is capable of demonstration, is, that " the precise real essence of the things moral words stand for may be perfectly known, and so the congruity or incongruity of the things themselves be certainly discovered, in which consists perfect knowledge." The field of demonstration is the various relations of things conceived abstractly, of which we may have perfect and adequate conceptions; and Mr. Locke, taking *all* the things which moral words stand for to be of this kind, concluded that morality is as capable of demonstration as mathematics.

Now I acknowledge that the names of the virtues and vices, of right and obligation, of liberty and property, stand for things abstract, which may be accurately defined, or, at least, conceived as distinctly and adequately as mathematical quantities. And thence, indeed, it follows, that their mutual relations may be perceived as clearly and certainly as mathematical truths. Of this Mr. Locke gives two pertinent examples: the first, " *Where there is no property, there is no injustice*, is," says he, " a proposition as certain as any demonstration in Euclid." When injustice is defined to be a violation of property, it is as necessary a truth, that there can be no injustice where there is no property, as that you cannot take from a man that which he has not. The second example is, that " *no government allows absolute liberty.*" This is a truth no less certain and necessary. But such abstract truths I would call *metaphysical* rather than *moral*. We give the name of *mathematical* to truths that express the relations of quantities considered abstractly; all other abstract truths may be called metaphysical. But if those mentioned by Mr. Locke are to be called moral truths, I agree with him that there are many such that are necessarily true, and that have all the evidence that mathematical truths can have.

It ought, however, to be remembered, that, as was before observed, the relations of things abstract, perceivable by us, excepting those of mathematical quantities, are few, and for the most part immediately discerned, so as not to require that train of reasoning which we call demonstration. Their evidence resembles more that of mathematical *axioms* than mathematical *propositions*. This appears in the two propositions given as examples by Mr. Locke. The first follows immediately from the definition of injustice; the second, from the definition of government. Their evidence may more properly be called *intuitive* than *demonstrative*. And this I apprehend to be the case, or nearly the case, with all abstract truths that are not mathematical, for the reason given above.

The propositions which I think are properly called *moral*, are those that affirm some moral obligation to be, or not to be, incumbent on one or more individual persons. To such propositions Mr. Locke's reasoning does not apply, because the subjects of the proposition are not things whose real essence may be perfectly known. They are the creatures of God; their obligation results from the constitution which God has given them, and the circumstances in which he has placed them. That an individual has such a constitution, and is placed in such circumstances, is not an abstract and necessary, but a contingent truth. It is a matter of fact, and therefore not capable of demonstrative evidence, which belongs only to necessary truths.

If a man had not the faculty given him by God of perceiving certain things in conduct to be right, and others to be wrong, and of perceiving his obligation to do what is right, and not to do what is wrong, he would not be a moral and accountable being. If a man be endowed with such a faculty, there must be some things which, by this faculty, are *immediately discerned* to be right, and others to be wrong; and therefore there must be in morals, as in other sciences, *first principles*, which do not derive their evidence from any antecedent principles, but may be said to be intuitively discerned.

37

Moral truths, therefore, may be divided into two classes, — to wit, such as are self-evident to every man whose understanding and moral faculty are ripe, and such as are deduced by reasoning from those that are self-evident. If the first be not discerned without reasoning, the last never can be by any reasoning. If any man could say with sincerity, that he is conscious of no obligation to consult his own present and future happiness; to be faithful to his engagements; to obey his Maker; to injure no man; I know not what reasoning, either probable or demonstrative, I could use to convince him of any moral duty. As you cannot reason in mathematics with a man who denies the axioms, as little can you reason with a man in morals who denies the first principles of morals. The man who does not, by the light of his own mind, perceive some things in conduct to be right, and others to be wrong, is as incapable of reasoning about morals as a blind man is about colors.

Every man knows certainly, that what he approves in other men he ought to do in like circumstances, and that he ought not to do what he condemns in other men. Every man knows that he ought, with candor, to use the best means of knowing his duty. To every man who has a conscience, these things are self-evident. They are immediate dictates of our moral faculty, which is a part of the human constitution; and every man condemns himself, whether he will or not, when he knowingly acts contrary to them.

Thus I think it appears, that every man of common understanding knows certainly, and without reasoning, the *ultimate ends* he ought to pursue, and that reasoning is necessary only to discover the *most proper means* of attaining them; and in this, indeed, a good man may often be in doubt. Thus, a magistrate knows that it is his duty to promote the good of the community which has intrusted him with authority; and to offer to prove this to him by reasoning would be to affront him. But whether such a scheme of conduct in his office, or another, may best serve that end, he may in many cases be doubtful. I believe, in such cases, he can very rarely have *demonstrative* evidence. His conscience determines the end he ought to pursue, and he has intuitive evidence that his end is good; but prudence must determine the means of attaining that end; and prudence can very rarely use demonstrative reasoning, but must rest in what appears *most probable*.

Upon the whole, I agree with Mr. Locke, that propositions expressing the congruities and incongruities of *things abstract*, which moral words stand for, *may have all the evidence of mathematical truths*. But this is not peculiar to things which moral words stand for. It is common to abstract propositions of *every* kind. For instance: — *You cannot take from a man what he has not; A man cannot be bound and perfectly free at the same time*. I think no man will call these moral truths, but they are necessary truths, and as evident as any in mathematics. Indeed, they are very nearly allied to the two which Mr. Locke gives as instances of moral propositions capable of demonstration. Of such abstract propositions, however, I think it may more properly be said that they have the evidence of mathematical axioms, than that they are capable of demonstration.

There are propositions of another kind, which alone deserve the name of moral propositions. They are such as affirm something to be the duty of persons that really exist. These are not abstract propositions; and therefore Mr. Locke's reasoning does not apply to them. The truth of all such propositions depends upon the constitution and circumstances of the persons to whom they are applied.

Of such propositions, there are some that are self-evident to every man that has a conscience; and these are the principles from which all moral reasoning must be drawn. They may be called the *axioms of morals*. But our reasoning from these axioms to any duty that is not self-evident, can very rarely be demonstrative. Nor is this any detriment to the cause of virtue, because to act against what appears *most probable* in a matter of duty is as real a trespass against the first principles of morality, as to act against demonstration; and because he who has but *one* talent in reasoning, and makes the proper use of it, shall be accepted, as well as he to whom God has given *ten.*

, 15th

CHAPTER II.

OF PROBABLE REASONING.

I. *Distinction between Probable and Demonstrative Reasoning.*] The field of demonstration, as has been observed, is necessary truth; the field of probable reasoning is *contingent* truth, — not what necessarily must be at all times, but what is, or was, or shall be.

No contingent truth is capable of strict demonstration; but necessary truths may sometimes have probable evidence. Dr. Wallis discovered many important mathematical truths, by that kind of induction which draws a general conclusion from particular premises. This is not strict demonstration, but, in some cases, gives as full conviction as demonstration itself; and a man may be certain that a truth is demonstrable before it ever has been demonstrated. In other cases, a mathematical proposition may have such probable evidence from induction or analogy, as encourages the mathematician to investigate its demonstration. But still the reasoning proper to mathematical and other necessary truths is demonstration; and that which is proper to contingent truths is probable reasoning.

These two kinds of reasoning differ in other respects. In demonstrative reasoning, one argument is as good as a thousand. One demonstration may be more elegant than another; it may be more easily comprehended, or it may be more subservient to some purpose beyond the present. On any of these accounts, it may deserve a preference: but then it is sufficient by itself; it needs no aid from another; it can receive none. To add more demonstrations of the same conclusion would be a kind of tautology in reasoning; because one demonstration, clearly comprehended, gives all the evidence we are capable of receiving.

The strength of probable reasoning, for the most part, depends, not upon any one argument, but upon many, which unite their force, and lead to the same conclusion. Any one of them by itself would be insufficient to convince; but the whole taken together may have a force that is irresistible, so that to desire more evidence would be absurd. Would any man seek new arguments to prove that there were such persons as King Charles the First, or Oliver Cromwell? Such evidence may be compared to a rope made up of many slender filaments twisted together. The rope has strength more than sufficient to bear the stress laid upon it, though no one of the filaments of which it is composed would be sufficient for that purpose.

It is a common observation, that it is unreasonable to require demonstration for things which do not admit of it. It is no less unreasonable to require reasoning of any kind for things which are known without reasoning. *All reasoning must be grounded upon truths which are known without reasoning.* In every branch of real knowledge there must be first principles whose truth is known intuitively, without reasoning, either probable or demonstrative. They are not grounded on reasoning, but all reasoning is grounded on them. It has been shown, that there are first principles of necessary truths, and first principles of contingent truths. Demonstrative reasoning is grounded upon the former, and probable reasoning upon the latter.

That we may not be embarrassed by the ambiguity of words, it is proper to observe, that there is a popular meaning of *probable evidence*, which ought not to be confounded with the philosophical meaning above explained. In common language, probable evidence is considered as an inferior degree of evidence, and is opposed to certainty; so that what is certain is more than probable, and what is only probable is not certain.

37 *

Philosophers consider probable evidence, not as *a degree*, but as *a species* of evidence which is opposed, not to *certainty*, but to another species of evidence called *demonstration*.

Demonstrative evidence has no degrees; but probable evidence, taken in the philosophical sense, has all degrees, from the very least to the greatest, which we call certainty. That there is such a city as Rome, I am as certain as of any proposition in Euclid; but the evidence is not demonstrative, but of that kind which philosophers call probable. Yet, in common language, it would sound oddly to say, *It is probable there is such a city as Rome*, because it would imply some degree of doubt or uncertainty.

Taking probable evidence, therefore, in the philosophical sense, as it is opposed to demonstrative, it may have any degree of evidence, from the least to the greatest.

I think, in most cases, we measure the degrees of evidence by the effect they have upon a sound understanding, when comprehended clearly, and without prejudice. Every degree of evidence perceived by the mind produces a proportioned degree of assent or belief. The judgment may be in perfect suspense between two contradictory opinions, when there is no evidence for either, or equal evidence for both. The least preponderancy on one side inclines the judgment in proportion. Belief is mixed with doubt, more or less, until we come to the highest degree of evidence, when all doubt vanishes, and the belief is firm and immovable. This degree of evidence, the highest the human faculties can attain, we call *certainty*.

II. *Different Kinds of Probable Evidence.*] Probable evidence not only differs in kind from demonstrative, but is itself of different kinds. The chief of these I shall mention, without pretending to make a complete enumeration.

1. The first kind is that of *human testimony*, upon which the greatest part of human knowledge is built.

The faith of history depends upon it, as well as the judgment of solemn tribunals with regard to men's acquired rights, and with regard to their guilt or innocence when they are charged with crimes. A great part of the business of the judge, of counsel at the bar, of the historian, the critic, and the antiquarian, is to canvass and weigh this kind of evidence; and no man can act with common prudence, in the ordinary occurrences of life, who has not ·some competent judgment of it. •

The belief we give to testimony, in many cases, is not solely grounded upon the veracity of the testifier. In a single testimony, we consider the motives a man might have to falsify. If there be no appearance of any such motive, much more if there be motives on the other side, his testimony has weight independent of his moral character. If the testimony be circumstantial, we consider how far the circumstances agree together, and with things that are known. It is so very difficult to fabricate a story, which cannot be detected by a judicious examination of the circumstances, that it acquires evidence by being able to bear such a trial. There is an art in detecting false evidence in judicial proceedings, well known to able judges and barristers; so that I believe few false witnesses leave the bar without suspicion of their guilt.

When there is an agreement of many witnesses, in a great variety of circumstances, without the possibility of a previous concert, the evidence may be equal to that of demonstration.[*]

2. A second kind of probable evidence is the *authority of those who are good judges of the point in question.* The supreme court of judicature of the British nation is often determined by the opinion of lawyers in a point of law, of physicians in a point of medicine, and of

---

[*] See Babbage's *Ninth Bridgewater Treatise*, Note E, *On Hume's Argument against Miracles;* in which it is demonstrated mathematically that " it is *always* possible to assign a number of independent witnesses, the improbability of the falsehood of whose *concurring* testimony shall be greater than the improbability of the alleged miracle." — ED.

other artists in what relates to their several professions. And, in the common affairs of life, we frequently rely upon the judgment of others, in points of which we are not proper judges ourselves.

3. A third kind of probable evidence is that *by which we recognize the identity of things, and persons of our acquaintance.* That two swords, two horses, or two persons may be so perfectly alike, as not to be distinguishable by those to whom they are best known, cannot be shown to be impossible. But we learn either from nature, or from experience, that it never happens; or so very rarely, that a person or thing well known to us is immediately recognized without any doubt, when we perceive the marks or signs by which we have been accustomed to distinguish it from all other individuals of the kind.

This evidence we rely upon in the most important affairs of life, and by this evidence the identity both of things and of persons is determined in courts of judicature.

4. A fourth kind of probable evidence is that *which we have of men's future actions and conduct, from the general principles of action in man, or from our knowledge of the individuals.*

Notwithstanding the folly and vice that are to be found among men, there is a certain degree of prudence and probity which we rely upon in every man that is not insane. If it were not so, no man would be safe in the company of another, and there could be no society among mankind. If men were as much disposed to hurt as to do good, to lie as to speak truth, they could not live together: they would keep at as great a distance from one another as possible, and the race would soon perish. We expect that men will take some care of themselves, of their family, friends, and reputation; that they will not injure others without some temptation; that they will have some gratitude for good offices, and some resentment of injuries.

Such maxims with regard to human conduct are the foundation of all political reasoning, and of common prudence in the conduct of life. Hardly can a man form any project in public or in private life, which does not depend upon the conduct of other men, as well as his own, and which does not go upon the supposition, that men will act such a part in such circumstances. This evidence may be probable in a very high degree, but can never be demonstrative. The best concerted project may fail, and wise counsels may be frustrated, because some individual acted a part which it would have been against all reason to expect.

5. Another kind of probable evidence, the counterpart of the last, is that *by which we collect men's characters and designs from their actions, speech, and other external signs.*

We see not men's hearts, nor the principles by which they are actuated; but there are external signs of their principles and dispositions, which, though not certain, may sometimes be more trusted than their professions; and it is from external signs that we must draw all the knowledge we can attain of men's characters.

6. The next kind of probable evidence I mention is that which mathematicians call *the probability of chances.*

We attribute some events to chance, because we know only the remote cause which must produce some one event of a number; but know not the more immediate cause which determines a particular event of that number, in preference to the others. I think all the chances about which we reason in mathematics are of this kind. Thus, in throwing a just die upon a table, we say it is an equal chance which of the six sides shall be turned up; because neither the person who throws, nor the by-standers, know the precise measure of force and direction necessary to turn up any one side rather than another. There are here, therefore, six events, one of which must happen; and as all are supposed to have equal probability, the probability of any one side being turned up — the ace, for instance — is as one to the remaining number, five. The probability of turning up two aces with two dice is as one to thirty-five; because here there are thirty-six events, each of which has equal probability.

Upon such principles as these, the doctrine of chances has furnished a field of demonstrative reasoning of great extent, although the events about which this reasoning is employed be not necessary, but contingent, and be not certain, but probable. This may seem to contradict a principle before advanced, that contingent truths are not capable of demonstration; but it does not: for in the mathematical reasonings about chance, the conclusion demonstrated is not that such an event *shall happen*, but that *the probability of its happening* bears such a ratio to *the probability of its failing;* and this conclusion is necessary upon the suppositions on which it is grounded.

7. The last kind of probable evidence I shall mention is that *by which the known laws of nature have been discovered, and the effects which have been produced by them in former ages, or which may be expected in time to come.*

The laws of nature are the rules by which the Supreme Being governs the world. We deduce them only from facts that fall within our own observation, or are properly attested by those who have observed them.

The knowledge of some of the laws of nature is necessary to all men in the conduct of life. These are soon discovered, even by savages. They know that fire burns, that water drowns, that bodies gravitate towards the earth. They know that day and night, summer and winter, regularly succeed each other. As far back as their experience and information reach, they know that these have happened regularly; and, upon this ground, they are led, by the constitution of human nature, to expect that they will happen in time to come, in like circumstances.

The knowledge which the philosopher attains of the laws of nature differs from that of the vulgar, not in the first principles on which it is grounded, but in its extent and accuracy. He collects with care the phenomena that lead to the same conclusion, and compares them with those that seem to contradict or to limit it. He observes the circumstances on which every phenomenon depends, and distinguishes them carefully from those that are accidentally conjoined with it. He puts natural bodies in various situations, and applies them to one another in various ways, on purpose to observe the effect; and thus acquires from his senses a more extensive knowledge of the course of nature in a short time, than could be collected by casual observation in many ages.

But what is the result of his laborious researches? It is, that, as far as he has been able to observe, such things have always happened in such circumstances, and such bodies have always been found to have such properties. These are matters of fact, attested by sense, memory, and testimony, just as the few facts which the vulgar know are attested to them.

And what conclusions does the philosopher draw from the facts he has collected? They are, that like events have happened in former times in like circumstances, and will happen in time to come; and these conclusions are built on the very same ground on which the simple rustic concludes that the sun will rise tomorrow.

Facts reduced to general rules, and the consequences of those general rules, are all that we really know of the material world. And the evidence that such general rules have no exceptions, as well as the evidence that they will be the same in time to come as they have been in time past, can never be demonstrative. It is only that species of evidence which philosophers call probable. General rules may have exceptions or limitations which no man ever had occasion to observe. The laws of nature may be changed by Him who established them. But we are led by our constitution to rely upon their continuance with as little doubt as if it was demonstrable.*

---

* As Reid gives an entire Essay to Reasoning, it is remarkable that he does not treat of *induction* by name, to which his last-mentioned form of

CHAPTER III.

OF MR. HUME'S SKEPTICISM WITH REGARD TO REASON.

I. *He reduces all Knowledge to Probability.*] In the *Treatise of Human Nature*, Book I. Part IV. Sect. I., the author undertakes to prove two points: — *First*, that all that is called human knowledge (meaning demonstrative knowledge) is only probability ; and *secondly*, that this probability, when duly examined, evanishes by degrees, and leaves at last no evidence at all : so that, in the issue, there is no ground to believe

---

probable reasoning belongs, nor mark the distinction between *inductive* and *deductive* reasoning. To supply this defect I copy a passage from Jouffroy (*Introduction to Ethics*, Lect. IX.), one of the most faithful of Reid's followers : —

"This is the process of *reasoning by induction :* — when several particular cases, which are analogous, have been ascertained by observation, and stored up in the memory, reason applies to this series of analogous observations the *a priori* principle, that the laws of nature are constant ; and, at once, what was true through observation in only twenty, thirty, or forty observed cases, becomes, by the application of this principle, *a general law*, as true of other cases not observed as of those which observation has ascertained. From the results of observation, and solely by the application to these results of a conception of reason, the mind arrives at a consequence that transcends them. Such is the method of reasoning by induction. Its characteristic is, that it proceeds from certain results, communicated by observation, to a general principle, within which they are included.

"The process of *reasoning by deduction* is as follows : — A truth of any kind, particular, general, or universal, being made known, reason deduces from it whatever other truths it includes. Sometimes the deduction is complete, in which case reason only presents the whole truth under two different aspects ; at other times the deduction is imperfect, and then reason passes from the whole to a part. But in either case, if we compare together the results of our reasoning and the premises from which we drew them, we shall always find that these results, and a part or the whole of the premises, are perfectly equivalent. This is the special characteristic of deductive reasoning."

The following admirable passage on the verification of inductions is from the *Quarterly Review*, Vol. LXVIII. p. 233 : —

"It is of great moment to distinguish the characters of a sound induction. One of them is its ready identification with our conceptions of facts, so as to make itself a part of them, to ingraft itself into language, and by no subsequent effort of the mind to be got rid of. The leading term of a true theory

any one proposition rather than its contrary, and "all those are certainly fools who reason, or believe any thing."

To pretend to prove by reasoning that there is no force in reason, does indeed look like a philosophical delirium. It is like a man's pretending to see clearly that he himself and all other men are blind.

Still, it may not be improper to inquire, whether, as the author thinks, this state of mind was produced by a just application of the rules of logic, or, as others may be apt to think, by the misapplication and abuse of them.

First, Because we are *fallible,* the author infers that all knowledge degenerates into probability.

That man, and probably every created being, is falli-

---

once pronounced, we cannot fall back, even in thought, to that helpless state of doubt and bewilderment in which we gazed on the facts before. The general proposition is more than a sum of the particulars. Our dots are filled in and connected by an ideal outline, which we pursue even beyond their limits, assign it a name, and speak of it as a *thing.* In all our propositions, this *new thing* is referred to, the elements of which it is formed are forgotten; and thus we arrive at an inductive *formula,* — a general, perhaps a universal, proposition.

"Another character of sound inductions is, that they *enable us to predict.* We feel secure that our rule is based upon the realities of nature, when it stands us in the stead of more experience; when it embodies facts, as an experience wider than our own would do, and in a way that our ordinary experience would never reach; when it will bear, not stress, but torture, and gives true results in cases studiously different from those which led to the discovery. The theories of Newton and Fresnel are full of such cases. In the latter, indeed [the theory of polarization], this test is carried to such an extreme, that *theory* has actually remanded back *experiment* to read her lesson anew, and convicted her of blindness and error. It has informed her of facts so strange as to appear to her impossible, and showed her all the singularities she would observe in critical cases she never dreamed of trying.

"Another character, which is exemplified only in the greatest theories, is the *consilience of inductions,* where many and widely different lines of experience spring together into one theory which explains them all, and that in a more simple manner than seemed to be required for either separately. Thus, in the infinitely varied phenomena of physical astronomy, when all are discussed and all explained, we hear from all quarters the consentaneous echoes of but one word, — *gravitation.*"

For recent authorities on the subject of induction, see Baden Powell's *Connection of Natural and Divine Truth,* Sect. I.; Whewell's *Philosophy of the Inductive Sciences,* Books I., XI., and XIII.; Mill's *Logic,* Book III.; Whewell, *On Induction with Special Reference to Mr. Mill's System of Logic.* — Ed.

ble, and that a fallible being cannot have that perfect comprehension and assurance of truth which an infallible being has, I think ought to be granted. It becomes a fallible being to be modest, open to new light, and sensible that, by some false bias, or by rash judging, he may be misled. If this be called a degree of skepticism, I cannot help approving of it, being persuaded that the man who makes the best use he can of the faculties which God has given him, without thinking them more perfect than they really are, may have all the belief that is necessary in the conduct of life, and all that is necessary to his acceptance with his Maker.

It is granted, then, that human judgments ought always to be formed with a humble sense of our fallibility in judging. This is all that can be inferred by the rules of logic from our being fallible. And if this be all that is meant by our knowledge degenerating into probability, I know no person of a different opinion. But it may be observed, that the author here uses the word *probability* in a sense for which I know no authority but his own. Philosophers understand probability as *opposed to demonstration;* the vulgar as *opposed to certainty;* but this author understands it as *opposed to infallibility,* which no man claims.

One who believes himself to be fallible may still hold it to be certain that two and two make four, and that two contradictory propositions cannot both be true. He may believe some things to be probable only, and other things to be demonstrable, without making any pretence to infallibility.

If we use words in their proper meaning, it is impossible that demonstration should degenerate into probability from the imperfection of our faculties. Our judgment cannot change the nature of the things about which we judge. What is really demonstration will still be so, whatever judgment we form concerning it. It may likewise be observed, that, when we mistake that for demonstration which really is not, the consequence of this mistake is, *not* that demonstration degenerates into probability, but that what we took to be demonstration is no proof at all ; for one false step in a demonstration destroys the whole, but cannot turn it into another kind of proof.

Upon the whole, then, this first conclusion of our author, that the fallibility of human judgment turns all knowledge into probability, if understood literally, is absurd ; but if it be only a figure of speech, and means no more than that, in all our judgments, we ought to be sensible of our fallibility, and ought to hold our opinions with that modesty that becomes fallible creatures, which I take to be what the author meant, this, I think, nobody denies, nor was it necessary to enter into a laborious proof of it.

II. *And all Probability to Nothing.*] The *second* point which he attempts to prove is, that this probability, when duly examined, suffers a *continual diminution, and at last a total extinction.*

The obvious consequence of this is, that no fallible being can have good reason to believe any thing at all. But let us hear the proof.

" In every judgment, we ought to correct the first judgment derived from the nature of the object, by another judgment derived from the nature of the understanding. Beside the original uncertainty inherent in the subject, there arises another, derived from the weakness of the faculty which judges. Having adjusted these two uncertainties together, we are obliged, by our reason, to add a new uncertainty, derived from the possibility of error in the estimation we make of the truth and fidelity of our faculties. This is a doubt of which, if we would closely pursue our reasoning, we cannot avoid giving a decision. But this decision, though it should be favorable to our preceding judgment, being founded only on probability, must weaken still further our first evidence. The third uncertainty must in like manner be criticized by a fourth, and so on without end.

" Now, as every one of these uncertainties takes away a part of the original evidence, it must at last be reduced to nothing. Let our first belief be ever so strong, it must infallibly perish by passing through so many examinations, each of which carries off somewhat of its force and vigor. No finite object can subsist under a decrease repeated *in infinitum*."

This is the author's Achillean argument against the evidence of reason, from which he concludes, that a man who would govern his belief by reason must believe nothing at all, and that belief is an act, not of the cogitative, but of the sensitive part of our nature. If there be any such thing as motion, said an ancient skeptic, the swift-footed Achilles could never overtake an old man in a journey. For, suppose the old man to set out a thousand paces before Achilles, and that, while Achilles has travelled the thousand paces, the old man has got five hundred; when Achilles has gone the five hundred, the old man has gone two hundred and fifty; and when Achilles has gone the two hundred and fifty, the old man is still one hundred and twenty-five before him. Repeat these estimations *in infinitum*, and you will still find the old man foremost; therefore Achilles can never overtake him; therefore there can be no such thing as motion.

The reasoning of the modern skeptic against reason is equally ingenious, and equally convincing. Indeed, they have a great similarity. If we trace the journey of Achilles two thousand paces, we shall find the very point where the old man is overtaken: but this short journey, by dividing it into an infinite number of stages, with corresponding estimations, is made to appear infinite. In like manner, our author, subjecting every judgment to an infinite number of successive probable estimations, reduces the evidence to nothing.

To return, then, to the argument of the modern skeptic. I examine the proof of a theorem of Euclid. It appears to me to be strict demonstration. But I may have overlooked some fallacy; therefore I examine it again and again, but can find no flaw in it. I find all that have examined it agree with me. I have now that evidence of the truth of the proposition which I and all men call demonstration, and that belief of it which we call certainty.

Here my skeptical friend interposes, and assures me, that the rules of logic reduce this demonstration to no evidence at all. I am willing to hear what step in it he thinks fallacious, and why. He makes no objection to any part of the demonstration, but pleads my fallibility in judging. I have made the proper allowance for this already, by being open to conviction. " But," says he, " there are *two* uncertainties, the *first* inherent in the subject, which I have already shown to have only probable evidence; the *second* arising from the weakness of the faculty that judges." I answer, it is the weakness of the faculty only that reduces this demonstration to what you call probability. You must not, therefore, make it a second uncertainty; for it is the same with the first. To take credit twice in an account for the same article is not agreeable to the rules of logic. Hitherto, therefore, there is but one uncertainty, — to wit, my fallibility in judging.

" But," says my friend, " you are obliged by reason to add a *new* uncertainty, derived from *the possibility of error in the estimation you make of the truth and fidelity of your faculties.*" I answer, — This estimation is ambiguously expressed; it may either mean an estimation of my liableness to err by the misapplication and abuse of my faculties, or it may mean an estimation of my liableness to err by conceiving my faculties to be true and faithful, while they may be false and fallacious in themselves, even when applied in the best manner. I shall consider this estimation in each of these senses.

If the first be the estimation meant, it is true that reason directs us, as fallible creatures, to carry along with us, in all our judgments, a sense of our fallibility. It is true, also, that we are in greater danger of erring in some cases, and less in others; and that this danger of erring may, according to the circumstances of the case, admit of an estimation, which we ought likewise to carry along with us in every judgment we form.

After repeated examination of a proposition of Euclid, I judge it to be strictly demonstrated; this is my first judgment. But as I am liable to err from various causes, I consider how far I may have been misled by any of these causes in this judgment. My decision upon this second point is favorable to my first judgment, and therefore, as I apprehend, must *strengthen* it. To say, that this decision, because it is only probable, must weaken the first evidence, seems to me contrary to all rules of logic, and to common sense. The first judgment may be compared to the testimony of a credible witness; the second, after a scrutiny into the character of the witness, wipes off every objection that can be made to it, and therefore surely must confirm, and not weaken, his testimony.

But let us suppose, that, in another case, I examine my first judgment upon some point, and find, that it was attended with unfavorable circumstances. What, in reason, and according to the rules of logic, ought to be the effect of this discovery?

The effect surely will be, and ought to be, to make me less confident in my first judgment, until I examine the point anew in more favorable circumstances. If it be a matter of importance, I return to weigh the evidence of my first judgment. If it was precipitate before, it must now be deliberate in every point. If at first I was in passion, I must now be cool. If I had an interest in the decision, I must place the interest on the other side.

It is evident, that this review of the subject may *confirm* my first judgment, notwithstanding the suspicious circumstances that attended it. Though the judge was biased or corrupted, it does not follow that the sentence was unjust. The rectitude of the decision does not depend upon the character of the judge, but upon the nature of the case. From that only it must be determined whether the decision be just. The circumstances that rendered it suspicious are mere presumptions, which have no force against direct evidence.

Thus, I have considered the effect of this estimation of our liableness to err in our first judgment, and have allowed to it all the effect that reason and the rules of logic permit. In the case I first supposed, and in every case where we can discover no cause of error, it affords a presumption *in favor* of the first judgment. In other cases, it may afford a presumption against it. But the rules of logic require that we should not judge by presumptions where we have direct evidence. The effect of an unfavorable presumption should only be, to make us examine the evidence with the greater care.

The skeptic urges, in the *last* place, that this estimation must be subjected to another estimation, that to another, and so on *in infinitum;* and as every new estimation takes away from the evidence of the first judgment, it must at last be *totally annihilated.*

I answer, *first,* it has been shown above, that the first estimation, supposing it unfavorable, can only afford a *presumption* against the first judgment; the second, upon the same supposition, will be only the presumption of a presumption; and the third, the presumption that there is a presumption of a presumption. This infinite series of presumptions resembles an infinite series of quantities decreasing in geometrical proportion, which amounts only to a *finite sum.* The infinite series of stages of Achilles's journey after the old man amounts only to two thousand paces; nor can this infinite series of presumptions outweigh one solid argument in favor of the first judgment, supposing them all to be unfavorable to it.

Secondly, I have shown, that the estimation of our first judgment may *strengthen* it; and the same thing may be said of *all the subsequent estimations.* It would, therefore, be as reasonable to conclude, that the first judgment will be brought to infallible certainty when this series of estimations is wholly in its favor, as that its evidence will be brought to nothing by such a series supposed to be wholly unfavorable to it. But, in reality, one serious and cool reëxamination of the evidence by which our first judgment is supported has, and, in reason, ought to have, more force to strengthen or weaken it, than an infinite series of such estimations as our author requires.

Thirdly, I know no reason nor rule in logic that requires that such a *series of estimations* should follow every particular judgment.

The author's reasoning supposes, that a man, when he forms his first judgment, conceives himself to be infallible; that by a second and subsequent judgment, he discovers that he is not infallible; and that by a third judgment, subsequent to the second, he estimates his liableness to err in such a case as the present.

If the man proceed in this order, I grant that his second judgment will, with good reason, bring down the first from supposed infallibility to fallibility; and that his third judgment will, in some degree, either strengthen or weaken the first, as it is corrected by the second. But every man of understanding proceeds in a contrary order. When about to judge in any particular point, he knows already that he is not infallible. He knows what are the cases in which he is most or least liable to err. The conviction of these things is always present to his mind, and influences the degree of his assent in his first judgment, as far as to him appears reasonable. If he should afterwards find reason to suspect his first judgment, and desires to have all the satisfaction his faculties can give, reason will direct him not to form such a series of estimations upon estimations as this author requires, but to examine the evidence of his first judgment carefully and coolly; and this review may very reasonably, according to its result, either strengthen or weaken, or totally overturn, his first judgment.

This infinite series of estimations, therefore, is not the method that reason directs in order to form our judgment in any case. It is introduced without necessity, without any use but to puzzle the understanding, and to make us think, that to judge, even in the simplest and plainest cases, is a matter of insurmountable difficulty and endless labor; just as the ancient skeptic, to make a journey of two thousand paces appear endless, divided it into an infinite number of stages.

But we observed, that the estimation which our author requires may admit of another meaning, which, indeed, is more agreeable to the expression, but inconsistent with what he advanced before.

By the possibility of error in the estimation of the truth and fidelity of our faculties, may be meant, that *we may err by esteeming our faculties true and faithful, while, in fact, they may be false and fallacious,* even when used according to the rules of reason and logic.

If this be meant, I answer, *first,* that the truth and fidelity of our faculty of judging are, and must be, *taken for granted* in every judgment and in every estimation.

If the skeptic can seriously doubt of the truth and fidelity of his faculty of judging when properly used, and suspend his judgment upon that point till he finds proof, his skepticism admits of no cure by reasoning, and he must even continue in it until he have new faculties given him, which shall have authority to sit in judgment upon the old. Nor is there any need of an endless succession of doubts upon this subject, for the first puts an end to all judgment and reasoning, and to the possibility of conviction by that means. The skeptic has here got possession of a stronghold which is impregnable to reasoning, and we must leave him in possession of it, till nature, by other means, makes him give it up.

Secondly, I observe, that this ground of skepticism, from the supposed infidelity of our faculties, contradicts what the author before advanced in this very argument, to wit, that " the rules of the demonstrative sciences are certain and infallible, and that truth is the natural effect of reason, and that error arises from the irruption of other causes."

But perhaps he made these concessions unwarily. He is therefore at liberty to retract them, and to rest his skepticism upon this sole foundation, *that no reasoning can prove the truth and fidelity of our faculties.* Here he stands upon firm ground : for it is evident, that every argument offered to prove the truth and fidelity of our faculties takes for granted the thing in question, and is therefore that kind of sophism which logicians call *petitio principii.*

All we would ask of this kind of skeptic is, that he would be uniform and consistent, and that his practice in life do not belie his profession of skepticism with regard to the fidelity of his faculties: for the want of faith, as well as faith itself, is best shown by works. If a skeptic avoid the fire as much as those who believe it dangerous to go into it, we can hardly avoid thinking his skepticism to be feigned, and not real.

Our author, indeed, was aware, that neither his skepticism, nor that of any other person, was able to endure this trial, and therefore enters a caveat against it. " Neither I," says he, " nor any other person, was ever sincerely and constantly of that opinion. Nature, by an absolute and uncontrollable necessity, has determined us to judge, as well as to breathe and feel."

Upon the whole, I see only two conclusions that can be fairly drawn from this profound and intricate reasoning against reason. The first is, that we are fallible in all our judgments and in all our reasonings. The second, that the truth and fidelity of our faculties can never be proved by reasoning; and therefore our trust in them cannot be founded on reasoning. If the last be what the author calls his hypothesis, I subscribe to it, and think it not an hypothesis, but a manifest truth; though I conceive it to be very improperly expressed by saying that belief is more properly an act of the sensitive than of the cogitative part of our nature.*

---

* On the general subject of skepticism, see Fichte's *Destination of Man;* Jouffroy's *Introduction to Ethics,* Lectures VIII.-X.; Ancillon, *Essai sur la Science et sur la Foi Philosophique;* Javary, *De la Certitude.* — ED.

ESSAY VIII.

OF TASTE.

CHAPTER I.

OF TASTE IN GENERAL.

THAT power of the mind by which we are capable of discerning and relishing the beauties of nature, and whatever is excellent in the fine arts, is called *taste*.

In treating of this as an *intellectual* power of the mind, I intend only to make some observations, first on its *nature*, and then on its *objects*.

1. In the external sense of taste, we are led by reason and reflection to distinguish between the *agreeable sensation* we feel, and the *quality in the object* which occasions it. Both have the same name, and on that account are apt to be confounded by the vulgar, and even by philosophers. The sensation I feel when I taste any sapid body is in my mind; but there is a real quality in the body which is the cause of this sensation. These two things have the same name in language, not from any similitude in their nature, but because the one is the sign of the other, and because there is little occasion in common life to distinguish them. This was fully explained in treating of the Secondary Qualities of Bodies. The reason of taking notice of it now is, that the internal power of taste bears a great analogy in this respect to the external.

When a beautiful object is before us, we may distinguish the agreeable emotion it produces in us from the quality of the object which causes that emotion. When

I hear an air in music that pleases me, I say it is fine, it is excellent. This excellence is not in me; it is *in the music.* But the pleasure it gives is not in the music; it is *in me.* Perhaps I cannot say what it is in the tune that pleases my ear, as I cannot say what it is in a sapid body that pleases my palate; but there is a quality in the sapid body which pleases my palate, and I call it a delicious taste; and there is a quality in the tune that pleases my taste, and I call it a fine or an excellent air.

But though some of the qualities that please a good taste resemble the secondary qualities of body, and therefore may be called *occult* qualities, as we only feel their effect, and have no more knowledge of the cause than that it is something which is adapted by nature to produce that effect, this is not always the case. Our judgment of beauty is, in many cases, more enlightened. A work of art may appear beautiful to the most ignorant, even to a child. It pleases, but he knows not why. To one who understands it perfectly, and perceives how every part is fitted with exact judgment to its end, the beauty is not mysterious; it is perfectly comprehended; and he knows wherein it consists, as well as how it affects him.

2. We may observe, that, though all the tastes we perceive by the palate are either agreeable or disagreeable, or indifferent; yet among those that are agreeable there is a great diversity, not in degree only, but in kind. And as we have not generical names for all the different kinds of taste, we distinguish them by the bodies in which they are found. In like manner, all the objects of our internal taste are either beautiful, or disagreeable, or indifferent; yet *of beauty there is a great diversity, not only of degree, but of kind :* the beauty of a demonstration, the beauty of a poem, the beauty of a palace, the beauty of a piece of music, the beauty of a fine woman, and many more that might be named, are different kinds of beauty; and we have no names to distinguish them, but the names of the different objects to which they belong.

As there is such diversity in the *kinds* of beauty as well as in the *degrees*, we need not think it strange that philosophers have gone into different systems in analyzing it, and enumerating its simple ingredients. They have made many just observations on the subject; but, from the love of simplicity, have reduced it to fewer principles than the nature of the thing will permit, having had in their eye some particular kinds of beauty, while they overlooked others.

There are moral beauties as well as natural; beauties in the objects of sense, and in intellectual objects; in the works of men, and in the works of God; in things inanimate, in brute animals, and in rational beings; in the constitution of the body of man, and in the constitution of his mind. There is no *real excellence* which has not its beauty to a discerning eye, when placed in a proper point of view; and it is as difficult to enumerate the ingredients of beauty as the ingredients of real excellence.

3. Those who conceive that there is *no standard* in nature by which taste may be regulated, and that the common proverb, that *there ought to be no dispute about taste*, is to be taken in the utmost latitude, go upon slender and insufficient ground. The same arguments might be used with equal force against any standard of truth. Whole nations by the force of prejudice are brought to believe the grossest absurdities; and why should it be thought that the taste is less capable of being perverted than the judgment? It must indeed be acknowledged, that men differ more in the faculty of taste than in what we commonly call judgment; and therefore it may be expected that they should be more liable to have their taste corrupted in matters of beauty and deformity, than their judgment in matters of truth and error.

If we make due allowance for this, we shall see that it is as easy to account for the variety of taste, though there be in nature a standard of true beauty, and consequently of good taste, as it is to account for the variety and contrariety of opinions, though there be in

39

nature a standard of truth, and consequently of right judgment.

4. Nay, if we speak accurately and strictly, we shall find that, *in every operation of taste, there is judgment implied.*

When a man pronounces a poem or a palace to be beautiful, he affirms something of that poem or that palace; and every affirmation or denial expresses judgment. For we cannot better define judgment, than by saying that it is an affirmation or denial of one thing concerning another. I had occasion to show, when treating of judgment, that it is implied in every perception of our external senses. There is an immediate conviction and belief of the existence of the quality perceived, whether it be color, or sound, or figure; and the same thing holds in the perception of beauty or deformity.

If it be said, that the perception of beauty is merely a feeling in the mind that perceives, without any belief of excellence in the object, the necessary consequence of this opinion is, that when I say Virgil's Georgics is a beautiful poem, I mean not to say any thing of the poem, but only something concerning myself and my feelings. Why should I use a language that expresses the contrary of what I mean? My language, according to the necessary rules of construction, can bear no other meaning but this, that there is something in the poem, and not in me, which I call beauty. Even those who hold beauty to be merely a feeling in the person that perceives it, find themselves under a necessity of expressing themselves as if beauty were solely a quality of the object, and not of the percipient.

Our judgment of beauty is not, indeed, a dry and unaffecting judgment, like that of a mathematical or metaphysical truth. By the constitution of our nature, it is accompanied with an agreeable feeling or emotion, for which we have no other name but *the sense of beauty.* This sense of beauty, like the perceptions of our other senses, implies not only a feeling, but an opinion of some quality in the object which occasions that feeling.

In objects that please the taste, we always judge that there is some real excellence, some superiority to those that do not please. In some cases, that superior excellence is distinctly perceived, and can be pointed out; in other cases, we have only a general notion of some excellence which we cannot describe. Beauties of the former kind may be compared to the primary qualities perceived by the external senses; those of the latter kind, to the secondary.

5. Beauty or deformity in an object results from its nature or structure. To perceive the -beauty, therefore, we must perceive the nature or structure from which it results. In this the internal sense differs from the external. Our external senses may discover qualities which do not depend upon any antecedent perception. Thus I can hear the sound of a bell, though I never perceived any thing else belonging to it. But it is impossible to perceive the beauty of an object without perceiving the object, or at least conceiving it. On this account, Dr. Hutcheson called the senses of beauty and harmony *reflex* or *secondary* senses; because the beauty cannot be perceived unless the object be perceived by some other power of the mind. Thus the sense of harmony and melody in sounds supposes the external sense of hearing, and is a kind of secondary to it. A man born deaf may be a good judge of beauties of another kind, but can have no notion of melody or harmony. The like may be said of beauties in coloring and in figure, which can never be perceived without the senses by which color and figure are perceived.

CHAPTER II.

OF THE OBJECTS OF TASTE.

A PHILOSOPHICAL analysis of the objects of taste is like applying the anatomical knife to a fine face. The design of the philosopher, as well as of the anatomist, is, not to gratify taste, but to improve knowledge. The reader ought to be aware of this, that he may not entertain an expectation in which he will be disappointed.

By the *objects of taste*, I mean *those qualities or attributes of things, which are by nature adapted to please a good taste*. Mr. Addison, and Dr. Akenside after him, have reduced them to three, to wit, *novelty, grandeur*, and *beauty*. This division is sufficient for all I intend to say upon the subject, and therefore I shall adopt it; — observing only, that *beauty* is often taken in so extensive a sense as to comprehend all the objects of taste; yet all the authors I have met with, who have given a division of the objects of taste, make beauty one species. I take the reason of this to be, that we have specific names for some of the qualities that please the taste, but not for all; and therefore all those fall under the general name of beauty for which there is no specific name in the division.

I. *First Object of Taste. — Novelty.*] *Novelty* is not properly a quality of the thing to which we attribute it, far less is it a sensation in the mind to which it is new: it is *a relation which the thing has to the knowledge of the person*. What is new to one man may not be so to another; what is new this moment may be familiar to the same person some time hence. When an object is first brought to our knowledge, it is new, whether it be agreeable or not. It is evident, therefore, with regard to novelty (whatever may be said of other objects of taste), that it is not merely a sensation in the mind of him to whom the thing is new; it is a *real relation* which the thing has to his knowledge at that time.

But we are so constituted, that what is new to us commonly gives pleasure upon that account, if it be not in itself disagreeable. It rouses our attention, and occasions an agreeable exertion of our faculties.

We can perhaps conceive a being so made, that his

happiness consists in a continuance of the same un-
varied sensations or feelings, without any active exertion on his part. Whether this be possible or not, it is
evident that man is not such a being. His good consists in the vigorous exertion of his active and intel-
lective powers upon their proper objects; he is made
for action and progress, and cannot be happy without
it; his enjoyments seem to be given by nature, not so
much for their own sake, as to encourage the exercise
of his various powers. That tranquillity of soul in
which some place human happiness is not a dead rest,
but a regular progressive motion.

Such is the constitution of man by the appointment
of nature. This constitution is perhaps a part of the
imperfection of our nature; but it is wisely adapted to
our state, which is not intended to be stationary, but
progressive. The eye is not satiated with seeing, nor
the ear with hearing; something is always wanted.
Desire and hope never cease, but remain to spur us on
to something yet to be acquired; and, if they could
cease, human happiness must end with them. That
our desire and hope be properly directed, is our part;
that they can never be extinguished, is the work of
nature.

But the pleasure derived from new objects, in many
cases, is not owing solely or chiefly to their being new,
but to some other circumstance that gives them value.
The new fashion in dress, furniture, equipage, and
other accommodations of life, gives pleasure, not so
much, as I apprehend, because it is new, as because it
is a sign of rank, and distinguishes a man from the
vulgar.

In some things novelty is due, and the want of it a
real imperfection. Thus, if an author adds to the
number of books with which the public is already
overloaded, we expect from him something new; and
if he says nothing but what has been said before, in as
agreeable a manner, we are justly disgusted.

When novelty is altogether separated from the conception of worth and utility, it makes but a slight im-

pression upon a truly correct taste. Every discovery in nature, in ·the arts, and in the sciences, has a real value, and gives a rational pleasure to a good taste. But things that have nothing to recommend them but novelty are fit only to entertain children, or those who are distressed from a vacuity of thought. This quality of objects may therefore be compared to the cipher in arithmetic, which adds greatly to the value of significant figures, but, when put by itself, signifies nothing at all.

II. *Second Object of Taste. — Grandeur.*] We are next to consider what *grandeur* in objects is. To me it seems to be nothing else than *such a degree of excellence, in one kind or another, as merits our admiration.*

There are some attributes of mind which have a real and intrinsic excellence, compared with their contraries, and which, in every degree, are the natural objects of esteem, but in an uncommon degree are objects of admiration. We put a value upon them because they are intrinsically valuable and excellent.

The spirit of modern philosophy would indeed lead us to think, that the worth and value we put upon things is only a sensation in our minds, and not any thing inherent in the object; and that we might have been so constituted as to put the highest value upon the things which we now despise, and to despise the qualities which we now highly esteem. But if we hearken to the dictates of common sense, we must be convinced that *there is real excellence in some things,* whatever our feelings or our constitution be. It depends, no doubt, upon our constitution, whether we do or do not *perceive* excellence where it really is; but the object has its excellence from its own constitution, and not from ours.

The common judgment of mankind in this matter sufficiently appears in the language of all nations, which uniformly ascribes excellence, grandeur, and beauty to the object, and not to the mind that perceives it. And I believe in this, as in most other things, we shall find the common judgment of mankind and true philosophy not to be at variance.

Is not power in its nature more excellent than weakness, knowledge than ignorance, wisdom than folly, fortitude than pusillanimity? Is there no intrinsic excellence in self-command, in generosity, in public spirit? Is not friendship a better affection of mind than hatred, — a noble emulation, than envy? Let us suppose, if possible, a being so constituted as to have a high respect for ignorance, weakness, and folly; to venerate cowardice, malice, and envy, and to hold the contrary qualities in contempt; to have an esteem for lying and falsehood, and to love most those who impose upon him, and use him worst. Could we believe such a constitution to be any thing else than madness and delirium? It is impossible. We can as easily conceive a constitution by which one should perceive two and three to make fifteen, or a part to be greater than the whole.

Every one who attends to the operations of his own mind will find it to be certainly true, as it is the common belief of mankind, that esteem is led by opinion, and that every person draws our esteem as far only as he appears, either to reason or fancy, to be amiable and worthy.

There is, therefore, a real intrinsic excellence in some qualities of mind, — as in power, knowledge, wisdom, virtue, magnanimity. These in every degree merit *esteem;* but in an uncommon degree they merit *admiration;* and that which merits admiration we call *grand.*

In the contemplation of uncommon excellence the mind feels a noble enthusiasm, which disposes it to the imitation of what it admires. When we contemplate the character of Cato, his greatness of soul, his superiority to pleasure, to toil, and to danger, his ardent zeal for the liberty of his country, — when we see him standing unmoved in misfortunes, the last pillar of the liberty of Rome, and falling nobly in his country's ruin, — who would not wish to be Cato, rather than Cæsar in all his triumph? Such a spectacle of a great soul struggling with misfortune, Seneca thought not unworthy of the attention of Jupiter himself. *Ecce spectaculum Deo dignum, ad quod respiciat Jupiter suo operi intentus, vir fortis cum mala fortuna compositus.*

As the Deity is, of all objects of thought, the most grand, the descriptions given in Holy Writ of his attributes and works, even when clothed in simple expression, are acknowledged to be sublime. The expression of Moses, " And God said, Let there be light; and there was light," * has not escaped the notice of Longinus, a heathen critic, as an example of the sublime.

Hitherto we have found grandeur only in qualities of mind; but it may be asked, Is there no real grandeur in *material objects?*

It will perhaps appear extravagant to deny that there is; yet it deserves to be considered, whether all the grandeur we ascribe to objects of sense be not derived from something intellectual, of which they are the effects or signs, or to which they bear some relation or analogy. Besides the relations of effect and cause, of sign and thing signified, there are innumerable similitudes and analogies between things of very different nature, which lead us to connect them in our imagination, and to ascribe to the one what properly belongs to the other. Every metaphor in language is an instance of this; and it must be remembered, that a very great part of language which we now account proper was originally metaphorical; for the metaphorical meaning becomes the proper as soon as it becomes the most usual; much more, when that which was at first the proper meaning falls into disuse.

Thus the names of *grand* and *sublime*, as well as their opposites, *mean* and *low*, are evidently borrowed from the dimensions of body; yet it must be acknowledged, that many things are truly grand and sublime, to which we cannot ascribe the dimensions of height and extension. Some analogy there is, without doubt, between greatness of dimension, which is an object of

---

* Better translated, " Be there light; and light there was."—H.

external sense, and that grandeur which is an object of taste. On account of this analogy, the last borrows its name from the first; and the name being common leads us to conceive that there is something common in the nature of the things. But we shall find many qualities of mind denoted by names taken from some quality of body to which they have some *analogy*, without any thing *common in their nature.*

Sweetness and austerity, simplicity and duplicity, rectitude and crookedness, are names common to certain qualities of mind, and to qualities of body to which they have some analogy; yet he would err greatly who ascribed to a body that sweetness or that simplicity which are the qualities of mind. In like manner, greatness and meanness are names common to qualities perceived by the external sense, and to qualities perceived by taste; yet he may be in an error, who ascribes to the objects of sense that greatness or that meanness which is only an object of taste.

As intellectual objects are made more level to our apprehension by giving them a visible form, so the objects of sense are dignified and made more august by ascribing to them intellectual qualities which have some analogy to those they really possess. The sea rages, the sky lowers, the meadows smile, the rivulets murmur, the breezes whisper, the soil is grateful or ungrateful, — such expressions are so familiar in common language, that they are scarcely accounted poetical or figurative; but they give a kind of dignity to inanimate objects, and make our conception of them more agreeable.

When we consider matter as an inert, extended, divisible, and movable substance, there seems to be nothing in these qualities which we can call grand; and when we ascribe grandeur to any portion of matter, however modified, may it not *borrow this quality from something intellectual,* of which it is the effect, or sign, or instrument, or to which it bears some analogy? or it may be because it produces in the mind an emotion that has some resemblance to that admiration which truly grand objects raise.

A very elegant writer on the sublime and beautiful [Burke] makes every thing grand or sublime that is terrible. Might he not be led to this by the similarity between *dread* and *admiration?* Both are grave and solemn passions ; both make a strong impression upon the mind ; and both are very infectious. But they differ specifically, in this respect, that admiration supposes some *uncommon excellence in its object,* which dread does not. We may admire what we see no reason to dread ; and we may dread what we do not admire. In dread there is nothing of that enthusiasm which naturally accompanies admiration, and is a chief ingredient of the emotion raised by what is truly grand or sublime.

Upon the whole, I humbly apprehend that true grandeur is such a degree of excellence as is fit to raise an enthusiastical admiration ; that this grandeur is found originally and properly in qualities of mind ; that it is discerned in objects of sense only by reflection, as the light we perceive in the moon and planets is truly the light of the sun ; and that those who look for grandeur in mere matter seek the living among the dead.

If this be a mistake, it ought at least to be granted that the grandeur which we perceive in qualities of mind ought to have a different name from that which belongs properly to the objects of sense, as they are very different in their nature, and produce very different emotions in the mind of the spectator.

III. *Third Object of Taste. — Beauty.*] All the objects we call *beautiful* agree in two things, which seem to concur in our sense of beauty. *First,* when they are perceived, or even imagined, they produce a certain agreeable emotion or feeling in the mind ; and *secondly,* this agreeable emotion is accompanied with an opinion or belief of their having some perfection or excellence belonging to them.

1. Whether the *pleasure we feel in contemplating beautiful objects* may have any necessary connection with the belief of their excellence, or whether that pleas-

ure be conjoined with this belief by the good pleasure only of our Maker, I will not determine. The reader may see Dr. Price's sentiments upon this subject, which merit consideration, in the second chapter of his *Review of the Questions concerning Morals.* At any rate, the pleasure exists. " There is nothing," says Mr. Addison, " that makes its way more directly to the soul than beauty, which immediately diffuses a secret satisfaction and complacence through the imagination, and gives a finishing to any thing that is great and uncommon. The very first discovery of it strikes the mind with an inward joy, and spreads a cheerfulness and delight through all its faculties."

As we ascribe beauty, not only to persons, but to inanimate things, we give the name of *love* or *liking* to the emotion which beauty, in both these kinds of objects, produces. It is evident, however, that liking to a person is a very different affection of mind from liking to an inanimate thing. The first always implies benevolence ; but what is inanimate cannot be the object of benevolence. Still, the two affections, however different, have a resemblance in some respects ; and, on account of that resemblance, have the same name : and perhaps beauty, in these two different kinds of objects, though it has one name, may be as different in its nature as the emotions which it produces in us.

2. Besides the agreeable emotion which beautiful objects produce in the mind of the spectator, they produce also *an opinion or judgment of some perfection or excellence in the object.*

The feeling is, no doubt, in the mind, and so also is the judgment we form of the object : but this judgment, like all others, must be true or false. If it be a true judgment, there is some real excellence in the object. And the use of all languages shows, that the name of *beauty* belongs to this excellence of the object, and not to the feelings of the spectator.

We have reason to believe, not only that the beauties we see in nature are real, and not fanciful, but that there are thousands which our faculties are too dull to perceive. The man who is skilled in painting or statuary sees more of the beauty of a fine picture or statue than a common spectator. The same thing holds in all the fine arts. The most perfect works of art have a beauty that strikes even the rude and ignorant; but they see only a small part of that beauty which is seen in such works by those who understand them perfectly, and can produce them. This may be applied with no less justice to the works of nature. They have a beauty that strikes even the ignorant and inattentive. But the more we discover of their structure, of their mutual relations, and of the laws by which they are governed, the greater beauty, and the more delightful marks of art, wisdom, and goodness, we discern. Superior beings may see more than we; but He only who made them, and upon a review pronounced them all to be " very good," can see all their beauty.

Our determinations with regard to the beauty of objects may, I think, be distinguished into two kinds; the first we may call *instinctive*, the other *rational.*

(1.) Some objects strike us at once, and appear beautiful at first sight, without any reflection, without our being able to say why we call them beautiful, or being able to specify any perfection which justifies our judgment. Something of this kind there seems to be in brute animals, and in children before the use of reason; nor does it end with infancy, but continues through life. In the plumage of birds, and of butterflies, in the colors and form of flowers, of shells, and of many other objects, we perceive a beauty that delights; but cannot say what it is in the object that should produce that emotion.

The beauty of the object may, in such cases, be called an *occult quality.* We know well how it affects our senses; but what it is in itself we know not. But this, as well as other occult qualities, is a proper subject of philosophical disquisition; and, by a careful examination of the objects to which nature has given this amiable quality, we may perhaps discover some real excellence in the object, or at least some valuable purpose that is served by the effect which it produces upon us.

This instinctive sense of beauty, in different species of animals, may differ as much as the external sense of taste, and in each species be adapted to its manner of life. By this, perhaps, the various tribes are led to associate with their kind, to dwell among certain objects rather than others, and to construct their habitation in a particular manner. There seem likewise to be varieties in the sense of beauty in the individuals of the same species, by which they are directed in the choice of a mate, and in the love and care of their offspring. "We see," says Mr. Addison, "that every different species of sensible creatures has its different notions of beauty, and that each of them is most affected with the beauties of its own kind. This is nowhere more remarkable than in birds of the same shape and proportion, where we often see the mate determined in his courtship by the single grain or tincture of a feather, and never discovering any charms but in the color of its own species."

> "Scit thalamo servare fidem, sanctasque veretur
> Connubii leges; non illum in pectore candor
> Sollicitat niveus; neque pravum accendit amorem
> Splendida lanugo, vel honesta in vertice crista;
> Purpureusve nitor pennarum; ast agmina latè
> Fœminea explorat cautus, maculasque requirit
> Cognatas, paribusque interlita corpora guttis:
> Ni faceret, pictis sylvam circum undique monstris
> Confusam aspiceres vulgo, partusque biformes,
> Et genus ambiguum, et veneris monumenta nefandæ.
>   Hinc merula in nigro se oblectat nigra marito;
> Hinc socium lasciva petit philomela canorum,
> Agnoscitque pares sonitus; hinc noctua tetram
> Canitiem alarum, et glaucos miratur ocellos.
> Nempe sibi semper constat, crescitque quotannis
> Lucida progenies, castos confessa parentes:
> Vere novo exultat, plumasque decora juventus
> Explicat ad solem, patriisque coloribus ardet."

As far as our determinations of the comparative beauty of objects are instinctive, they are no subject of reasoning or of criticism; they are purely the gift of nature, and we have no standard by which they may be measured.

40

(2.) But there are judgments of beauty that may be called *rational*, being grounded on some agreeable quality of the object which is distinctly conceived, and may be specified.

This distinction between a rational judgment of beauty and that which is instinctive, may be illustrated by an instance. In a heap of pebbles, one that is remarkable for brilliancy of color and regularity of figure will be picked out of the heap by a child. He perceives a beauty in it, puts a value upon it, and is fond of the property of it. For this preference no reason can be given, but that children are, by their constitution, fond of brilliant colors, and of regular figures. Suppose, again, that an expert mechanic views a well-constructed machine. He sees all its parts to be made of the fittest materials, and of the most proper form; nothing superfluous, nothing deficient; every part adapted to its use, and the whole fitted in the most perfect manner to the end for which it is intended. He pronounces it to be a beautiful machine. He views it with the same agreeable emotion as the child viewed the pebble; but he can give a reason for his judgment, and point out the particular perfections of the object on which it is grounded.

Although the instinctive and the rational sense of beauty may be perfectly distinguished in speculation, yet, in passing judgment upon particular objects, they are often so mixed and confounded, that it is difficult to assign to each its own province. Nay, it may often happen, that a judgment of the beauty of an object, which was at first merely instinctive, shall afterwards become rational, when we discover some latent perfection of which that beauty in the object is a sign.

As the sense of beauty may be distinguished into instinctive and rational; so, I think, beauty itself may be distinguished into *original* and *derived*.

The attributes of body we ascribe to mind, and the attributes of mind to material objects. To inanimate things we ascribe life, and even intellectual and moral qualities. And although the qualities that are thus made common belong to one of the subjects in the proper sense, and to the other metaphorically, these different senses are often so mixed in our imagination, as to produce the same sentiment with regard to both. It is therefore natural, and agreeable to the strain of human sentiments and of human language, that in many cases the beauty which originally and properly is in the thing signified, should be transferred to the sign; that which is in the cause, to the effect; that which is in the end, to the means; and that which is in the agent, to the instrument.

If what was just said of the distinction between the grandeur which we ascribe to qualities of mind, and that which we ascribe to material objects, be well founded, this distinction of the beauty of objects will easily be admitted as perfectly analogous to it. I shall, therefore, only illustrate it by an example.

There is nothing in the exterior of a man more lovely and more attractive than perfect good breeding. But what is this good breeding? It consists of all the external signs of due respect to our superiors, condescension to our inferiors, politeness to all with whom we converse or have to do, joined in the fair sex with that delicacy of outward behaviour which becomes them. And how comes it to have such charms in the eyes of all mankind? For this reason only, as I apprehend, that it is a natural sign of that temper, and those affections and sentiments with regard to others, and with regard to ourselves, which are in themselves truly amiable and beautiful. This is the original, of which good breeding is the picture; and it is the beauty of the original that is reflected to our sense by the picture. The beauty of good breeding, therefore, is not originally in the external behaviour in which it consists, but is derived from the qualities of mind which it expresses. And though there may be good breeding without the amiable qualities of mind, its beauty is still derived from what it naturally expresses.

Having explained these distinctions of our *sense of beauty* into *instinctive* and *rational*, and of *beauty itself* into *original* and *derived*, I would now proceed to give a general view of those qualities in objects to which we may justly and rationally ascribe beauty, whether original or derived.

But here some embarrassment arises from the vague meaning of the word *beauty*, which I had occasion before to observe. Sometimes it is extended, so as to include every thing that pleases a good taste, and so comprehends grandeur and novelty, as well as what in a more restricted sense is called beauty. At other times, it is even by good writers confined to the objects of sight, when they are either seen, or remembered, or imagined. Yet it is admitted by all men, that there are beauties in music; that there is beauty as well as sublimity in composition, both in verse and in prose; that there is beauty in characters, in affections, and in actions. These are not objects of sight; and a man may be a good judge of beauty of various kinds, who has not the faculty of sight.

To give a determinate meaning to a word so variously extended and restricted, I know no better way than what is suggested by the common division of the objects of taste into *novelty, grandeur,* and *beauty.* Novelty, it is plain, is no quality of the new object, but merely a relation which it has to the knowledge of the person to whom it is new. Therefore, if this general division be just, every quality in an object that pleases a good taste must, in one degree or another, have either grandeur or beauty. It may still be difficult to fix the precise limit betwixt grandeur and beauty; but they must together comprehend every thing fitted by its nature to please a good taste, — that is, every real perfection and excellence in the objects we contemplate.

In a poem, in a picture, in a piece of music, it is real excellence that pleases a good taste. In a person, every perfection of the mind, moral or intellectual, and every perfection of the body, gives pleasure to the spectator as well as to the owner, when there is no envy or malignity to destroy that pleasure. It is therefore in *the scale* of perfection and real excellence that we must look for what is either grand or beautiful in objects. What is the proper object of *admiration* is *grand*, and what is the proper object of *love and esteem* is *beautiful.*

This, I think, is the only notion of beauty that corresponds with the division of the objects of taste which has been generally received by philosophers. And this connection of beauty with real perfection was a capital doctrine of the Socratic school. It is often ascribed to Socrates in the dialogues of Plato and of Xenophon.

I apprehend, therefore, that it is in the moral and intellectual perfections of *mind*, and in its active powers, that beauty originally dwells; and that from this, as the fountain, all the beauty which we perceive in the *visible world* is derived.

This, I think, was the opinion of the ancient philosophers before named; and it has been adopted by Lord Shaftesbury and Dr. Akenside among the moderns.

> " *Mind, mind alone!* bear witness earth and heaven,
> The living fountains in itself contains
> Of beauteous and sublime. Here hand in hand
> Sit paramount the graces. Here enthroned,
> Celestial Venus, with divinest airs,
> Invites the soul to never-fading joy."

But neither mind, nor any of its qualities or powers, is an immediate object of perception to man. We are, indeed, immediately conscious of the operations of our own mind; and every degree of perfection in them gives the purest pleasure, with a proportional degree of self-esteem, so flattering to self-love, that the great difficulty is to keep it within just bounds, so that we may not think of ourselves above what we ought to think.

Other minds we perceive only through the medium of material objects, on which their signatures are impressed. It is through this medium that we perceive life, activity, wisdom, and every moral and intellectual quality in other beings. The signs of those qualities are immediately perceived by the senses; by them the qualities themselves are reflected to our understanding; and we are very apt to attribute to the sign the beauty or the grandeur which is properly and originally in the things signified.

Thus the beauties of mind, though invisible in themselves, are perceived in the objects of sense, on which their image is impressed.

If we consider, on the other hand, the qualities in sensible objects to which we ascribe beauty, I apprehend we shall find in all of them some relation to mind, and the greatest in those that are most beautiful.

The qualities of inanimate matter, in which we perceive beauty, are *sound, color, form,* and *motion;* the first an object of *hearing,* the other three of *sight;* which we may consider in order.

1. In *a single note,* sounded by a very fine voice, there is a beauty which we do not perceive in the same note, sounded by a bad voice, or an imperfect instrument. I need not attempt to enumerate the perfections in a single note which give beauty to it. Some of them have names in the science of music, and there perhaps are others which have no names. But I think it will be allowed, that every quality which gives beauty to a single note is a sign of some perfection, either in the organ, whether it be the human voice or an instrument, or in the execution. The beauty of the sound is both the sign and the effect of this perfection; and the perfection of the cause is the only reason we can assign for the beauty of the effect.

In a composition of sounds, or a piece of music, the beauty is either in the *harmony,* the *melody,* or the *expression.* The beauty of expression must be derived either from the beauty of the thing expressed, or from the art and skill employed in expressing it properly.

In harmony, the very names of concord and discord are metaphorical, and suppose some analogy between the relations of sound, to which they are figuratively applied, and the relations of minds and affections which they originally and properly signify. As far as I can judge by my ear, when two or more persons of a good voice and ear converse together in amity and friendship, the tones of their different voices are concordant, but become discordant when they give vent to angry passions; so that, without hearing what is said, one may know by the tones of the different voices whether they quarrel or converse amicably. This, indeed, is not so easily perceived in those who have been taught, by good breeding, to suppress angry tones of voice, even when they are angry, as in the lowest ranks, who express their angry passions without any restraint.

When discord arises occasionally in conversation, but soon terminates in perfect amity, we receive more pleasure than from perfect unanimity. In like manner, in the harmony of music, discordant sounds are occasionally introduced, but it is always in order to give a relish to the most perfect concord that follows.

Whether these analogies between the harmony of a piece of music and harmony in the intercourse of minds be merely fanciful, or have any real foundation in fact, I submit to those who have a nicer ear, and have applied it to observations of this kind. If they have any just foundation, as they seem to me to have, they serve to account for the metaphorical application of the names of concord and discord to the relations of sounds; to account for the pleasure we have from harmony in music; and to show that the beauty of harmony is derived from the relation it has to agreeable affections of *mind*.

With regard to melody, I leave it to the adepts in the science of music to determine whether music, composed according to the established rules of harmony and melody, can be altogether void of expression; and whether music that has no expression can have any beauty. To me it seems, that every strain in melody that is agreeable is an imitation of the tones of the human voice in the expression of some sentiment or passion, or an imitation of some other object in nature; and that music, as well as poetry, is an imitative art.

2. The sense of beauty in the *colors* and in the *motions* of inanimate objects is, I believe, in some cases,

instinctive. We see that children and savages are pleased with brilliant colors and sprightly motions. In persons of an improved and rational taste, there are many sources from which colors and motions may derive their beauty. They, as well as the forms of objects, admit of regularity and variety. The motions produced by machinery indicate the perfection or imperfection of the mechanism, and may be better or worse adapted to their end, and from that derive their beauty or deformity.

The colors of natural objects are commonly signs of some good or bad quality in the object; or they may suggest to the imagination something agreeable or disagreeable. A number of clouds of different and ever-changing hue, seen on the ground of a serene azure sky at the going down of the sun, present to the eye of every man a glorious spectacle. It is hard to say, whether we should call it grand or beautiful. It is both in a high degree. Clouds towering above clouds, variously tinged, according as they approach nearer to the direct rays of the sun, enlarge our conceptions of the regions above us. They give us a view of the furniture of those regions, which, in an unclouded air, seem to be a perfect void; but are now seen to contain the stores of wind and rain, bound up for the present, but to be poured down upon the earth in due season. Even the simple rustic does not look upon this beautiful sky merely as a show to please the eye, but as a happy omen of fine weather to come.

3. If we consider, in the last place, the beauty of *form* or *figure* in inanimate objects, this, according to Dr. Hutcheson, results from regularity, mixed with variety. Here it ought to be observed, that regularity, in all cases, expresses design and art: for nothing regular was ever the work of chance; and where regularity is joined with variety, it expresses design more strongly. Besides, it has been justly observed, that regular figures are more easily and more perfectly comprehended by the mind than the irregular, of which we can never form an adequate conception.

Although straight lines and plane surfaces have a beauty from their regularity, they admit of no variety, and therefore are beauties of the lowest order. Curve lines and surfaces admit of infinite variety, joined with every degree of regularity; and therefore, in many cases, excel in beauty those that are straight.

But the beauty arising from regularity and variety must always yield to that which arises from the fitness of the form for the end intended. In every thing made for an end, the form must be adapted to that end; and every thing in the form that suits the end is a beauty; every thing that unfits it for its end is a deformity. The forms of a pillar, of a sword, and of a balance, are very different. Each may have great beauty; but that beauty is derived from the fitness of the form and of the matter for the purpose intended.

The beauties of the vegetable kingdom are far superior to those of inanimate matter, in any form which human art can give it. The beauties of the field, of the forest, and of the flower-garden, strike a child long before he can reason. He is delighted with what he sees; but he knows not why. This is instinct, but it is not confined to childhood; it continues through all the stages of life. It leads the florist, the botanist, the philosopher, to examine and compare the objects which nature, by this powerful instinct, recommends to his attention. By degrees he becomes a critic in beauties of this kind, and can give a reason why he prefers one to another. In every species he sees the greatest beauty in the plants or flowers that are most perfect in their kind, which have neither suffered from unkindly soil nor inclement weather; which have not been robbed of their nourishment by other plants, nor hurt by any accident. When he examines the internal structure of those productions of nature, and traces them from their embryo state in the seed to their maturity, he sees a thousand beautiful contrivances of nature, which feast his understanding more than their external form delighted his eye.

In the animal kingdom we perceive still greater beauties than in the vegetable. Here we observe life, and sense, and activity, various instincts and affections, and in many cases great sagacity. These are attributes of mind, and have an original beauty. As we allow to brute animals a thinking principle or mind, though far inferior to that which is in man, and as, in many of their intellectual and active powers, they very much resemble the human species, their actions, their motions, and even their looks, derive a beauty from the powers of thought which they express. There is a wonderful variety in their manner of life; and we find the powers they possess, their outward form, and their inward structure, exactly adapted to it. In every species, the more perfectly any individual is fitted for its end and manner of life, the greater is its beauty.

But of all the objects of sense, the most striking and attractive beauty is perceived in the human species, and particularly in woman. Milton represents Satan himself, in surveying the furniture of this globe, as struck with the beauty of the first happy pair.

> " Two of far nobler shape, erect and tall,
> Godlike erect ! with native honor clad
> In naked majesty, seemed lords of all.
> And worthy seemed, for in their looks divine,
> The image of their glorious Maker, shone
> Truth, wisdom, sanctitude severe and pure ;
> Severe, but in true filial freedom placed,
> Whence true authority in man ; though both
> Not equal, as their sex not equal, seemed ;
> For contemplation he and valor formed,
> For softness she, and sweet attractive grace."

In this well-known passage of Milton, we see that this great poet derives the beauty of the first pair in paradise from those expressions of *moral and intellectual* qualities which appeared in their outward form and demeanour.

It cannot, indeed, be denied, that the expression of a fine countenance may be unnaturally disjoined from the amiable qualities which it naturally expresses : but we presume the contrary till we have clear evidence ; and even then we pay homage to the expression, as we do to the throne when it happens to be unworthily filled.*

---

* Of later works on the philosophy of taste, the following are among the most important: — Kant, *Kritik der Urtheilskraft und Beobachtungen über das Gefühl des Schönen und Erhabenen* (translated into French by J. Barni, *Critique du Jugement*, &c.); Schleiermacher, *Vorlesungen über die Æsthetik*; Weisse, *System der Æsthetik als Wissenschaft von der Idee der Schönheit*; Hegel, *Cours d'Esthetique analysé et traduit de l'Allemand*, par M. Bénard; Jouffroy, *Cours d'Esthetique*; Alison's *Essays on the Nature and Principles of Taste*; Stewart's *Philosophical Essays*, Part II.; Knight's *Analytical Inquiry into the Principles of Taste*; Schiller's *Æsthetic Letters, Essays*, &c., translated by J. Weiss; Daniel's *Philosophy of the Beautiful, from the French of Cousin*. — ED.

APPENDIX.

SIR W. HAMILTON'S DOCTRINE OF COMMON SENSE AND
THEORY OF PERCEPTION. — NATURAL REALISM. —
PRESENTATIVE KNOWLEDGE.*

OUR cognitions, it is evident, are not all at second hand.
Consequents cannot, by an infinite regress, be evolved out of
antecedents, which are themselves only consequents. Demonstration, if proof be possible, behooves to repose at last on
propositions, which, carrying their own evidence, necessitate
their own admission ; and which being, as primary, inexplicable, as inexplicable, incomprehensible, must consequently manifest themselves less in the character of cognitions than of *facts*,
of which consciousness assures us under the simple form of
feeling or *belief.*

Without at present attempting to determine the character,
number, and relations — waiving, in short, all attempt at an
articulate analysis and classification — of the primary elements
of cognition, as carrying us into a discussion beyond our limits,
and not of indispensable importance for the end we have in
view ;† it is sufficient to have it conceded, in general, *that such*

---

* This Appendix consists of selections from the Supplementary Dissertations to Hamilton's edition of Reid, Notes A, B, and C. They will give,
it is hoped, a faithful sketch of his doctrine on some of the cardinal points
in his system ; but justice to the author — one of the most acute philosophers of the present age, and one of the most erudite philosophers of any
age — requires that they should be read and studied in the connection in
which they stand. Here, as elsewhere, the references of the author to his
own Notes are retained, though but a small proportion, numerically considered, have as yet appeared. — ED.

† Such an analysis and classification is, however, in itself certainly one
of the most interesting and important problems of philosophy ; and it is

41

elements there are ; and this concession of their existence being
supposed, I shall proceed to hazard some observations, principally in regard to their authority as warrants and criteria of
truth.   Nor can this assumption of the existence of some original bases of knowledge in the mind itself be refused by any.
For even those philosophers who profess to derive all our
knowledge from experience, and who admit no universal truths
of intelligence but such as are generalized from individual
truths of fact, — even these philosophers are forced virtually to
acknowledge, at the root of the several acts of observation from
which their generalization starts, some law or principle to which
they can appeal as guaranteeing the procedure, should the
validity of these primordial acts themselves be called in question.   This acknowledgment is, among others, made even by
Locke ; and on such fundamental guarantee of induction he
even bestows the name of Common Sense.
   Limiting, therefore, our consideration to the question of authority, how, it is asked, do these primary propositions, these
cognitions at first hand, these fundamental facts, feelings, beliefs, certify us of their own -veracity ?   To this the only possible answer is, that, as elements of our mental constitution, as
the essential conditions of our knowledge, they *must* by us be

---

one in which much remains to be accomplished. Principles of cognition,
which now stand as ultimate, may, I think, be reduced to simpler elements ; and some, which are now viewed as direct and positive, may be
shown to be merely indirect and negative ; their cogency depending, not
on the immediate necessity of thinking them, — for if carried unconditionally out they are themselves incogitable, — but in the impossibility of
thinking something to which they are directly opposed, and from which
they are the immediate recoils.   An exposition of the axiom, — that positive thought lies in the limitation or conditioning of one or other of two
opposite extremes, neither of which, as unconditioned, can be realized to
the mind as possible, and yet of which, as contradictories, one or other
must, by the fundamental laws of thought, be recognized as necessary ; —
the exposition of this great but unenounced axiom would show that some
of the most illustrious principles are only its subordinate modifications, as
applied to certain primary notions, intuitions, data, forms, or categories of
intelligence, as Existence, Quantity (protensive, Time ; extensive, Space ;
intensive, Degree), Quality, &c.   Such modifications, for example, are the
principles of Cause and Effect, Substance and Phenomenon, &c.
   I may here also observe, that, though *the primary truths of fact* and the
primary truths of intelligence (the *contingent* and *necessary* truths of Reid)
form two very distinct classes of the original beliefs or intuitions of consciousness, there appears no sufficient ground to regard their sources as
different, and therefore to be distinguished by different names.   In this I
regret that I am unable to agree with Mr. Stewart. See his *Elements*,
Vol. II. Chap. I., and his *Account of Reid*, Sect. II., near the end.

accepted as true. To suppose their falsehood is to suppose that we are created capable of intelligence in order to be made the victims of delusion; that God is a deceiver, and the root of our nature a lie. But such a supposition, if gratuitous, is manifestly illegitimate. For, on the contrary, the data of our original consciousness must, it is evident, *in the first instance*, be presumed true. It is only if proved false, that their authority can, *in consequence of that proof*, be, in the second instance, disallowed.

Speaking, therefore, generally, *to argue from common sense* is simply to show, that the denial of a given proposition would involve the denial of some original datum of consciousness. In this case, as every original datum of consciousness is to be presumed true, the proposition in question, as dependent on such a principle, must be admitted.

This being understood, the following propositions are either self-evident, or admit of easy proof: —

1. The end of philosophy is truth; and consciousness is the instrument and criterion of its acquisition. In other words, philosophy is the development and application of the constitutive and normal truths which consciousness immediately reveals.

2. Philosophy is thus wholly dependent upon consciousness; the possibility of the former supposing the trustworthiness of the latter.

3. Consciousness is to be presumed trustworthy, until proved mendacious.

4. The mendacity of consciousness is proved, if its data, immediately in themselves, or mediately in their necessary consequences, be shown to stand in mutual contradiction.

5. The immediate or mediate repugnance of any two of its data being established, the presumption in favor of the general veracity of consciousness is abolished, or rather reversed. For while, on the one hand, all that is not contradictory is not therefore true; on the other, a positive proof of falsehood, in one instance, establishes a presumption of probable falsehood in all; for the maxim, " *Falsus in uno, falsus in omnibus*," must determine the credibility of consciousness, as the credibility of every other witness.

6. No attempt to show that the data of consciousness are (either in themselves or in their necessary consequences) mutually contradictory has yet succeeded; and the presumption in favor of the truth of consciousness and the possibility of phi-

losophy has, therefore, never been redargued. In other words, an original, universal, dogmatic subversion of knowledge has hitherto been found impossible.

7. No philosopher has ever formally denied the truth or disclaimed the authority of consciousness; but few or none have been content implicitly to accept and consistently to follow out its dictates. Instead of humbly resorting to consciousness, to draw from thence his doctrines and their proof, each dogmatic speculator looked only into consciousness, there to discover his preadopted opinions. In philosophy, men have abused the code of natural, as, in theology, the code of positive, revelation; and the epigraph of a great Protestant divine on the book of Scripture is certainly not less applicable to the book of consciousness : —

> " Hic liber est in quo quærit sua dogmata quisque;
> Invenit, et pariter dogmata quisque sua."

8. The first and most obtrusive consequence of this procedure has been, the multiplication of philosophical systems in every conceivable aberration from the unity of truth.

9. The second, but less obvious, consequence has been, the virtual surrender, by each several system, of the possibility of philosophy in general. For, as the possibility of philosophy supposes the absolute truth of consciousness, every system which proceeded on the hypothesis, that even a single deliverance of consciousness is untrue, did, however it might eschew the overt declaration, thereby invalidate the general credibility of consciousness, and supply to the skeptic the premises he required to subvert philosophy, in so far as that system represented it.

10. And yet, although the past history of philosophy has, in a great measure, been only a history of variation and error (*variasse erroris est*); yet, the cause of this variation being known, we obtain a valid ground of hope for the destiny of philosophy in future. Because, since philosophy has hitherto been inconsistent with itself only in being inconsistent with the dictates of our natural beliefs, —

> "For Truth is catholic and Nature one,"—

it follows, that philosophy has simply to return to natural consciousness, to return to unity and truth.

In doing this, we have only to attend to the three following maxims or precautions : —

1°, That we omit nothing, not either an original datum of consciousness, or the legitimate consequence of such a datum;

2°, That we embrace all the original data of consciousness, and all their legitimate consequences; and,

3°, That we exhibit each of these in its individual integrity, neither distorted nor mutilated, and in its relative place, whether of preëminence or subordination.

Nor can it be contended that consciousness has spoken in so feeble or ambiguous a voice, that philosophers have misapprehended or misunderstood her enouncements. On the contrary, they have been usually agreed about the fact and purport of the deliverance, differing only as to the mode in which they might evade or qualify its acceptance.

This I shall illustrate by a memorable example, — by one in reference to the very cardinal point of philosophy. In the act of sensible perception, I am conscious of two things; — of *myself* as the *perceiving subject*, and of an *external reality*, in relation with my sense, as the *object perceived*. Of the existence of both these things I am convinced; because I am conscious of knowing each of them, not mediately in something else, *as represented*, but immediately in itself, *as existing*. Of their mutual independence I am no less convinced; because each is apprehended equally, and at once, in the same indivisible energy, the one not preceding or determining, the other not following or determined; and because each is apprehended out of, and in direct contrast to, the other.

Such is the fact of perception, as given in consciousness, and as it affords to mankind in general the conjunct assurance they possess of their own existence, and of the existence of an external world. Nor are the contents of the deliverance, considered *as a phenomenon*, denied by those who still hesitate to admit the truth of its testimony.

The contents of the *fact* of perception, *as given* in consciousness, being thus established, what are the consequences to philosophy, according as the *truth* of its testimony (I.) *is*, or (II.) *is not, admitted?*

I. On the *former* alternative, the veracity of consciousness, in the fact of perception, being unconditionally acknowledged, we have established at once, without hypothesis or demonstration, the reality of mind and the reality of matter; while no concession is yielded to the skeptic, through which he may subvert philosophy in manifesting its self-contradiction. The *one*

41 *

legitimate doctrine, thus possible, may be called *Natural Realism* or *Natural Dualism.*

II. On the *latter* alternative, *five* great variations from truth and nature may be conceived, — and all of these have actually found their advocates, — according as the testimony of consciousness, in the fact of perception, (A.) is *wholly*, or (B.) is *partially*, rejected.

A. If *wholly* rejected, that is, if nothing but the phenomenal reality of the fact itself be allowed, the result is *Nihilism.* This may be conceived either as a dogmatical or as a skeptical opinion; and Hume and Fichte have competently shown, that, if the truth of consciousness be not unconditionally recognized, Nihilism is the conclusion in which our speculation, if consistent with itself, must end.

B. On the other hand, if *partially* rejected, *four* schemes emerge, according to the way in which the fact is tampered with:

i. If the veracity of consciousness be allowed to the equipoise of the subject and object in the act, but disallowed to the reality of their antithesis, the system of *Absolute Identity* (whereof Pantheism is the corollary) arises, which reduces mind and matter to phenomenal modifications of the same common substance.

ii., iii. Again, if the testimony of consciousness be refused to the equal originality and reciprocal independence of the subject and object in perception, two unitarian schemes are determined, according as the one or as the other of these correlatives is supposed the prior and genetic. Is the object educed from the subject? *Idealism;* is the subject educed from the object? *Materialism*, is the result.

iv. Finally, if the testimony of consciousness to our *knowledge* of an external world existing be rejected, with the Idealist, but, with the Realist, the *existence* of that world be affirmed; we have a scheme which, as it by many various hypotheses endeavours, on the one hand, not to give up the reality of an unknown material universe, and, on the other, to explain the ideal illusion of its cognition, may be called the doctrine of *Cosmothetic Idealism, Hypothetical Realism*, or *Hypothetical Dualism.* This last, though the most vacillating, inconsequent, and self-contradictory of all systems, is the one which, as less obnoxious in its acknowledged consequences (being a kind of compromise between speculation and common sense), has found favor with the immense majority of philosophers.

From the rejection of the fact of consciousness in this example of perception, we have thus, in the first place, multiplicity, speculative variation, error; in the second, systems practically dangerous; and, in the third, the incompetence of an appeal to the common sense of mankind by any of these systems against the conclusions of others.

Now, there are only *two* of the preceding theories of perception, with one or other of which Reid's doctrine can possibly be identified. He is a Dualist; — and the only doubt is, whether he be a *Natural Realist,* or a *Hypothetical Realist,* under the finer form of *Egoistical Representationism.*

The cause why Reid left the character of his doctrine ambiguous on this the very cardinal point of his philosophy, is to be found in the following circumstances : —

1°, That, in general, (although the same may be said of all other philosophers,) he never discriminated, either speculatively or historically, the three theories of Real Presentationism, of Egoistical, and of Non-Egoistical, Representationism.

2°, That, in particular, he never clearly distinguished the first and second of these, as not only different, but contrasted, theories.

3°, That, while right in regarding philosophers, in general, as Cosmothetic Idealists, he erroneously supposed that they were all, or nearly all, Non-Egoistical Representationists. And, —

4°, That he viewed the theory of Non-Egoistical Representationism as that form alone of Cosmothetic Idealism which, when carried to its legitimate issue, ended in Absolute Idealism; whereas the other form of Cosmothetic Idealism, the theory of Egoistical Representationism, whether speculatively or historically considered, is, with at least equal rigor, to be developed into the same result.

Dr. Thomas Brown considers Reid to be, like himself, a Cosmothetic Idealist, under the finer form of Egoistical Representationism; but without assigning any reason for this belief, except one which, as I have elsewhere shown, is altogether nugatory.* For my own part, I am decidedly of opinion, that,

---

* *Edinburgh Review,* Vol. LII. pp. 173 – 175. In saying, however, on that occasion, that Dr. Brown was guilty of "a reversal of the real and even *unambiguous* import" of Reid's doctrine of perception, I feel called upon to admit that the latter epithet is too strong; — for, on grounds totally different from the untenable one of Brown, I am now about to show that Reid's doctrine on this point is doubtful. This admission does

as the great end, the governing principle, of Reid's doctrine
was to reconcile philosophy with the necessary convictions of
mankind, he intended a doctrine of *natural*, consequently a
doctrine of *presentative, realism;* and that he would have at
once surrendered, as erroneous, every statement which was
found at variance with such a doctrine.

The distinction of immediate and mediate cognition it is of
the highest importance to establish; for it is one without which
the whole philosophy of knowledge must remain involved in
ambiguities.   What, for example, can be more various, vacillating, and contradictory, than the employment of the all-impor-
tant terms *object* and *objective*, in contrast to *subject* and *subjective*, in the writings of Kant? — though the same is true of those
of other recent philosophers.   This arose from the want of a preliminary determination of the various, and even opposite, meanings of which these terms are susceptible, — a selection of the
one proper meaning, — and a rigorous adherence to the meaning thus preferred.   But, in particular, the doctrine of Natural
Realism cannot, without this distinction, be adequately understood, developed, and discriminated.   Reid, accordingly, in
consequence of the want of it, has not only failed in giving to
his philosophy its precise and appropriate expression, he has
failed even in withdrawing it from equivocation and confusion;
— insomuch, that it even remains a question, whether his doctrine be one of Natural Realism at all.   The following is a
more articulate development of this important distinction than
that which I gave some ten years ago; and since, by more than
one philosopher, adopted.*

1. A thing is known *immediately* or *proximately*, when we
cognize it *in itself; mediately* or *remotely*, when we cognize it
in or *through something numerically different from itself.*   Immediate cognition, thus the knowledge of a thing in itself, involves the *fact* of its existence; mediate cognition, thus the
knowledge of a thing in or through something not itself, involves
only the *possibility* of its existence.

2. An immediate cognition, inasmuch as the thing known is

---

not, however, imply that Brown is not, from first to last, — is not in one
and all of his strictures on Reid's doctrine of perception, as there shown, —
wholly in error.

* See *Edinburgh Review*, Vol. LII. p. 166 *et seq.*; Cross's *Selections from
the Edinburgh Review*, Vol. III. p. 200 *et seq.*; Peisse, *Fragments Philosophiques*, p. 75 *et seq.*

itself presented to observation, may be called a *presentative*, and inasmuch as the thing presented is, as it were, *viewed by the mind face to face*, may be called an *intuitive*, cognition. — A mediate cognition, inasmuch as the thing known is *held up or mirrored to the mind in a vicarious representation*, may be called a *representative* * cognition.

3. A *thing known* is called an *object* of knowledge.

4. In a presentative or immediate cognition there is *one sole object*; the thing (immediately) known and the thing existing being one and the same. — In a representative or mediate cognition there may be discriminated *two objects*; the thing (immediately) known and the thing existing being numerically different.

5. A thing known *in itself* is the (sole) *presentative* or *intuitive object* of knowledge, or the (sole) object of a *presentative* or *intuitive knowledge*. — A thing known *in and through something else* is the *primary, mediate, remote, real, existent,* or *represented object* of (mediate) knowledge, — *objectum quod;* and a thing *through which something else is known* is the *secondary, immediate, proximate, ideal,†* *vicarious,* or *representative object* of (mediate) knowledge, — *objectum quo,* or *per quod.* The former may likewise be styled *objectum entitativum.*

6. The Ego as the subject of thought and knowledge is now commonly styled by philosophers simply *the Subject;* and *Subjective* is a familiar expression for what pertains to the mind or thinking principle. In contrast and correlation to these, the terms *Object* and *Objective* are, in like manner, now in general use to denote the Non-Ego, its affections and properties, — and in general the Really existent as opposed to the Ideally known. These expressions, more especially Object and Objective, are ambiguous; for though the Non-Ego may be the more frequent

---

* The term *Representation* I employ always strictly, as in contrast to *Presentation,* and therefore with exclusive reference to individual objects, and not in the vague generality of *Representatio* or *Vorstellung* in the Leibnitzian and subsequent philosophies of Germany, where it is used for any cognitive act, considered, not in relation to what knows, but to what is known; that is, as the genus, including under it Intuitions, Perceptions, Sensations, Conceptions, Notions, Thoughts proper, &c., as species.

† I eschew, in general, the employment of the words *Idea* and *Ideal,* — they are so vague and various in meaning. (See Note G.) But they cannot always be avoided, as the conjugates of the indispensable term *Idealism.* Nor is there, as I use them, any danger from their ambiguity; for I always manifestly employ them simply for subjective (what is in or of the mind), in contrast to objective (what is out of, or external to, the mind).

and obtrusive object of cognition, still a *mode of mind* constitutes an *object* of thought and knowledge, no less than a mode of matter. Without, therefore, disturbing the preceding nomenclature, which is not only ratified, but convenient, I would propose that, when we wish to be precise, or where any ambiguity is to be dreaded, we should employ, — on the one hand, either the terms *subject-object*, or *subjective object* (and this we could again distinguish as *absolute* or as *relative*), — on the other, either *object-object*, or *objective object*.

7. If the representative object be supposed (according to one theory) a mode of the conscious mind or self, it may be distinguished as *Egoistical;* if it be supposed (according to another) something numerically different from the conscious mind or self, it may be distinguished as *Non-Egoistical.* The former theory supposes *two* things numerically different; — 1°, the object represented; 2°, the representing and cognizant mind: the latter *three;* — 1°, the object represented; 2°, the object representing; 3°, the cognizant mind. Compared merely with each other, the former, as simpler, may, *by contrast* to the latter, be considered, but still inaccurately, as an immediate cognition. The latter of these, as limited in its application to certain faculties, and now in fact wholly exploded, may be thrown out of account.

8. *External Perception*, or *Perception* simply, is the faculty *presentative* or *intuitive* of the phenomena of the Non-Ego or Matter, — if there be any *intuitive* apprehension allowed of the Non-Ego at all. *Internal Perception* or *Self-Consciousness* is the faculty *presentative* or *intuitive* of the phenomena of the Ego or Mind.

9. *Imagination* or *Phantasy*, in its most extensive meaning, is the faculty *representative* of the phenomena both of the external and internal worlds.

10. A representation considered as an *object* is logically, not really, different from a representation considered as an *act.* Here object and act are merely the same indivisible mode of mind viewed in two different relations. Considered by reference to a (mediate) object represented, it is a representative object; considered by reference to the mind representing and contemplating the representation, it is a representative act. A representative *object*, being viewed as posterior in the order of nature, but not of time, to the representative *act*, is viewed as a *product;* and the representative act being viewed as prior in the order of nature, though not of time, to the representative

object, is viewed as a *producing process.* The same may be said of Image and Imagination.

11. A thing to be known *in itself* must be known as *actually existing ;* and it cannot be known as actually existing unless it be known as existing in its *When* and its *Where.* But the When and Where of an object are *immediately* cognizable by the subject only if the When be *now* (i. e. at the same moment with the cognitive act), and the Where be *here* (i. e. within the sphere of the cognitive faculty); therefore a presentative or intuitive knowledge is only competent of an object *present* to the mind, both in *time* and in *space.*

12. *E converso,* — whatever is known, but not as *actually* existing *now* and *here,* is known not in itself, as the presentative object of an intuitive, but only as the remote object of a representative, cognition.

13. A representative object, considered irrespectively of what it represents, and simply as a mode of the conscious subject, is an intuitive or presentative object. For it is known in itself, as a mental mode, actually existing now and here.

14. *Consciousness* is a knowledge *solely of what is now and here present* to the mind. It is therefore only intuitive, and its objects exclusively presentative. Again, Consciousness is a knowledge of *all that is now and here present* to the mind : every immediate object of cognition is thus an object of consciousness, and every intuitive cognition itself, simply a special form of consciousness.

15. *Consciousness comprehends every cognitive act ;* in other words, whatever we are not conscious of, that we do not know. But consciousness is an immediate cognition. Therefore *all our mediate cognitions are contained in our immediate.*

16. The *actual* modifications, the *present* acts and affections, of the *Ego* are objects of immediate cognition, as themselves objects of consciousness. (Pr. 14.) The *past* and *possible* modifications of the Ego are objects of mediate cognition, as represented to consciousness in a present or actual modification.

17. The *Primary Qualities of matter or body, now* and *here,* that is, in proximate relation to our organs, are objects of immediate cognition to the Natural Realists ; of mediate, to the Cosmothetic Idealists : the former, on the testimony of consciousness, asserting to mind the capability of intuitively perceiving what is not itself ; the latter denying this capability, but asserting to the mind the power of representing, and truly representing, what it does not know. To the Absolute Idealists matter

has no existence as an object of cognition, either immediate or mediate.

18. The *Secondary Qualities* of body *now* and *here*, as only present affections of the conscious subject, determined by an unknown external cause, are, on every theory, now allowed to be objects of immediate cognition. (Pr. 16.)

19. As not *now present in time*, an immediate knowledge of the *past* is impossible. The past is only mediately cognizable in and through a present modification relative to, and representative of, it, as having been. To speak of an immediate knowledge of the past involves a contradiction *in adjecto*. For to know the past immediately, it must be known *in itself;* — and to be known in itself, it must be known as *now existing*. But the past is just a negation of the now-existent; its very notion, therefore, excludes the possibility of its being immediately known. — So much for Memory, or Recollective Imagination.

20. In like manner, supposing that a knowledge of the *future* were competent, this can only be conceived possible in and through a now present representation; that is, only as a mediate cognition. For, as *not yet existent*, the future cannot be known in itself, or as *actually* existent. As *not here present*, an immediate knowledge of an object *distant in space* is likewise impossible.* For, as beyond the sphere of our organs and faculties, it cannot be known by them in itself; it can only, therefore, if known at all, be known through something different from itself, that is, mediately, in a reproductive or a constructive act of imagination.

21. A *possible* object — an *ens rationis* — is a mere fabrication of the mind itself; it exists only ideally in and through an act of imagination, and has only a logical existence, apart from that act with which it is really identical. (Pr. 10.) It is therefore an intuitive object in itself; but in so far as not involving a contradiction, it is conceived as prefiguring something which may possibly exist somewhere and some-when, — this something, too, being constructed out of elements which had been previously given in Presentation, — it is Representative. See Note C, § 1.

---

* On the assertions of Reid, Stewart, &c., that the mind is *immediately* percipient of *distant* objects, see Note B, § 2, and Note C, § 2.

THE END.

Lightning Source UK Ltd.
Milton Keynes UK
UKHW020103231222
414357UK00005B/153